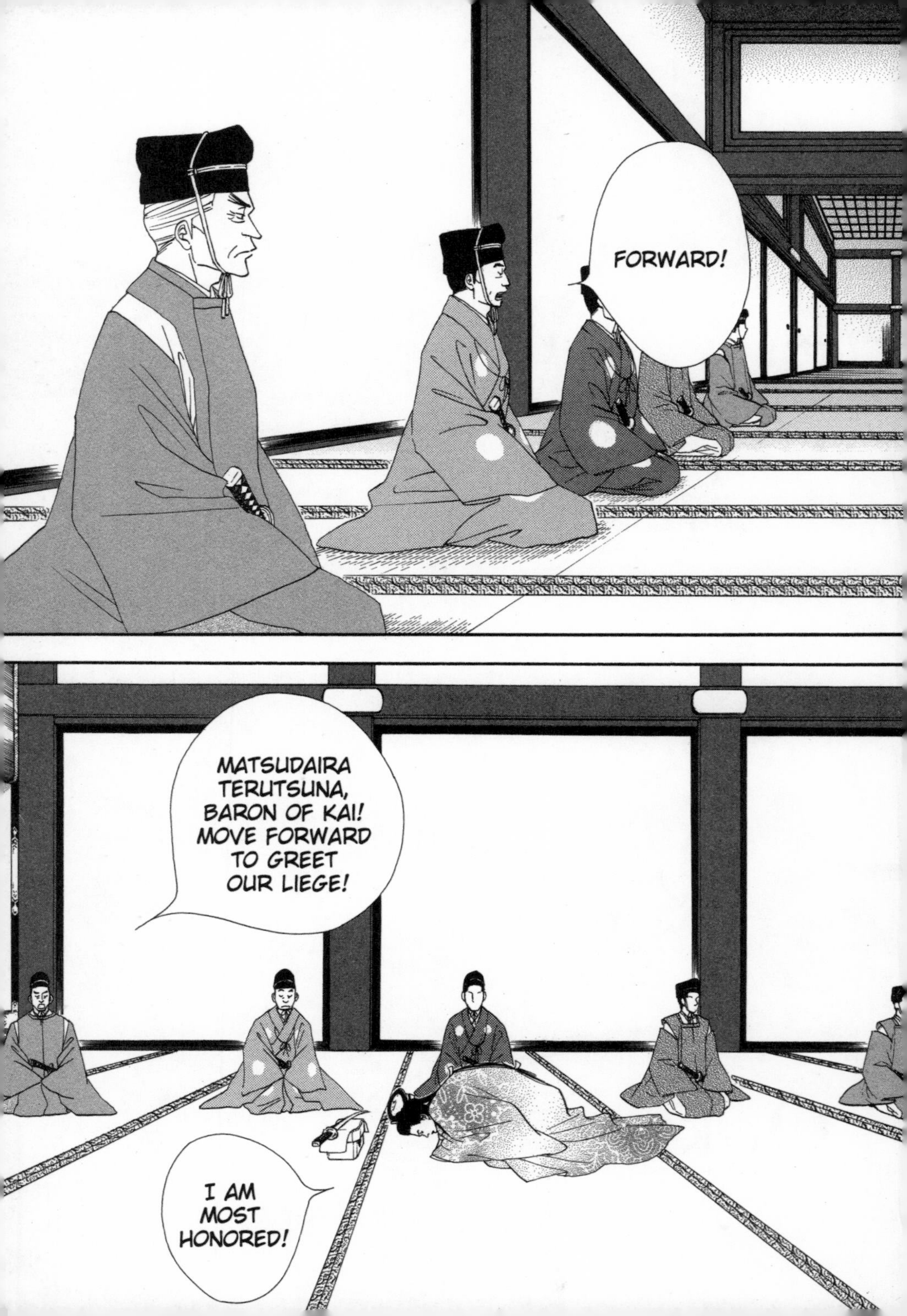
FORWARD!
MATSUDAIRA TERUTSUNA, BARON OF KAI! MOVE FORWARD TO GREET OUR LIEGE!
I AM MOST HONORED!

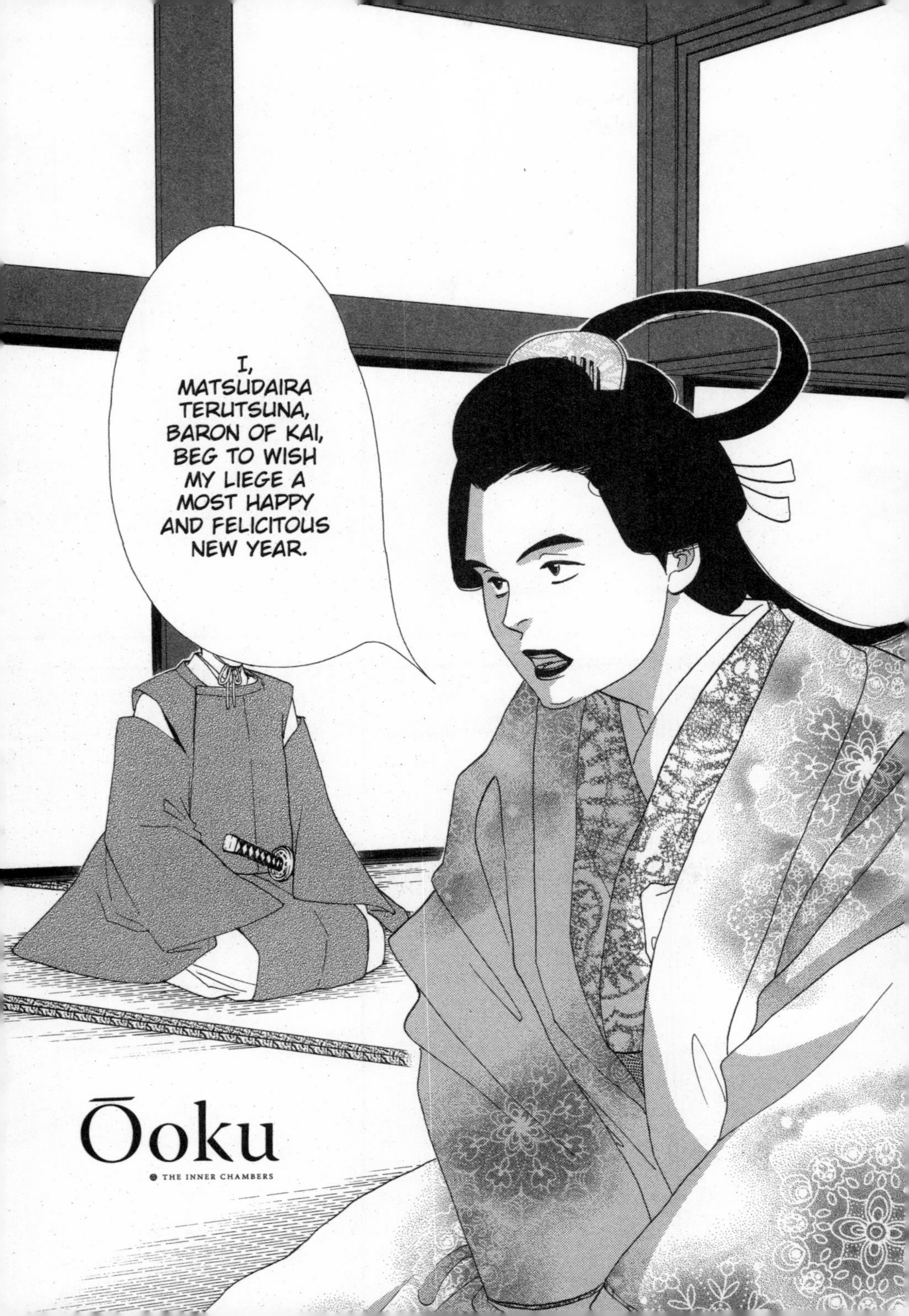
I, MATSUDAIRA TERUTSUNA, BARON OF KAI, BEG TO WISH MY LIEGE A MOST HAPPY AND FELICITOUS NEW YEAR.
Ōoku
THE INNER CHAMBERS

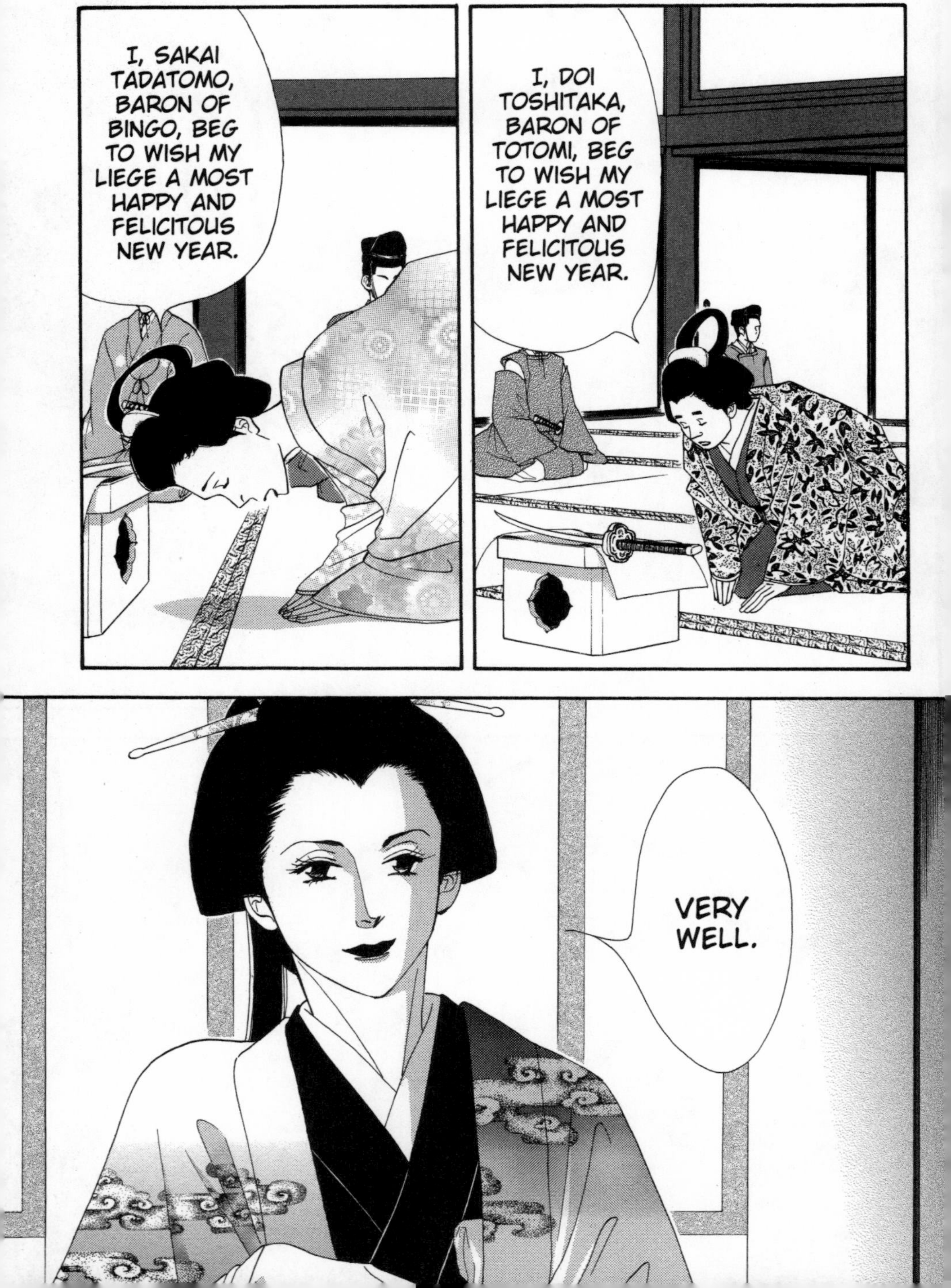
I, DOI TOSHITAKA, BARON OF TOTOMI, BEG TO WISH MY LIEGE A MOST HAPPY AND FELICITOUS NEW YEAR.
I, SAKAI TADATOMO, BARON OF BINGO, BEG TO WISH MY LIEGE A MOST HAPPY AND FELICITOUS NEW YEAR.
VERY WELL.

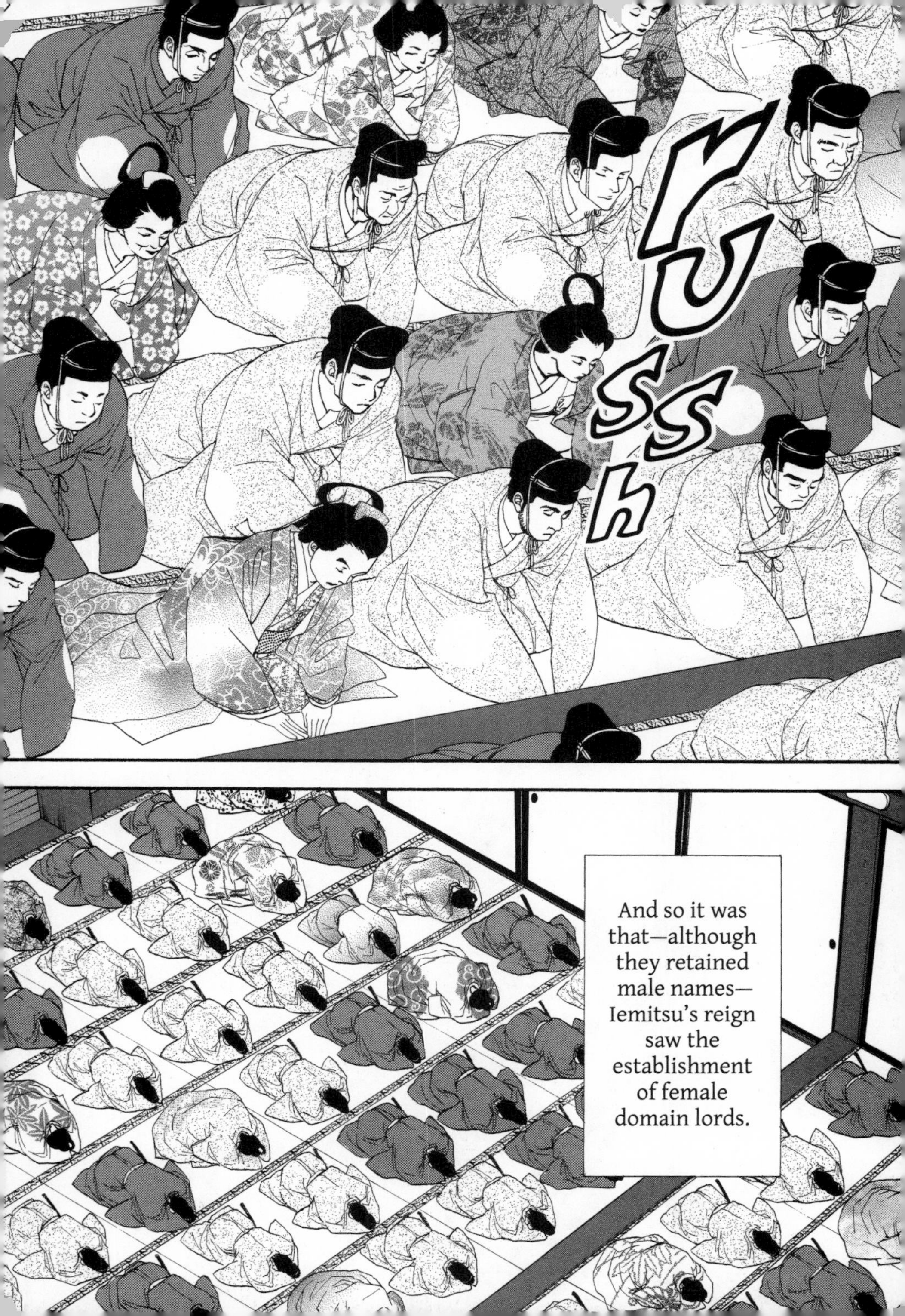
russh
And so it was that—although they retained male names—Iemitsu's reign saw the establishment of female domain lords.

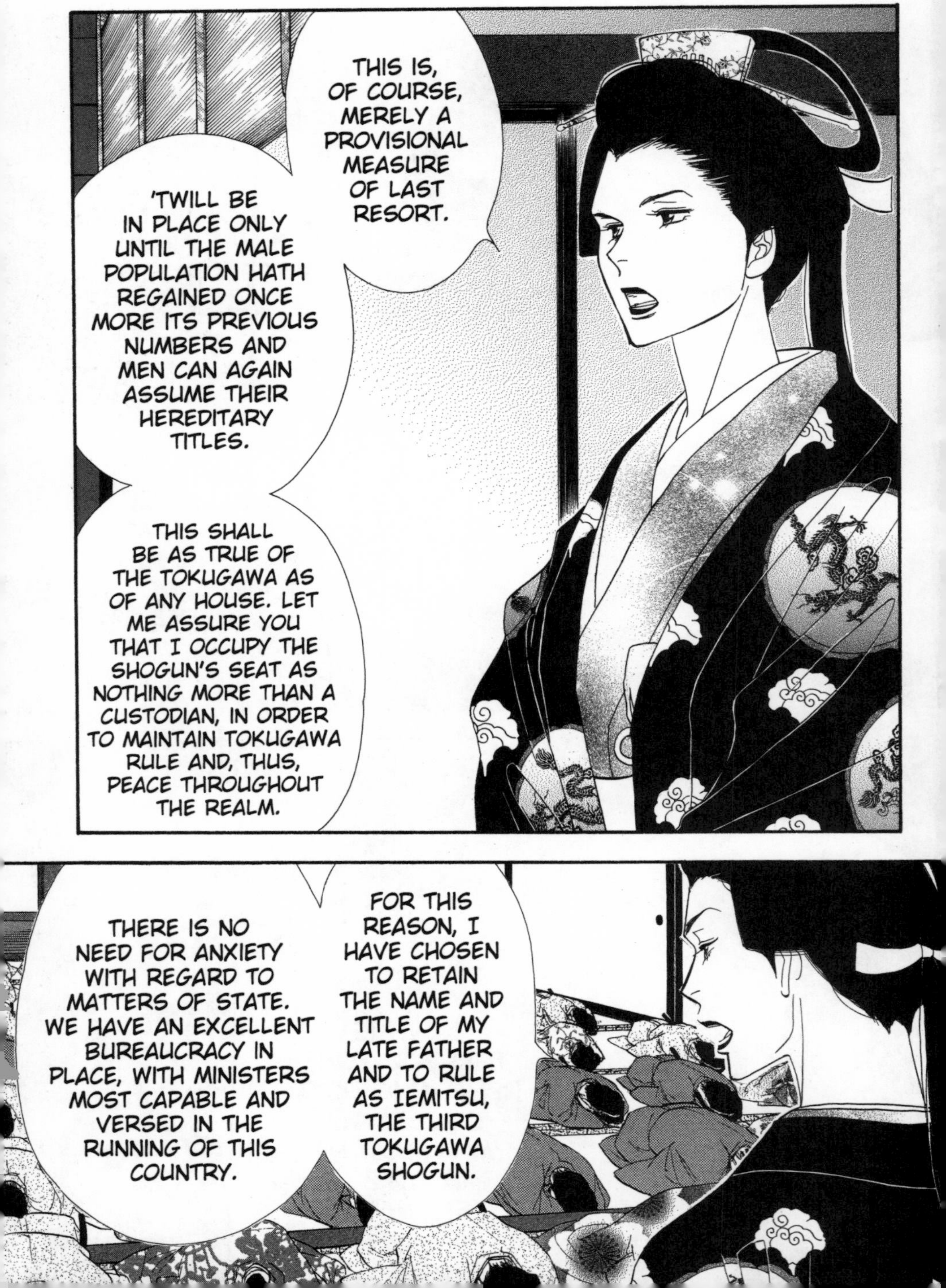
THIS IS, OF COURSE, MERELY A PROVISIONAL MEASURE OF LAST RESORT.
'TWILL BE IN PLACE ONLY UNTIL THE MALE POPULATION HATH REGAINED ONCE MORE ITS PREVIOUS NUMBERS AND MEN CAN AGAIN ASSUME THEIR HEREDITARY TITLES.
THIS SHALL BE AS TRUE OF THE TOKUGAWA AS OF ANY HOUSE. LET ME ASSURE YOU THAT I OCCUPY THE SHOGUN'S SEAT AS NOTHING MORE THAN A CUSTODIAN, IN ORDER TO MAINTAIN TOKUGAWA RULE AND, THUS, PEACE THROUGHOUT THE REALM.
FOR THIS REASON, I HAVE CHOSEN TO RETAIN THE NAME AND TITLE OF MY LATE FATHER AND TO RULE AS IEMITSU, THE THIRD TOKUGAWA SHOGUN.
THERE IS NO NEED FOR ANXIETY WITH REGARD TO MATTERS OF STATE. WE HAVE AN EXCELLENT BUREAUCRACY IN PLACE, WITH MINISTERS MOST CAPABLE AND VERSED IN THE RUNNING OF THIS COUNTRY.

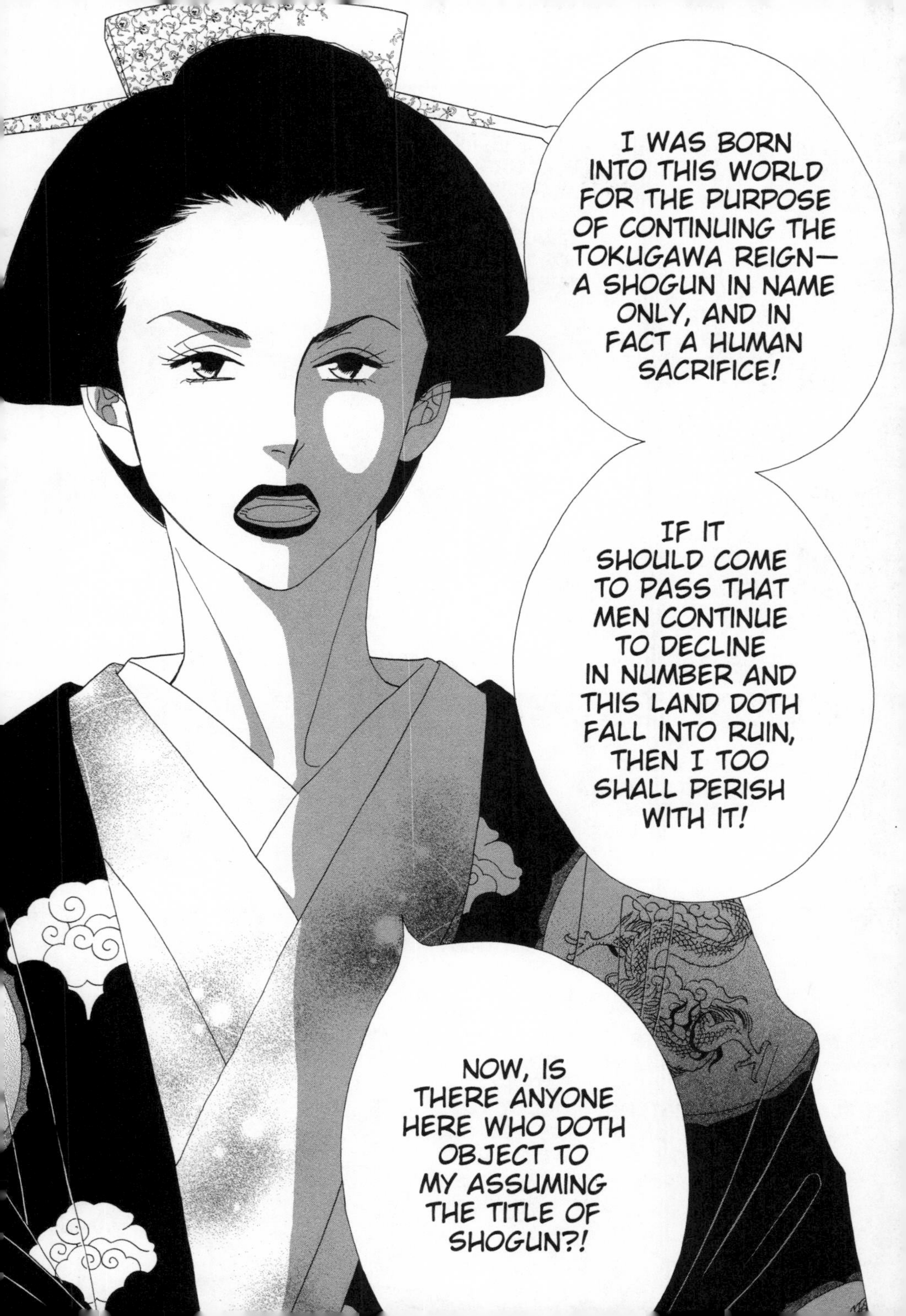
I WAS BORN INTO THIS WORLD FOR THE PURPOSE OF CONTINUING THE TOKUGAWA REIGN—A SHOGUN IN NAME ONLY, AND IN FACT A HUMAN SACRIFICE!
IF IT SHOULD COME TO PASS THAT MEN CONTINUE TO DECLINE IN NUMBER AND THIS LAND DOTH FALL INTO RUIN, THEN I TOO SHALL PERISH WITH IT!
NOW, IS THERE ANYONE HERE WHO DOTH OBJECT TO MY ASSUMING THE TITLE OF SHOGUN?!

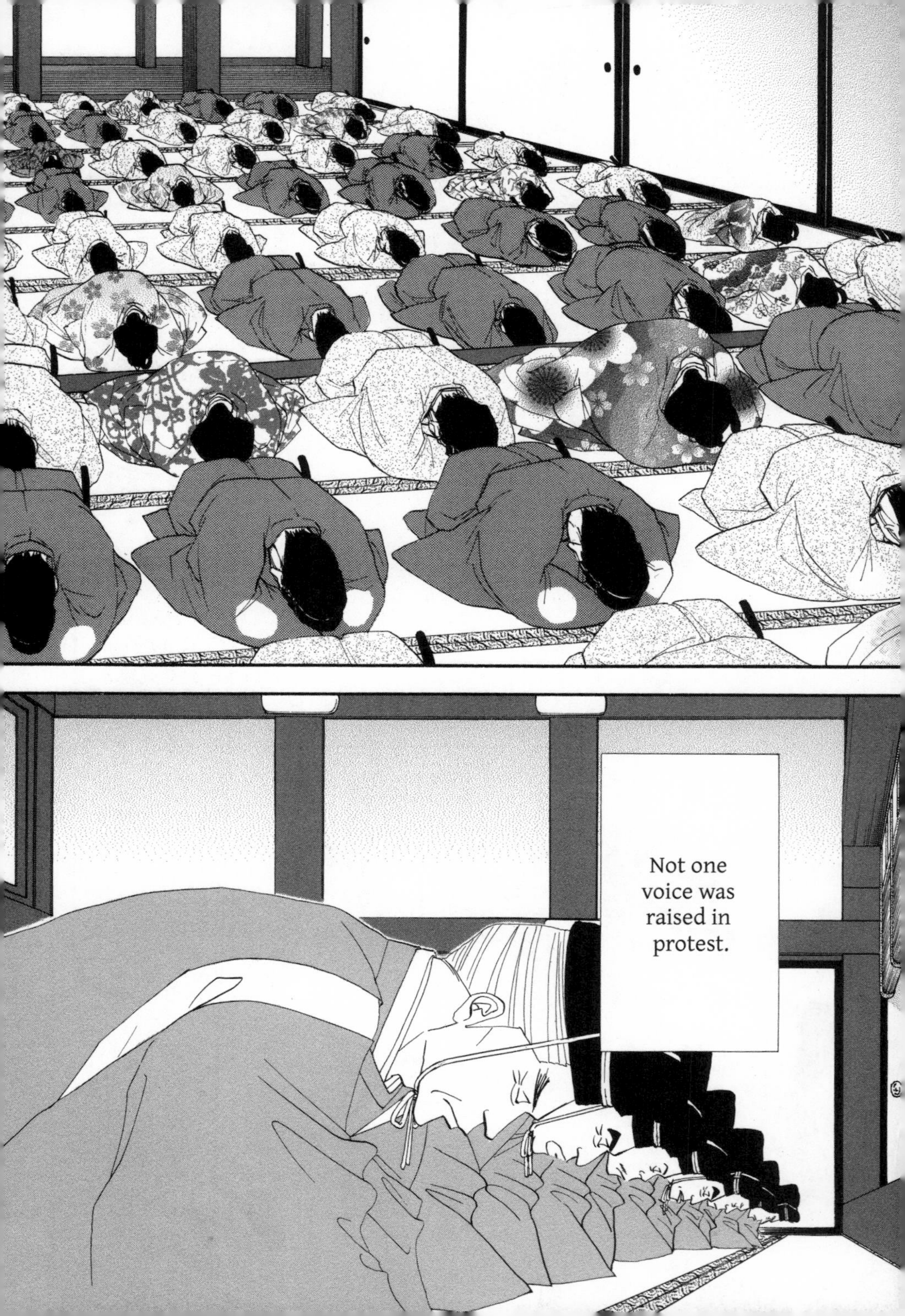
Not one voice was raised in protest.

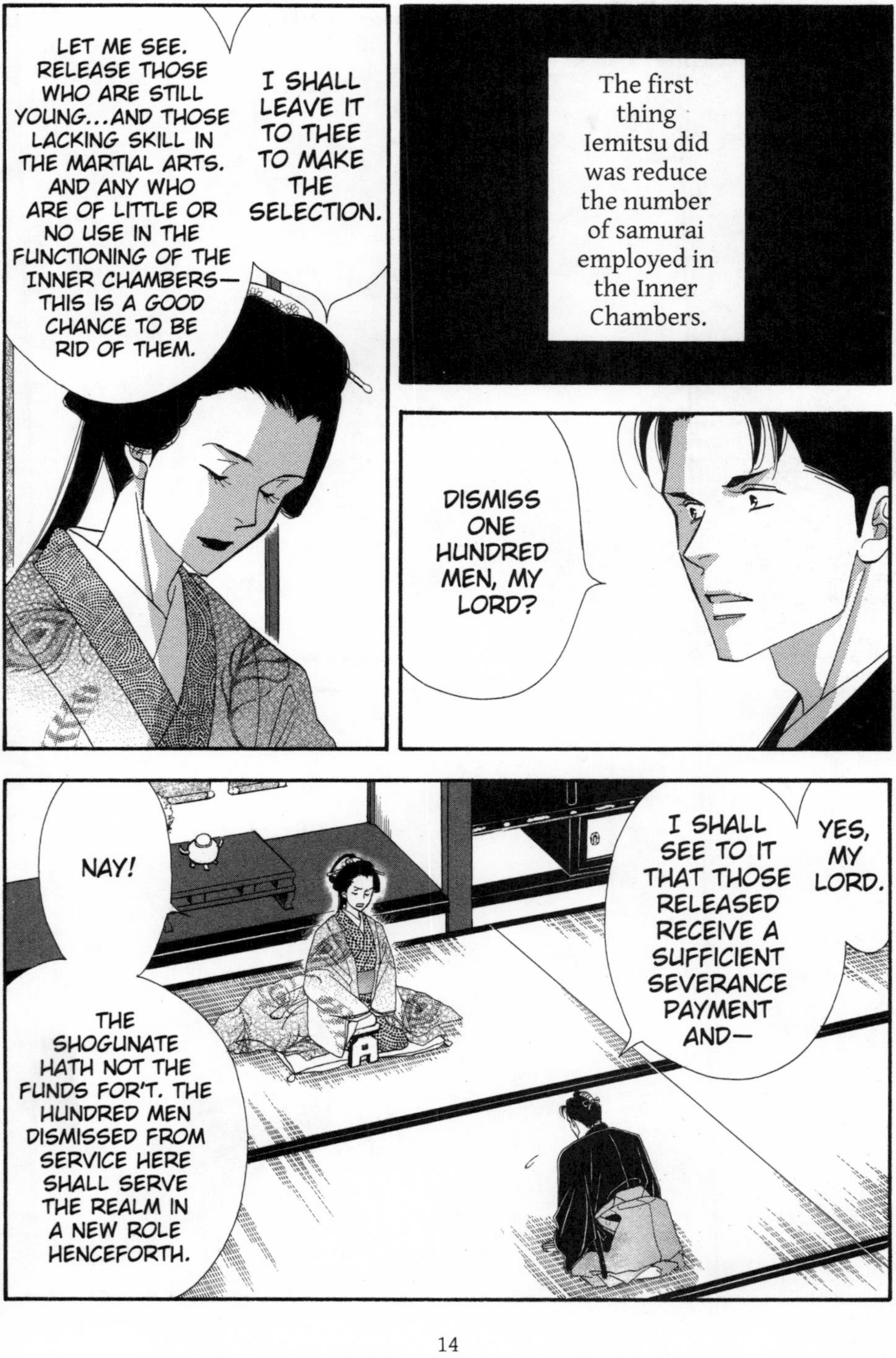
The first thing Iemitsu did was reduce the number of samurai employed in the Inner Chambers.
DISMISS ONE HUNDRED MEN, MY LORD?
LET ME SEE. RELEASE THOSE WHO ARE STILL YOUNG...AND THOSE LACKING SKILL IN THE MARTIAL ARTS. AND ANY WHO ARE OF LITTLE OR NO USE IN THE FUNCTIONING OF THE INNER CHAMBERS—THIS IS A GOOD CHANCE TO BE RID OF THEM.
I SHALL LEAVE IT TO THEE TO MAKE THE SELECTION.
YES, MY LORD.
I SHALL SEE TO IT THAT THOSE RELEASED RECEIVE A SUFFICIENT SEVERANCE PAYMENT AND—
NAY!
THE SHOGUNATE HATH NOT THE FUNDS FOR'T. THE HUNDRED MEN DISMISSED FROM SERVICE HERE SHALL SERVE THE REALM IN A NEW ROLE HENCEFORTH.

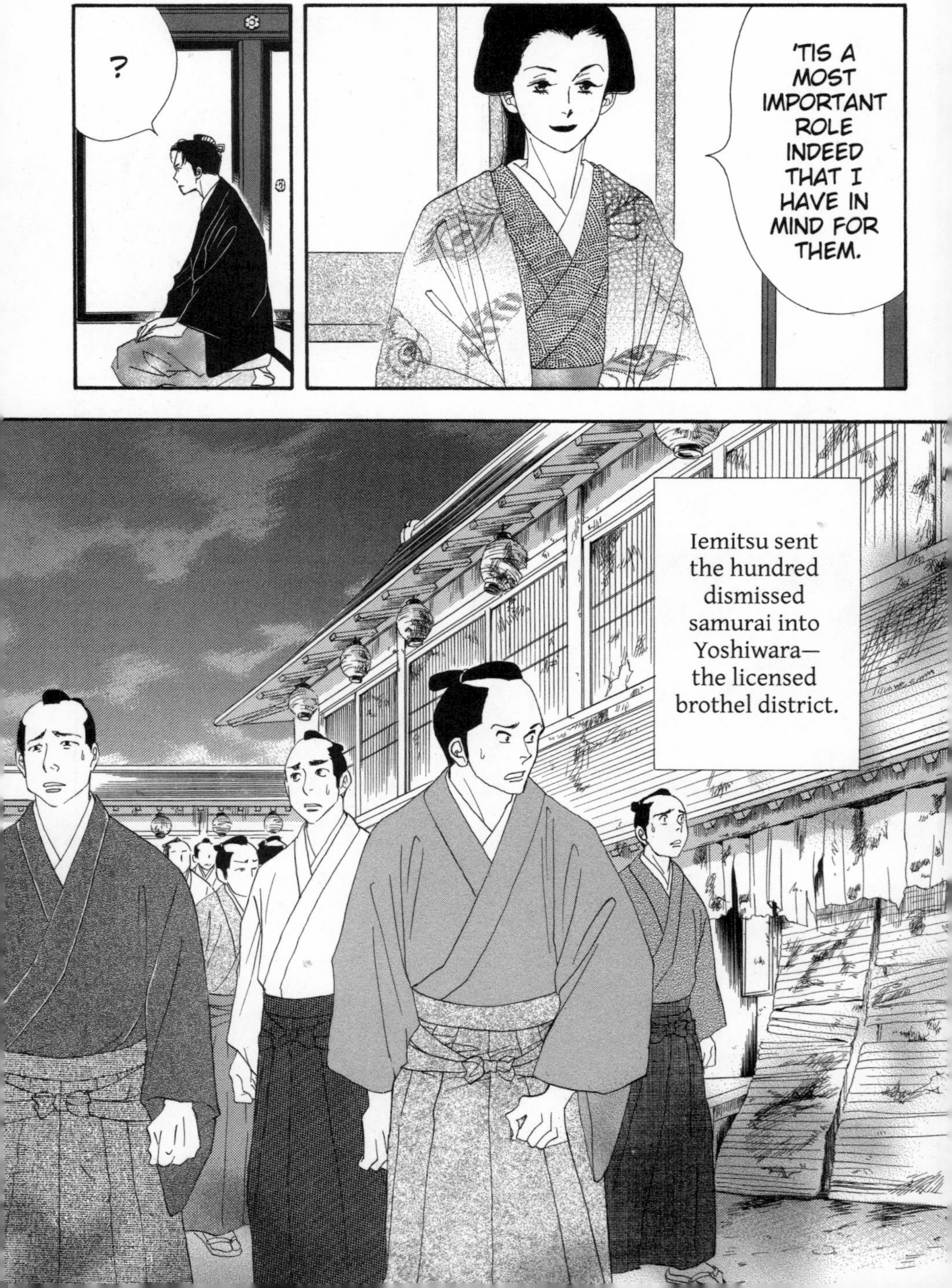
'TIS A MOST IMPORTANT ROLE INDEED THAT I HAVE IN MIND FOR THEM.
?
Iemitsu sent the hundred dismissed samurai into Yoshiwara—the licensed brothel district.

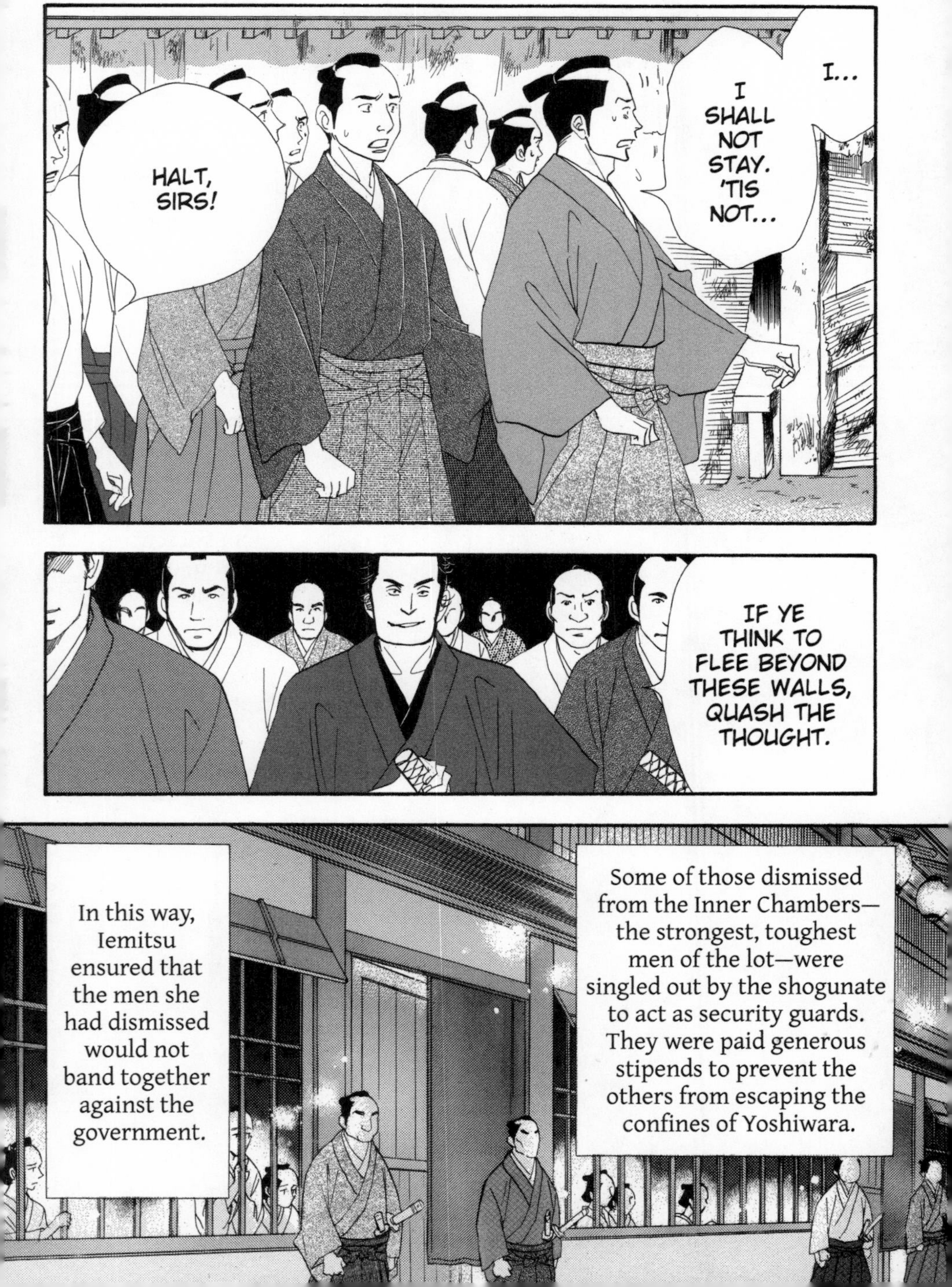
I...
I SHALL NOT STAY. 'TIS NOT...
HALT, SIRS!
IF YE THINK TO FLEE BEYOND THESE WALLS, QUASH THE THOUGHT.
Some of those dismissed from the Inner Chambers—the strongest, toughest men of the lot—were singled out by the shogunate to act as security guards. They were paid generous stipends to prevent the others from escaping the confines of Yoshiwara.
In this way, Iemitsu ensured that the men she had dismissed would not band together against the government.

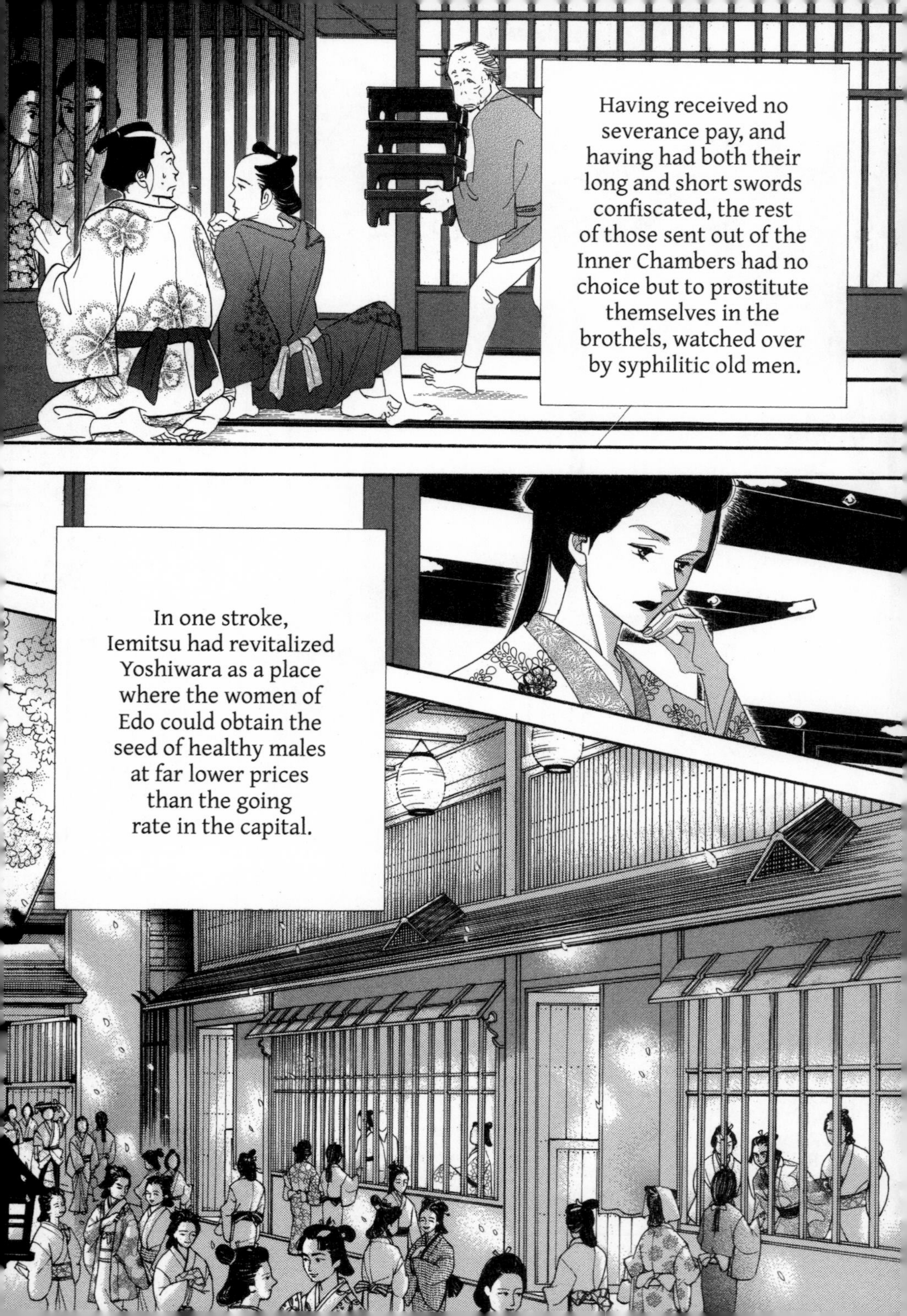
Having received no severance pay, and having had both their long and short swords confiscated, the rest of those sent out of the Inner Chambers had no choice but to prostitute themselves in the brothels, watched over by syphilitic old men.
In one stroke, Iemitsu had revitalized Yoshiwara as a place where the women of Edo could obtain the seed of healthy males at far lower prices than the going rate in the capital.

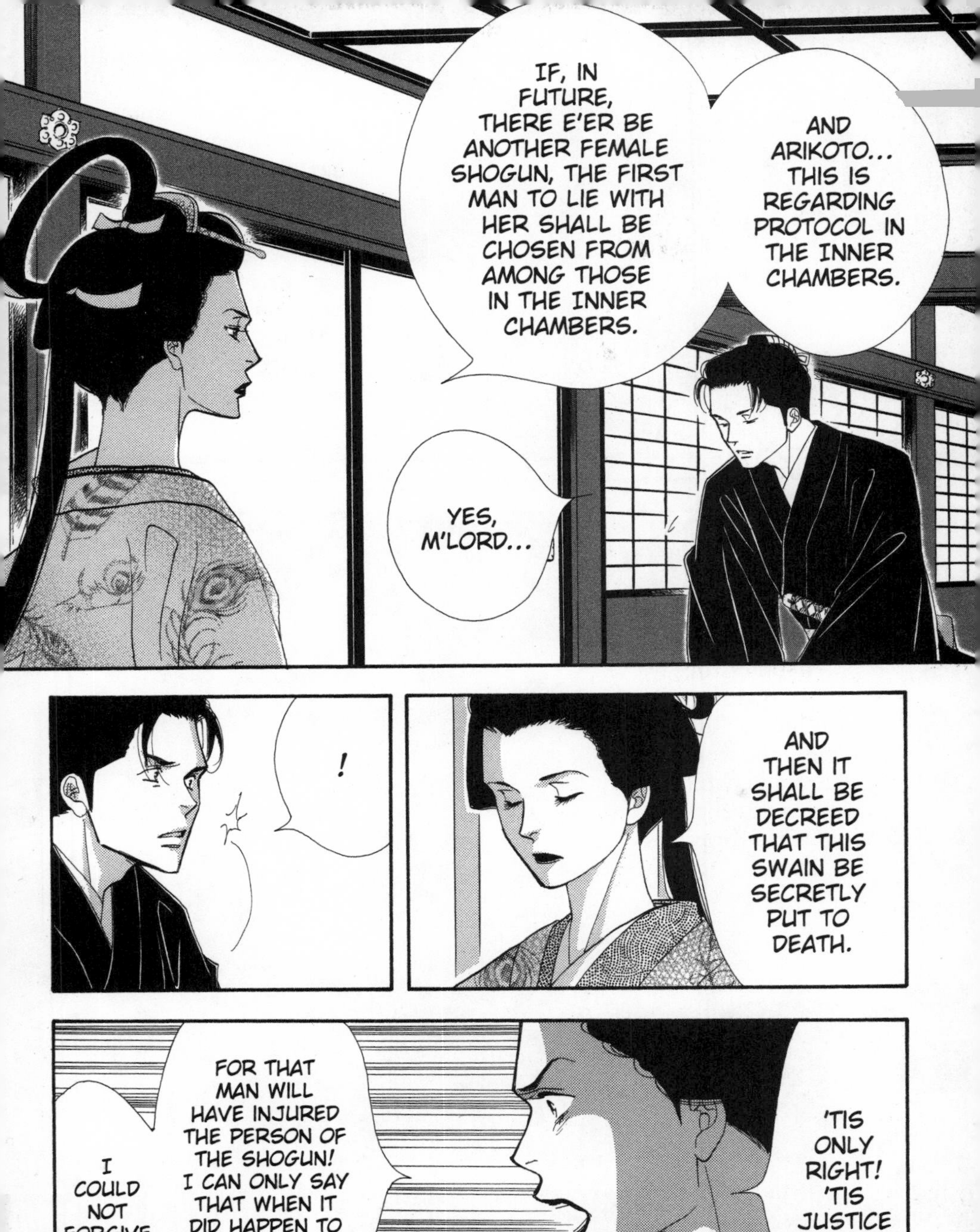
AND ARIKOTO... THIS IS REGARDING PROTOCOL IN THE INNER CHAMBERS.
IF, IN FUTURE, THERE E'ER BE ANOTHER FEMALE SHOGUN, THE FIRST MAN TO LIE WITH HER SHALL BE CHOSEN FROM AMONG THOSE IN THE INNER CHAMBERS.
YES, M'LORD...
AND THEN IT SHALL BE DECREED THAT THIS SWAIN BE SECRETLY PUT TO DEATH.
!
'TIS ONLY RIGHT! 'TIS JUSTICE DONE!
FOR THAT MAN WILL HAVE INJURED THE PERSON OF THE SHOGUN! I CAN ONLY SAY THAT WHEN IT DID HAPPEN TO ME, I COULD NOT FORGIVE THE FELLOW!
I COULD NOT FORGIVE THE FELLOW!!

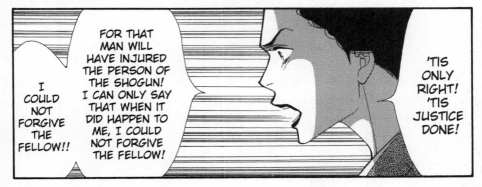

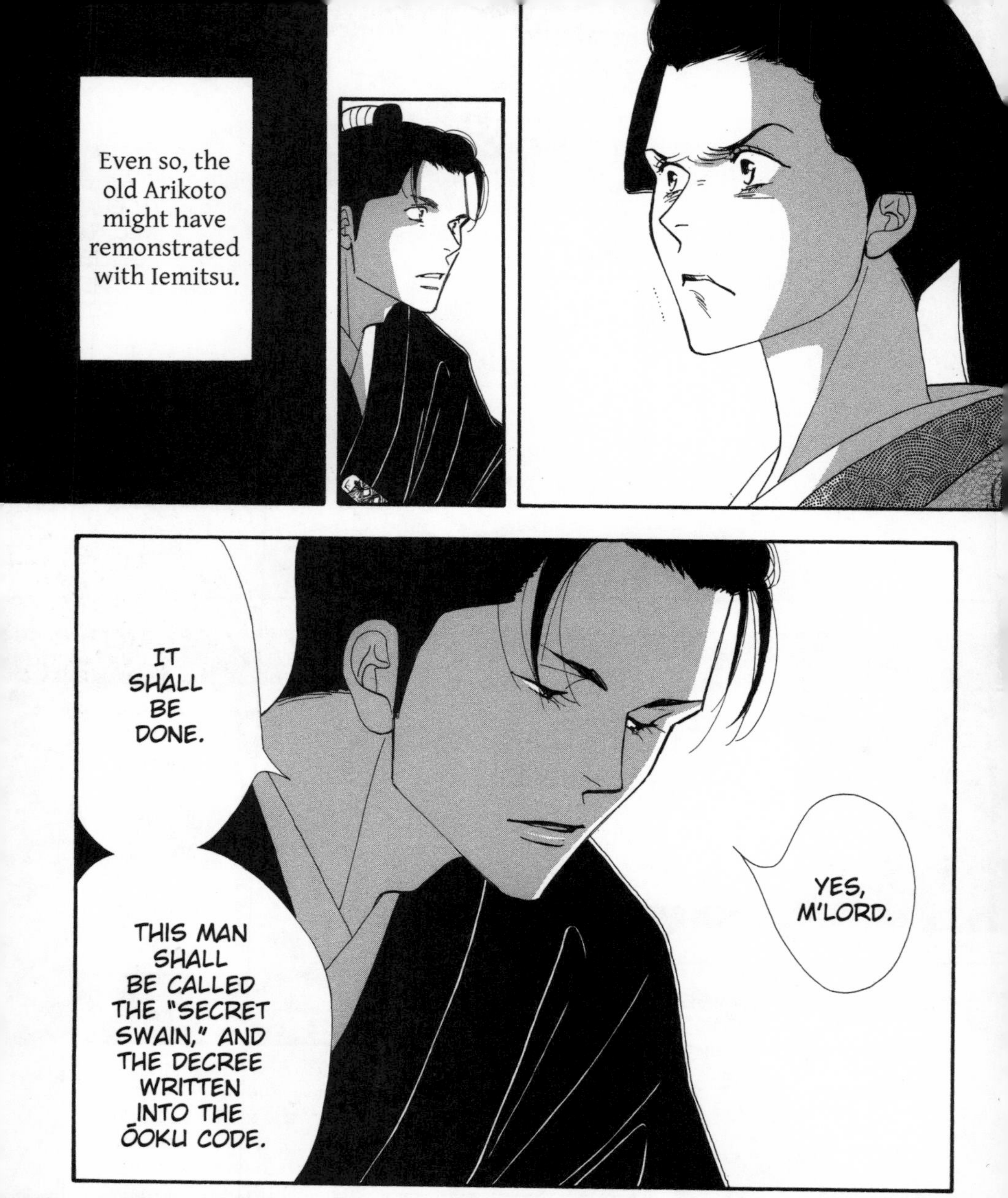
Even so, the old Arikoto might have remonstrated with Iemitsu.
IT SHALL BE DONE.
THIS MAN SHALL BE CALLED THE "SECRET SWAIN," AND THE DECREE WRITTEN INTO THE ŌOKU CODE.
YES, M'LORD.

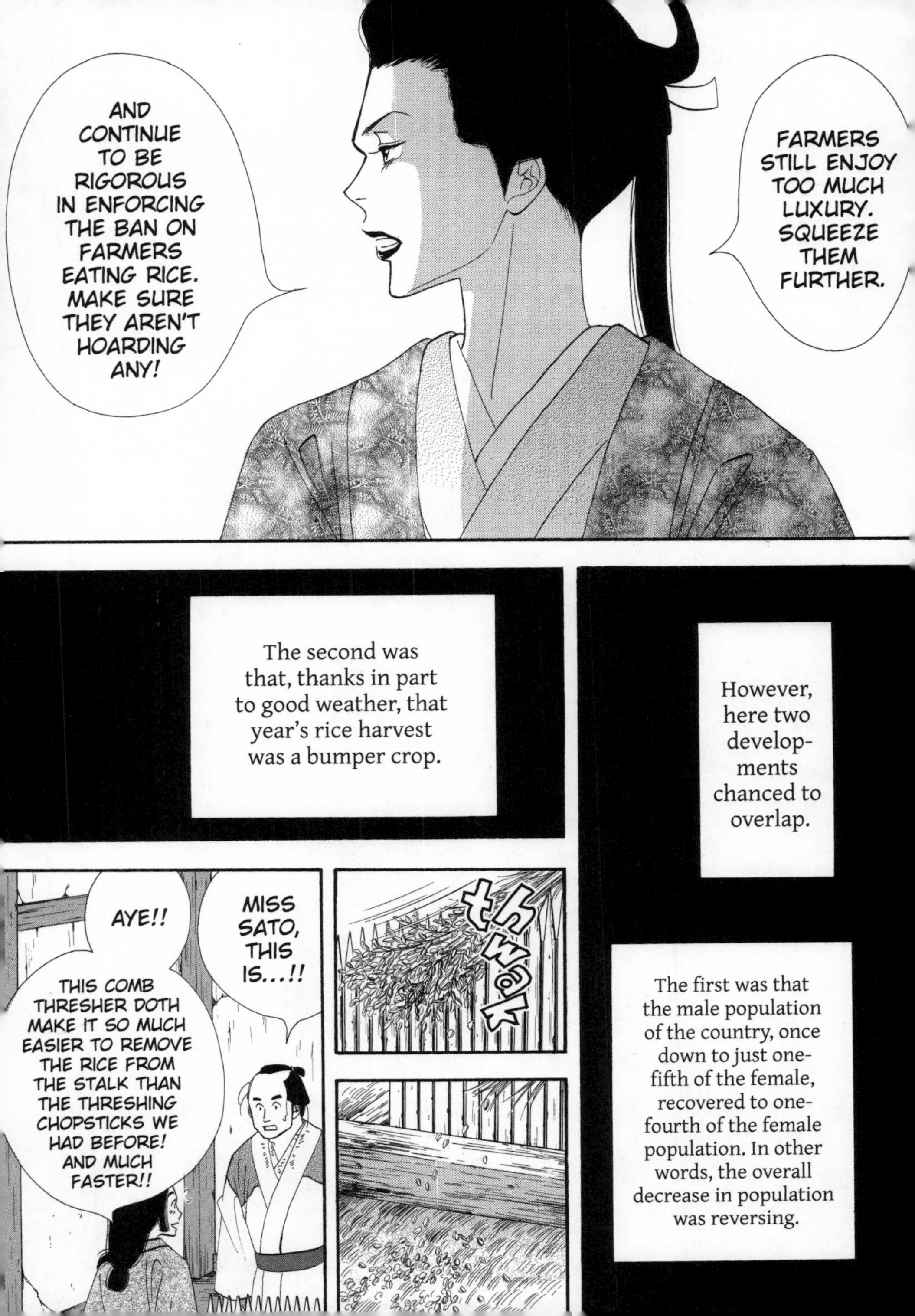
FARMERS STILL ENJOY TOO MUCH LUXURY. SQUEEZE THEM FURTHER.
AND CONTINUE TO BE RIGOROUS IN ENFORCING THE BAN ON FARMERS EATING RICE. MAKE SURE THEY AREN'T HOARDING ANY!
However, here two develop-ments chanced to overlap.
The first was that the male population of the country, once down to just one-fifth of the female, recovered to one-fourth of the female population. In other words, the overall decrease in population was reversing.
The second was that, thanks in part to good weather, that year's rice harvest was a bumper crop.
thwak
MISS SATO, THIS IS...!!
AYE!!
THIS COMB THRESHER DOTH MAKE IT SO MUCH EASIER TO REMOVE THE RICE FROM THE STALK THAN THE THRESHING CHOPSTICKS WE HAD BEFORE! AND MUCH FASTER!!

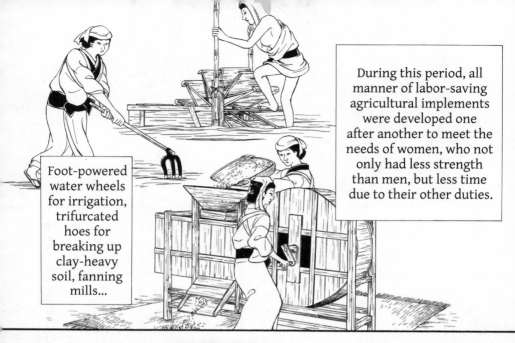

During this period, all manner of labor-saving agricultural implements were developed one after another to meet the needs of women, who not only had less strength than men, but less time due to their other duties.
Foot-powered water wheels for irrigation, trifurcated hoes for breaking up clay-heavy soil, fanning mills...
THANKS TO THE GOOD HARVEST WE HAD THIS YEAR, WE WERE ABLE TO BUY THIS COMB THRESHER.
IF ALL IN OUR VILLAGE USE IT, THE WOMEN WILL HAVE MORE TIME FOR ALL THEIR OTHER CHORES...
EVER SINCE WE GOT A NEW SHOGUN, THE FARMER'S LOT HAS IMPROVED, IT SEEMS TO ME. GOOD WEATHER, GOOD HARVEST, NEW TOOLS...
THE LADY SHOGUN DOTH BRING US GOOD FORTUNE! EVERYONE SAYETH SO.
IT MAY BE SO, SANPEITA... IT MAY BE SO.

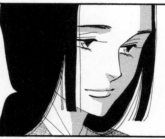

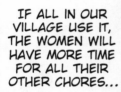

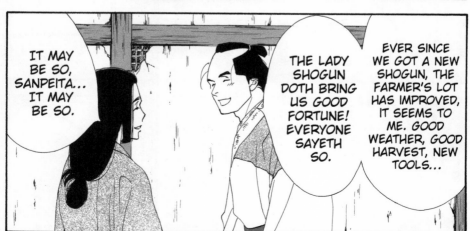

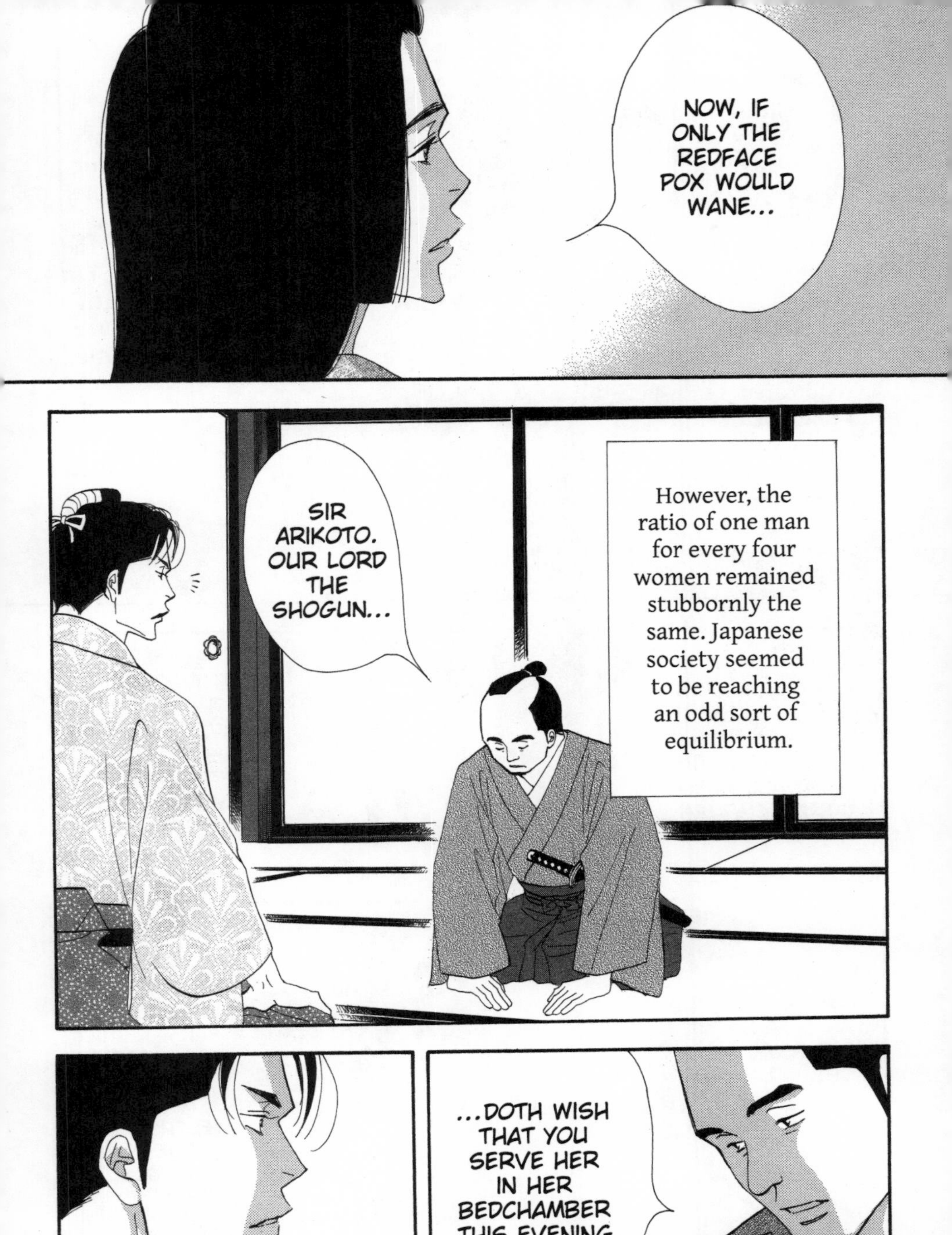
NOW, IF ONLY THE REDFACE POX WOULD WANE...
However, the ratio of one man for every four women remained stubbornly the same. Japanese society seemed to be reaching an odd sort of equilibrium.
SIR ARIKOTO. OUR LORD THE SHOGUN...
...DOTH WISH THAT YOU SERVE HER IN HER BEDCHAMBER THIS EVENING.

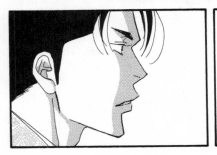

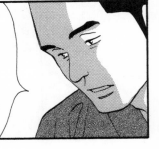

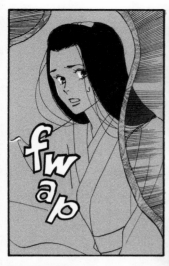

fwap

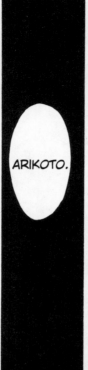

ARIKOTO.

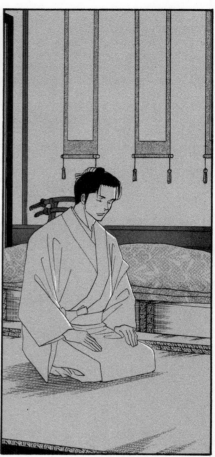

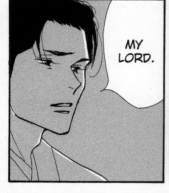

MY LORD.

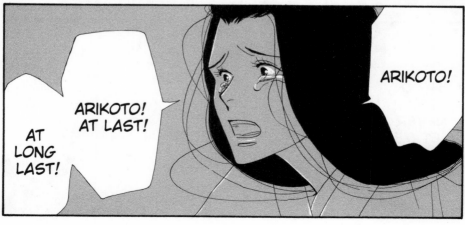

AT LONG LAST!

ARIKOTO! AT LAST!

ARIKOTO!

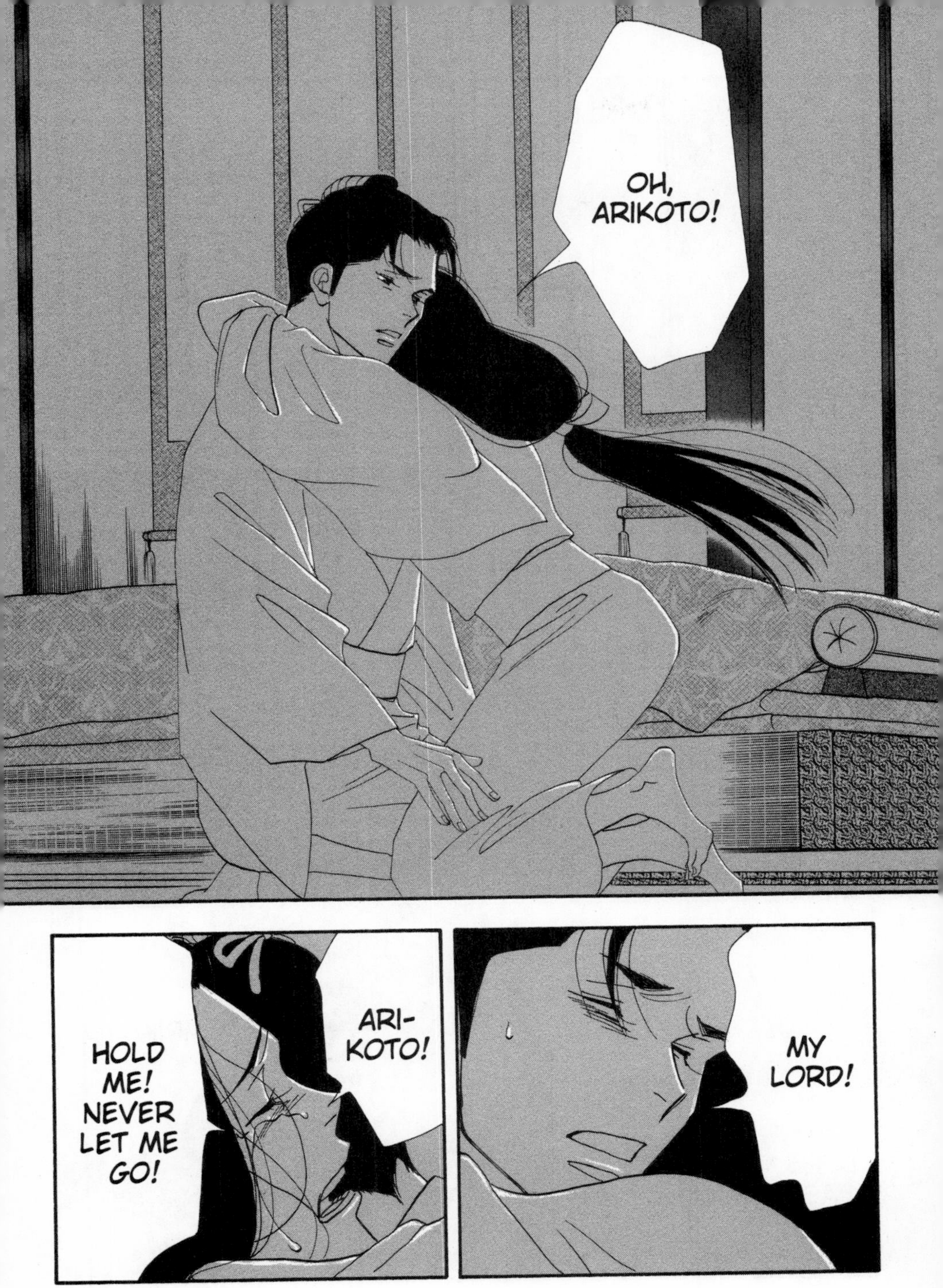
OH, ARIKOTO!
MY LORD!
ARI-KOTO!
HOLD ME! NEVER LET ME GO!

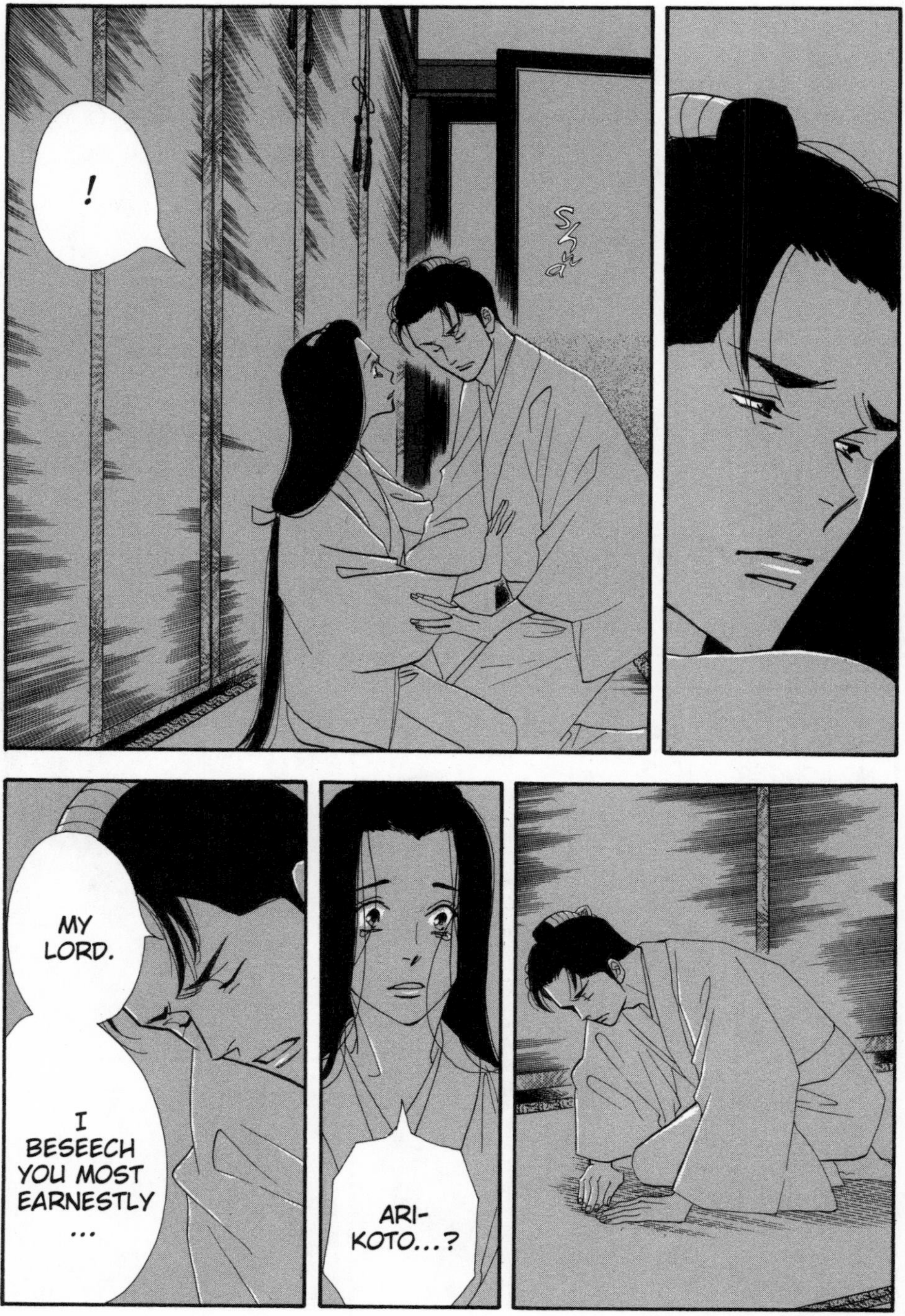
!
ARI-KOTO...?
MY LORD.
I BESEECH YOU MOST EARNESTLY ...

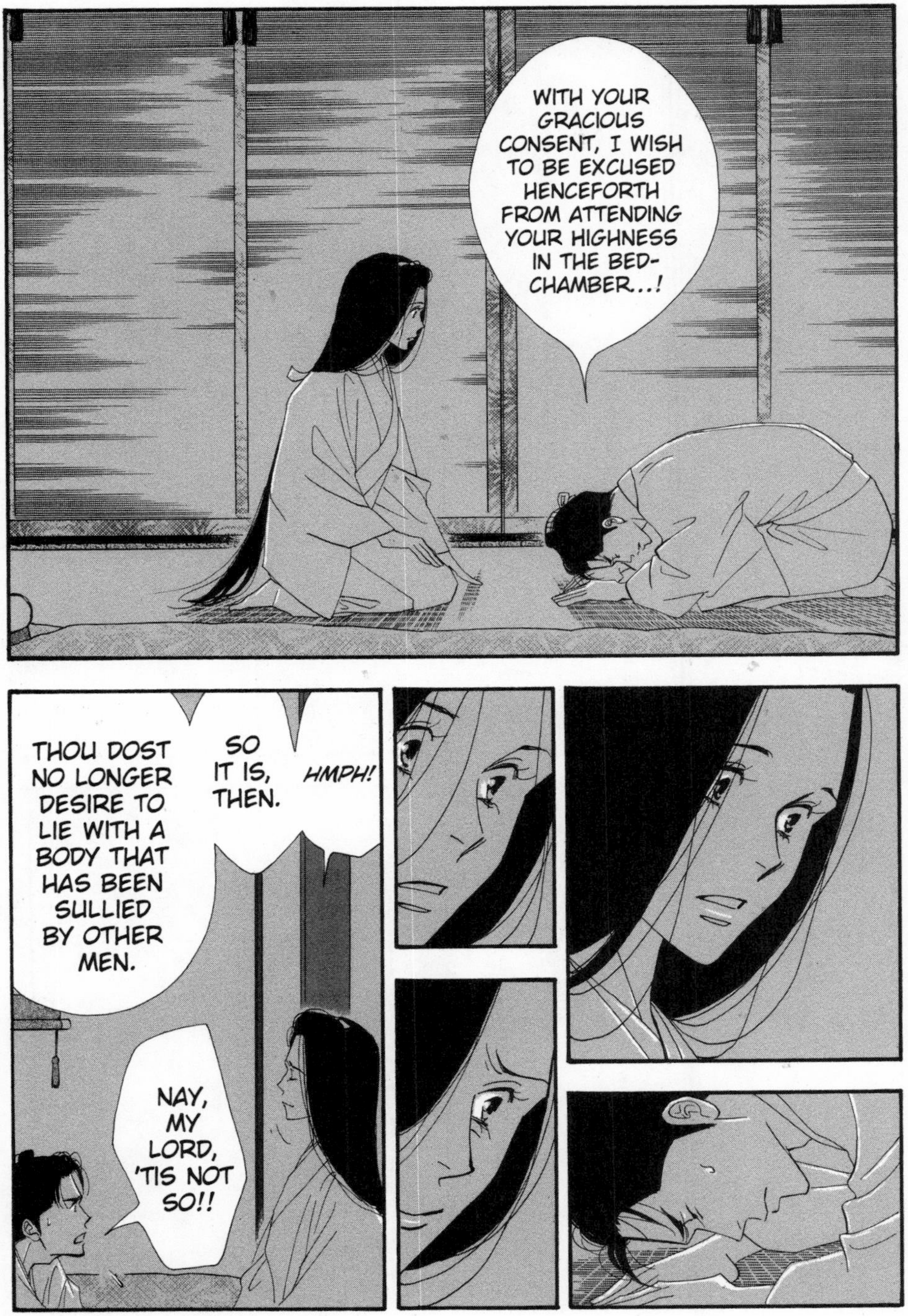
WITH YOUR GRACIOUS CONSENT, I WISH TO BE EXCUSED HENCEFORTH FROM ATTENDING YOUR HIGHNESS IN THE BED-CHAMBER...!
HMPH!
SO IT IS, THEN.
THOU DOST NO LONGER DESIRE TO LIE WITH A BODY THAT HAS BEEN SULLIED BY OTHER MEN.
NAY, MY LORD, 'TIS NOT SO!!

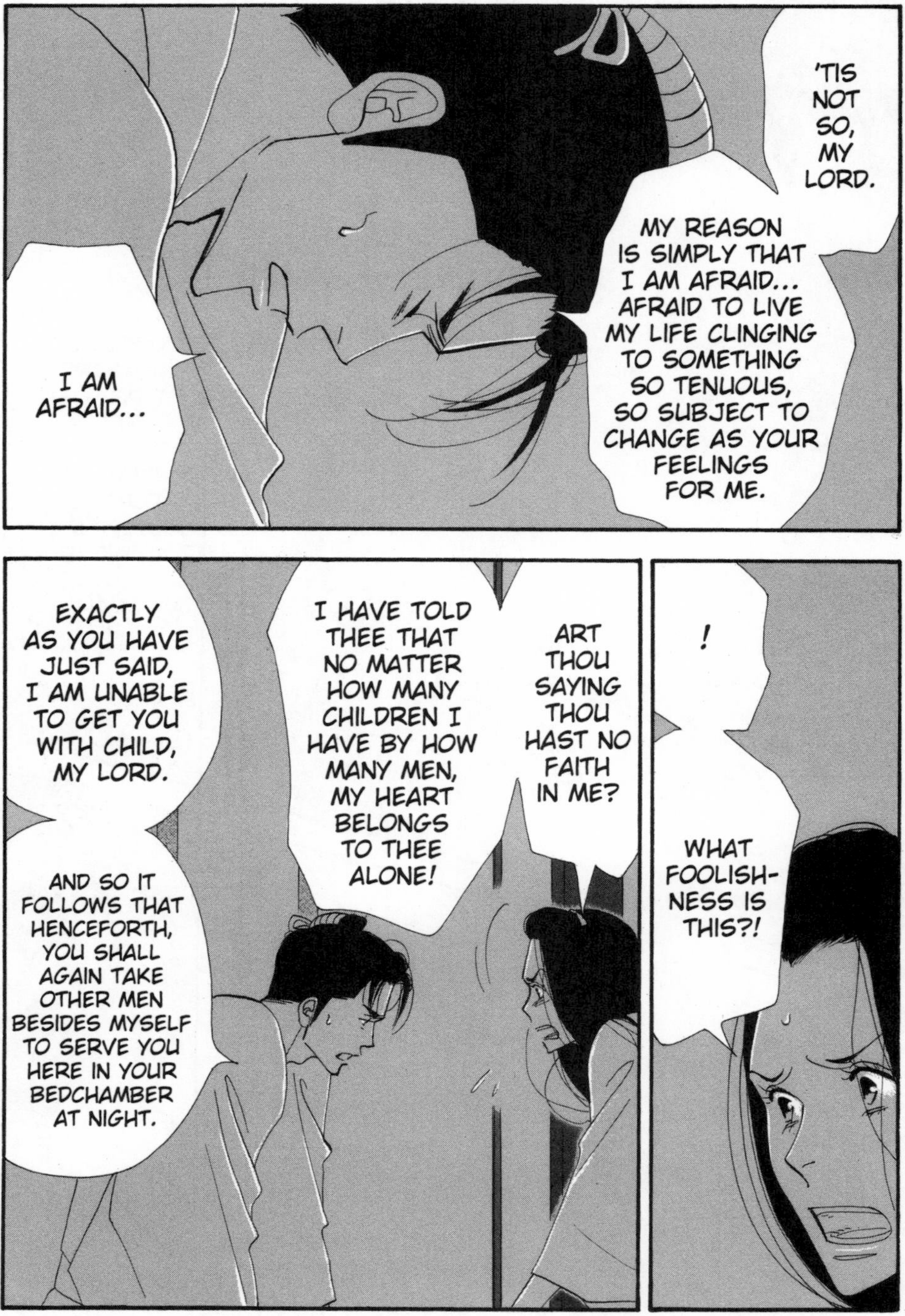
'TIS NOT SO, MY LORD.
MY REASON IS SIMPLY THAT I AM AFRAID... AFRAID TO LIVE MY LIFE CLINGING TO SOMETHING SO TENUOUS, SO SUBJECT TO CHANGE AS YOUR FEELINGS FOR ME.
I AM AFRAID...
!
WHAT FOOLISH-NESS IS THIS?!
ART THOU SAYING THOU HAST NO FAITH IN ME?
I HAVE TOLD THEE THAT NO MATTER HOW MANY CHILDREN I HAVE BY HOW MANY MEN, MY HEART BELONGS TO THEE ALONE!
EXACTLY AS YOU HAVE JUST SAID, I AM UNABLE TO GET YOU WITH CHILD, MY LORD.
AND SO IT FOLLOWS THAT HENCEFORTH, YOU SHALL AGAIN TAKE OTHER MEN BESIDES MYSELF TO SERVE YOU HERE IN YOUR BEDCHAMBER AT NIGHT.

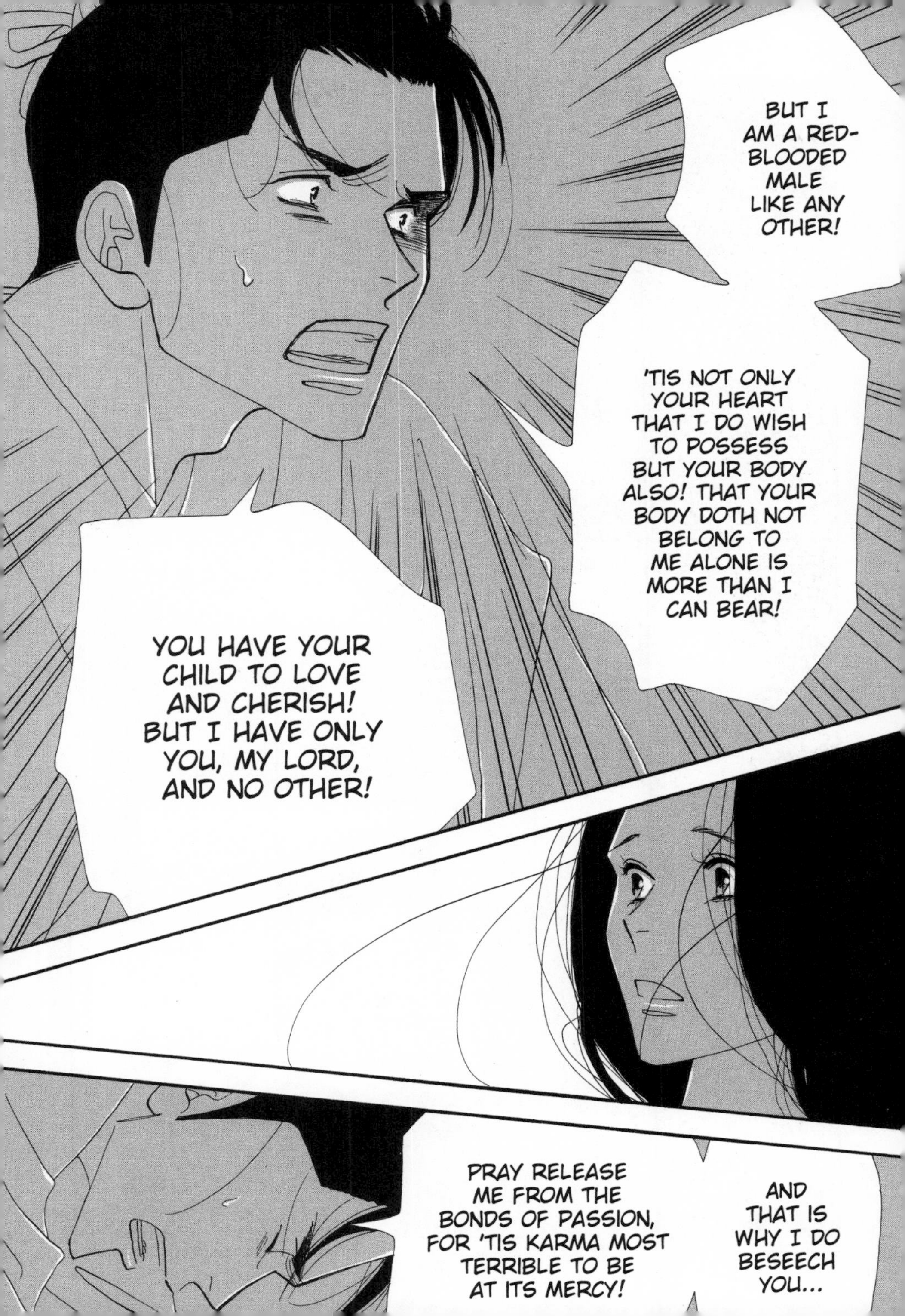
BUT I AM A RED-BLOODED MALE LIKE ANY OTHER!
'TIS NOT ONLY YOUR HEART THAT I DO WISH TO POSSESS BUT YOUR BODY ALSO! THAT YOUR BODY DOTH NOT BELONG TO ME ALONE IS MORE THAN I CAN BEAR!
YOU HAVE YOUR CHILD TO LOVE AND CHERISH! BUT I HAVE ONLY YOU, MY LORD, AND NO OTHER!
AND THAT IS WHY I DO BESEECH YOU...
PRAY RELEASE ME FROM THE BONDS OF PASSION, FOR 'TIS KARMA MOST TERRIBLE TO BE AT ITS MERCY!

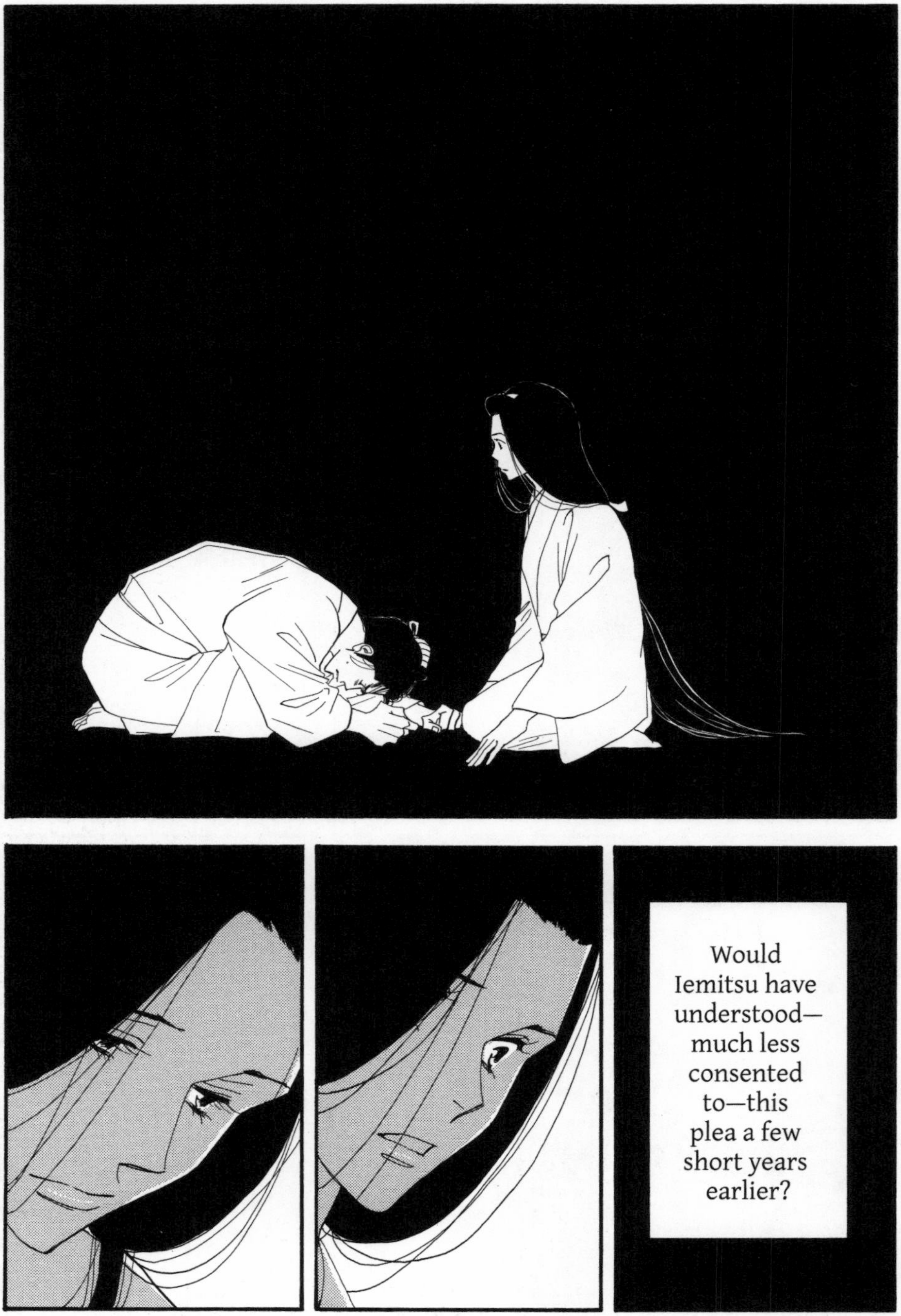
Would Iemitsu have understood—much less consented to—this plea a few short years earlier?

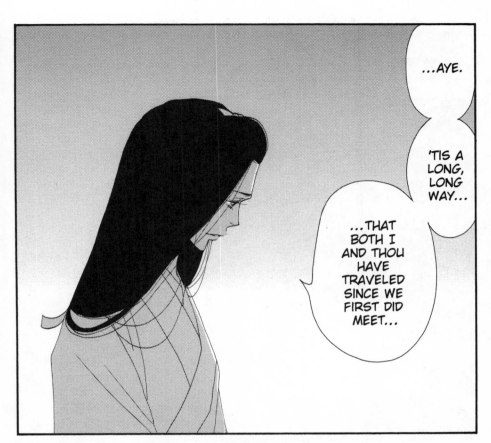

...AYE.
'TIS A LONG, LONG WAY...
...THAT BOTH I AND THOU HAVE TRAVELED SINCE WE FIRST DID MEET...
AYE, MY LORD.
INDEED IT IS...
YOUR HIGHNESS.
IF I MAY, THERE IS MORE.

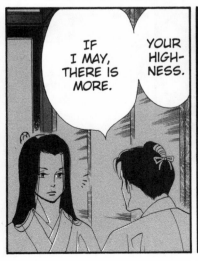

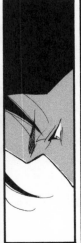

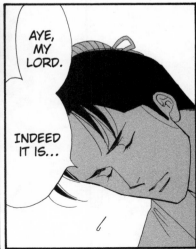

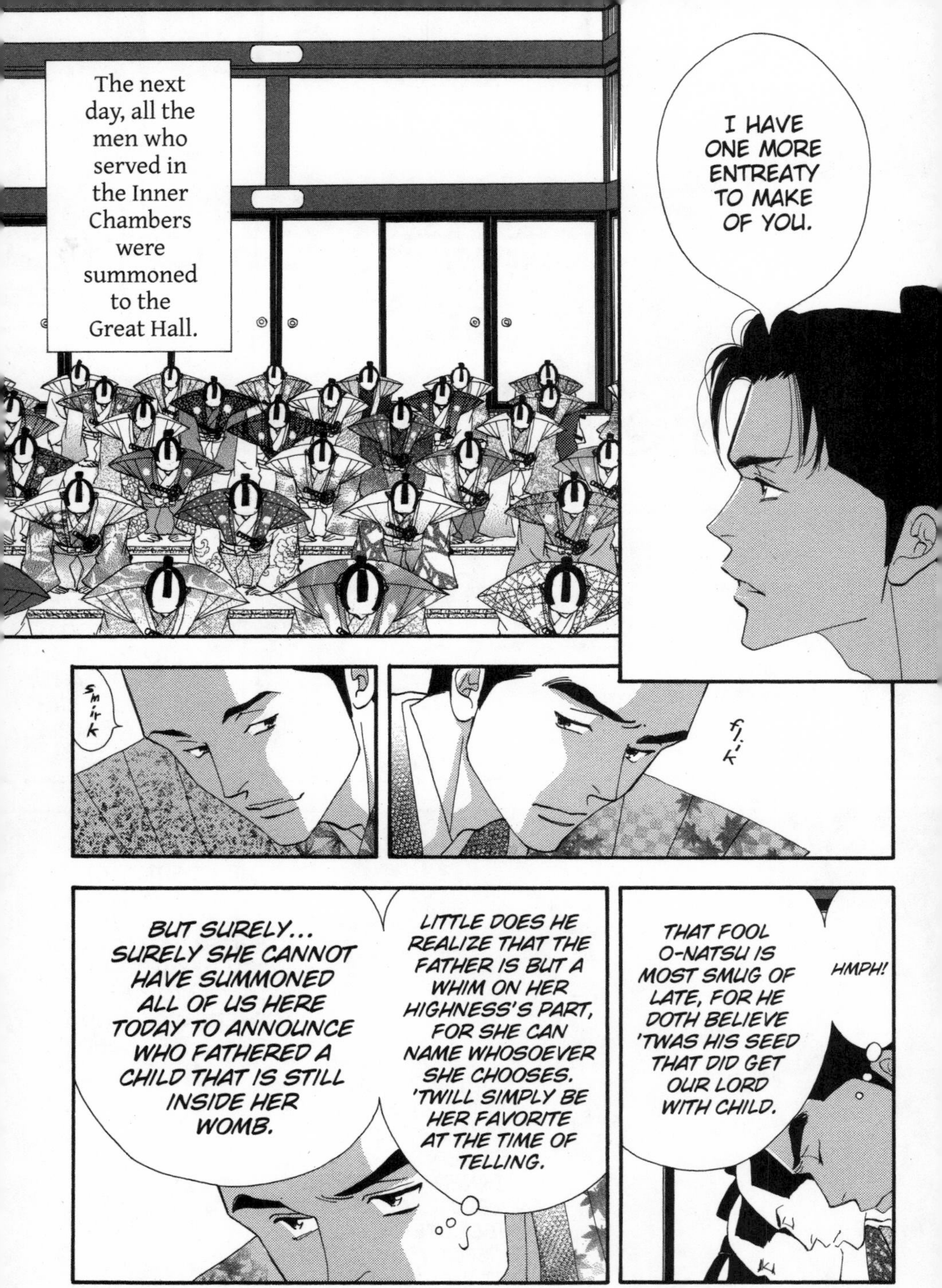
I HAVE ONE MORE ENTREATY TO MAKE OF YOU.
The next day, all the men who served in the Inner Chambers were summoned to the Great Hall.
flik
smirk
THAT FOOL O-NATSU IS MOST SMUG OF LATE, FOR HE DOTH BELIEVE 'TWAS HIS SEED THAT DID GET OUR LORD WITH CHILD.
HMPH!
LITTLE DOES HE REALIZE THAT THE FATHER IS BUT A WHIM ON HER HIGHNESS'S PART, FOR SHE CAN NAME WHOSOEVER SHE CHOOSES. 'TWILL SIMPLY BE HER FAVORITE AT THE TIME OF TELLING.
BUT SURELY... SURELY SHE CANNOT HAVE SUMMONED ALL OF US HERE TODAY TO ANNOUNCE WHO FATHERED A CHILD THAT IS STILL INSIDE HER WOMB.

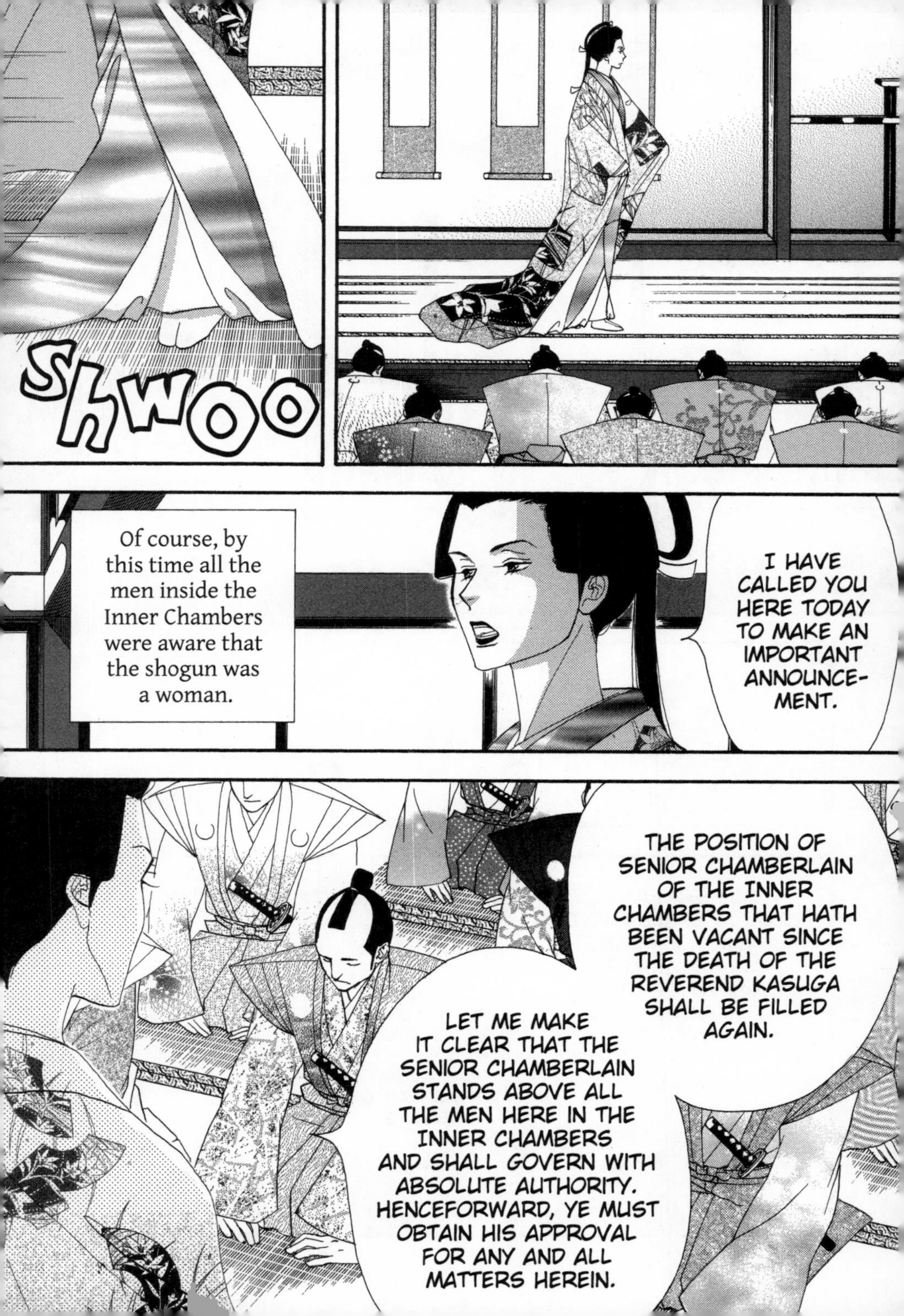
SHWOO
I HAVE CALLED YOU HERE TODAY TO MAKE AN IMPORTANT ANNOUNCE-MENT.
Of course, by this time all the men inside the Inner Chambers were aware that the shogun was a woman.
THE POSITION OF SENIOR CHAMBERLAIN OF THE INNER CHAMBERS THAT HATH BEEN VACANT SINCE THE DEATH OF THE REVEREND KASUGA SHALL BE FILLED AGAIN.
LET ME MAKE IT CLEAR THAT THE SENIOR CHAMBERLAIN STANDS ABOVE ALL THE MEN HERE IN THE INNER CHAMBERS AND SHALL GOVERN WITH ABSOLUTE AUTHORITY. HENCEFORWARD, YE MUST OBTAIN HIS APPROVAL FOR ANY AND ALL MATTERS HEREIN.

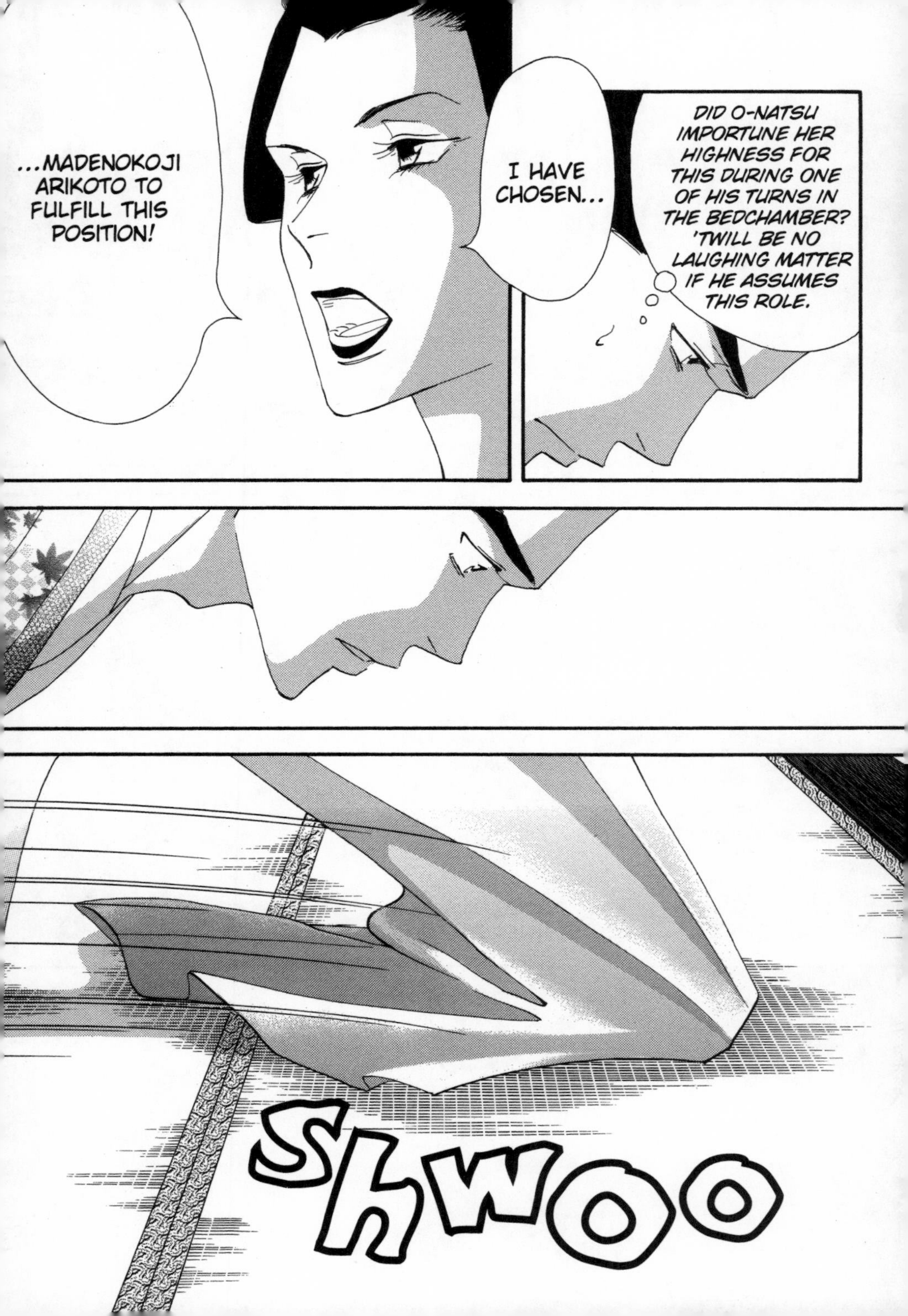
DID O-NATSU IMPORTUNE HER HIGHNESS FOR THIS DURING ONE OF HIS TURNS IN THE BEDCHAMBER? 'TWILL BE NO LAUGHING MATTER IF HE ASSUMES THIS ROLE.
I HAVE CHOSEN...
...MADENOKOJI ARIKOTO TO FULFILL THIS POSITION!
SHWOO

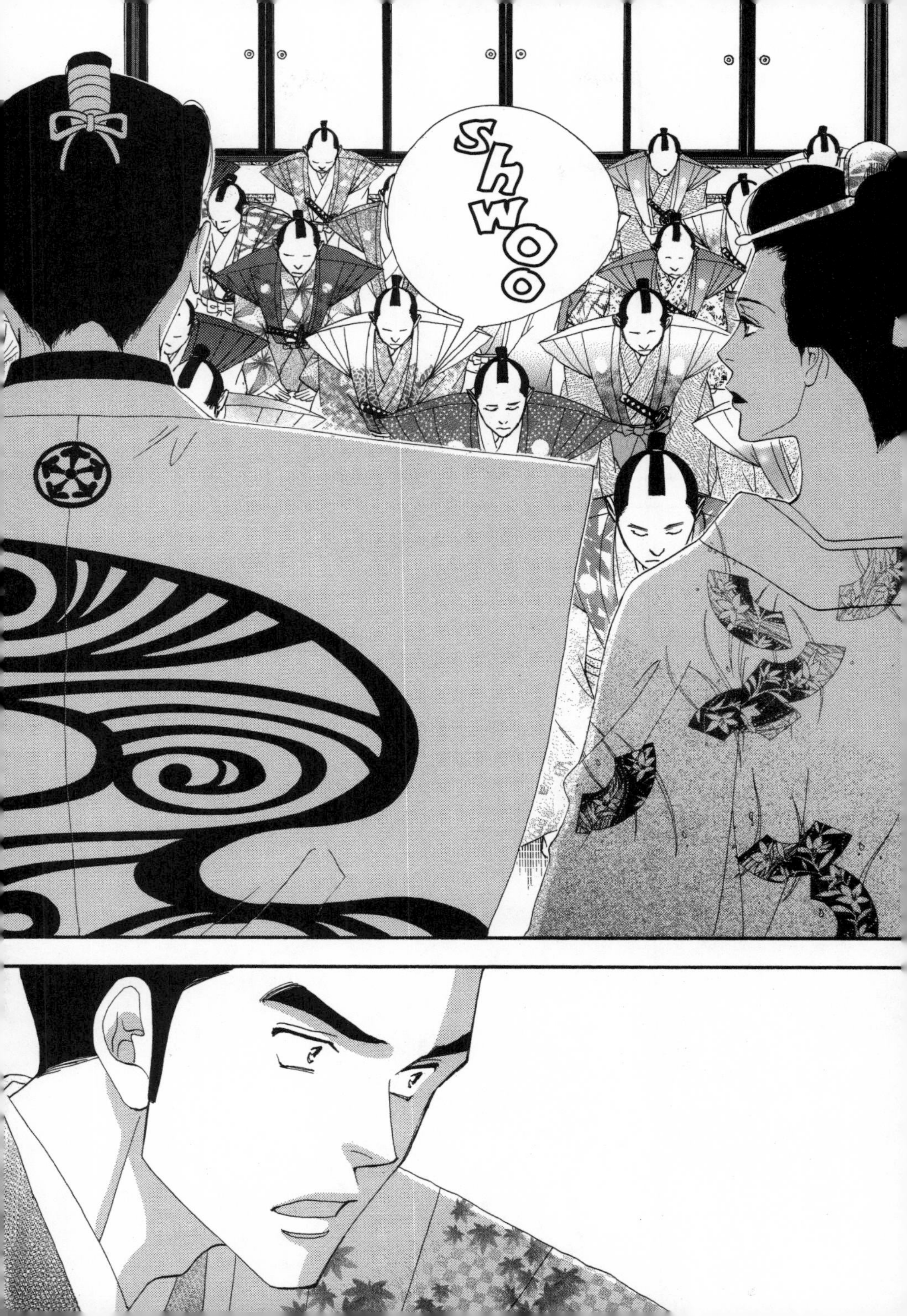
SHWOO

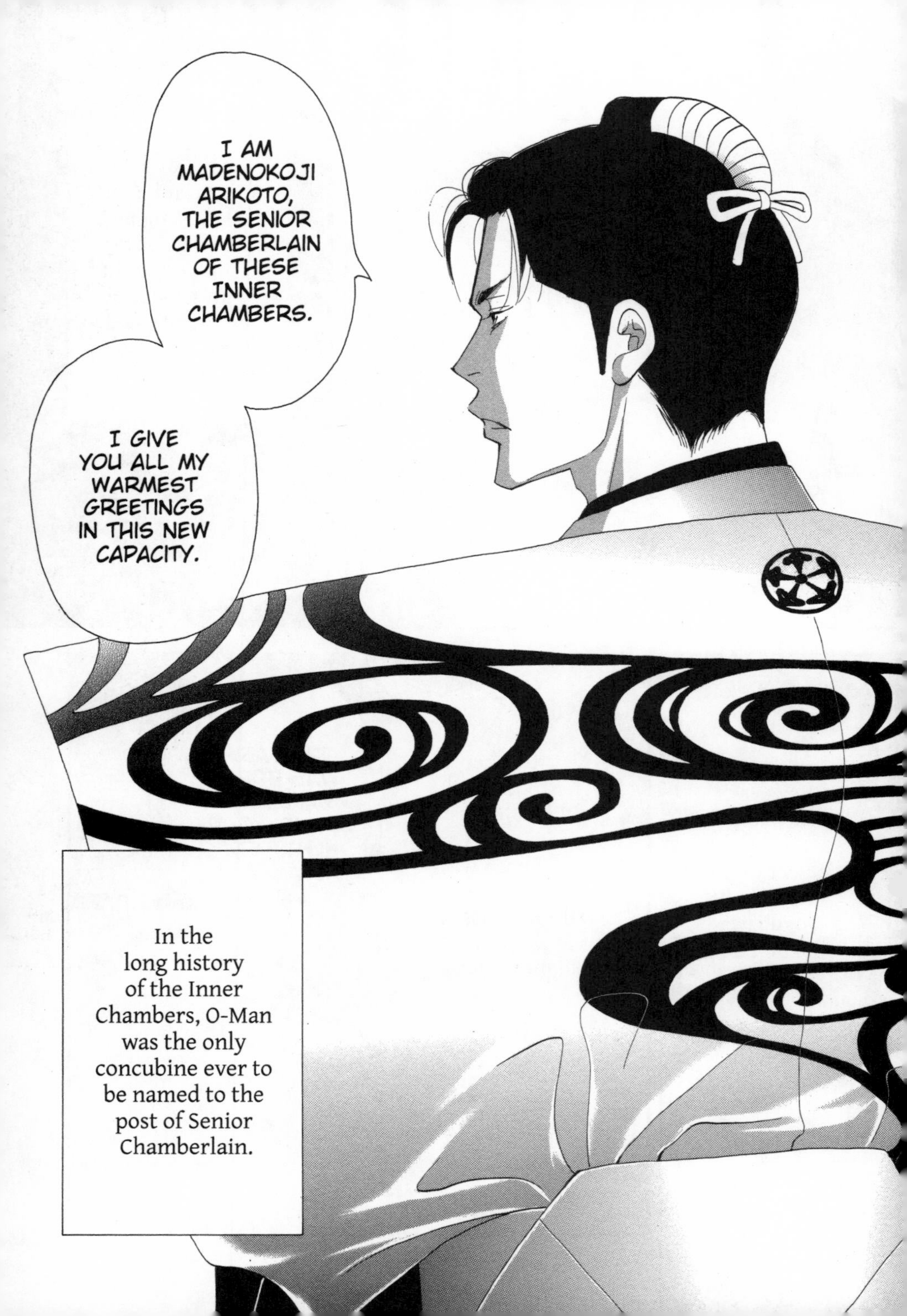
I AM MADENOKOJI ARIKOTO, THE SENIOR CHAMBERLAIN OF THESE INNER CHAMBERS.
I GIVE YOU ALL MY WARMEST GREETINGS IN THIS NEW CAPACITY.
In the long history of the Inner Chambers, O-Man was the only concubine ever to be named to the post of Senior Chamberlain.

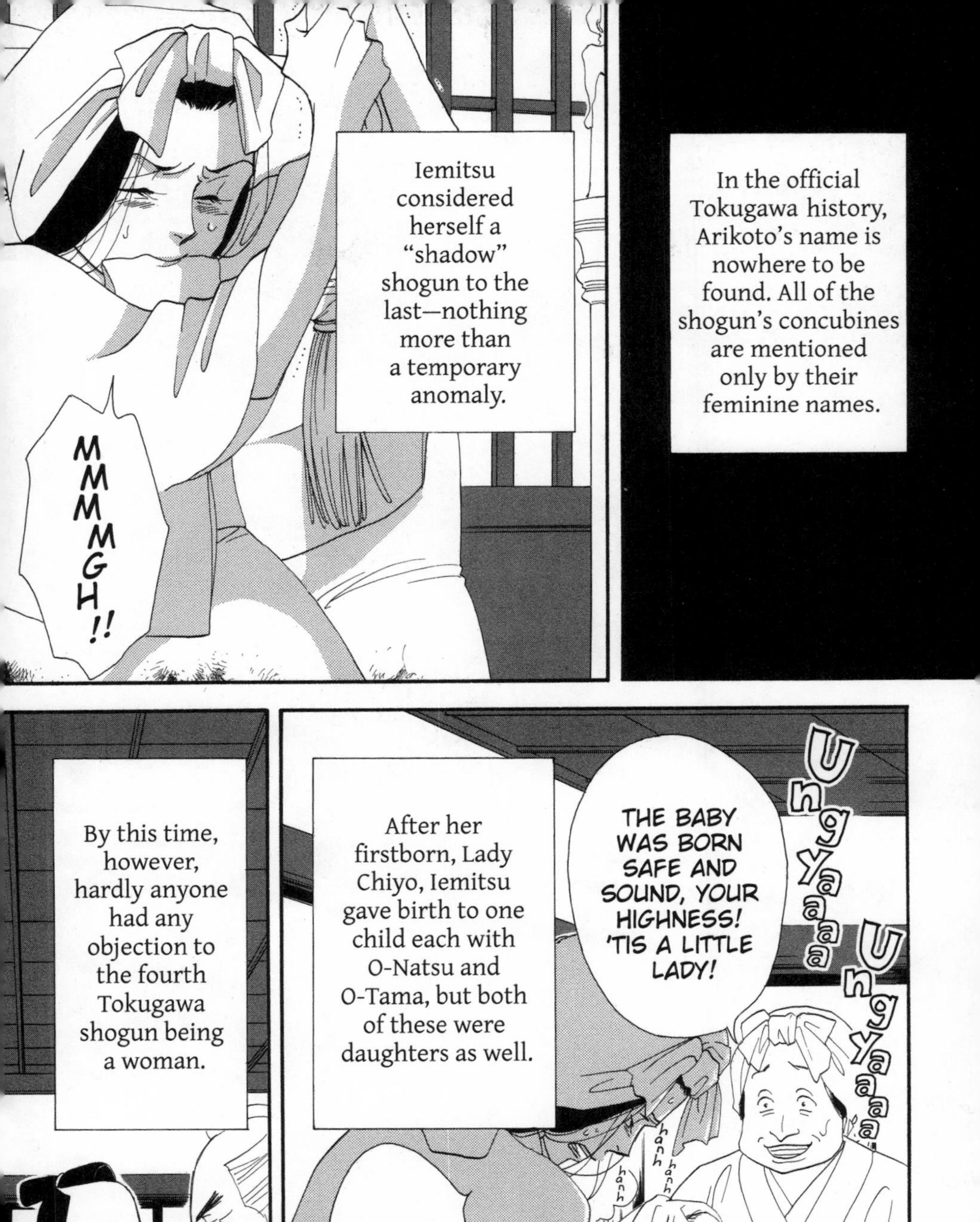
In the official Tokugawa history, Arikoto's name is nowhere to be found. All of the shogun's concubines are mentioned only by their feminine names.
Iemitsu considered herself a "shadow" shogun to the last—nothing more than a temporary anomaly.
MMMMGH!!
Ungyaaaa
Ungyaaaa
THE BABY WAS BORN SAFE AND SOUND, YOUR HIGHNESS! 'TIS A LITTLE LADY!
After her firstborn, Lady Chiyo, Iemitsu gave birth to one child each with O-Natsu and O-Tama, but both of these were daughters as well.
hanh hanh
hanh hanh
AH... AYE.
By this time, however, hardly anyone had any objection to the fourth Tokugawa shogun being a woman.

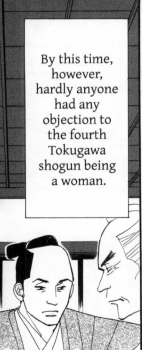

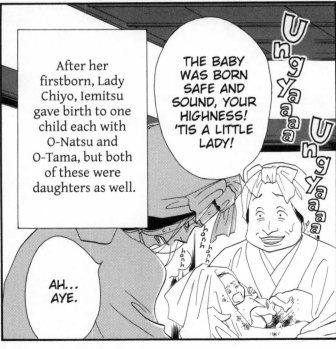

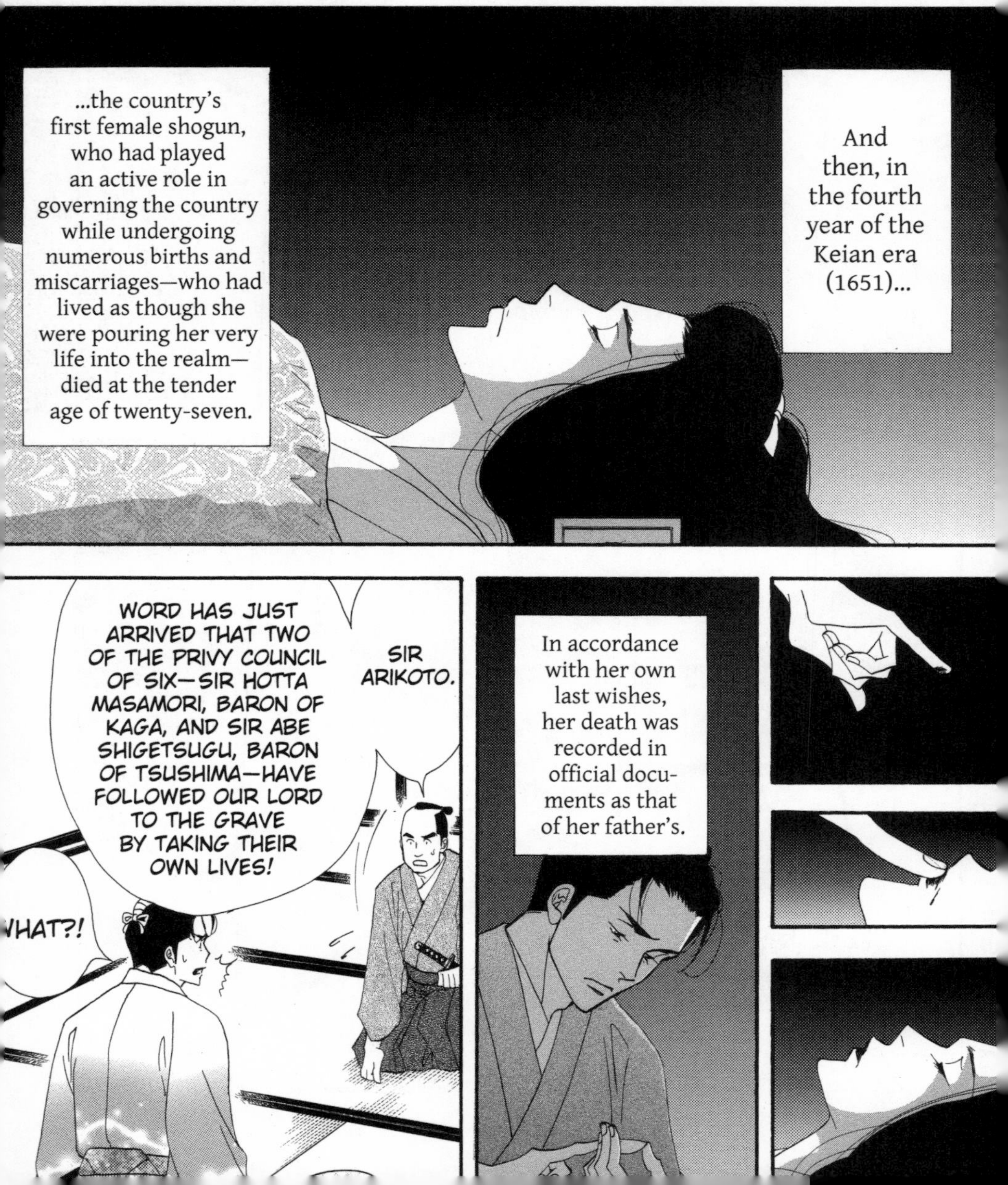
And then, in the fourth year of the Keian era (1651)...
...the country's first female shogun, who had played an active role in governing the country while undergoing numerous births and miscarriages—who had lived as though she were pouring her very life into the realm—died at the tender age of twenty-seven.
In accordance with her own last wishes, her death was recorded in official documents as that of her father's.
SIR ARIKOTO.
WORD HAS JUST ARRIVED THAT TWO OF THE PRIVY COUNCIL OF SIX—SIR HOTTA MASAMORI, BARON OF KAGA, AND SIR ABE SHIGETSUGU, BARON OF TSUSHIMA—HAVE FOLLOWED OUR LORD TO THE GRAVE BY TAKING THEIR OWN LIVES!
WHAT?!

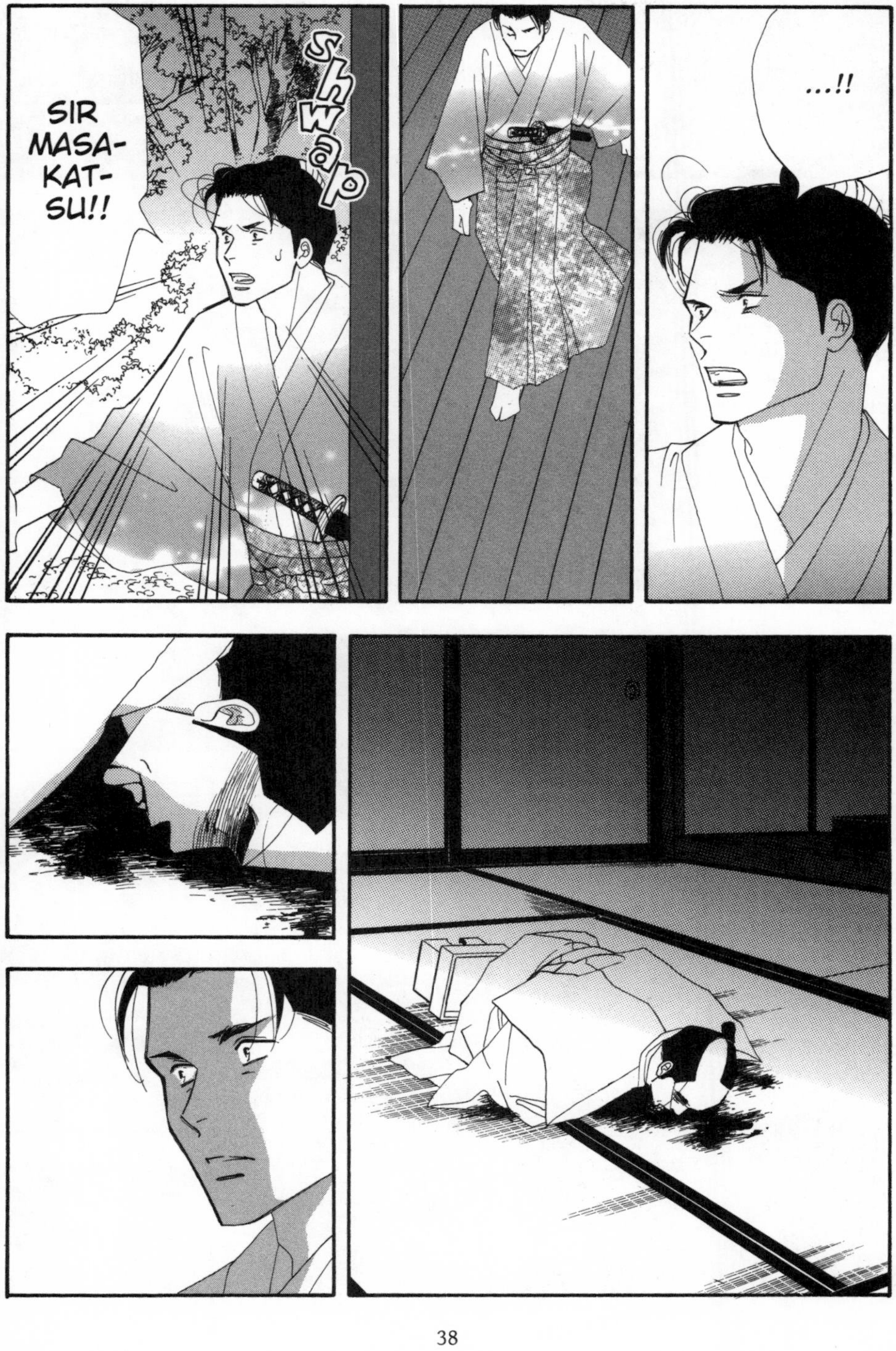
...!!
shwap
SIR MASA-KAT-SU!!

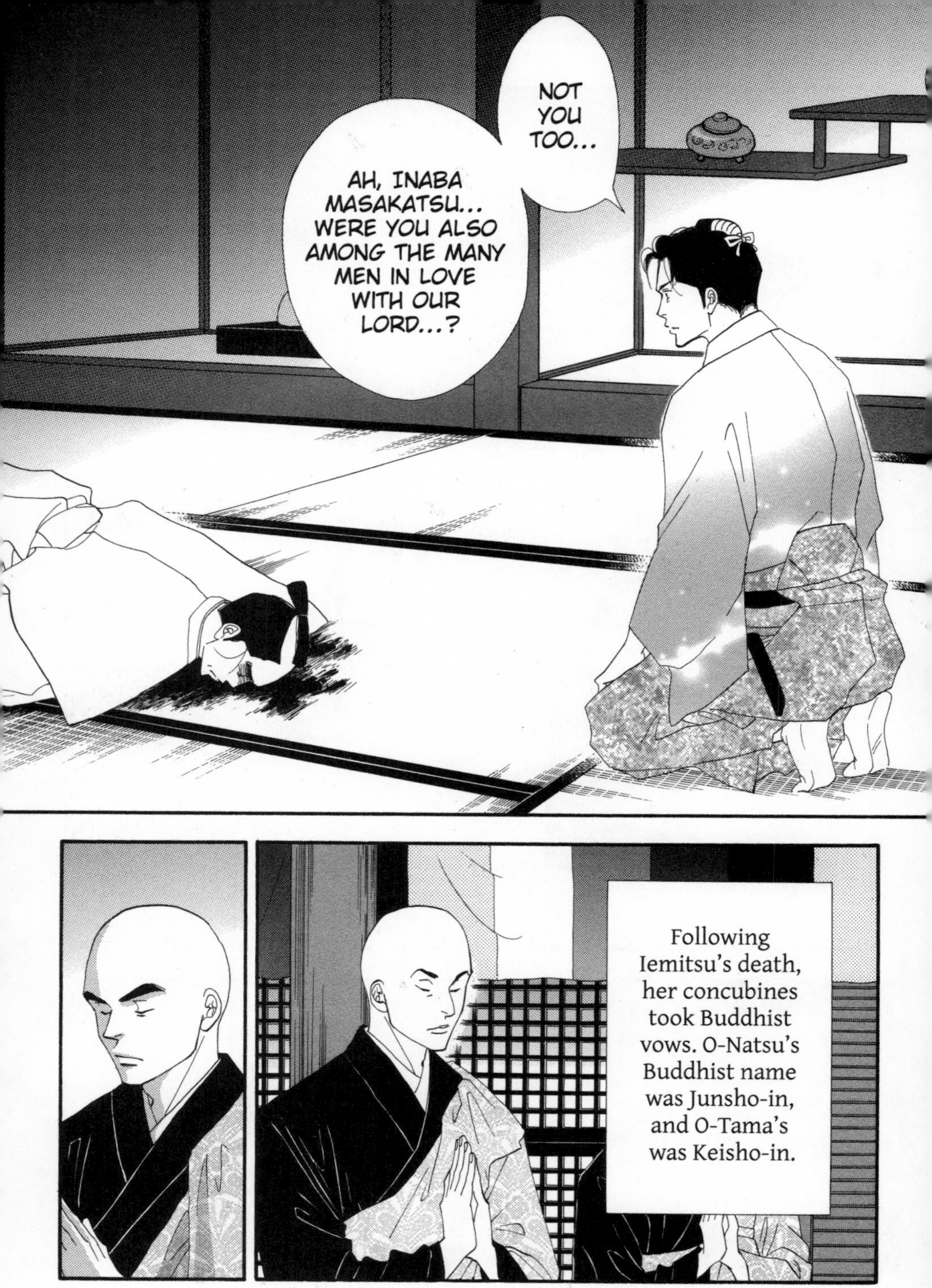
NOT YOU TOO...
AH, INABA MASAKATSU... WERE YOU ALSO AMONG THE MANY MEN IN LOVE WITH OUR LORD...?
Following Iemitsu's death, her concubines took Buddhist vows. O-Natsu's Buddhist name was Junsho-in, and O-Tama's was Keisho-in.

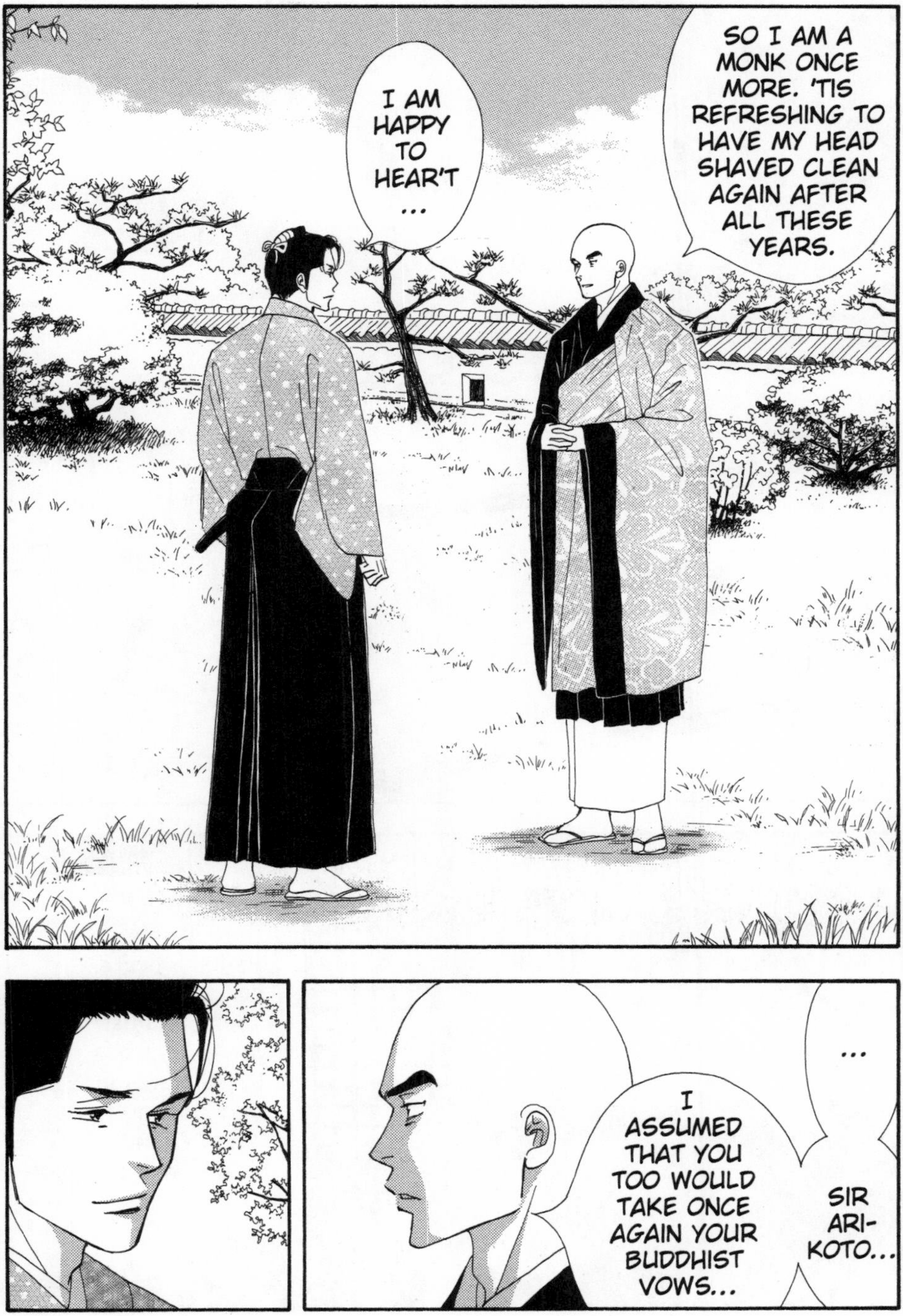
SO I AM A MONK ONCE MORE. 'TIS REFRESHING TO HAVE MY HEAD SHAVED CLEAN AGAIN AFTER ALL THESE YEARS.
I AM HAPPY TO HEAR'T ...
...
SIR ARI-KOTO...
I ASSUMED THAT YOU TOO WOULD TAKE ONCE AGAIN YOUR BUDDHIST VOWS...

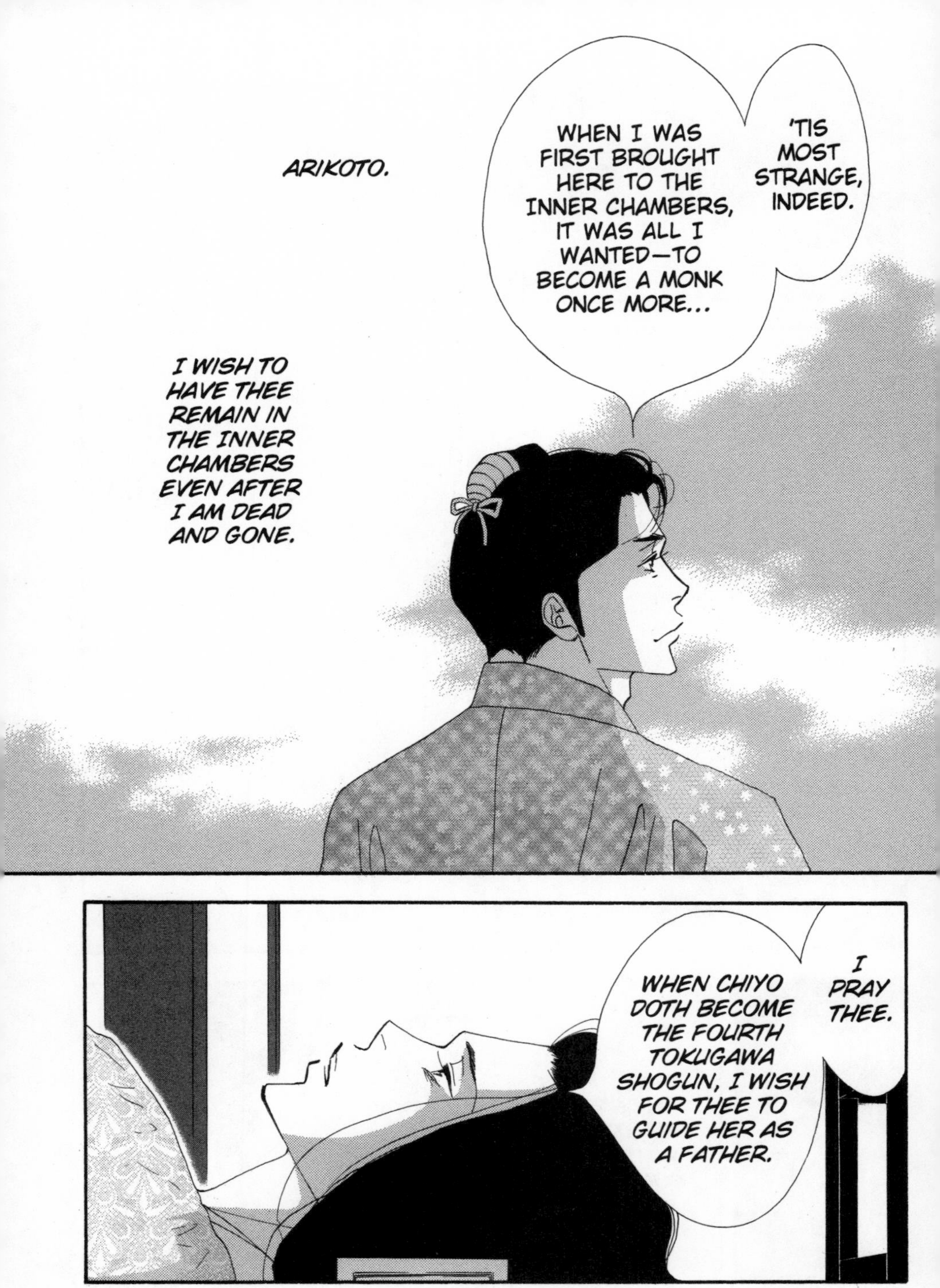
'TIS MOST STRANGE, INDEED.
WHEN I WAS FIRST BROUGHT HERE TO THE INNER CHAMBERS, IT WAS ALL I WANTED—TO BECOME A MONK ONCE MORE...
ARIKOTO.
I WISH TO HAVE THEE REMAIN IN THE INNER CHAMBERS EVEN AFTER I AM DEAD AND GONE.
I PRAY THEE.
WHEN CHIYO DOTH BECOME THE FOURTH TOKUGAWA SHOGUN, I WISH FOR THEE TO GUIDE HER AS A FATHER.

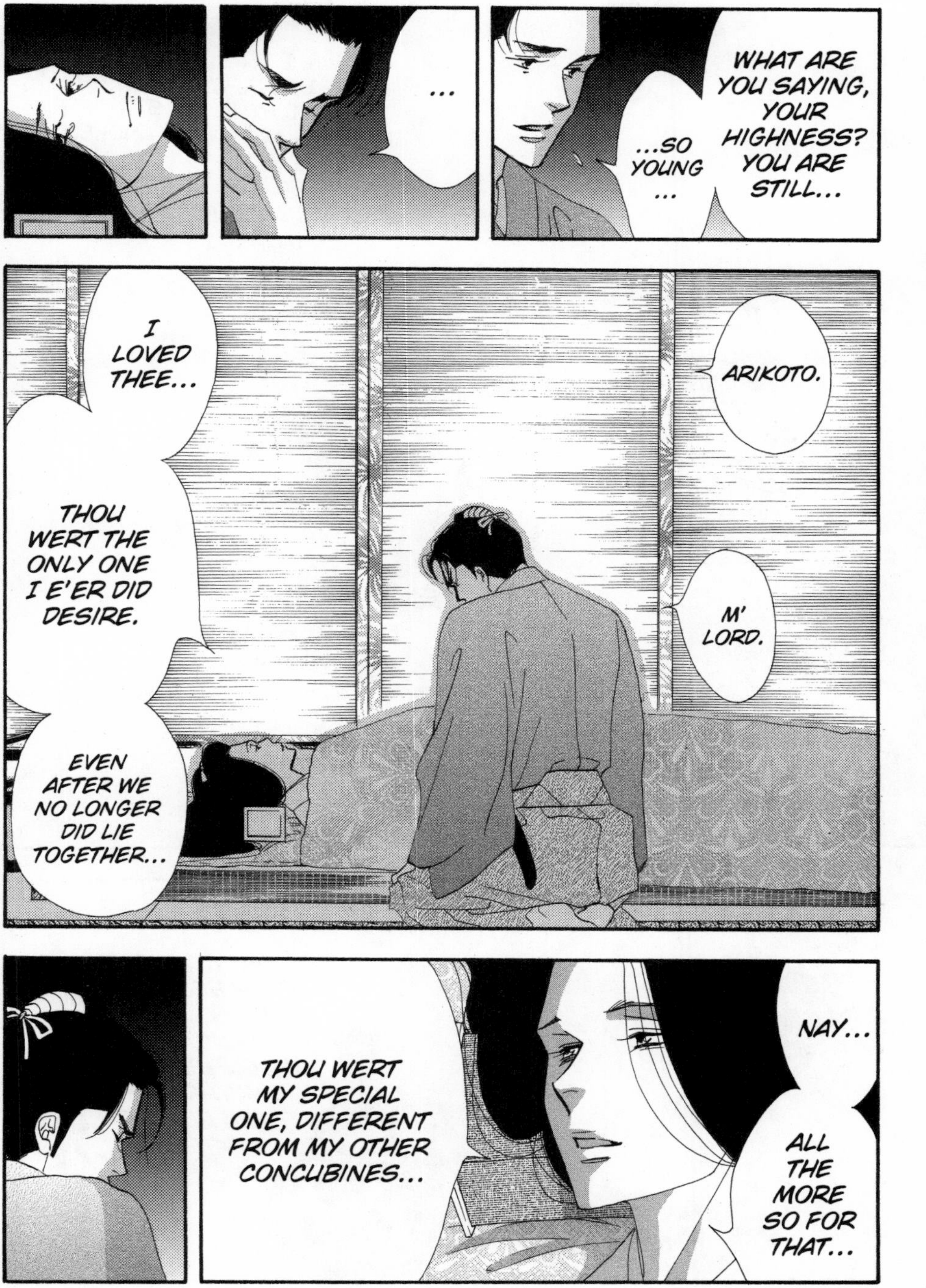
WHAT ARE YOU SAYING, YOUR HIGHNESS? YOU ARE STILL...
...SO YOUNG...
...
ARIKOTO.
M' LORD.
I LOVED THEE...
THOU WERT THE ONLY ONE I E'ER DID DESIRE.
EVEN AFTER WE NO LONGER DID LIE TOGETHER...
NAY...
ALL THE MORE SO FOR THAT...
THOU WERT MY SPECIAL ONE, DIFFERENT FROM MY OTHER CONCUBINES...

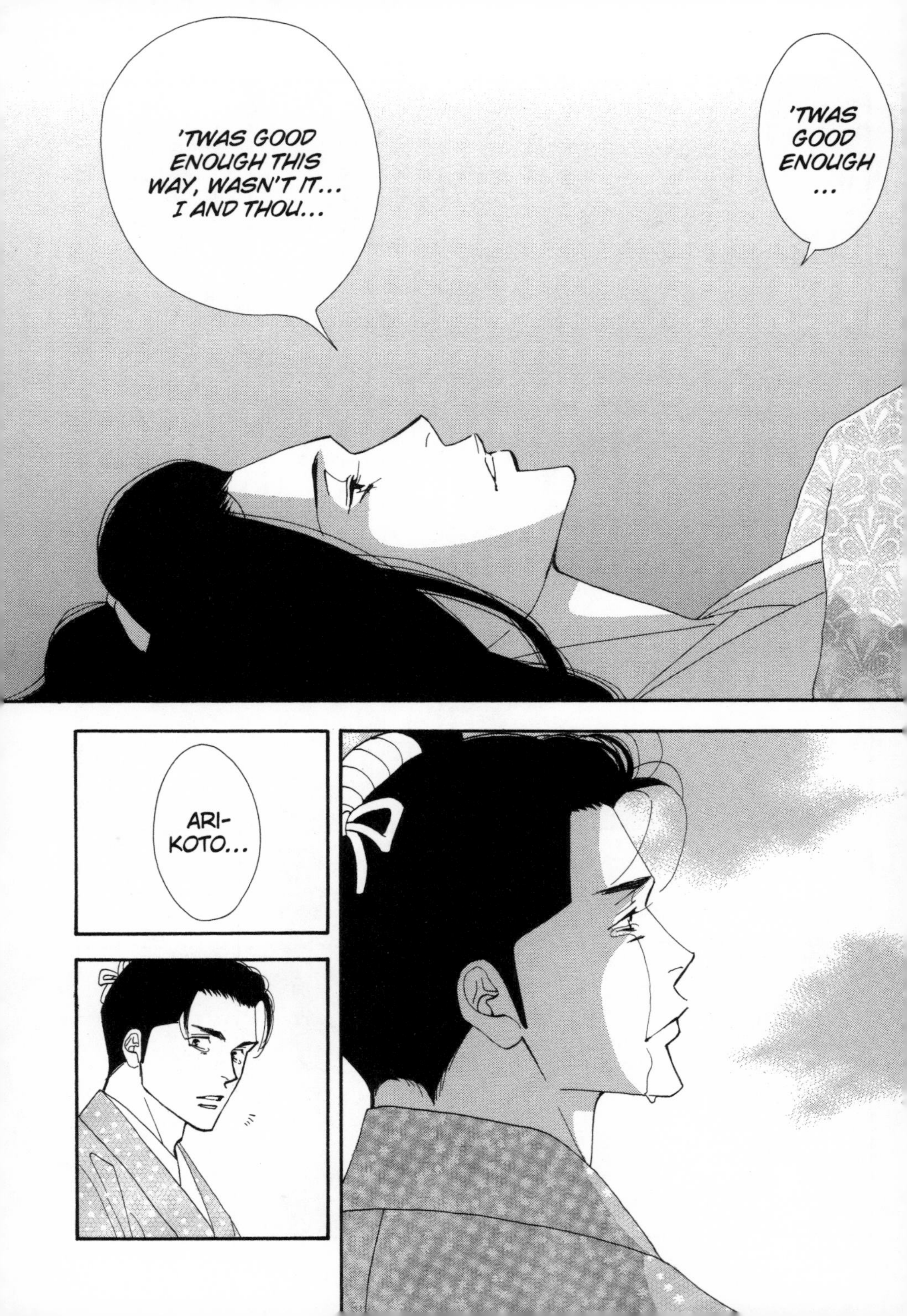
'TWAS GOOD ENOUGH ...
'TWAS GOOD ENOUGH THIS WAY, WASN'T IT... I AND THOU...
ARI-KOTO...

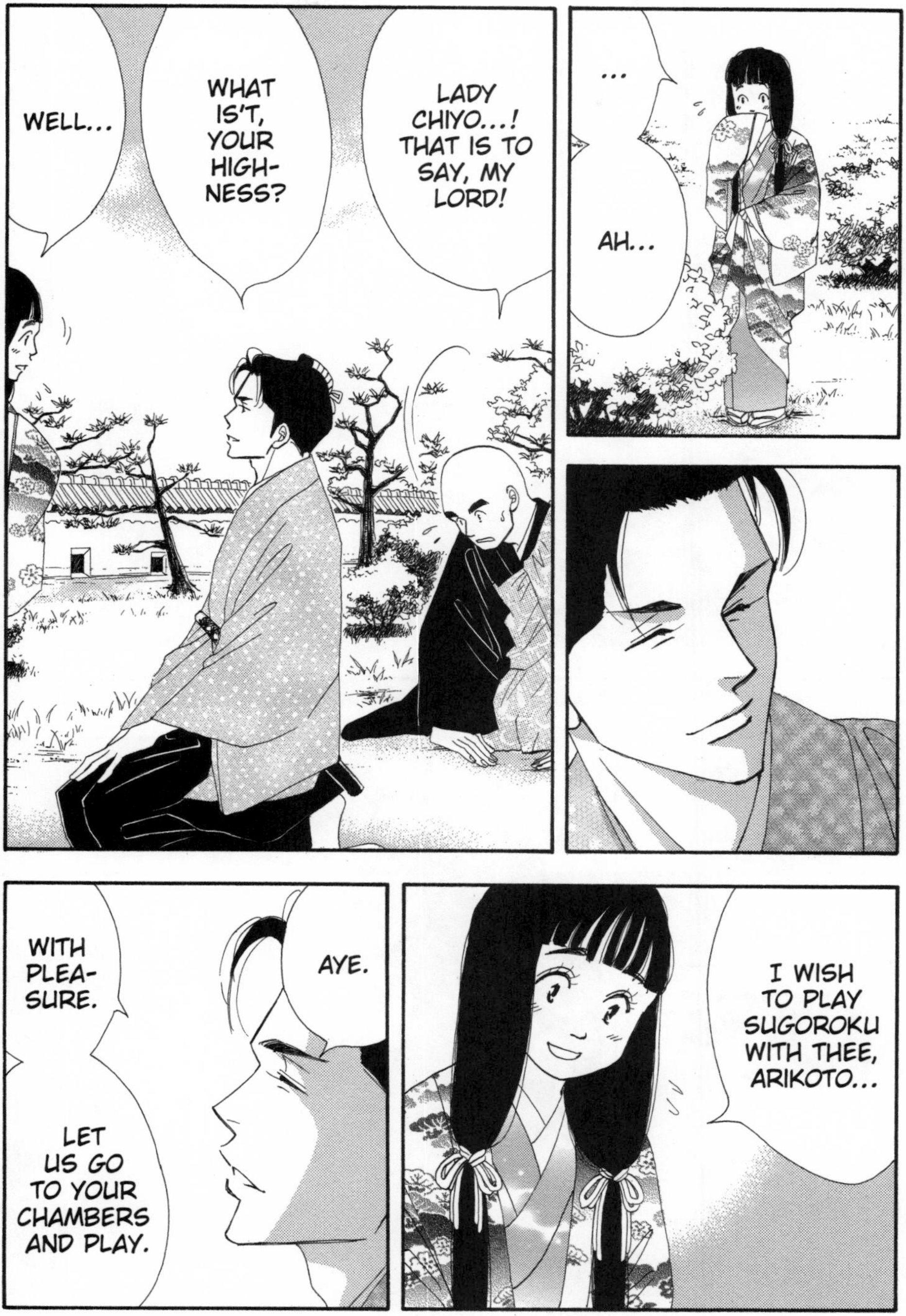
...
AH...
LADY CHIYO...! THAT IS TO SAY, MY LORD!
WHAT IS'T, YOUR HIGHNESS?
WELL...
I WISH TO PLAY SUGOROKU WITH THEE, ARIKOTO...
AYE.
WITH PLEASURE.
LET US GO TO YOUR CHAMBERS AND PLAY.

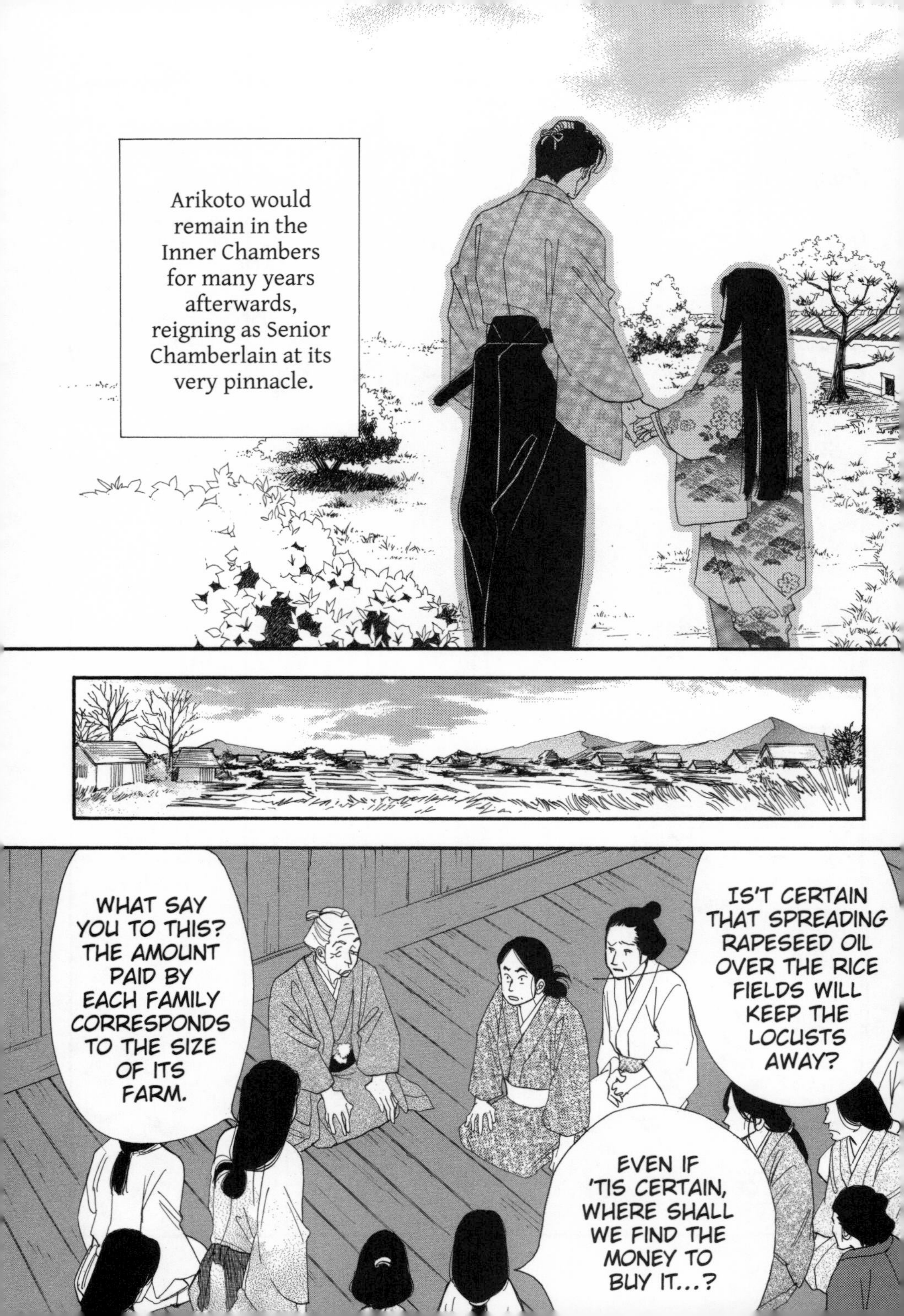
Arikoto would remain in the Inner Chambers for many years afterwards, reigning as Senior Chamberlain at its very pinnacle.
IS'T CERTAIN THAT SPREADING RAPESEED OIL OVER THE RICE FIELDS WILL KEEP THE LOCUSTS AWAY?
WHAT SAY YOU TO THIS? THE AMOUNT PAID BY EACH FAMILY CORRESPONDS TO THE SIZE OF ITS FARM.
EVEN IF 'TIS CERTAIN, WHERE SHALL WE FIND THE MONEY TO BUY IT...?

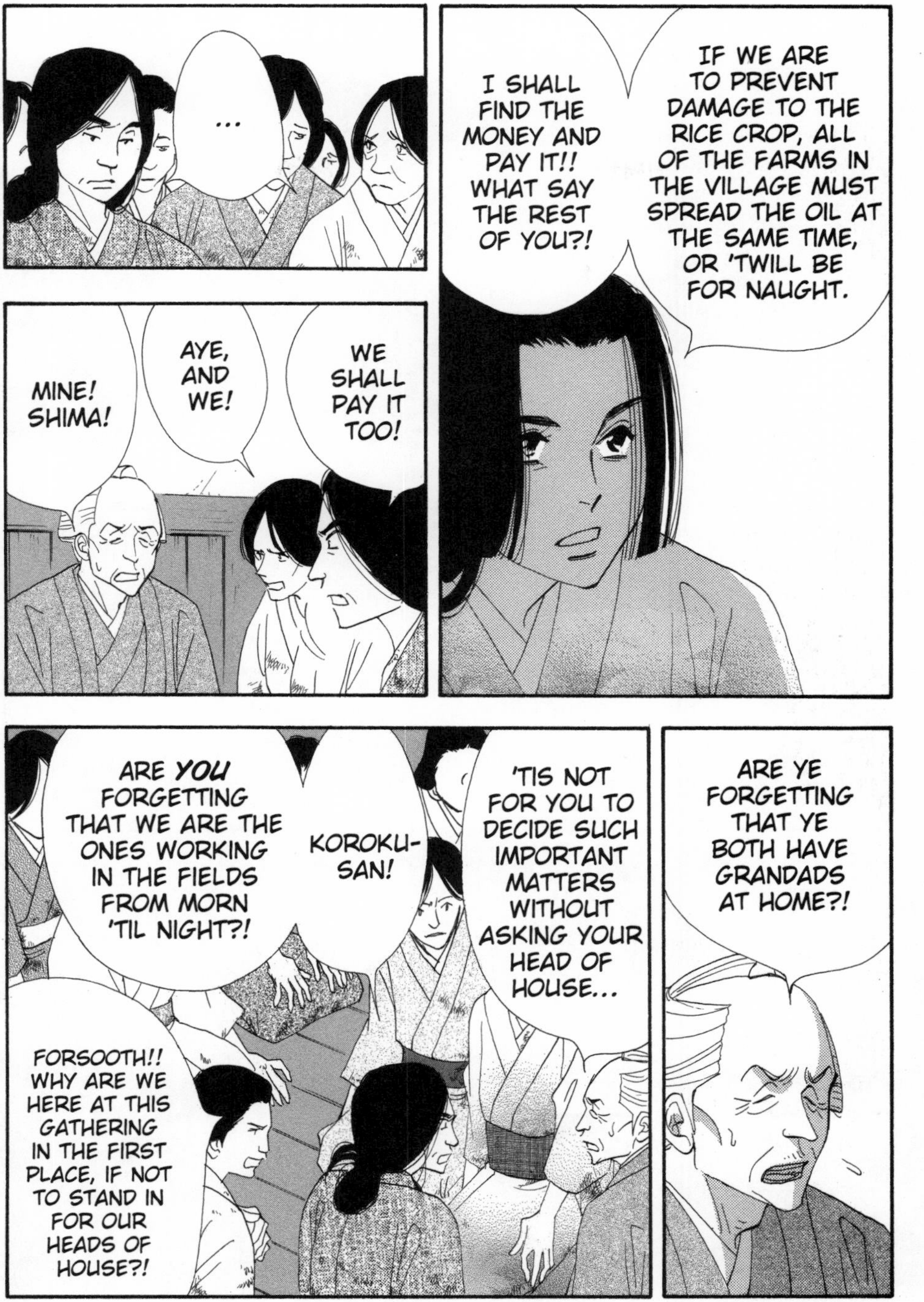
IF WE ARE TO PREVENT DAMAGE TO THE RICE CROP, ALL OF THE FARMS IN THE VILLAGE MUST SPREAD THE OIL AT THE SAME TIME, OR 'TWILL BE FOR NAUGHT.
I SHALL FIND THE MONEY AND PAY IT!! WHAT SAY THE REST OF YOU?!
...
WE SHALL PAY IT TOO!
AYE, AND WE!
MINE! SHIMA!
ARE YE FORGETTING THAT YE BOTH HAVE GRANDADS AT HOME?!
'TIS NOT FOR YOU TO DECIDE SUCH IMPORTANT MATTERS WITHOUT ASKING YOUR HEAD OF HOUSE...
KOROKU-SAN!
ARE YOU FORGETTING THAT WE ARE THE ONES WORKING IN THE FIELDS FROM MORN 'TIL NIGHT?!
FORSOOTH!! WHY ARE WE HERE AT THIS GATHERING IN THE FIRST PLACE, IF NOT TO STAND IN FOR OUR HEADS OF HOUSE?!

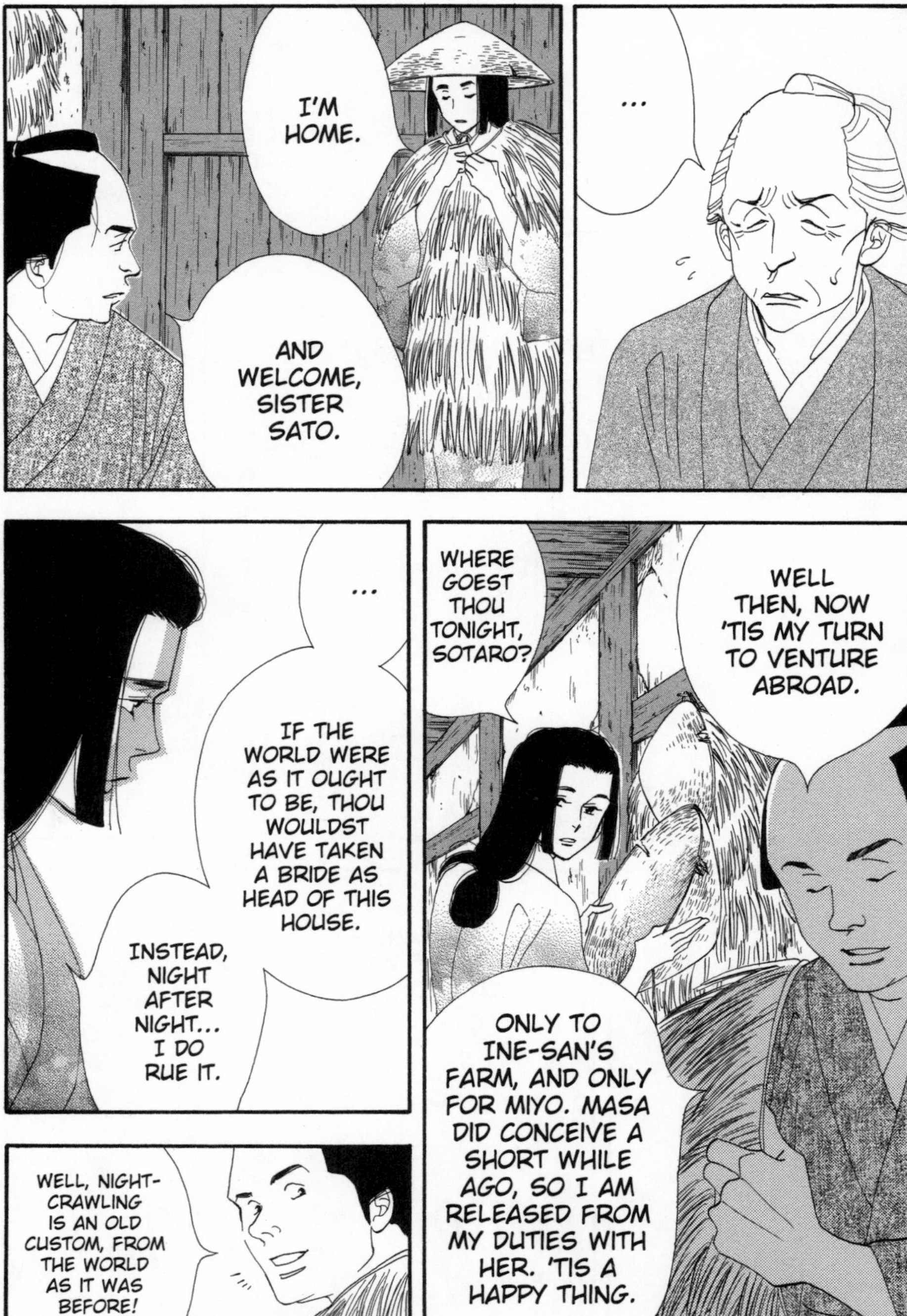
...
I'M HOME.
AND WELCOME, SISTER SATO.
WELL THEN, NOW 'TIS MY TURN TO VENTURE ABROAD.
WHERE GOEST THOU TONIGHT, SOTARO?
ONLY TO INE-SAN'S FARM, AND ONLY FOR MIYO. MASA DID CONCEIVE A SHORT WHILE AGO, SO I AM RELEASED FROM MY DUTIES WITH HER. 'TIS A HAPPY THING.
...
IF THE WORLD WERE AS IT OUGHT TO BE, THOU WOULDST HAVE TAKEN A BRIDE AS HEAD OF THIS HOUSE.
INSTEAD, NIGHT AFTER NIGHT... I DO RUE IT.
WELL, NIGHT-CRAWLING IS AN OLD CUSTOM, FROM THE WORLD AS IT WAS BEFORE!

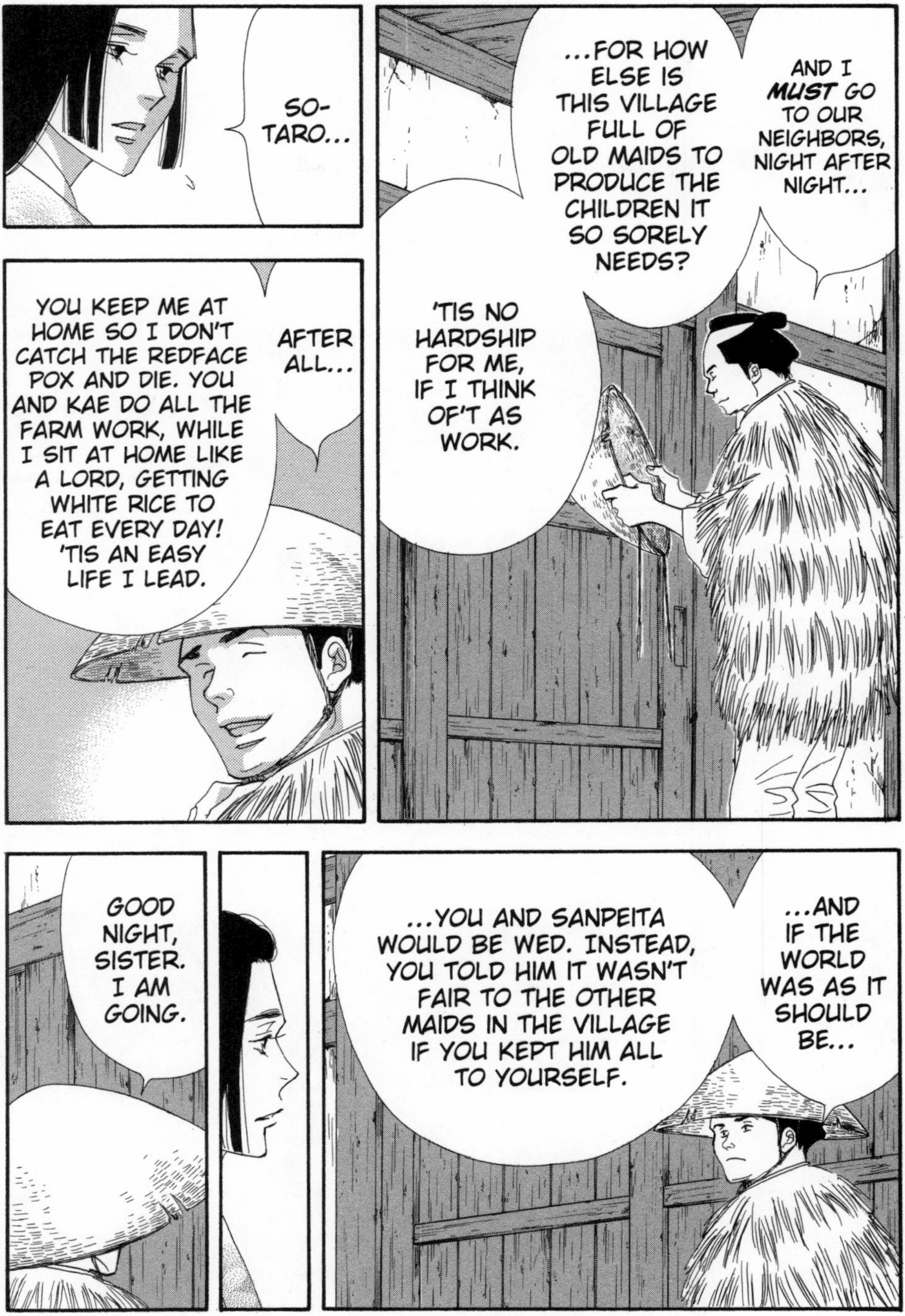
AND I **MUST** GO TO OUR NEIGHBORS, NIGHT AFTER NIGHT...
...FOR HOW ELSE IS THIS VILLAGE FULL OF OLD MAIDS TO PRODUCE THE CHILDREN IT SO SORELY NEEDS?
'TIS NO HARDSHIP FOR ME, IF I THINK OF'T AS WORK.
SO-TARO...
AFTER ALL...
YOU KEEP ME AT HOME SO I DON'T CATCH THE REDFACE POX AND DIE. YOU AND KAE DO ALL THE FARM WORK, WHILE I SIT AT HOME LIKE A LORD, GETTING WHITE RICE TO EAT EVERY DAY! 'TIS AN EASY LIFE I LEAD.
...AND IF THE WORLD WAS AS IT SHOULD BE...
...YOU AND SANPEITA WOULD BE WED. INSTEAD, YOU TOLD HIM IT WASN'T FAIR TO THE OTHER MAIDS IN THE VILLAGE IF YOU KEPT HIM ALL TO YOURSELF.
GOOD NIGHT, SISTER. I AM GOING.

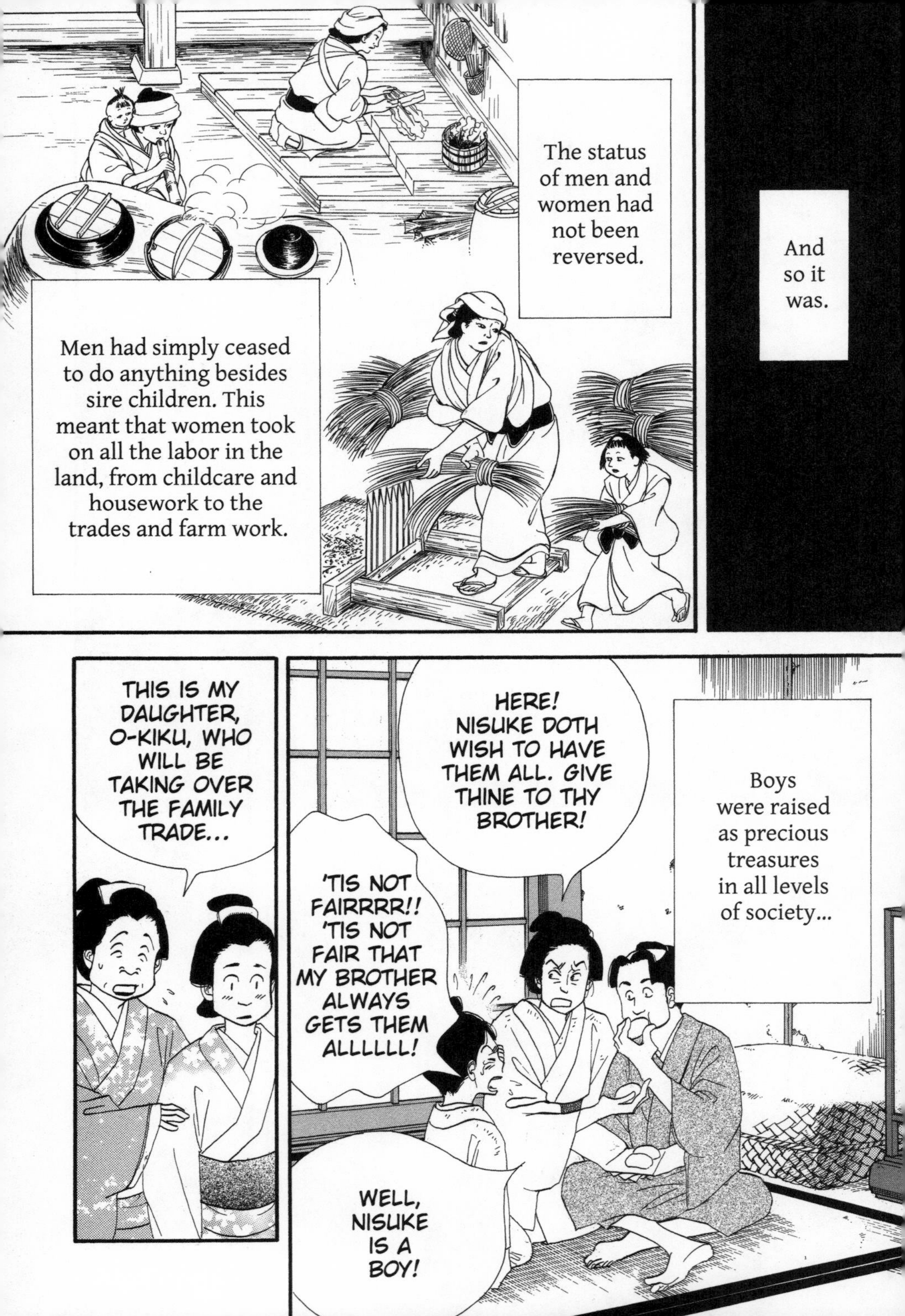
And so it was.
The status of men and women had not been reversed.
Men had simply ceased to do anything besides sire children. This meant that women took on all the labor in the land, from childcare and housework to the trades and farm work.
Boys were raised as precious treasures in all levels of society...
HERE! NISUKE DOTH WISH TO HAVE THEM ALL. GIVE THINE TO THY BROTHER!
'TIS NOT FAIRRRR!! 'TIS NOT FAIR THAT MY BROTHER ALWAYS GETS THEM ALLLLLL!
WELL, NISUKE IS A BOY!
THIS IS MY DAUGHTER, O-KIKU, WHO WILL BE TAKING OVER THE FAMILY TRADE...

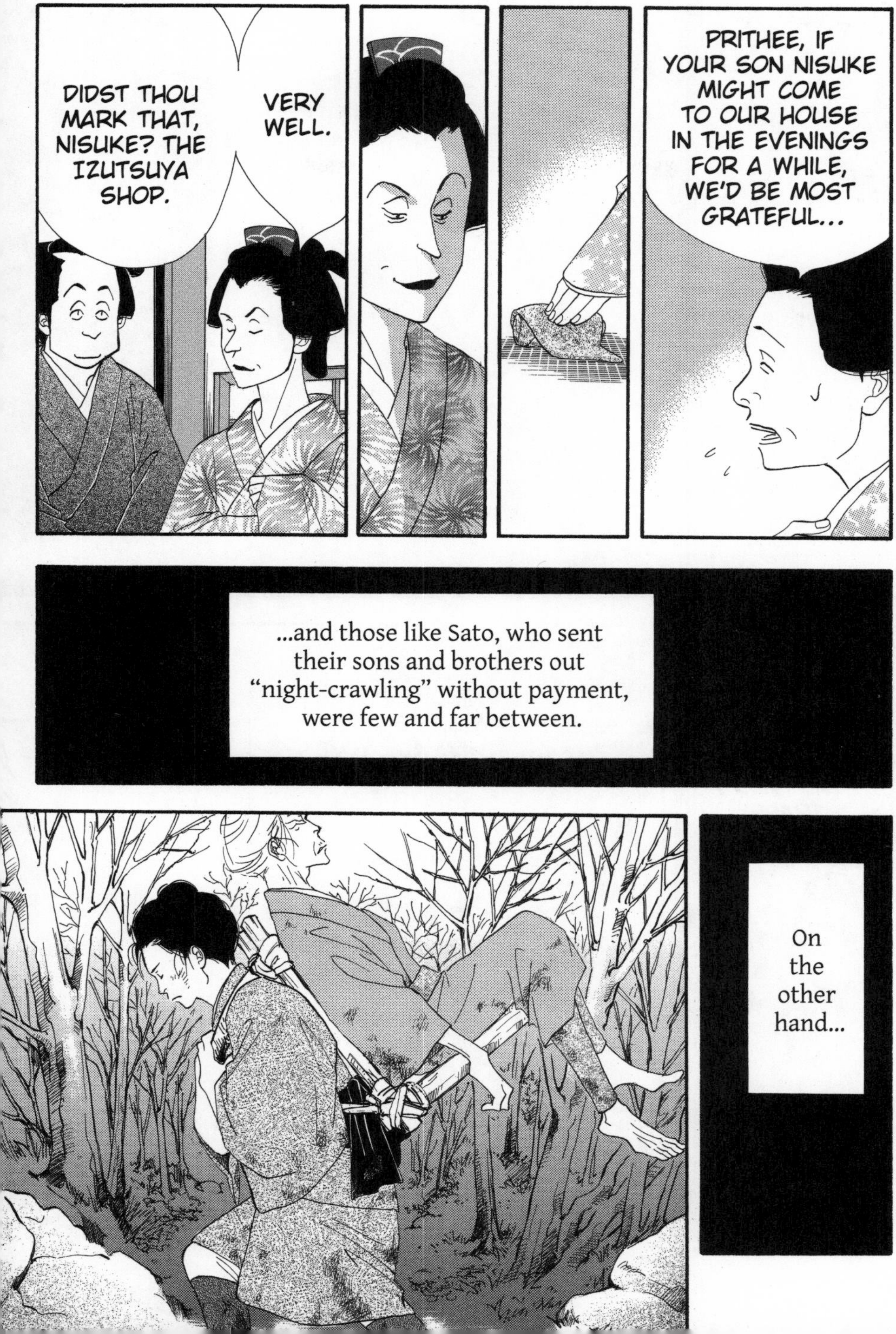
PRITHEE, IF YOUR SON NISUKE MIGHT COME TO OUR HOUSE IN THE EVENINGS FOR A WHILE, WE'D BE MOST GRATEFUL...
VERY WELL.
DIDST THOU MARK THAT, NISUKE? THE IZUTSUYA SHOP.
...and those like Sato, who sent their sons and brothers out "night-crawling" without payment, were few and far between.
On the other hand...

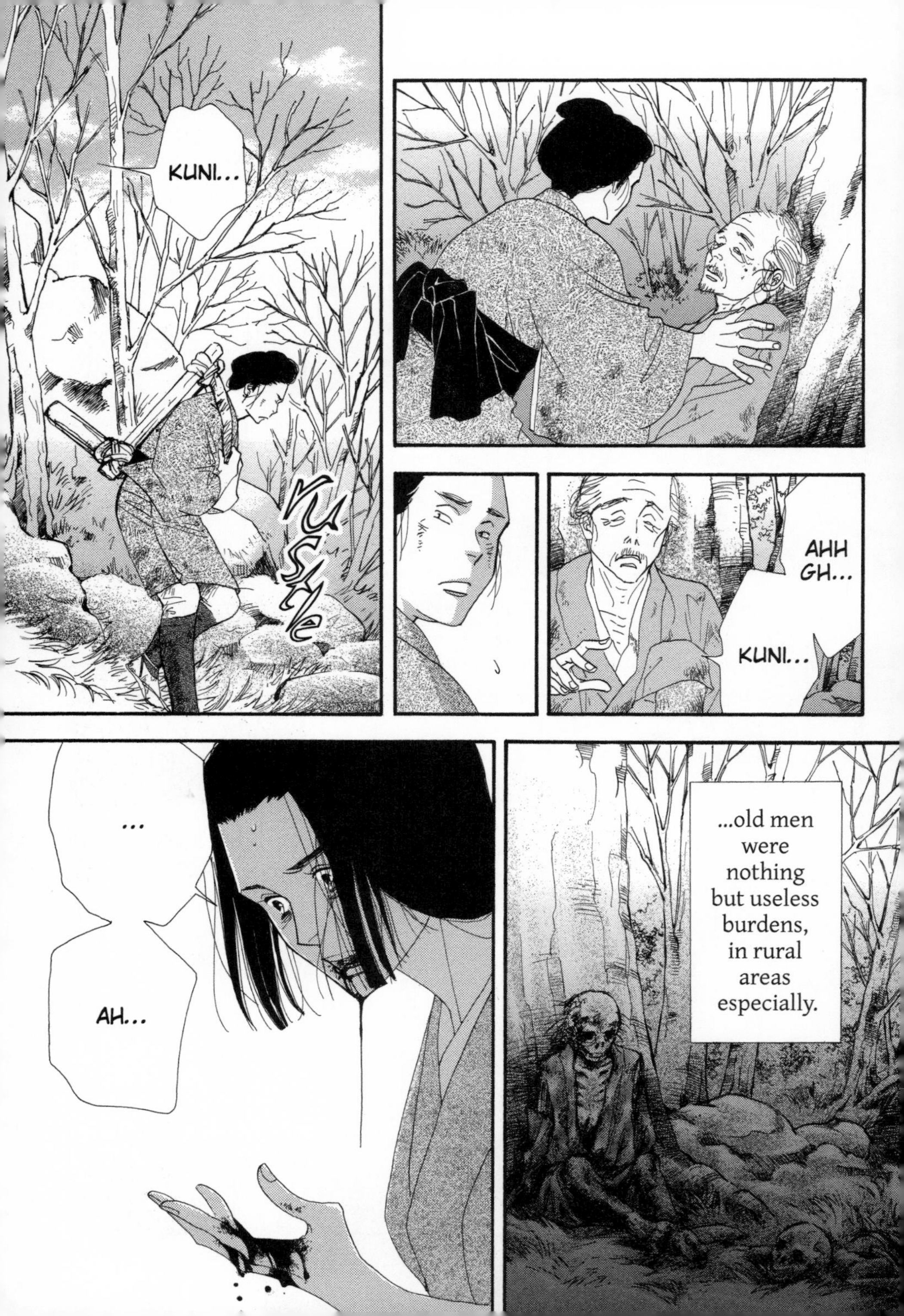
AHH GH...
KUNI...
KUNI...
RUSTLE
...old men were nothing but useless burdens, in rural areas especially.
...
AH...

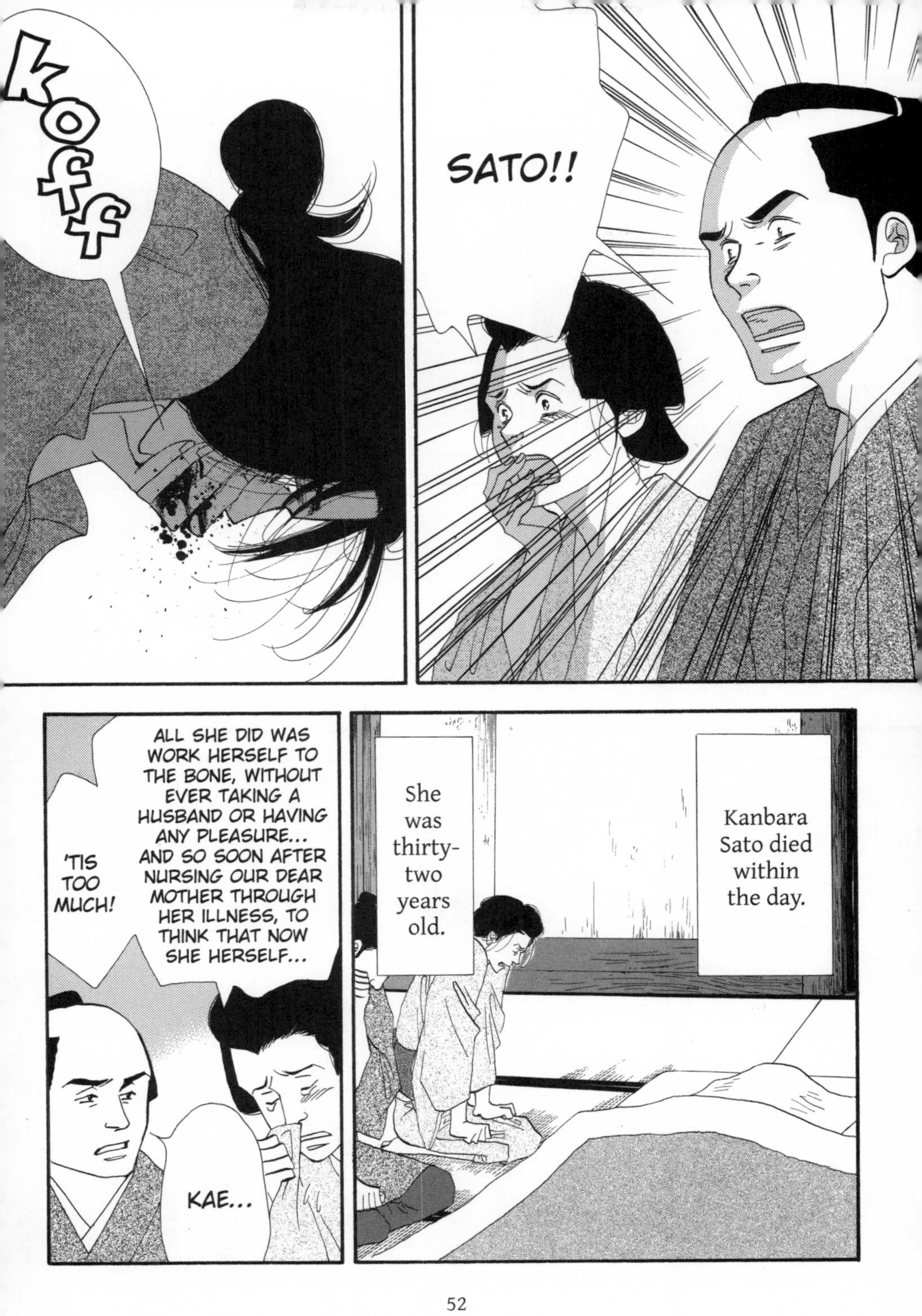
SATO!!
koff
Kanbara Sato died within the day.
She was thirty-two years old.
ALL SHE DID WAS WORK HERSELF TO THE BONE, WITHOUT EVER TAKING A HUSBAND OR HAVING ANY PLEASURE... AND SO SOON AFTER NURSING OUR DEAR MOTHER THROUGH HER ILLNESS, TO THINK THAT NOW SHE HERSELF...
'TIS TOO MUCH!
KAE...

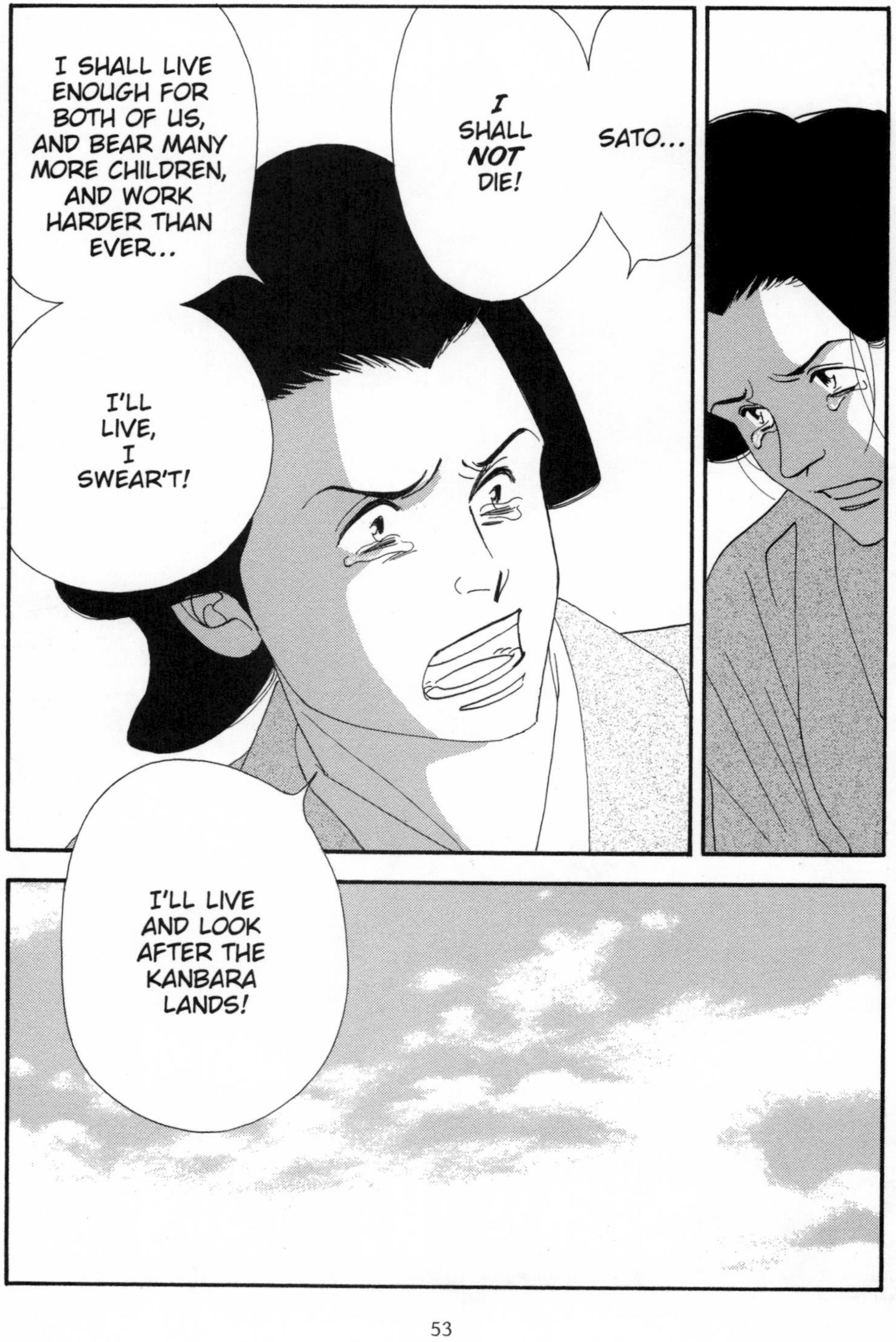
SATO...
I SHALL *NOT* DIE!
I SHALL LIVE ENOUGH FOR BOTH OF US, AND BEAR MANY MORE CHILDREN, AND WORK HARDER THAN EVER...
I'LL LIVE, I SWEAR'T!
I'LL LIVE AND LOOK AFTER THE KANBARA LANDS!

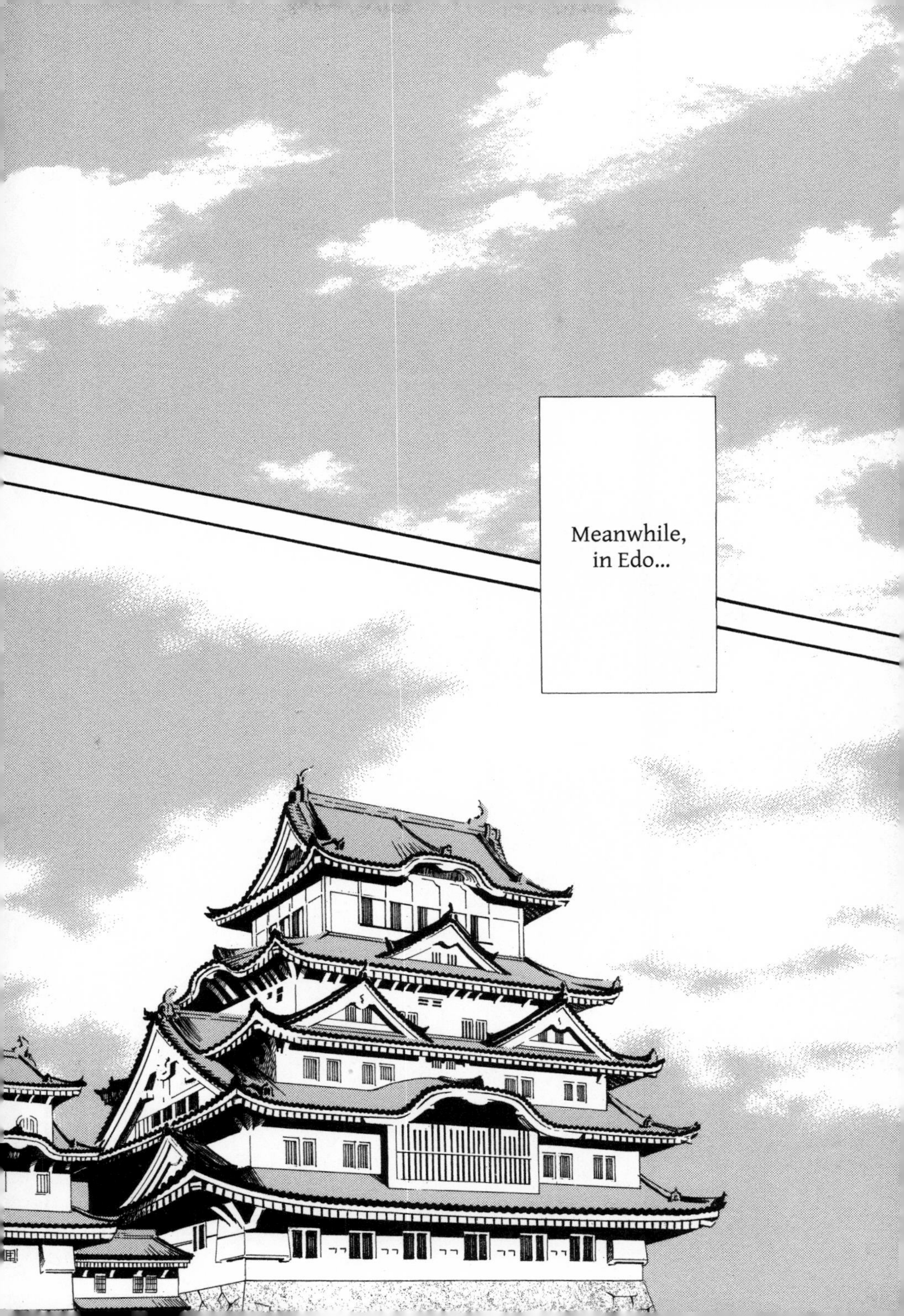
Meanwhile, in Edo...

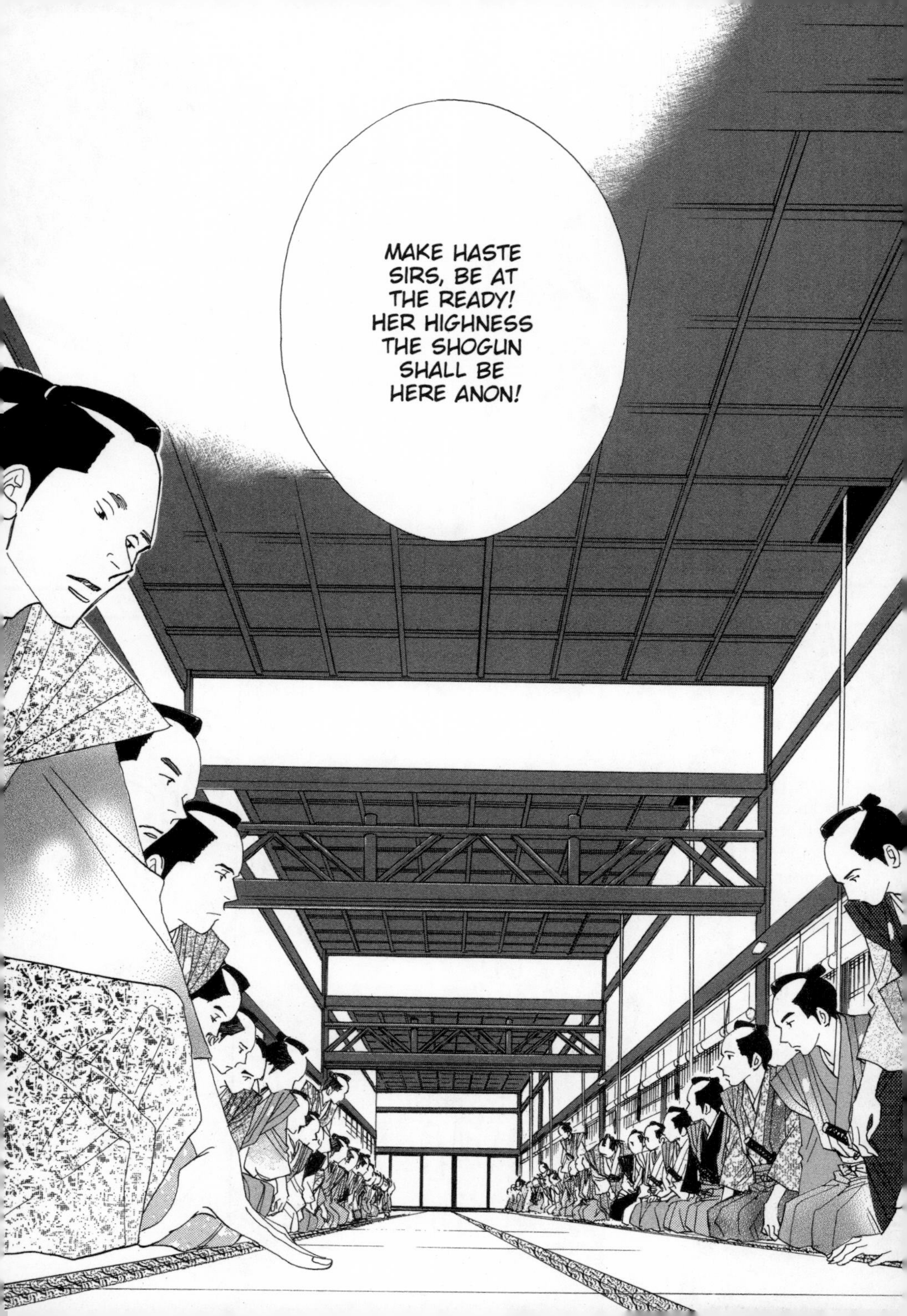
MAKE HASTE SIRS, BE AT THE READY! HER HIGHNESS THE SHOGUN SHALL BE HERE ANON!

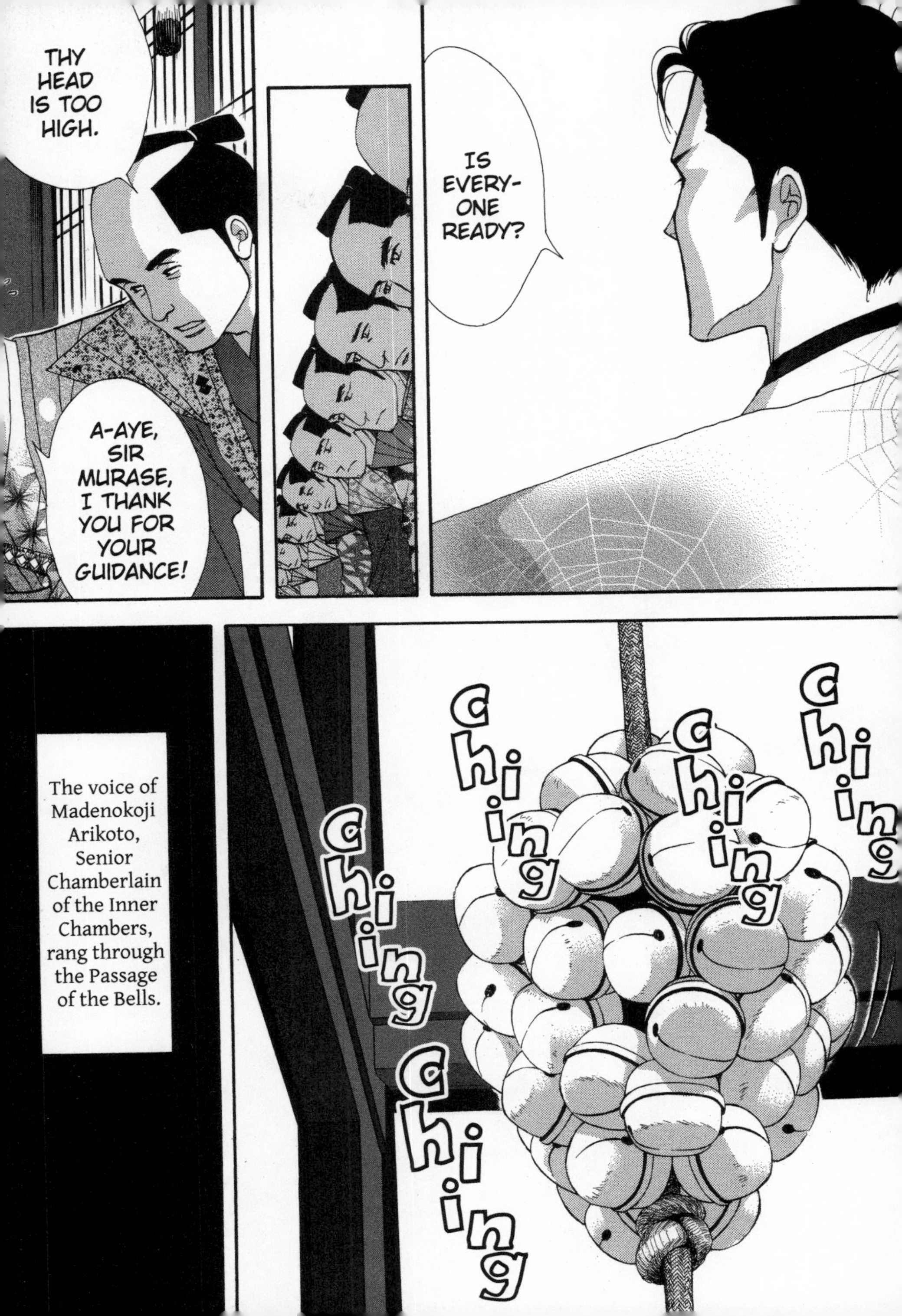
IS EVERYONE READY?
THY HEAD IS TOO HIGH.
A-AYE, SIR MURASE, I THANK YOU FOR YOUR GUIDANCE!
ching
ching
ching
ching
The voice of Madenokoji Arikoto, Senior Chamberlain of the Inner Chambers, rang through the Passage of the Bells.

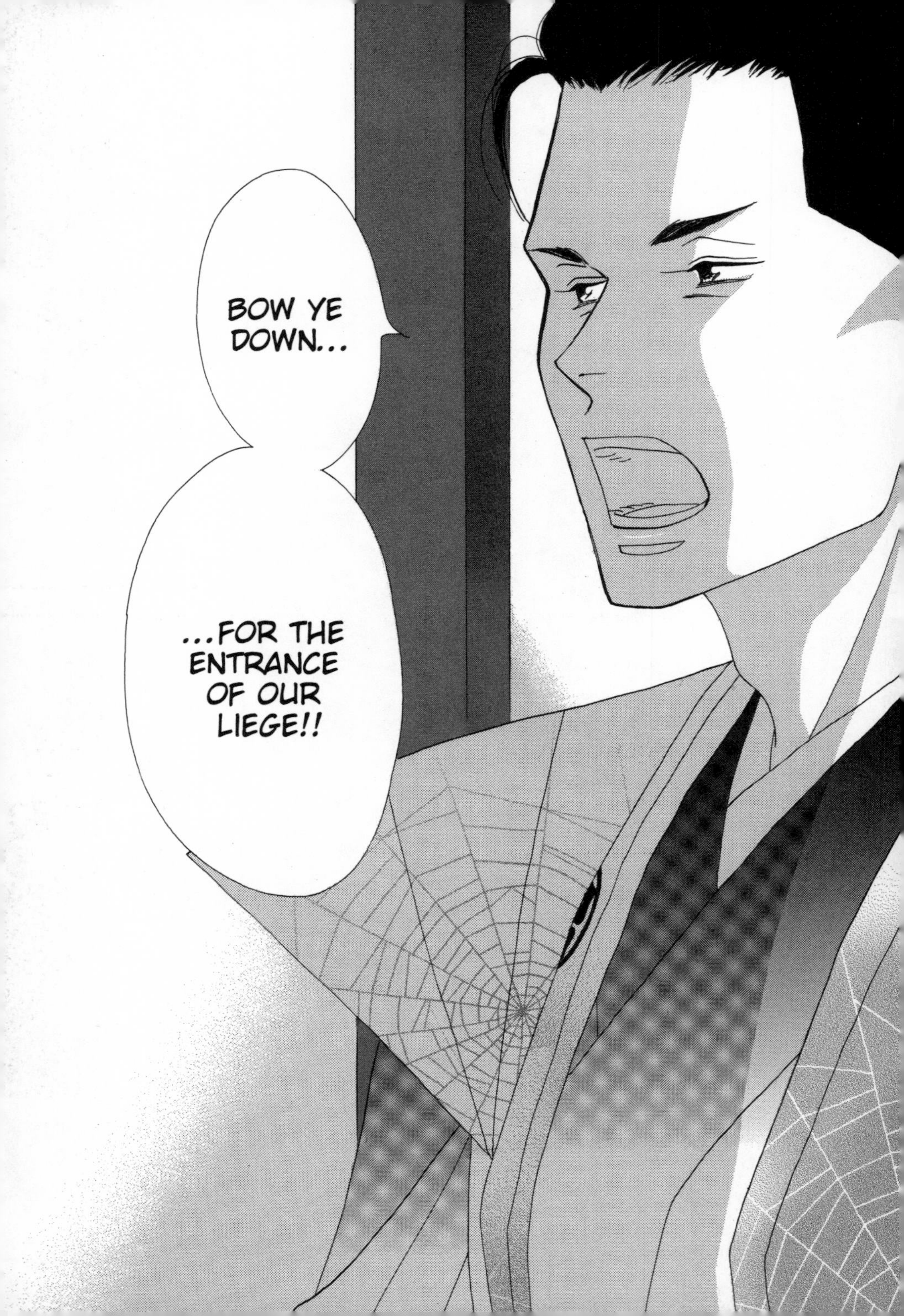
BOW YE DOWN...
...FOR THE ENTRANCE OF OUR LIEGE!!

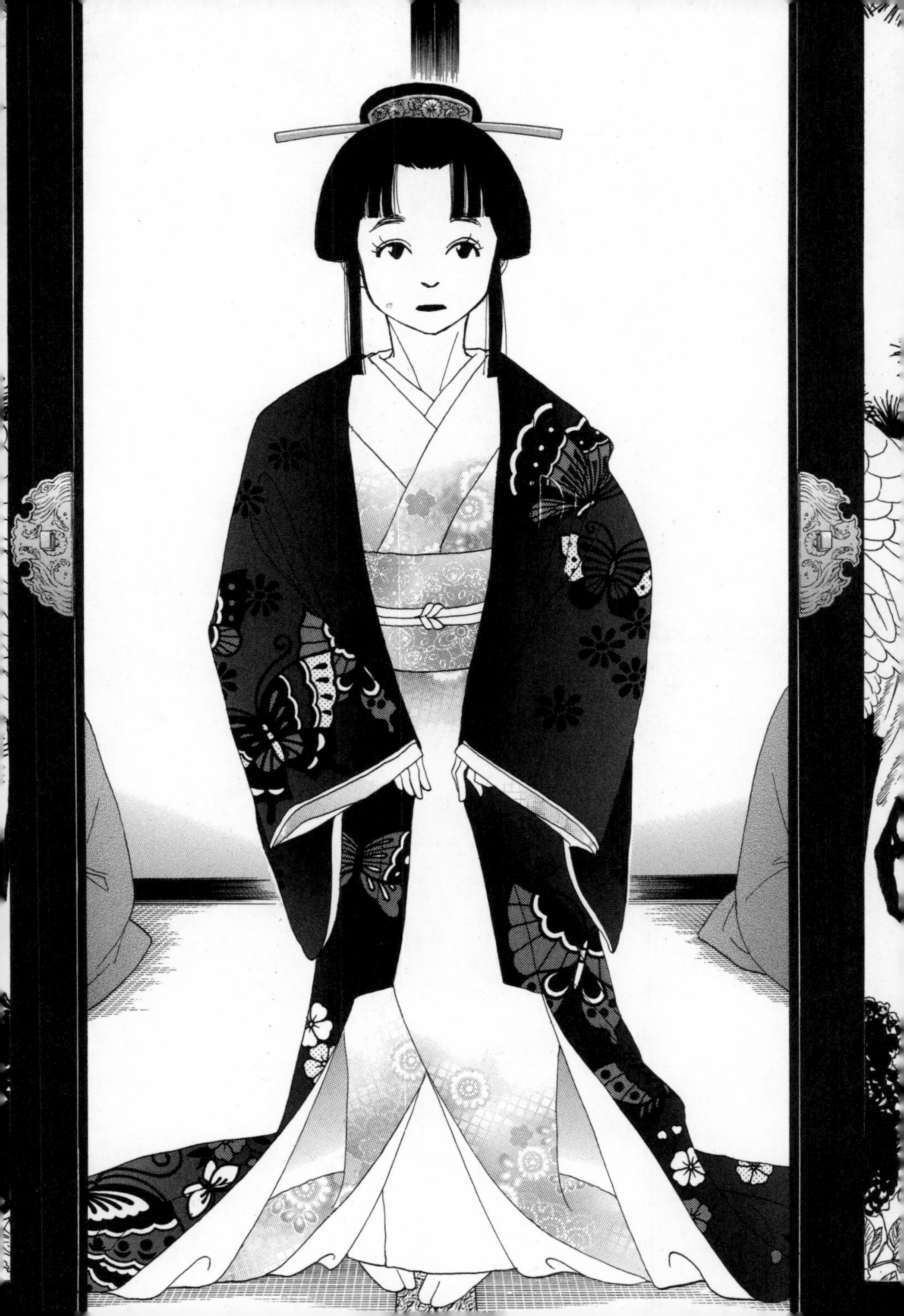

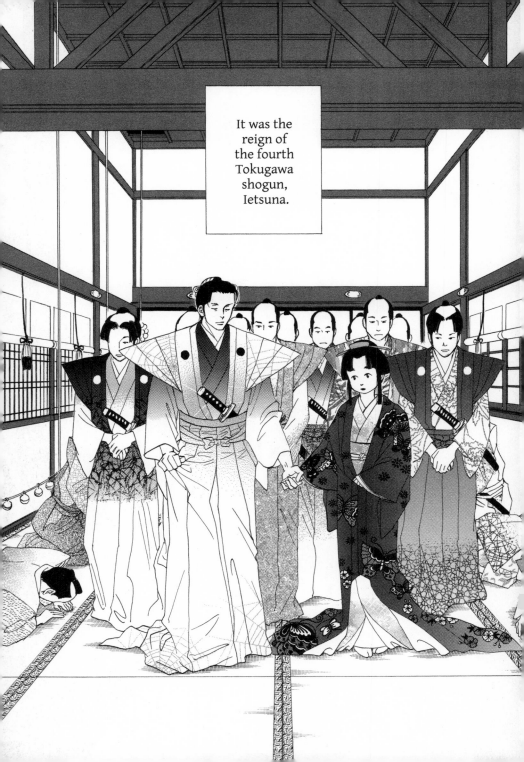

It was the reign of the fourth Tokugawa shogun, Ietsuna.

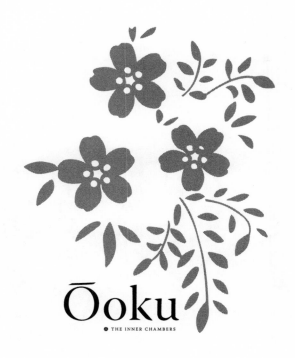

Ōoku
● THE INNER CHAMBERS

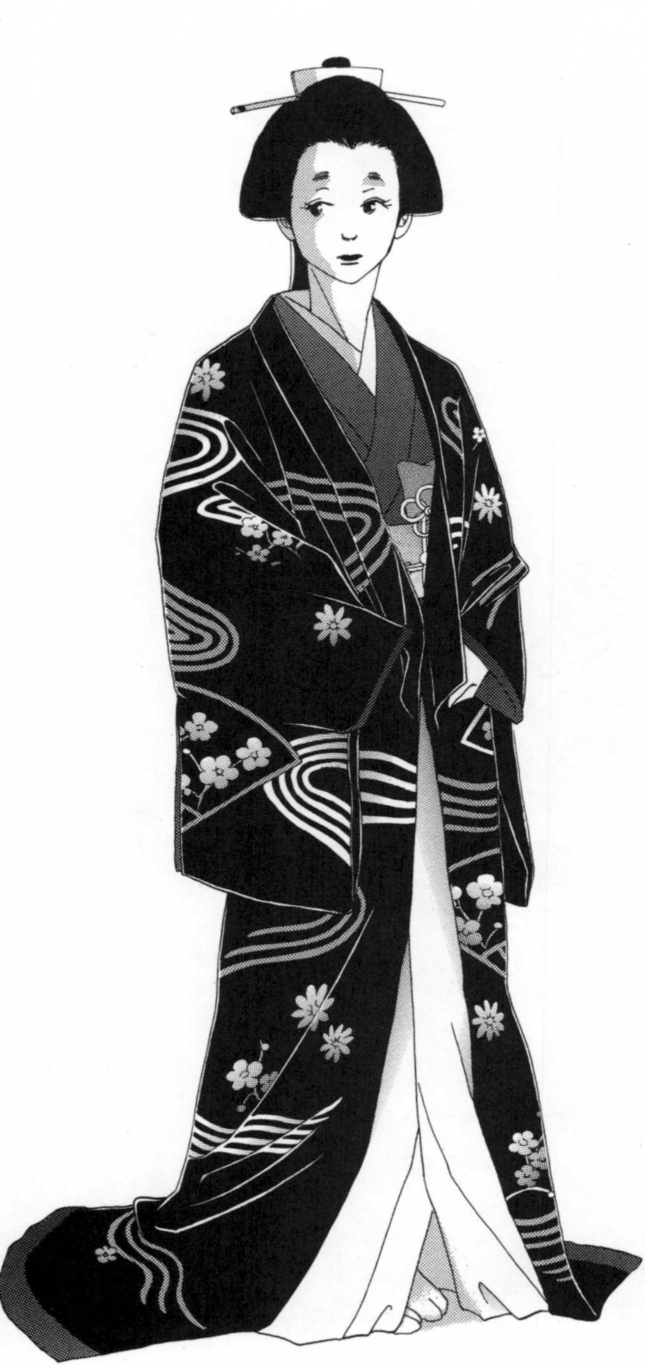

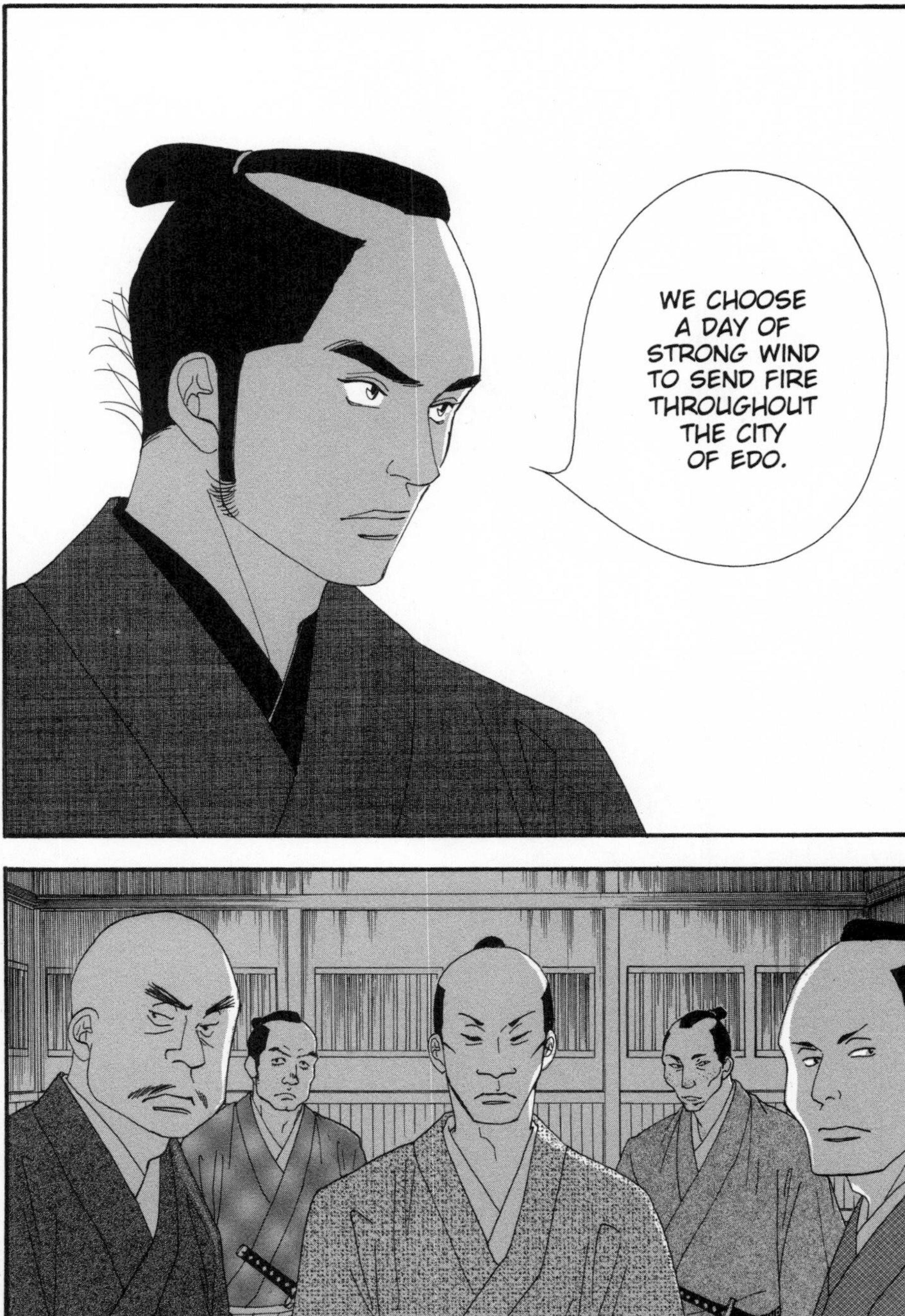
WE CHOOSE A DAY OF STRONG WIND TO SEND FIRE THROUGHOUT THE CITY OF EDO.

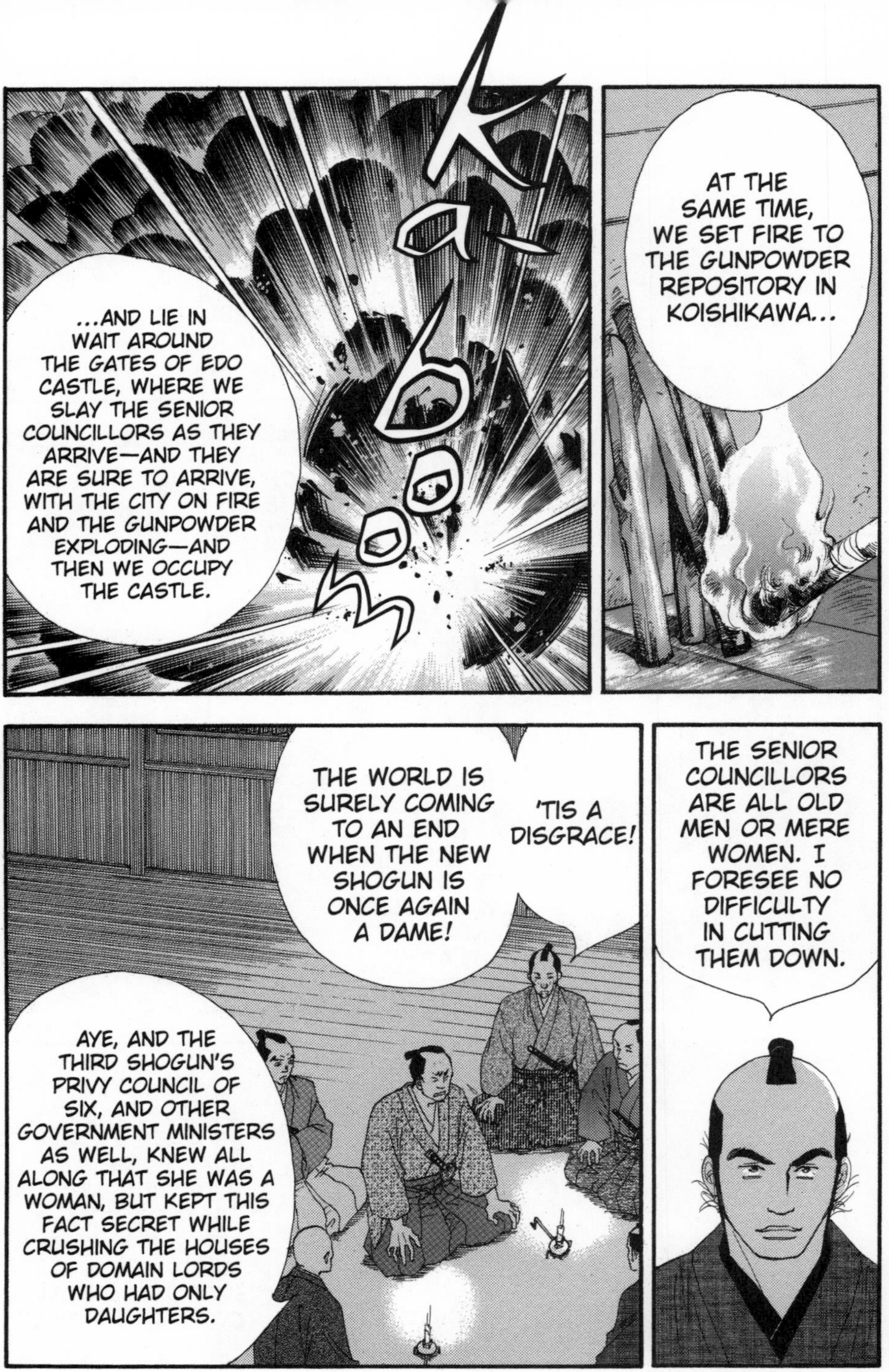
AT THE SAME TIME, WE SET FIRE TO THE GUNPOWDER REPOSITORY IN KOISHIKAWA...
KABOOM
...AND LIE IN WAIT AROUND THE GATES OF EDO CASTLE, WHERE WE SLAY THE SENIOR COUNCILLORS AS THEY ARRIVE—AND THEY ARE SURE TO ARRIVE, WITH THE CITY ON FIRE AND THE GUNPOWDER EXPLODING—AND THEN WE OCCUPY THE CASTLE.
THE SENIOR COUNCILLORS ARE ALL OLD MEN OR MERE WOMEN. I FORESEE NO DIFFICULTY IN CUTTING THEM DOWN.
'TIS A DISGRACE!
THE WORLD IS SURELY COMING TO AN END WHEN THE NEW SHOGUN IS ONCE AGAIN A DAME!
AYE, AND THE THIRD SHOGUN'S PRIVY COUNCIL OF SIX, AND OTHER GOVERNMENT MINISTERS AS WELL, KNEW ALL ALONG THAT SHE WAS A WOMAN, BUT KEPT THIS FACT SECRET WHILE CRUSHING THE HOUSES OF DOMAIN LORDS WHO HAD ONLY DAUGHTERS.

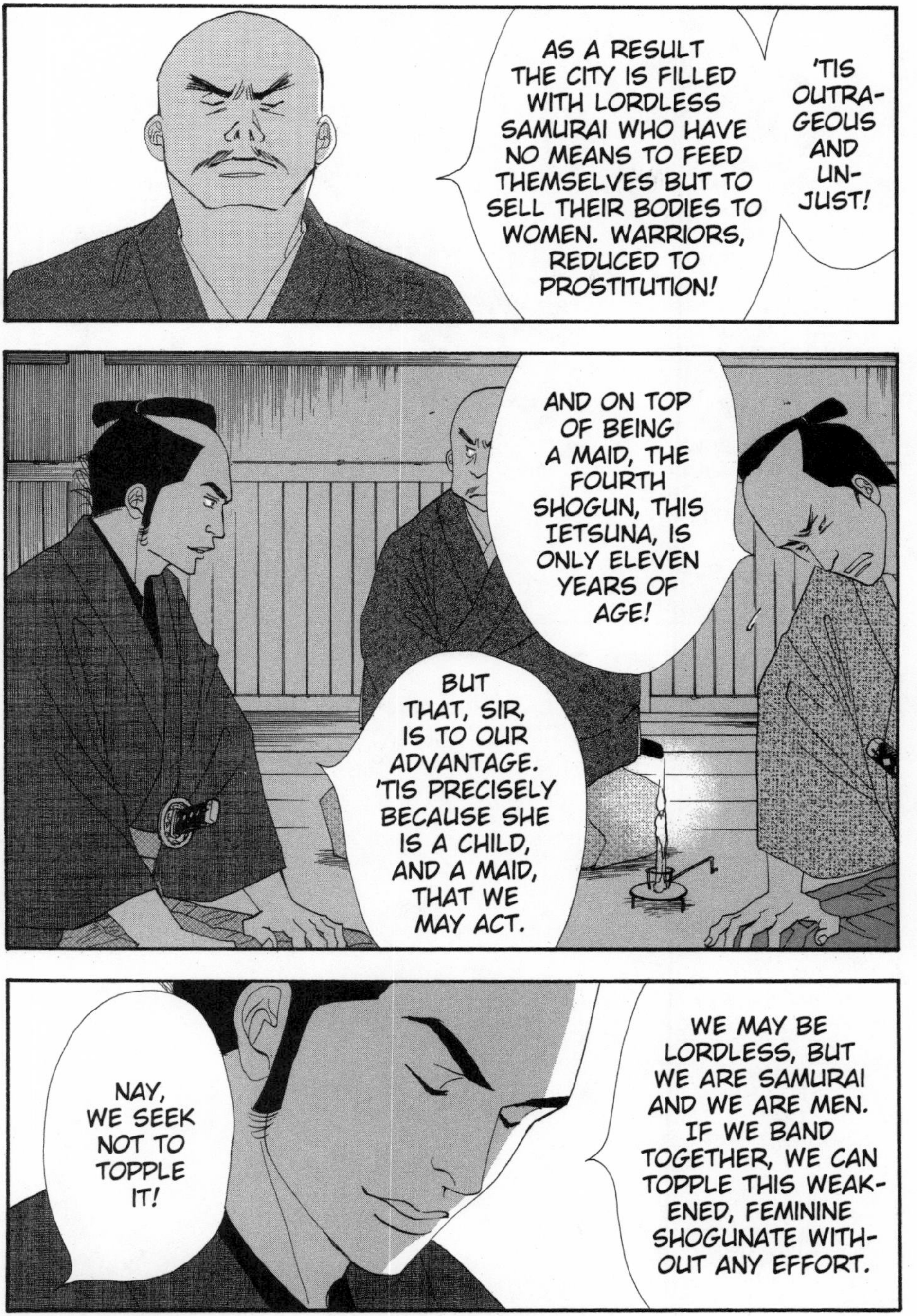
'TIS OUTRAGEOUS AND UNJUST!
AS A RESULT THE CITY IS FILLED WITH LORDLESS SAMURAI WHO HAVE NO MEANS TO FEED THEMSELVES BUT TO SELL THEIR BODIES TO WOMEN. WARRIORS, REDUCED TO PROSTITUTION!
AND ON TOP OF BEING A MAID, THE FOURTH SHOGUN, THIS IETSUNA, IS ONLY ELEVEN YEARS OF AGE!
BUT THAT, SIR, IS TO OUR ADVANTAGE. 'TIS PRECISELY BECAUSE SHE IS A CHILD, AND A MAID, THAT WE MAY ACT.
WE MAY BE LORDLESS, BUT WE ARE SAMURAI AND WE ARE MEN. IF WE BAND TOGETHER, WE CAN TOPPLE THIS WEAKENED, FEMININE SHOGUNATE WITHOUT ANY EFFORT.
NAY, WE SEEK NOT TO TOPPLE IT!

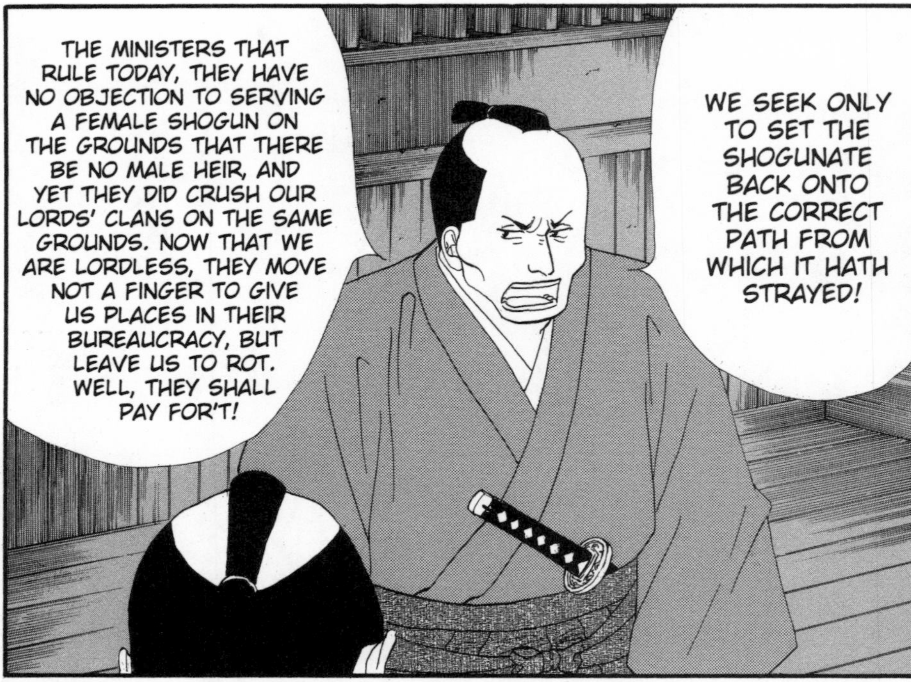
WE SEEK ONLY TO SET THE SHOGUNATE BACK ONTO THE CORRECT PATH FROM WHICH IT HATH STRAYED!
THE MINISTERS THAT RULE TODAY, THEY HAVE NO OBJECTION TO SERVING A FEMALE SHOGUN ON THE GROUNDS THAT THERE BE NO MALE HEIR, AND YET THEY DID CRUSH OUR LORDS' CLANS ON THE SAME GROUNDS. NOW THAT WE ARE LORDLESS, THEY MOVE NOT A FINGER TO GIVE US PLACES IN THEIR BUREAUCRACY, BUT LEAVE US TO ROT. WELL, THEY SHALL PAY FOR'T!

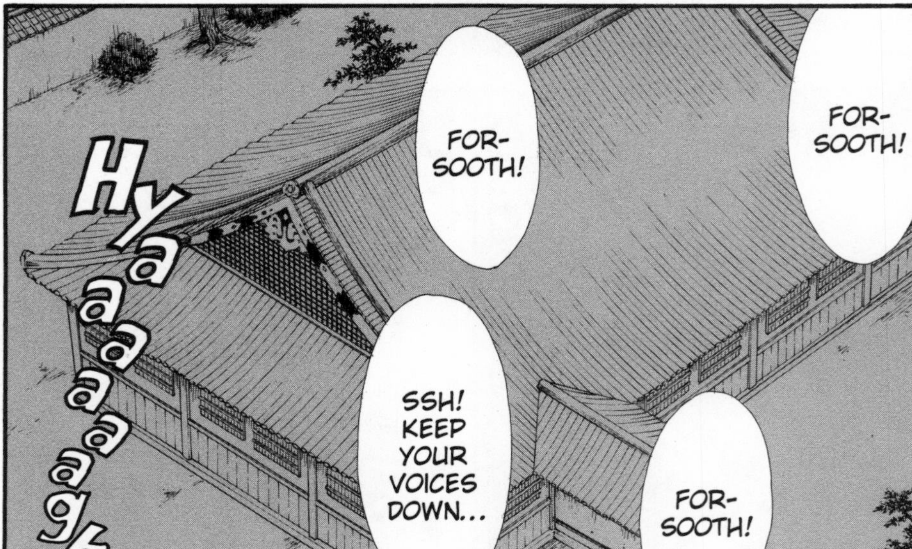
FOR-SOOTH!
FOR-SOOTH!
FOR-SOOTH!
SSH! KEEP YOUR VOICES DOWN...
Hyaaaaaagh!

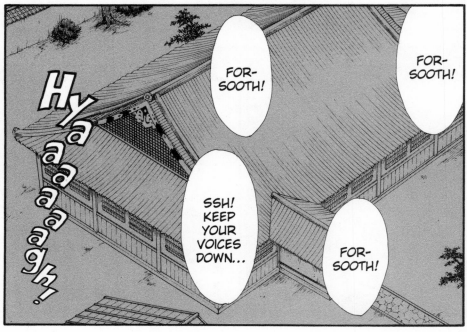

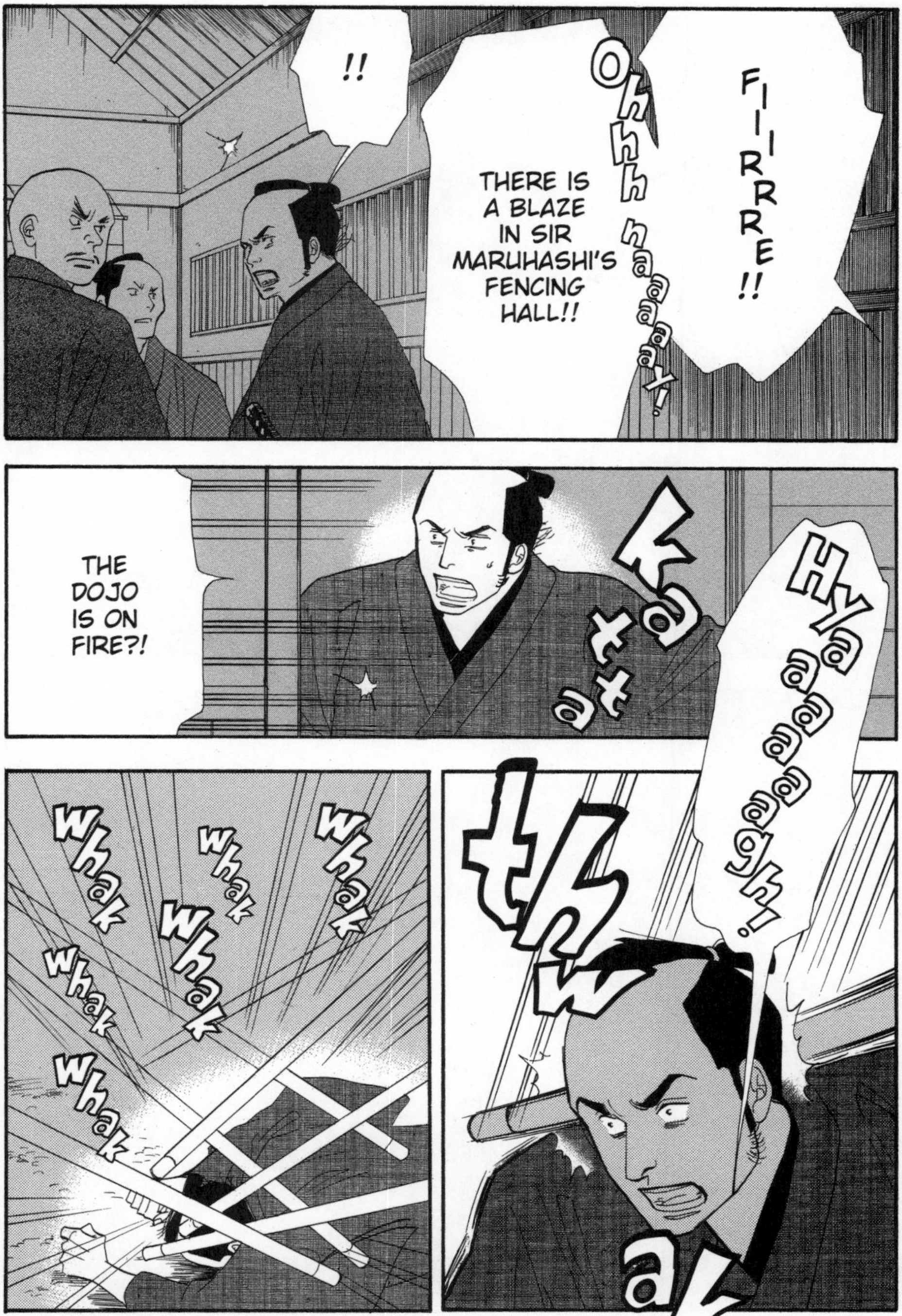
FIIIRRRE!!
Ohhhh naaaaay!
THERE IS A BLAZE IN SIR MARUHASHI'S FENCING HALL!!
!!
Hyaaaaaaagh!
katta
THE DOJO IS ON FIRE?!
thwak
whak
whak
whak
whak
whak

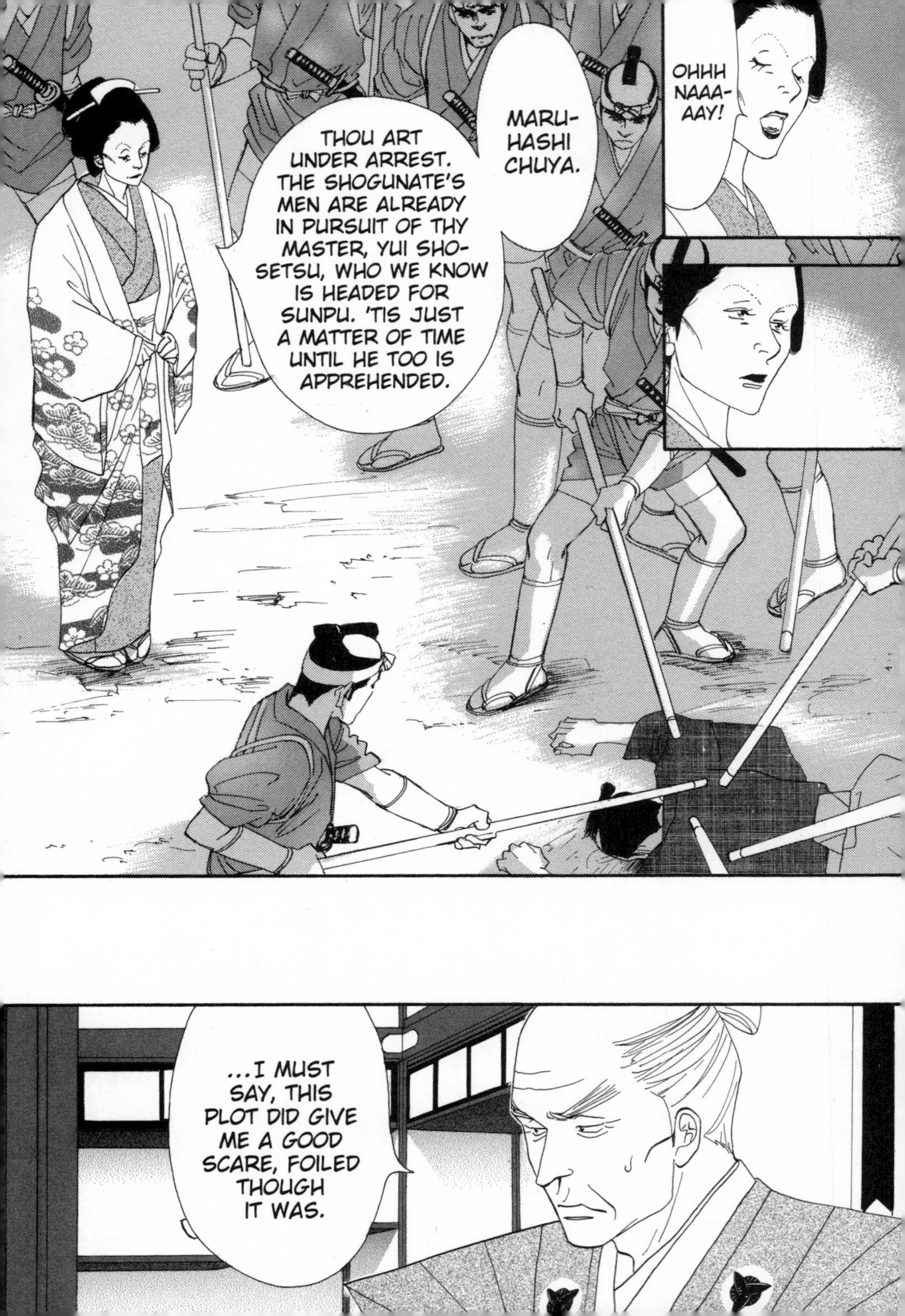
OHHH NAAAA-AAY!
MARU-HASHI CHUYA.
THOU ART UNDER ARREST. THE SHOGUNATE'S MEN ARE ALREADY IN PURSUIT OF THY MASTER, YUI SHO-SETSU, WHO WE KNOW IS HEADED FOR SUNPU. 'TIS JUST A MATTER OF TIME UNTIL HE TOO IS APPREHENDED.
...I MUST SAY, THIS PLOT DID GIVE ME A GOOD SCARE, FOILED THOUGH IT WAS.

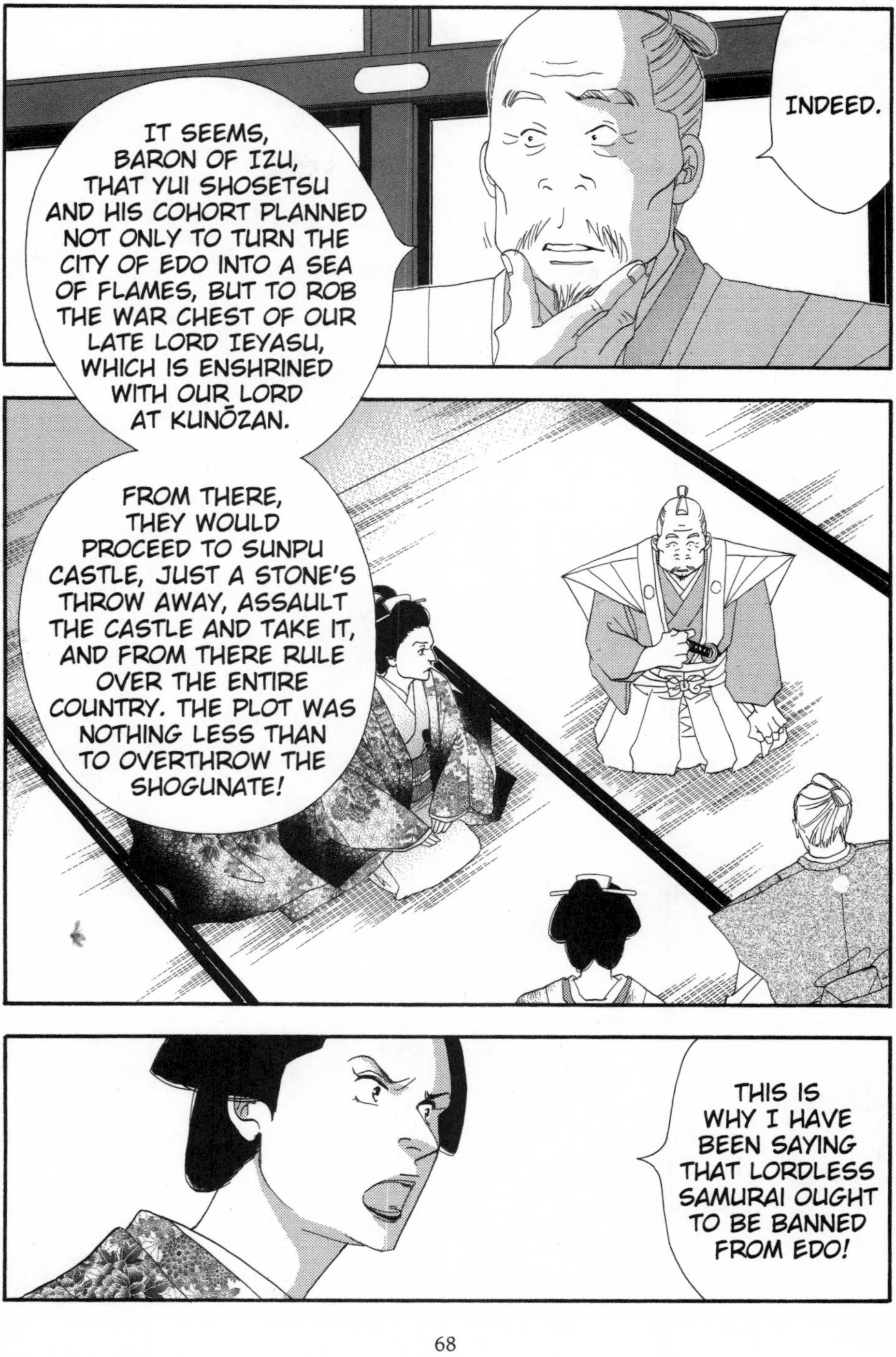
INDEED.
IT SEEMS, BARON OF IZU, THAT YUI SHOSETSU AND HIS COHORT PLANNED NOT ONLY TO TURN THE CITY OF EDO INTO A SEA OF FLAMES, BUT TO ROB THE WAR CHEST OF OUR LATE LORD IEYASU, WHICH IS ENSHRINED WITH OUR LORD AT KUNŌZAN.
FROM THERE, THEY WOULD PROCEED TO SUNPU CASTLE, JUST A STONE'S THROW AWAY, ASSAULT THE CASTLE AND TAKE IT, AND FROM THERE RULE OVER THE ENTIRE COUNTRY. THE PLOT WAS NOTHING LESS THAN TO OVERTHROW THE SHOGUNATE!
THIS IS WHY I HAVE BEEN SAYING THAT LORDLESS SAMURAI OUGHT TO BE BANNED FROM EDO!

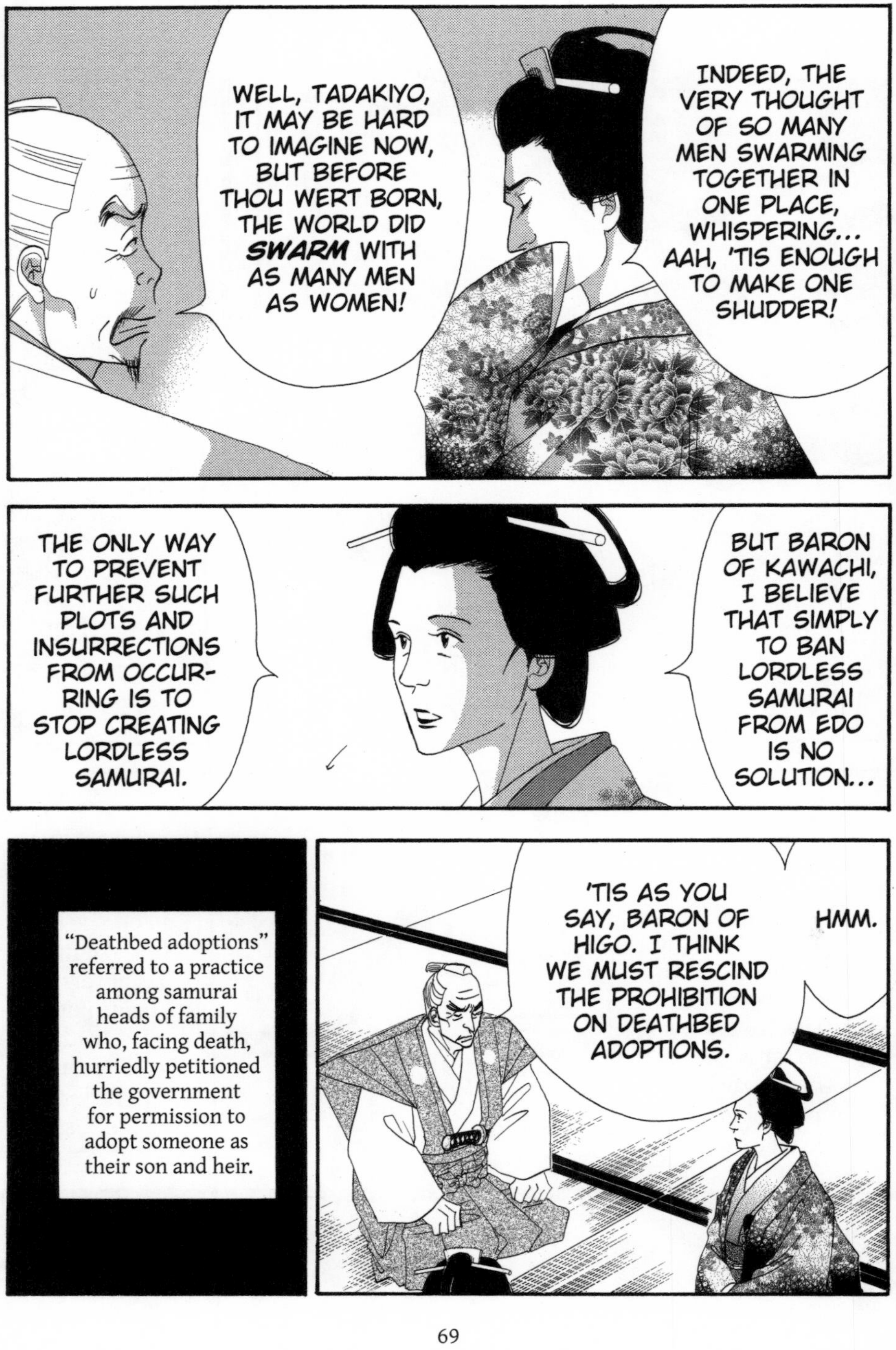
INDEED, THE VERY THOUGHT OF SO MANY MEN SWARMING TOGETHER IN ONE PLACE, WHISPERING... AAH, 'TIS ENOUGH TO MAKE ONE SHUDDER!
WELL, TADAKIYO, IT MAY BE HARD TO IMAGINE NOW, BUT BEFORE THOU WERT BORN, THE WORLD DID ***SWARM*** WITH AS MANY MEN AS WOMEN!
BUT BARON OF KAWACHI, I BELIEVE THAT SIMPLY TO BAN LORDLESS SAMURAI FROM EDO IS NO SOLUTION...
THE ONLY WAY TO PREVENT FURTHER SUCH PLOTS AND INSURRECTIONS FROM OCCUR-RING IS TO STOP CREATING LORDLESS SAMURAI.
HMM.
'TIS AS YOU SAY, BARON OF HIGO. I THINK WE MUST RESCIND THE PROHIBITION ON DEATHBED ADOPTIONS.
"Deathbed adoptions" referred to a practice among samurai heads of family who, facing death, hurriedly petitioned the government for permission to adopt someone as their son and heir.

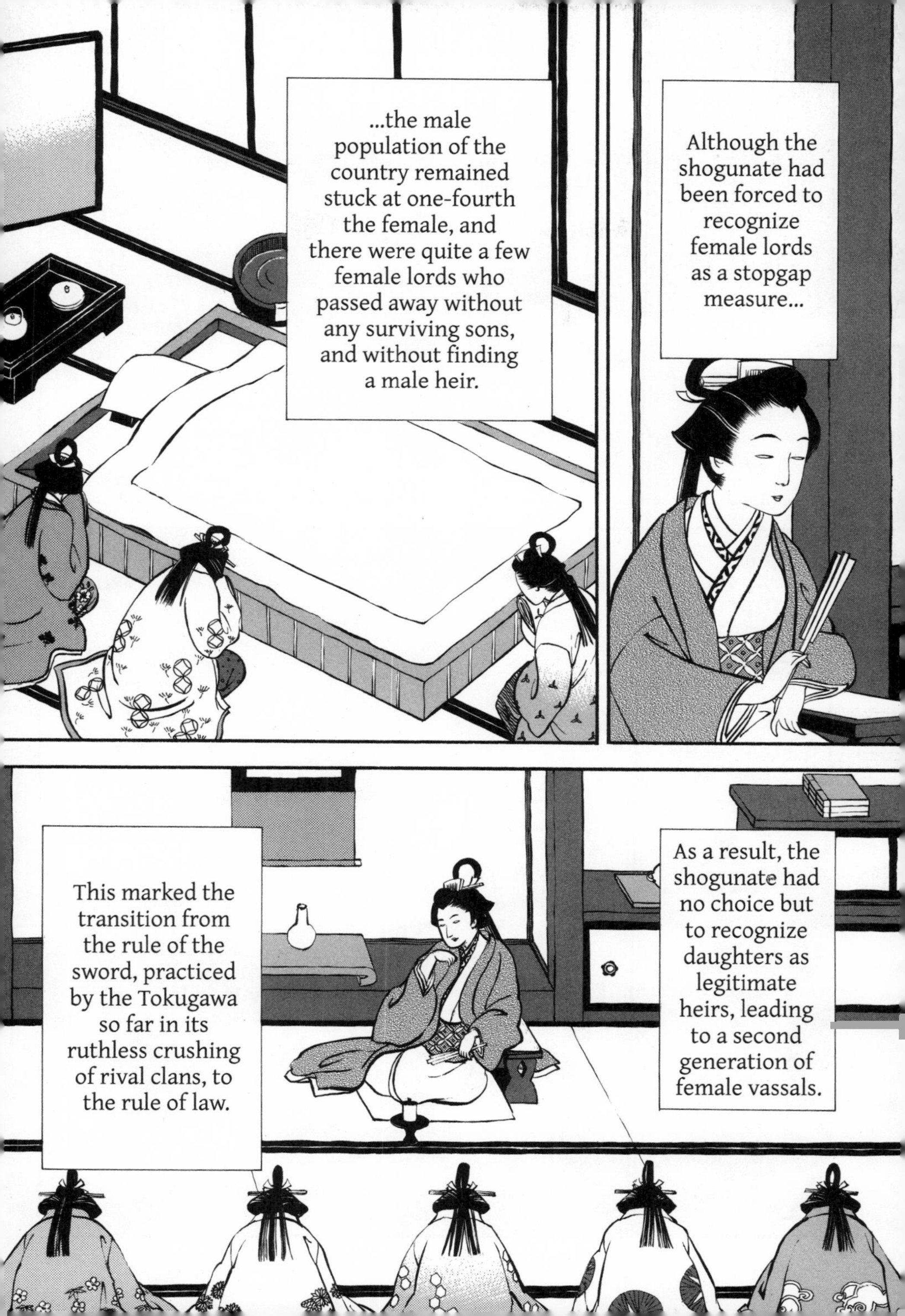
Although the shogunate had been forced to recognize female lords as a stopgap measure...
...the male population of the country remained stuck at one-fourth the female, and there were quite a few female lords who passed away without any surviving sons, and without finding a male heir.
As a result, the shogunate had no choice but to recognize daughters as legitimate heirs, leading to a second generation of female vassals.
This marked the transition from the rule of the sword, practiced by the Tokugawa so far in its ruthless crushing of rival clans, to the rule of law.

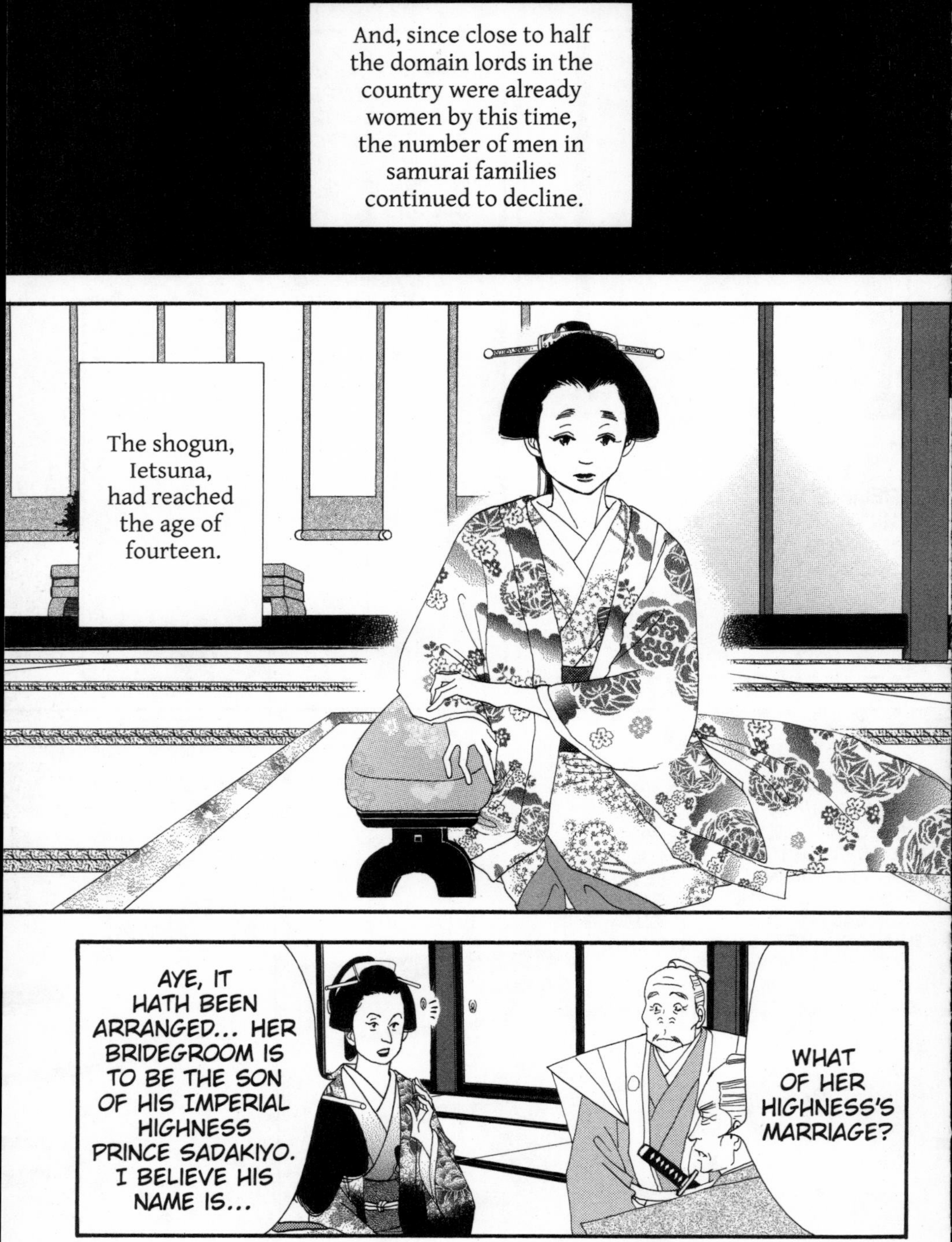
And, since close to half the domain lords in the country were already women by this time, the number of men in samurai families continued to decline.
The shogun, Ietsuna, had reached the age of fourteen.
WHAT OF HER HIGHNESS'S MARRIAGE?
AYE, IT HATH BEEN ARRANGED... HER BRIDEGROOM IS TO BE THE SON OF HIS IMPERIAL HIGHNESS PRINCE SADAKIYO. I BELIEVE HIS NAME IS...

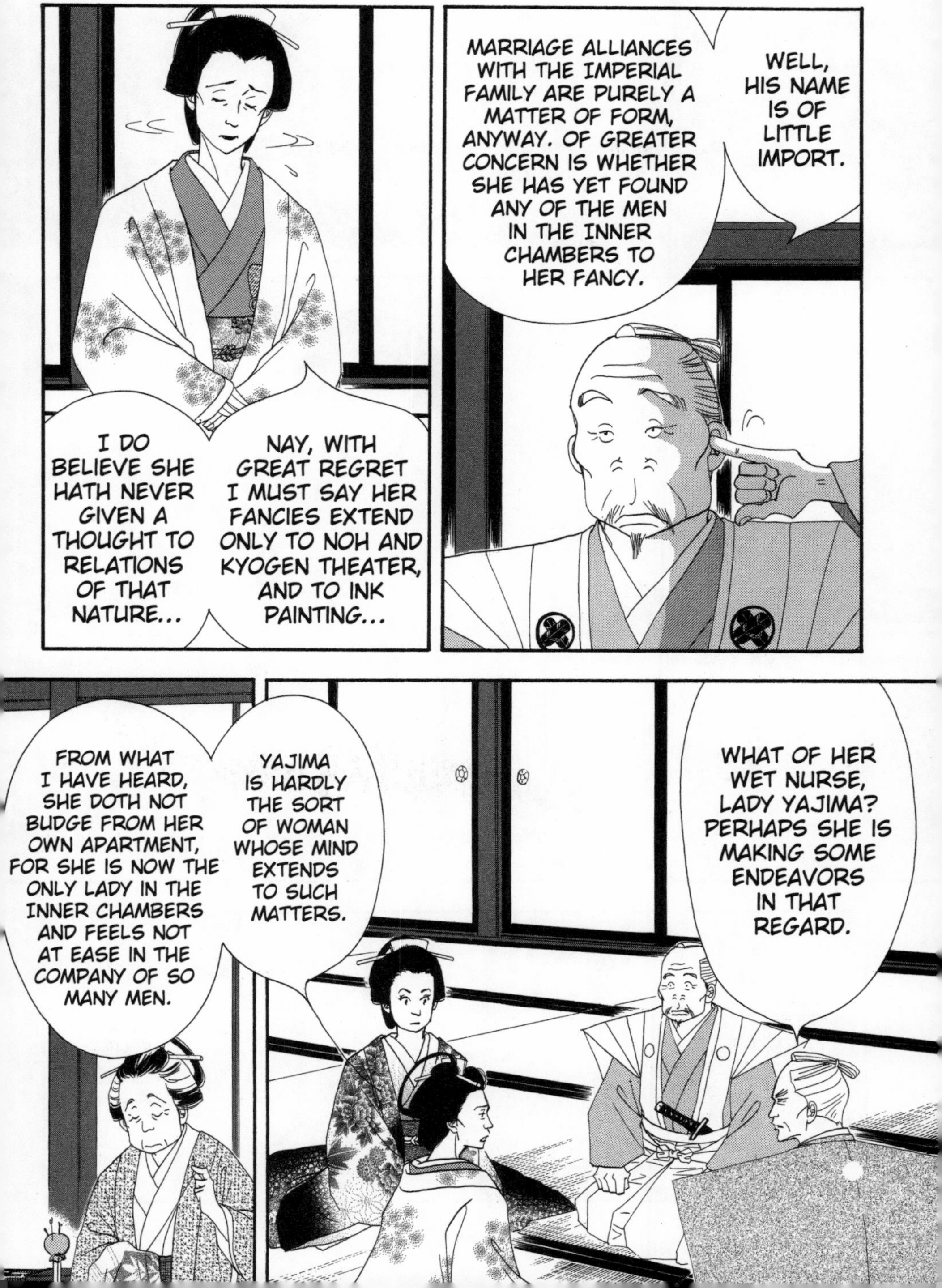
WELL, HIS NAME IS OF LITTLE IMPORT.
MARRIAGE ALLIANCES WITH THE IMPERIAL FAMILY ARE PURELY A MATTER OF FORM, ANYWAY. OF GREATER CONCERN IS WHETHER SHE HAS YET FOUND ANY OF THE MEN IN THE INNER CHAMBERS TO HER FANCY.
NAY, WITH GREAT REGRET I MUST SAY HER FANCIES EXTEND ONLY TO NOH AND KYOGEN THEATER, AND TO INK PAINTING...
I DO BELIEVE SHE HATH NEVER GIVEN A THOUGHT TO RELATIONS OF THAT NATURE...
WHAT OF HER WET NURSE, LADY YAJIMA? PERHAPS SHE IS MAKING SOME ENDEAVORS IN THAT REGARD.
YAJIMA IS HARDLY THE SORT OF WOMAN WHOSE MIND EXTENDS TO SUCH MATTERS.
FROM WHAT I HAVE HEARD, SHE DOTH NOT BUDGE FROM HER OWN APARTMENT, FOR SHE IS NOW THE ONLY LADY IN THE INNER CHAMBERS AND FEELS NOT AT EASE IN THE COMPANY OF SO MANY MEN.

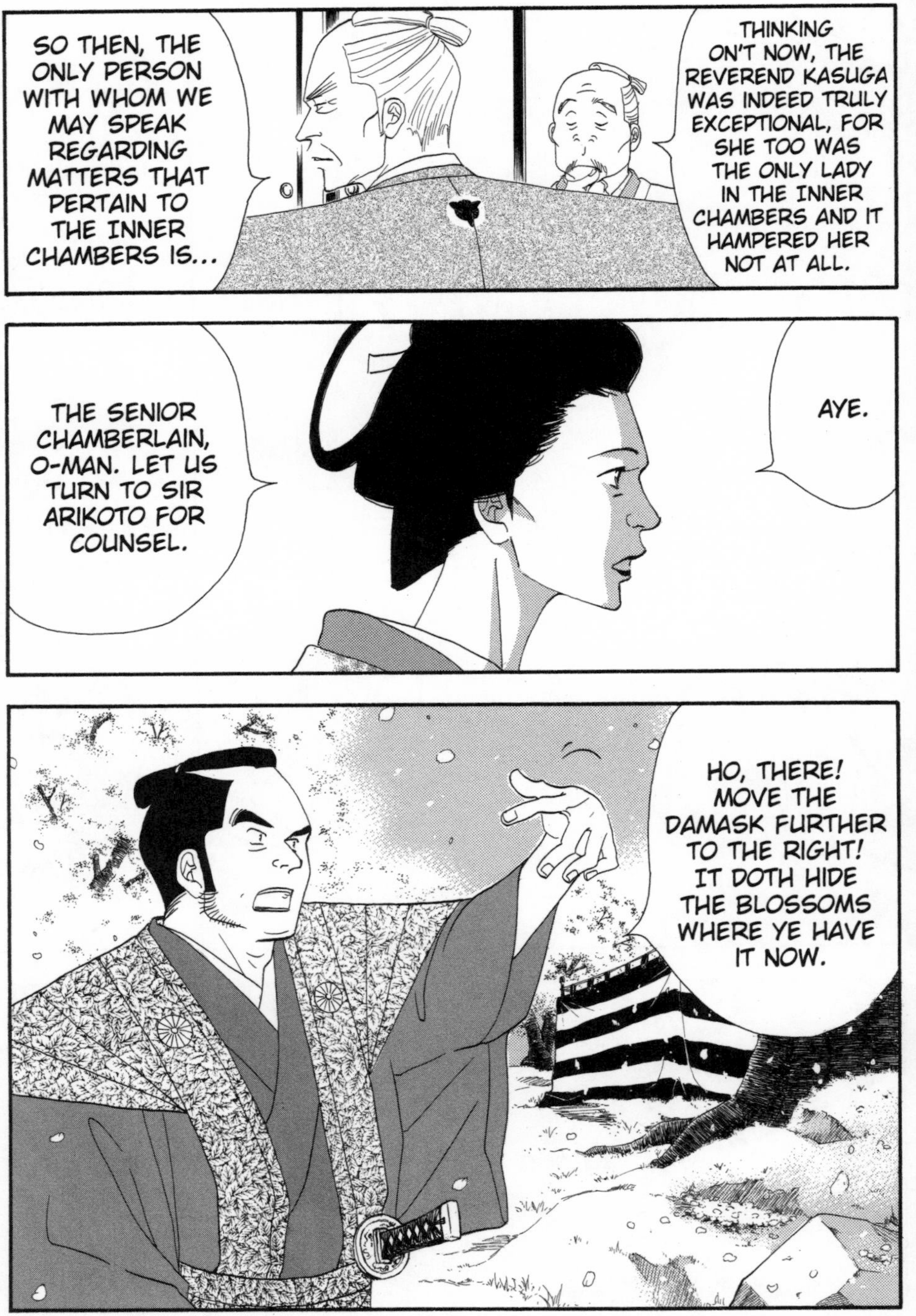
THINKING ON'T NOW, THE REVEREND KASUGA WAS INDEED TRULY EXCEPTIONAL, FOR SHE TOO WAS THE ONLY LADY IN THE INNER CHAMBERS AND IT HAMPERED HER NOT AT ALL.
SO THEN, THE ONLY PERSON WITH WHOM WE MAY SPEAK REGARDING MATTERS THAT PERTAIN TO THE INNER CHAMBERS IS...
AYE.
THE SENIOR CHAMBERLAIN, O-MAN. LET US TURN TO SIR ARIKOTO FOR COUNSEL.
HO, THERE! MOVE THE DAMASK FURTHER TO THE RIGHT! IT DOTH HIDE THE BLOSSOMS WHERE YE HAVE IT NOW.

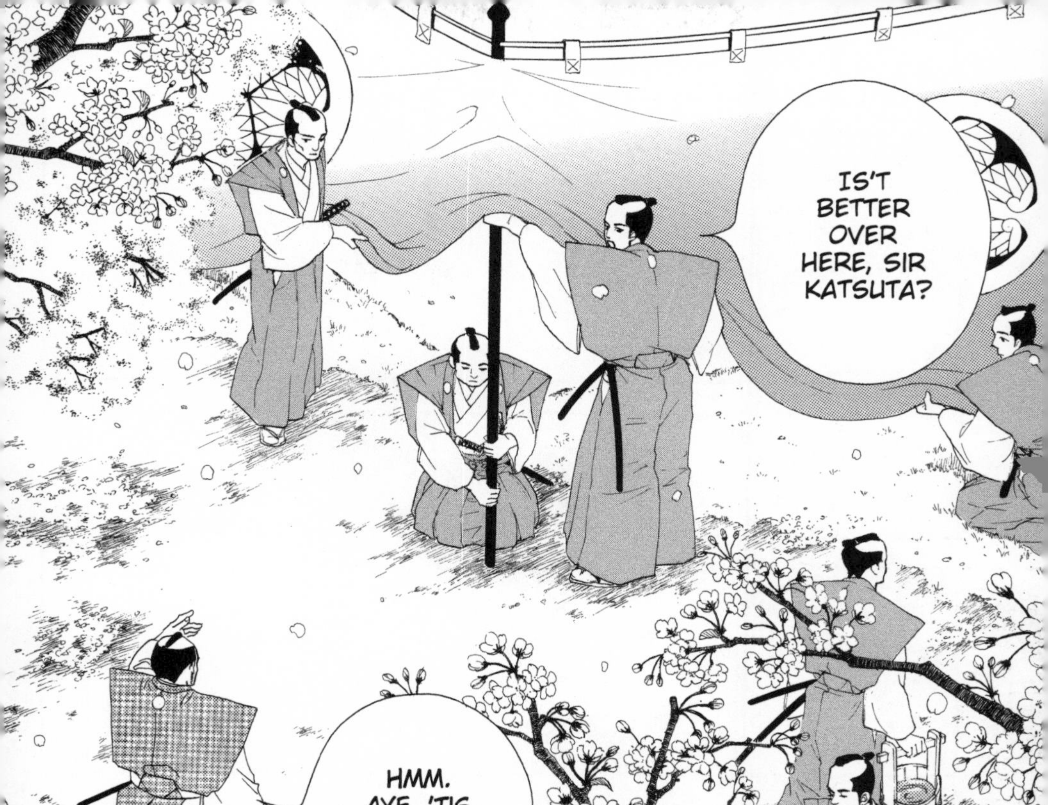
IS'T BETTER OVER HERE, SIR KATSUTA?
HMM. AYE, 'TIS GOOD THERE.

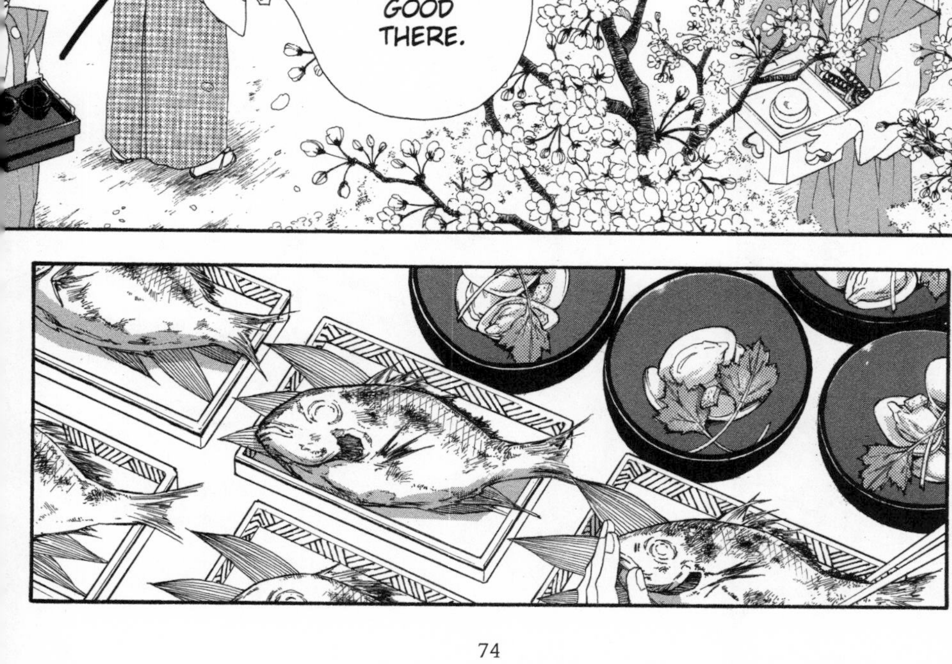

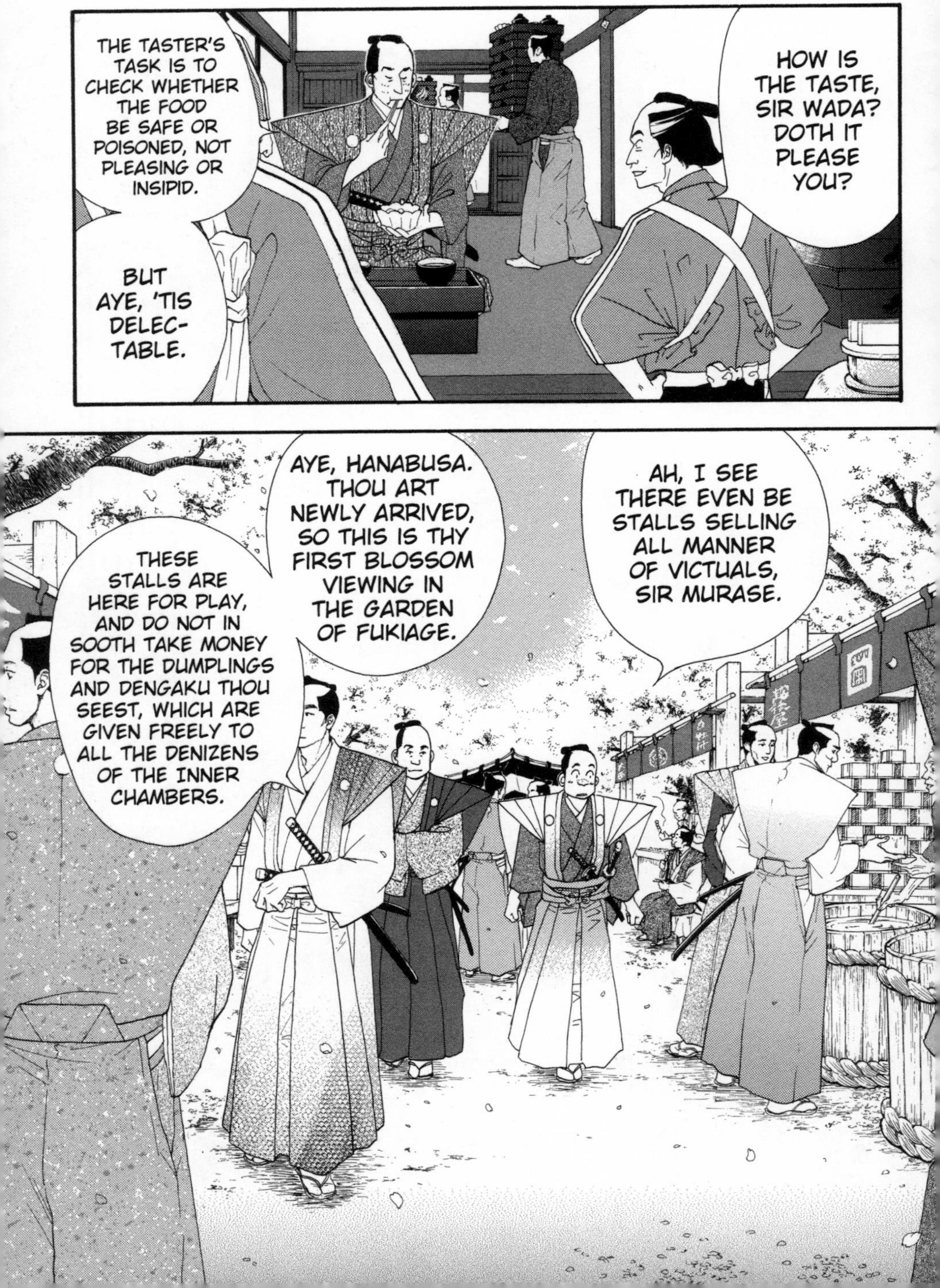
HOW IS THE TASTE, SIR WADA? DOTH IT PLEASE YOU?
THE TASTER'S TASK IS TO CHECK WHETHER THE FOOD BE SAFE OR POISONED, NOT PLEASING OR INSIPID.
BUT AYE, 'TIS DELEC-TABLE.
AH, I SEE THERE EVEN BE STALLS SELLING ALL MANNER OF VICTUALS, SIR MURASE.
AYE, HANABUSA. THOU ART NEWLY ARRIVED, SO THIS IS THY FIRST BLOSSOM VIEWING IN THE GARDEN OF FUKIAGE.
THESE STALLS ARE HERE FOR PLAY, AND DO NOT IN SOOTH TAKE MONEY FOR THE DUMPLINGS AND DENGAKU THOU SEEST, WHICH ARE GIVEN FREELY TO ALL THE DENIZENS OF THE INNER CHAMBERS.

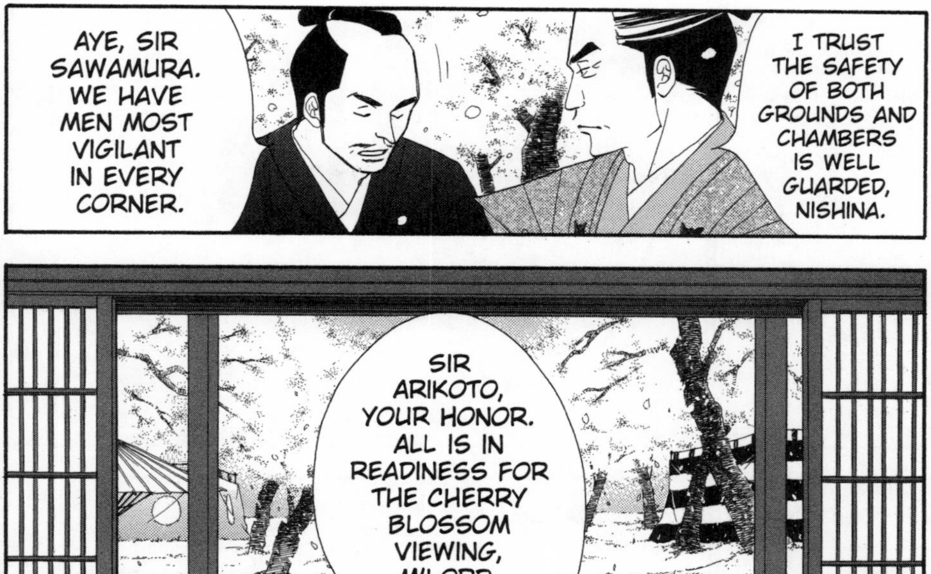
I TRUST THE SAFETY OF BOTH GROUNDS AND CHAMBERS IS WELL GUARDED, NISHINA.
AYE, SIR SAWAMURA. WE HAVE MEN MOST VIGILANT IN EVERY CORNER.
SIR ARIKOTO, YOUR HONOR. ALL IS IN READINESS FOR THE CHERRY BLOSSOM VIEWING, M'LORD..

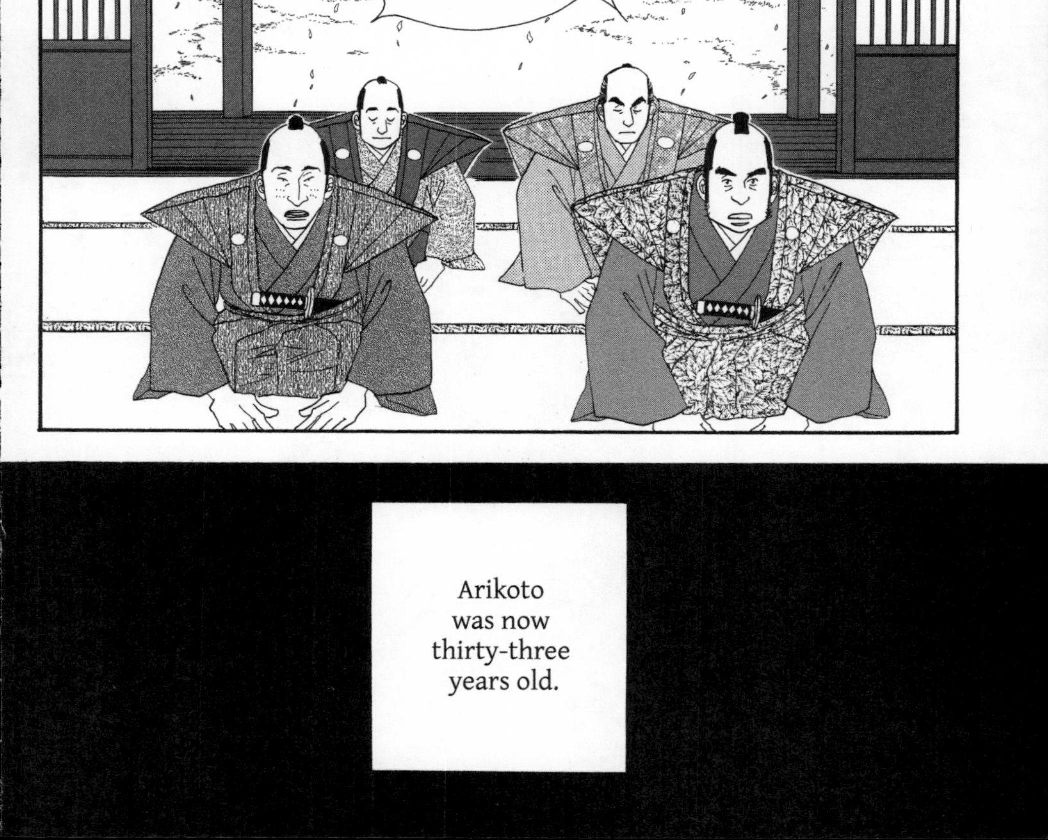
Arikoto was now thirty-three years old.

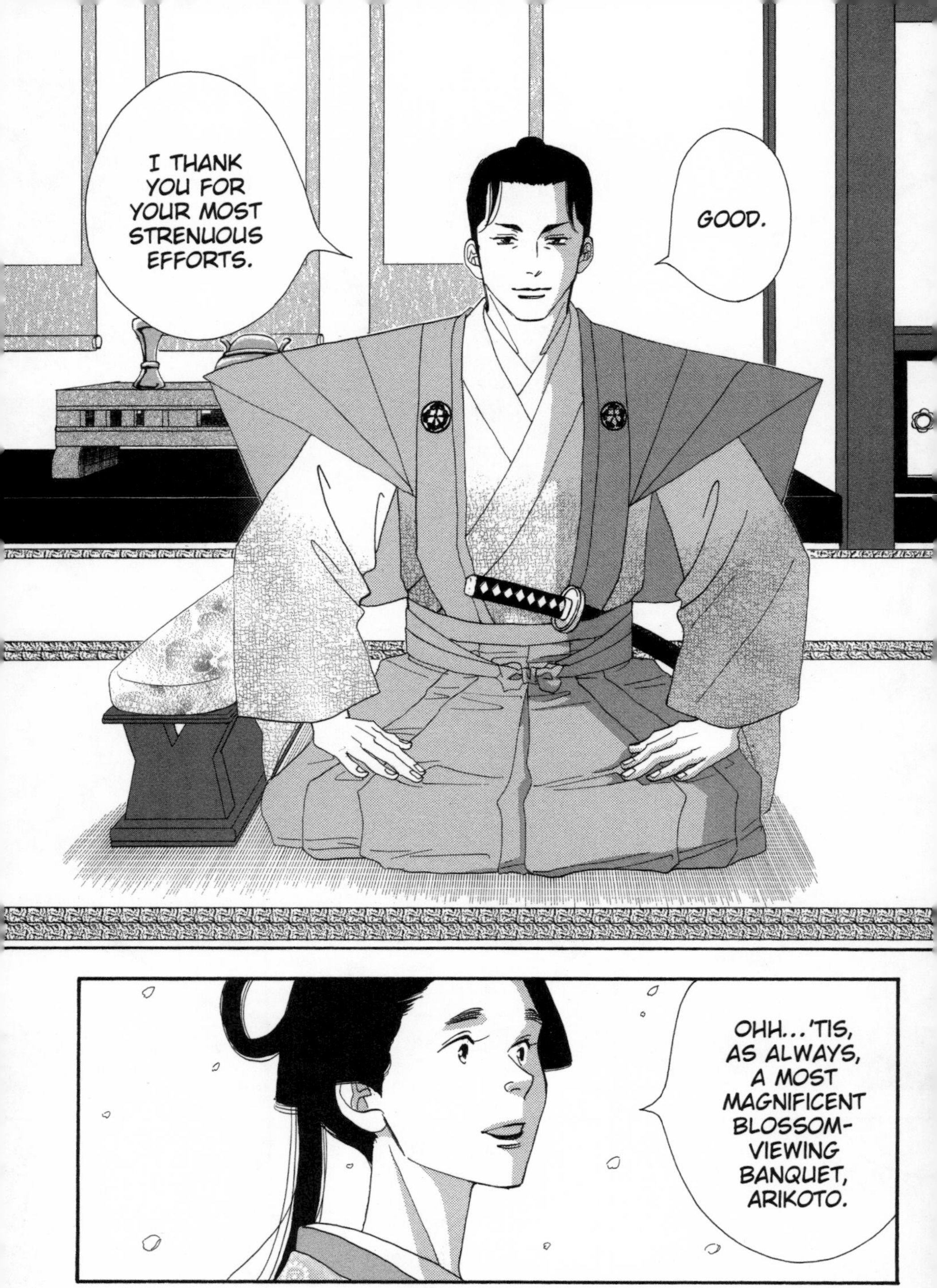
GOOD.
I THANK YOU FOR YOUR MOST STRENUOUS EFFORTS.
OHH...'TIS, AS ALWAYS, A MOST MAGNIFICENT BLOSSOM-VIEWING BANQUET, ARIKOTO.

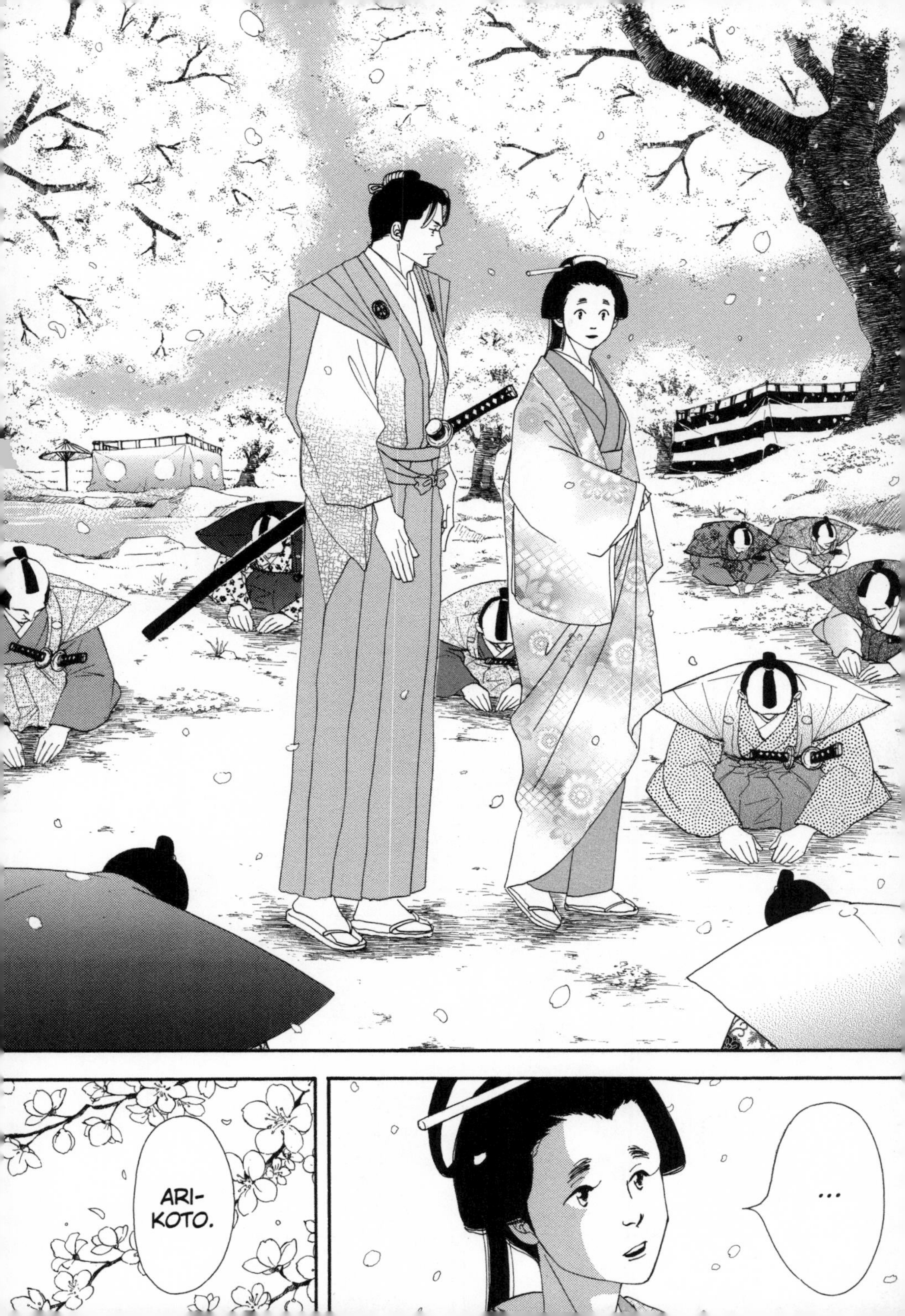
...
ARI-KOTO.

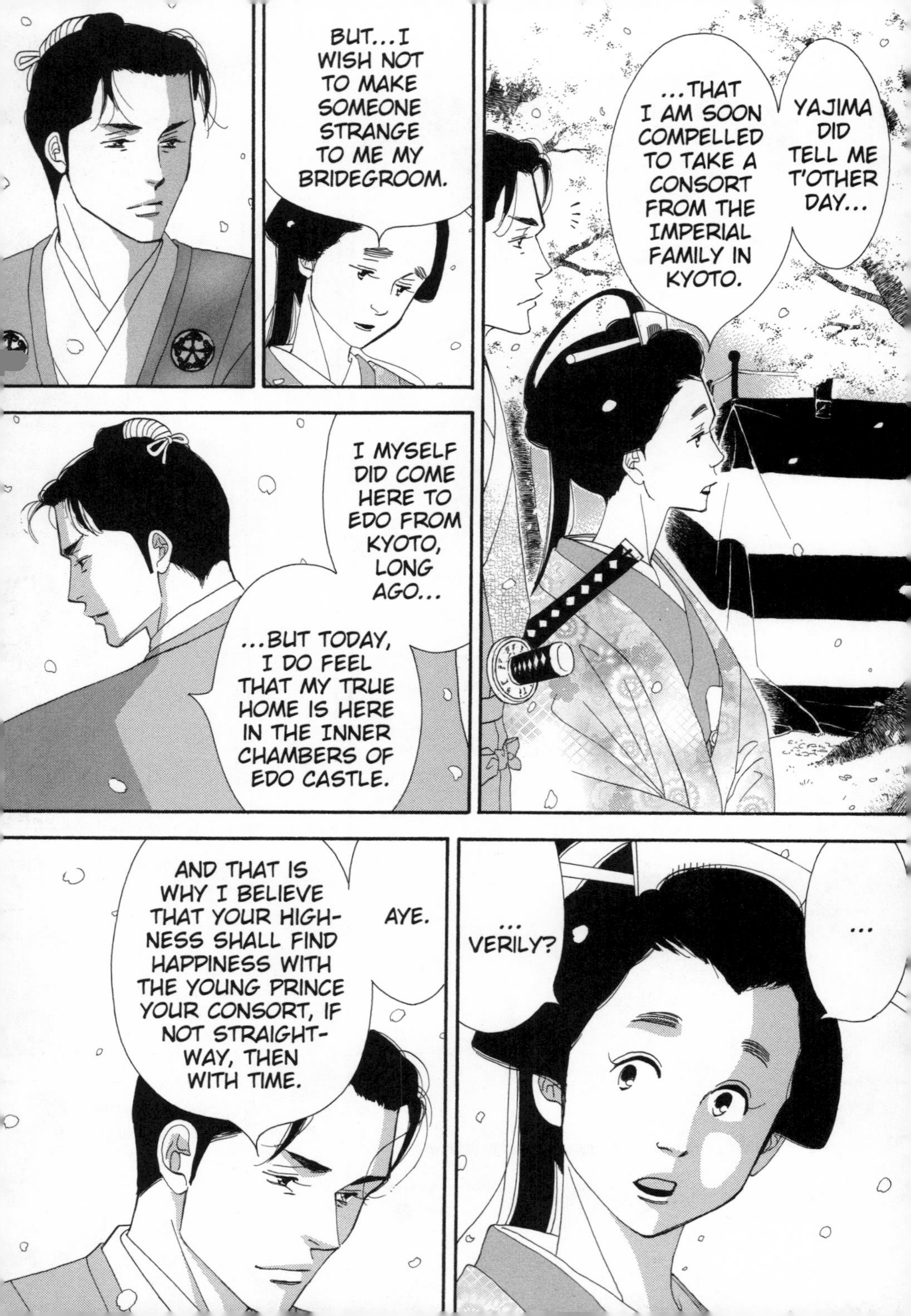

YAJIMA DID TELL ME T'OTHER DAY...
...THAT I AM SOON COMPELLED TO TAKE A CONSORT FROM THE IMPERIAL FAMILY IN KYOTO.
BUT...I WISH NOT TO MAKE SOMEONE STRANGE TO ME MY BRIDEGROOM.
I MYSELF DID COME HERE TO EDO FROM KYOTO, LONG AGO...
...BUT TODAY, I DO FEEL THAT MY TRUE HOME IS HERE IN THE INNER CHAMBERS OF EDO CASTLE.
...
... VERILY?
AYE.
AND THAT IS WHY I BELIEVE THAT YOUR HIGHNESS SHALL FIND HAPPINESS WITH THE YOUNG PRINCE YOUR CONSORT, IF NOT STRAIGHTWAY, THEN WITH TIME.

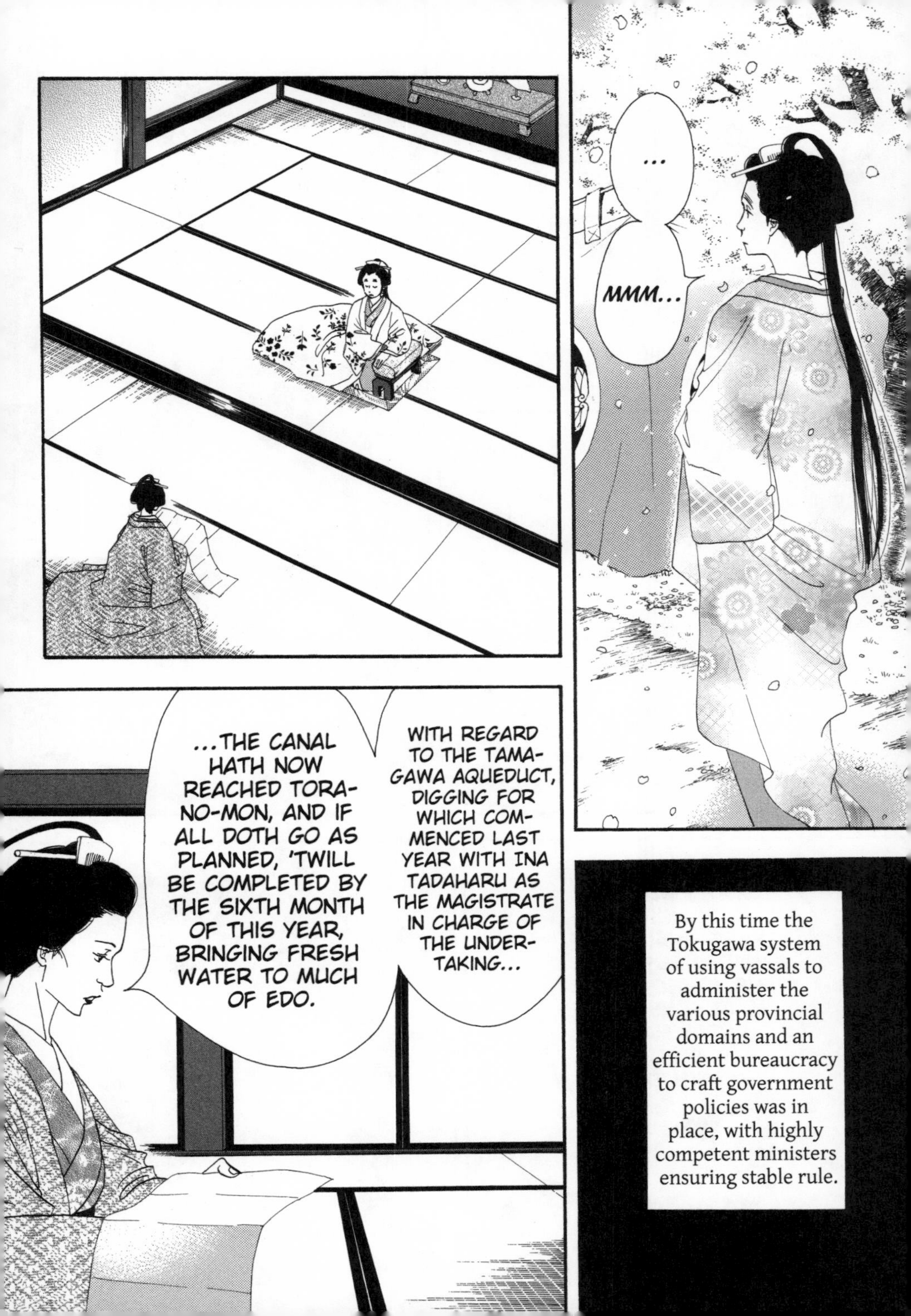
...
MMM...
By this time the Tokugawa system of using vassals to administer the various provincial domains and an efficient bureaucracy to craft government policies was in place, with highly competent ministers ensuring stable rule.
WITH REGARD TO THE TAMA-GAWA AQUEDUCT, DIGGING FOR WHICH COM-MENCED LAST YEAR WITH INA TADAHARU AS THE MAGISTRATE IN CHARGE OF THE UNDER-TAKING...
...THE CANAL HATH NOW REACHED TORA-NO-MON, AND IF ALL DOTH GO AS PLANNED, 'TWILL BE COMPLETED BY THE SIXTH MONTH OF THIS YEAR, BRINGING FRESH WATER TO MUCH OF EDO.

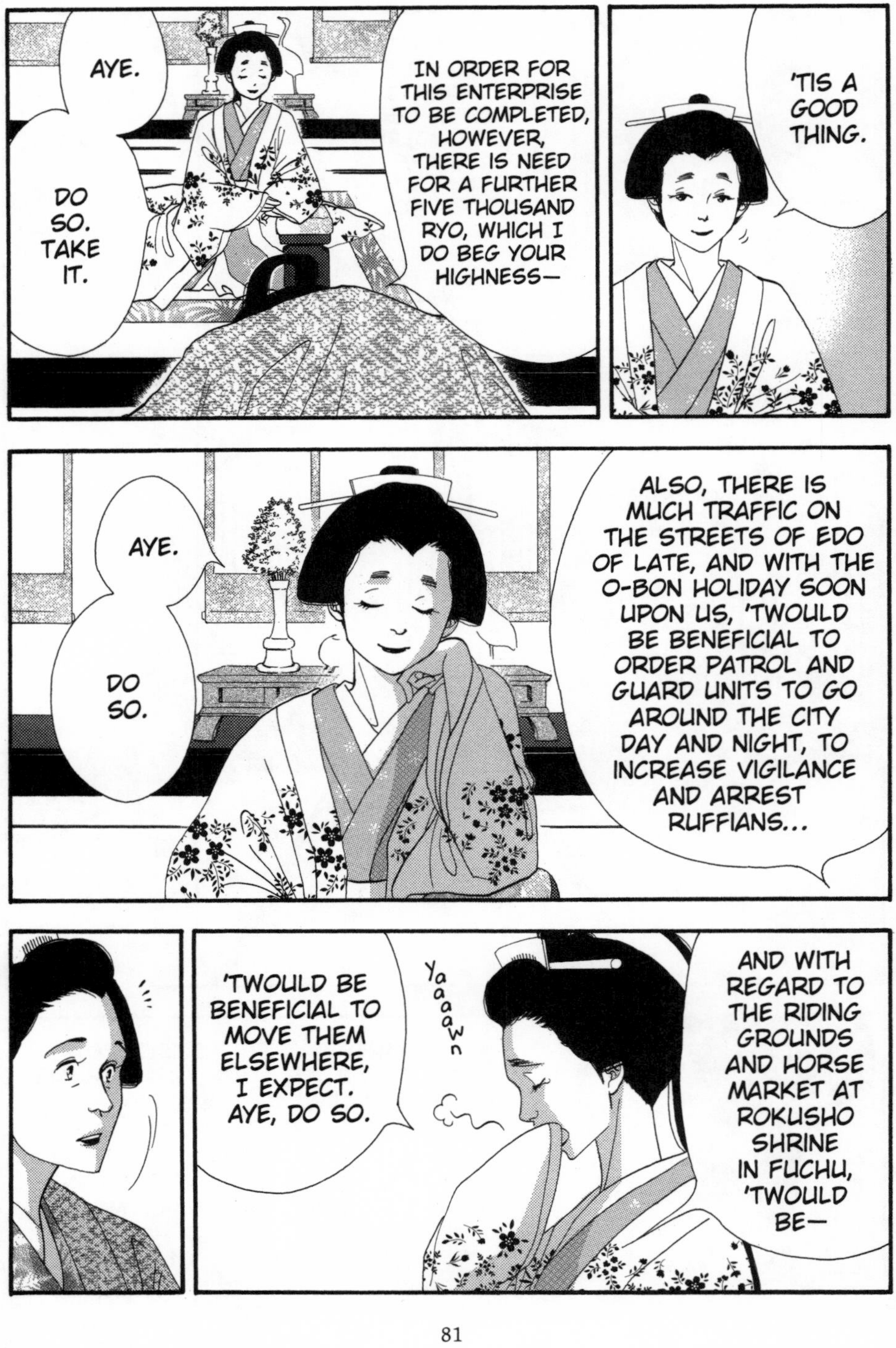
'TIS A GOOD THING.
IN ORDER FOR THIS ENTERPRISE TO BE COMPLETED, HOWEVER, THERE IS NEED FOR A FURTHER FIVE THOUSAND RYO, WHICH I DO BEG YOUR HIGHNESS—
AYE.
DO SO. TAKE IT.
ALSO, THERE IS MUCH TRAFFIC ON THE STREETS OF EDO OF LATE, AND WITH THE O-BON HOLIDAY SOON UPON US, 'TWOULD BE BENEFICIAL TO ORDER PATROL AND GUARD UNITS TO GO AROUND THE CITY DAY AND NIGHT, TO INCREASE VIGILANCE AND ARREST RUFFIANS...
AYE.
DO SO.
AND WITH REGARD TO THE RIDING GROUNDS AND HORSE MARKET AT ROKUSHO SHRINE IN FUCHU, 'TWOULD BE—
Yaaaawn
'TWOULD BE BENEFICIAL TO MOVE THEM ELSEWHERE, I EXPECT. AYE, DO SO.

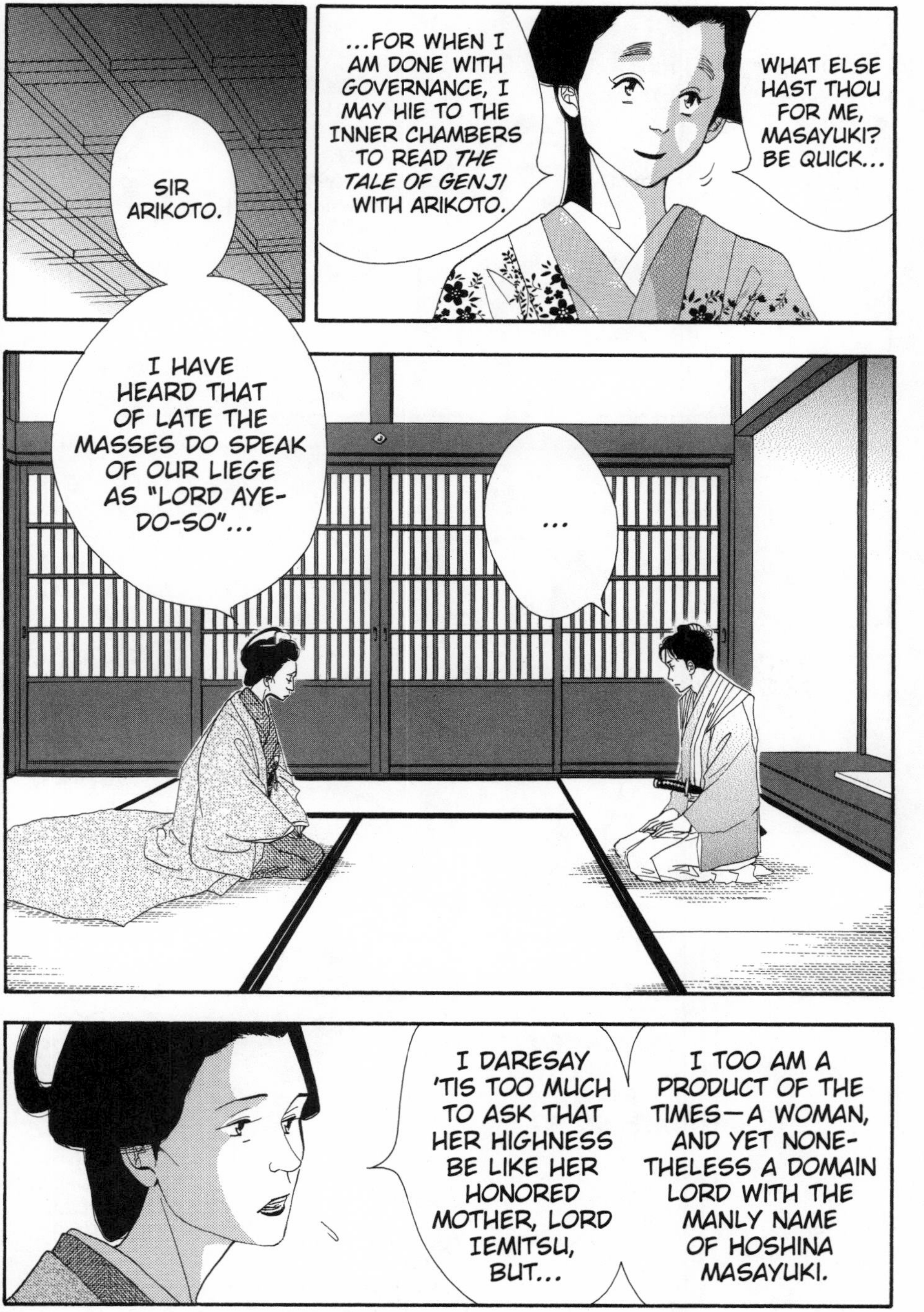
WHAT ELSE HAST THOU FOR ME, MASAYUKI? BE QUICK...
...FOR WHEN I AM DONE WITH GOVERNANCE, I MAY HIE TO THE INNER CHAMBERS TO READ *THE TALE OF GENJI* WITH ARIKOTO.
SIR ARIKOTO.
I HAVE HEARD THAT OF LATE THE MASSES DO SPEAK OF OUR LIEGE AS "LORD AYE-DO-SO"...
...
I TOO AM A PRODUCT OF THE TIMES—A WOMAN, AND YET NONETHELESS A DOMAIN LORD WITH THE MANLY NAME OF HOSHINA MASAYUKI.
I DARESAY 'TIS TOO MUCH TO ASK THAT HER HIGHNESS BE LIKE HER HONORED MOTHER, LORD IEMITSU, BUT...

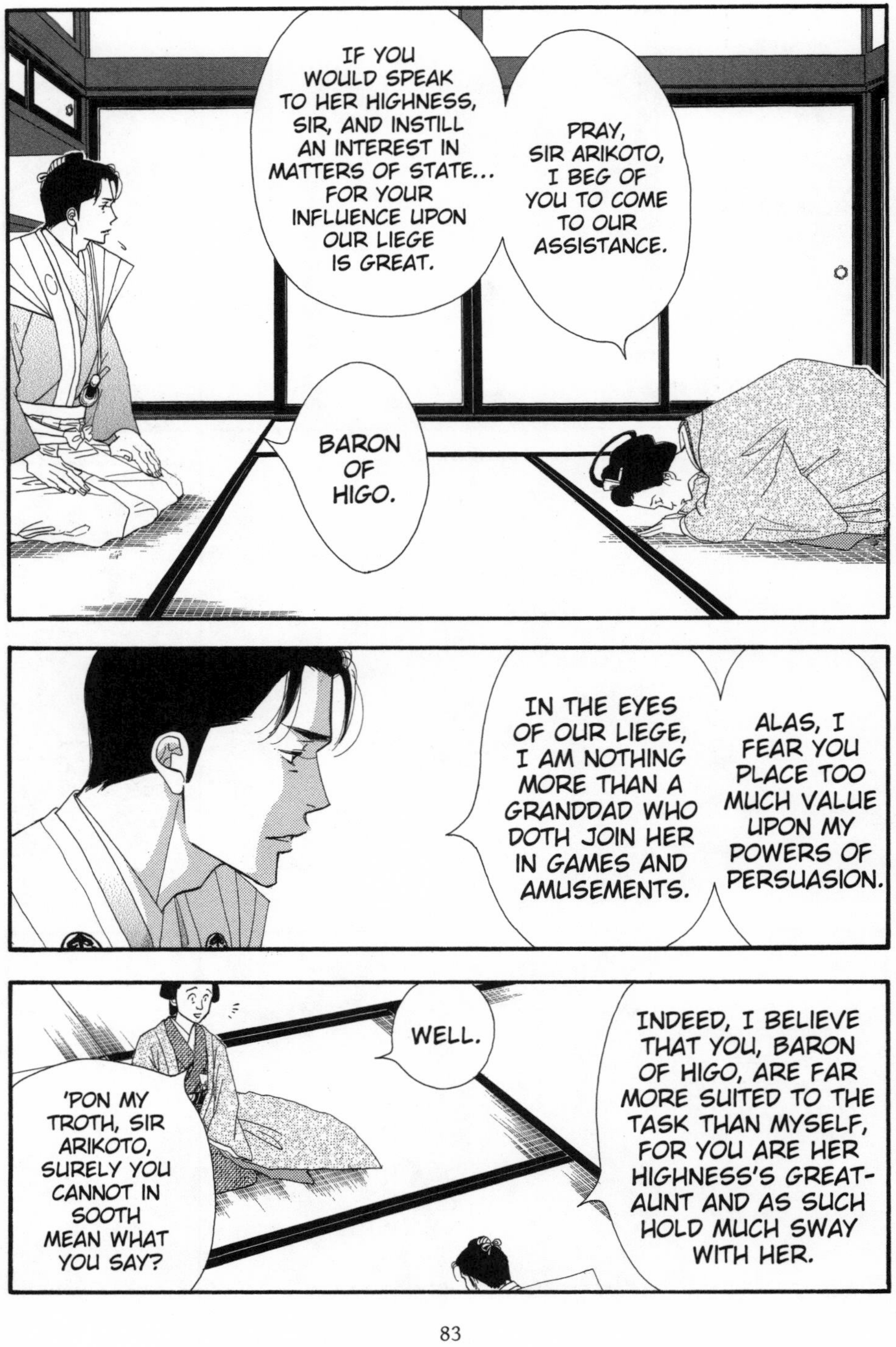
PRAY, SIR ARIKOTO, I BEG OF YOU TO COME TO OUR ASSISTANCE.
IF YOU WOULD SPEAK TO HER HIGHNESS, SIR, AND INSTILL AN INTEREST IN MATTERS OF STATE... FOR YOUR INFLUENCE UPON OUR LIEGE IS GREAT.
BARON OF HIGO.
ALAS, I FEAR YOU PLACE TOO MUCH VALUE UPON MY POWERS OF PERSUASION.
IN THE EYES OF OUR LIEGE, I AM NOTHING MORE THAN A GRANDDAD WHO DOTH JOIN HER IN GAMES AND AMUSEMENTS.
INDEED, I BELIEVE THAT YOU, BARON OF HIGO, ARE FAR MORE SUITED TO THE TASK THAN MYSELF, FOR YOU ARE HER HIGHNESS'S GREAT-AUNT AND AS SUCH HOLD MUCH SWAY WITH HER.
WELL.
'PON MY TROTH, SIR ARIKOTO, SURELY YOU CANNOT IN SOOTH MEAN WHAT YOU SAY?

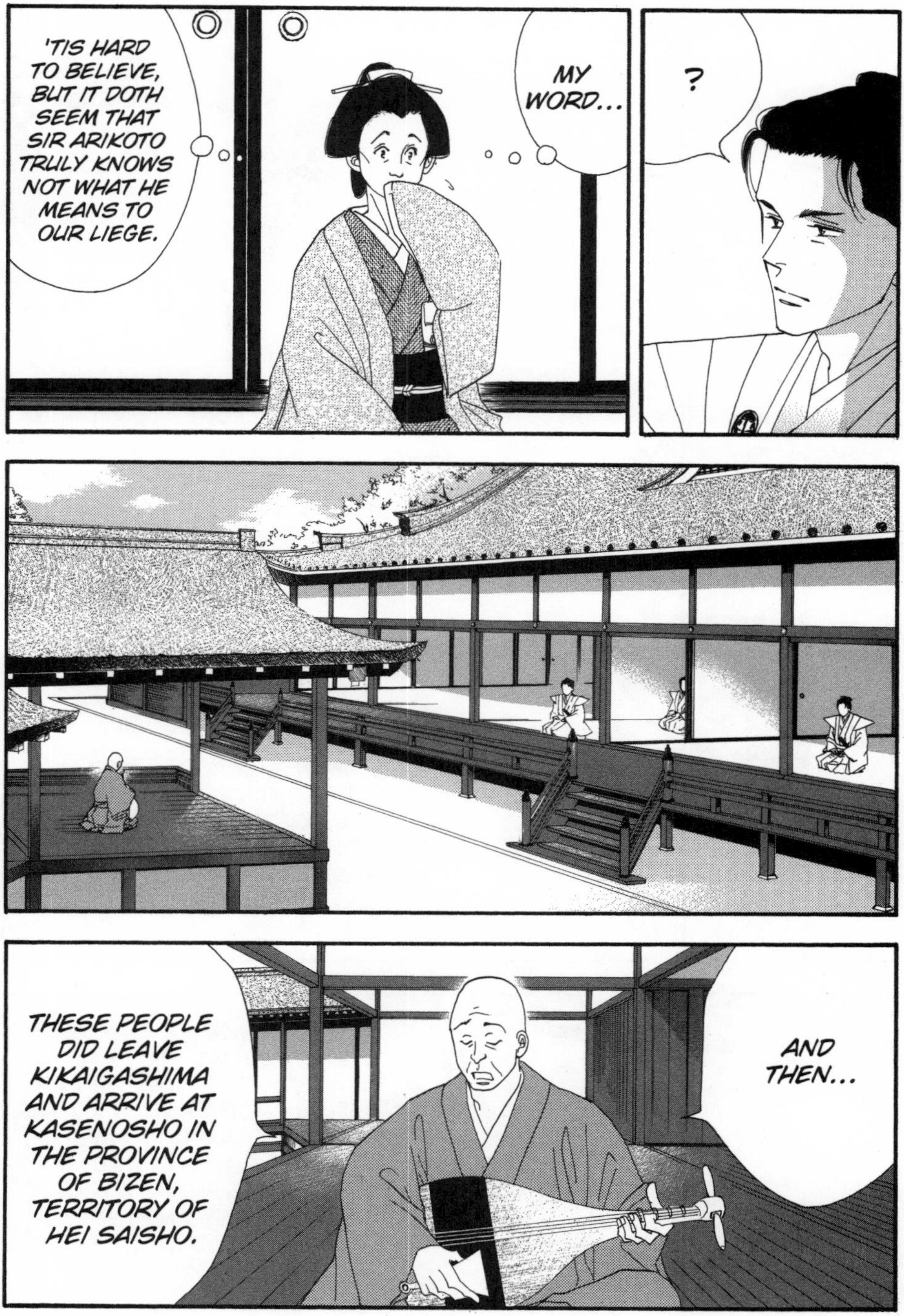
?
MY WORD...
'TIS HARD TO BELIEVE, BUT IT DOTH SEEM THAT SIR ARIKOTO TRULY KNOWS NOT WHAT HE MEANS TO OUR LIEGE.
AND THEN...
THESE PEOPLE DID LEAVE KIKAIGASHIMA AND ARRIVE AT KASENOSHO IN THE PROVINCE OF BIZEN, TERRITORY OF HEI SAISHO.

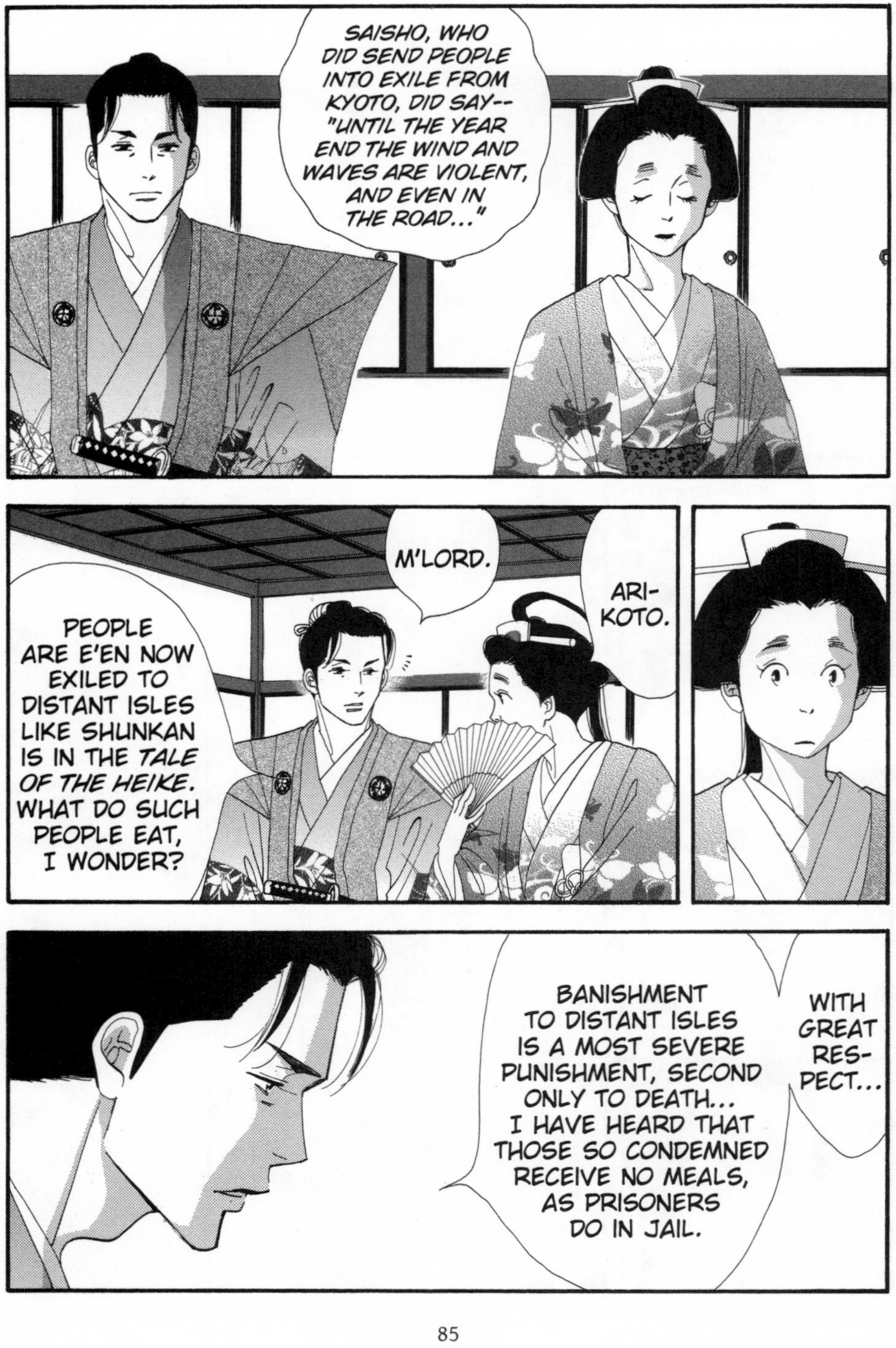
SAISHO, WHO DID SEND PEOPLE INTO EXILE FROM KYOTO, DID SAY-- "UNTIL THE YEAR END THE WIND AND WAVES ARE VIOLENT, AND EVEN IN THE ROAD..."
ARI-KOTO.
M'LORD.
PEOPLE ARE E'EN NOW EXILED TO DISTANT ISLES LIKE SHUNKAN IS IN THE *TALE OF THE HEIKE*. WHAT DO SUCH PEOPLE EAT, I WONDER?
WITH GREAT RES-PECT...
BANISHMENT TO DISTANT ISLES IS A MOST SEVERE PUNISHMENT, SECOND ONLY TO DEATH... I HAVE HEARD THAT THOSE SO CONDEMNED RECEIVE NO MEALS, AS PRISONERS DO IN JAIL.

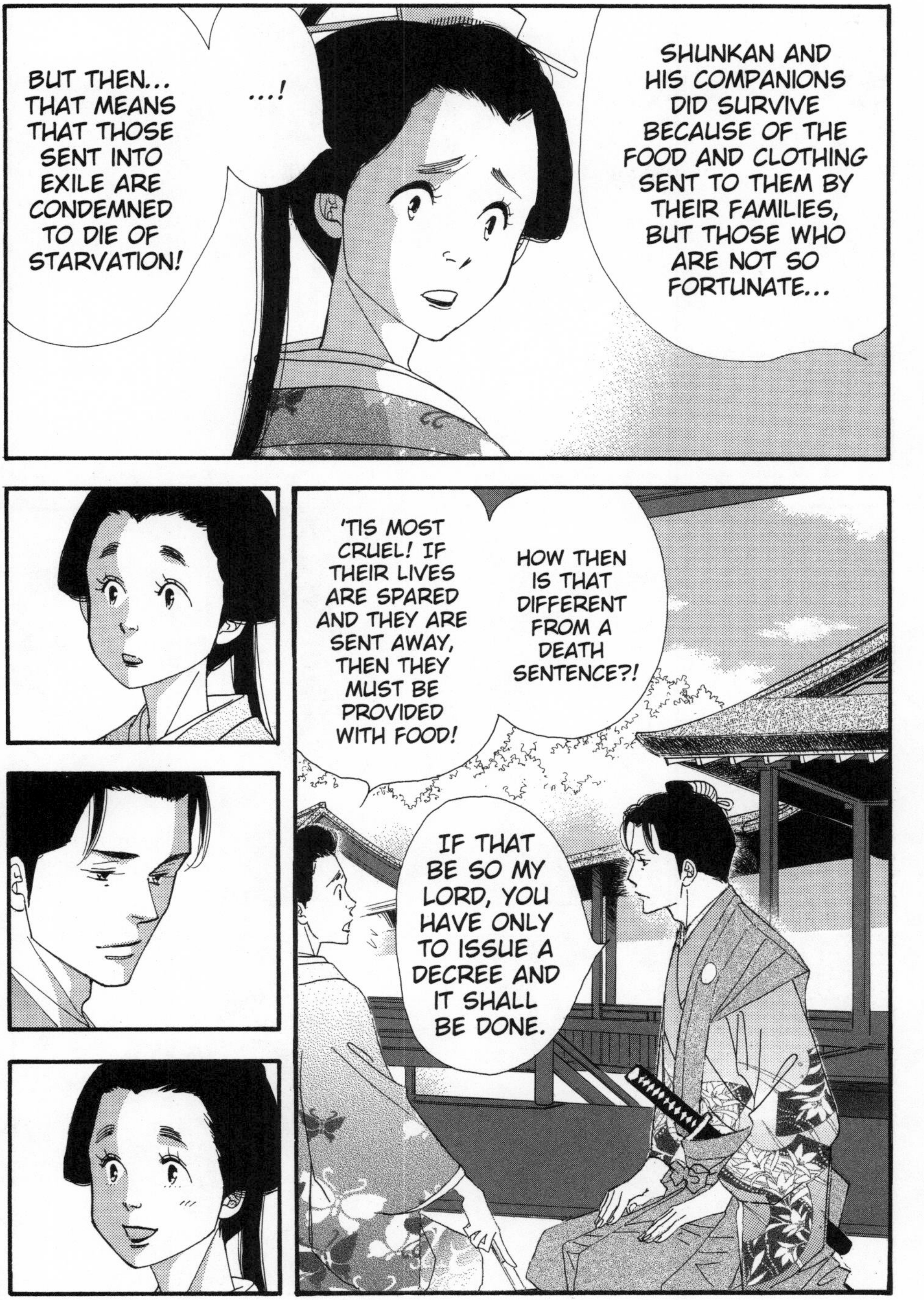
SHUNKAN AND HIS COMPANIONS DID SURVIVE BECAUSE OF THE FOOD AND CLOTHING SENT TO THEM BY THEIR FAMILIES, BUT THOSE WHO ARE NOT SO FORTUNATE...
...!
BUT THEN... THAT MEANS THAT THOSE SENT INTO EXILE ARE CONDEMNED TO DIE OF STARVATION!
'TIS MOST CRUEL! IF THEIR LIVES ARE SPARED AND THEY ARE SENT AWAY, THEN THEY MUST BE PROVIDED WITH FOOD!
HOW THEN IS THAT DIFFERENT FROM A DEATH SENTENCE?!
IF THAT BE SO MY LORD, YOU HAVE ONLY TO ISSUE A DECREE AND IT SHALL BE DONE.

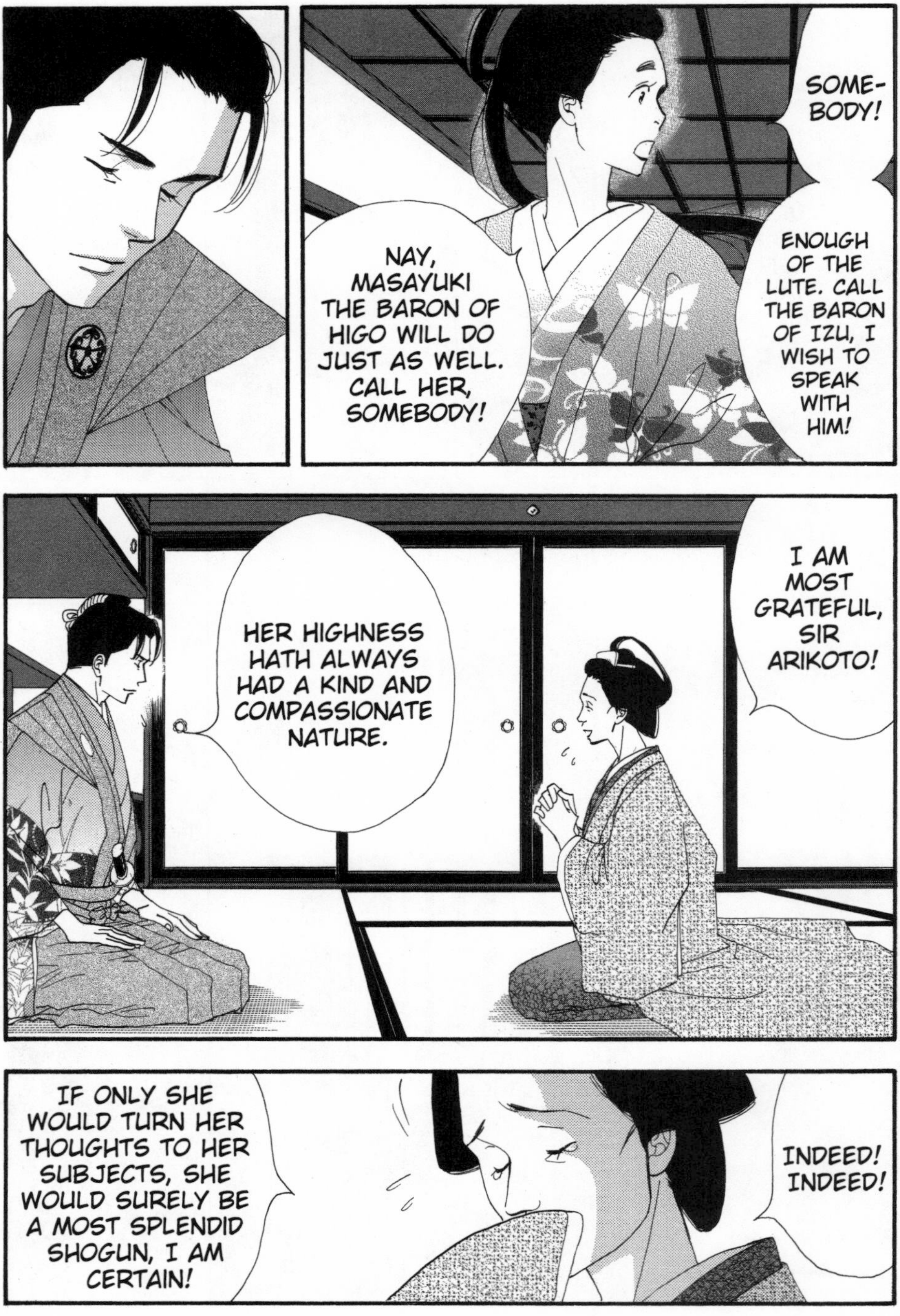
SOME-BODY!
ENOUGH OF THE LUTE. CALL THE BARON OF IZU, I WISH TO SPEAK WITH HIM!
NAY, MASAYUKI THE BARON OF HIGO WILL DO JUST AS WELL. CALL HER, SOMEBODY!
I AM MOST GRATEFUL, SIR ARIKOTO!
HER HIGHNESS HATH ALWAYS HAD A KIND AND COMPASSIONATE NATURE.
INDEED! INDEED!
IF ONLY SHE WOULD TURN HER THOUGHTS TO HER SUBJECTS, SHE WOULD SURELY BE A MOST SPLENDID SHOGUN, I AM CERTAIN!

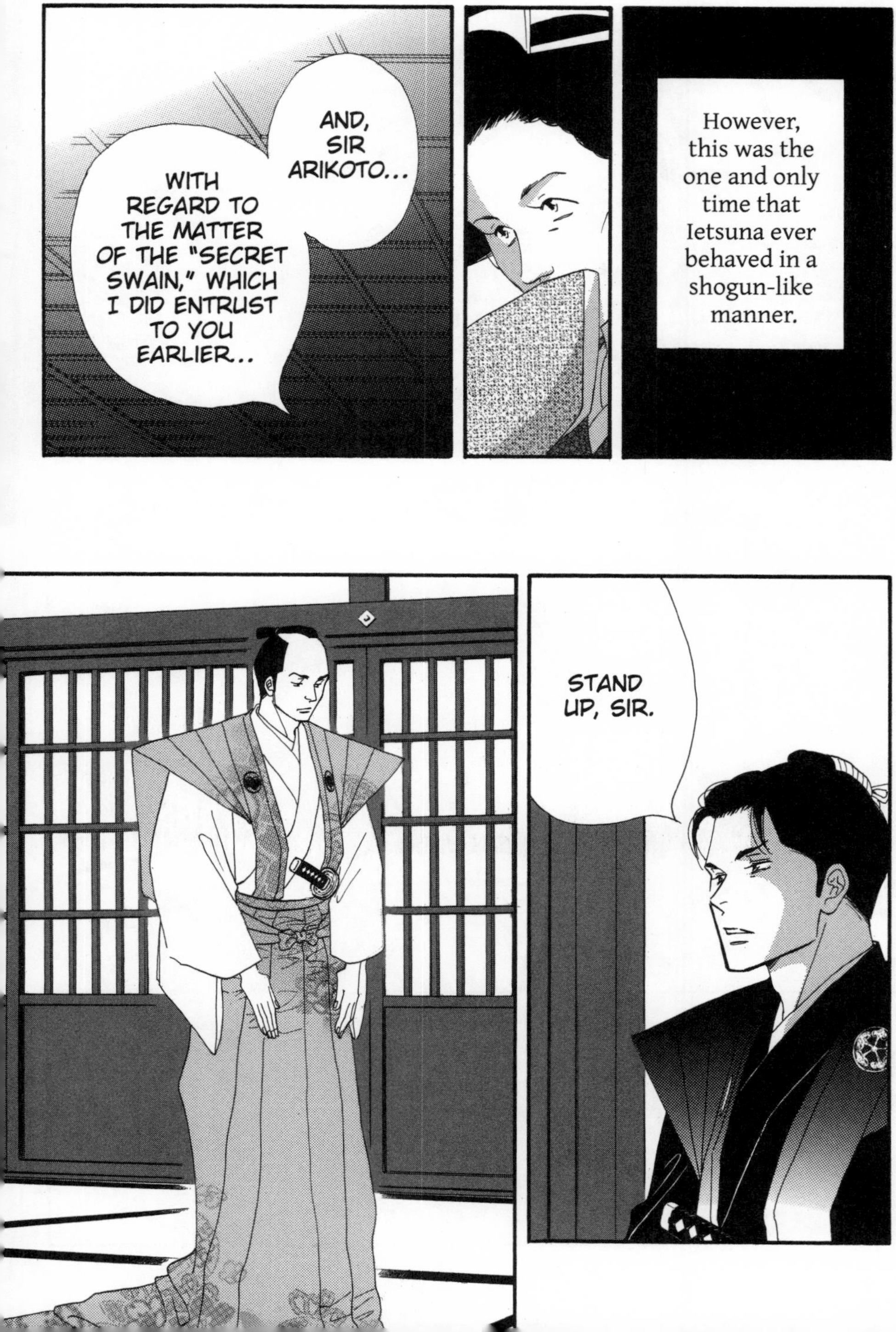
However, this was the one and only time that Ietsuna ever behaved in a shogun-like manner.
AND, SIR ARIKOTO...
WITH REGARD TO THE MATTER OF THE "SECRET SWAIN," WHICH I DID ENTRUST TO YOU EARLIER...
STAND UP, SIR.

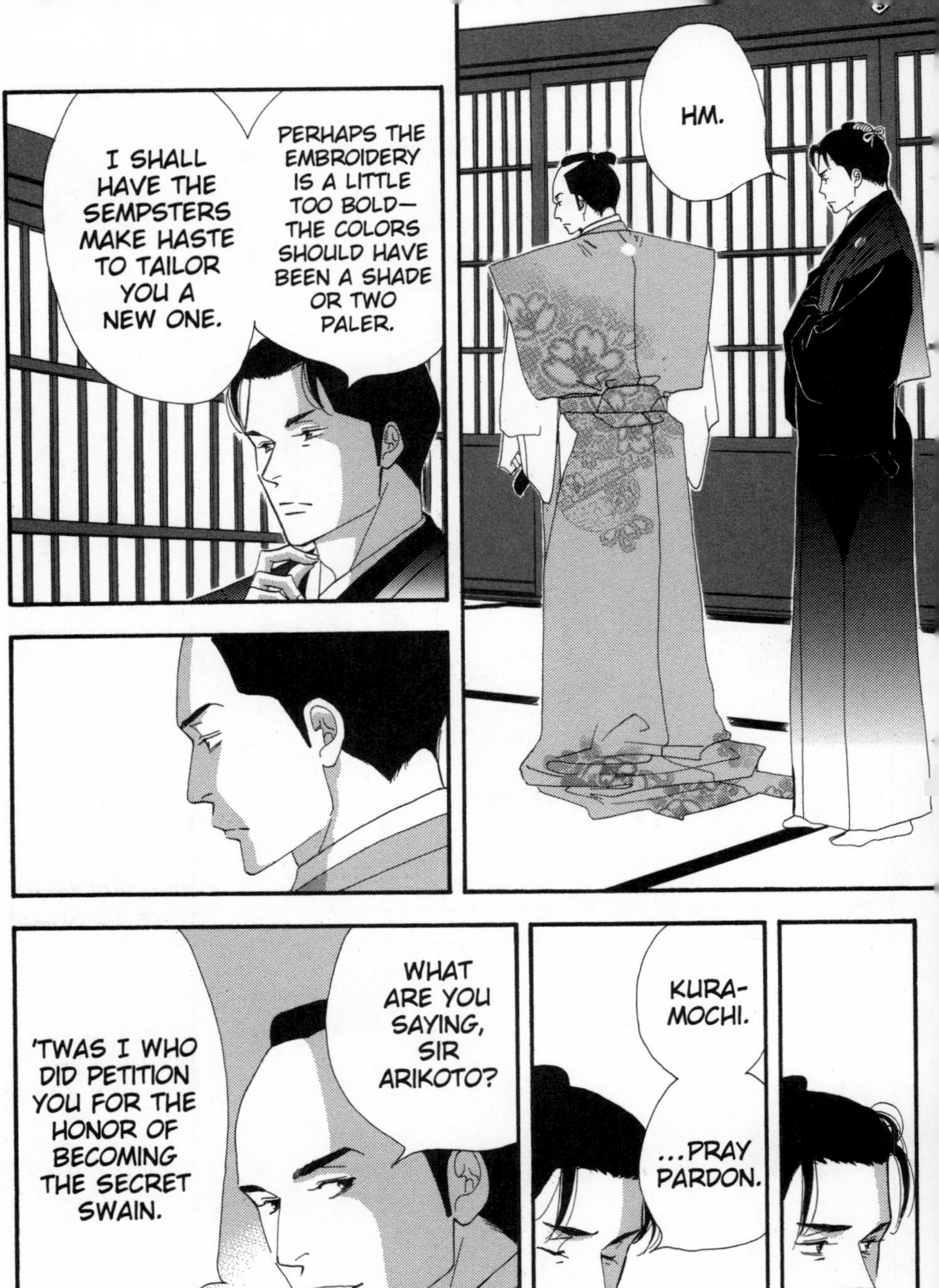
HM.
PERHAPS THE EMBROIDERY IS A LITTLE TOO BOLD— THE COLORS SHOULD HAVE BEEN A SHADE OR TWO PALER.
I SHALL HAVE THE SEMPSTERS MAKE HASTE TO TAILOR YOU A NEW ONE.
KURA-MOCHI.
...PRAY PARDON.
WHAT ARE YOU SAYING, SIR ARIKOTO?
'TWAS I WHO DID PETITION YOU FOR THE HONOR OF BECOMING THE SECRET SWAIN.

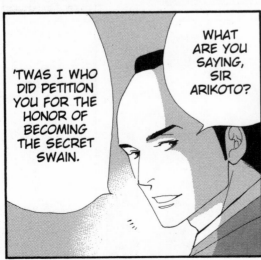

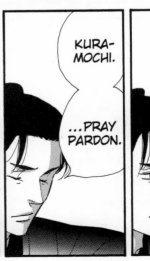

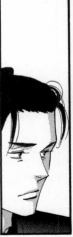

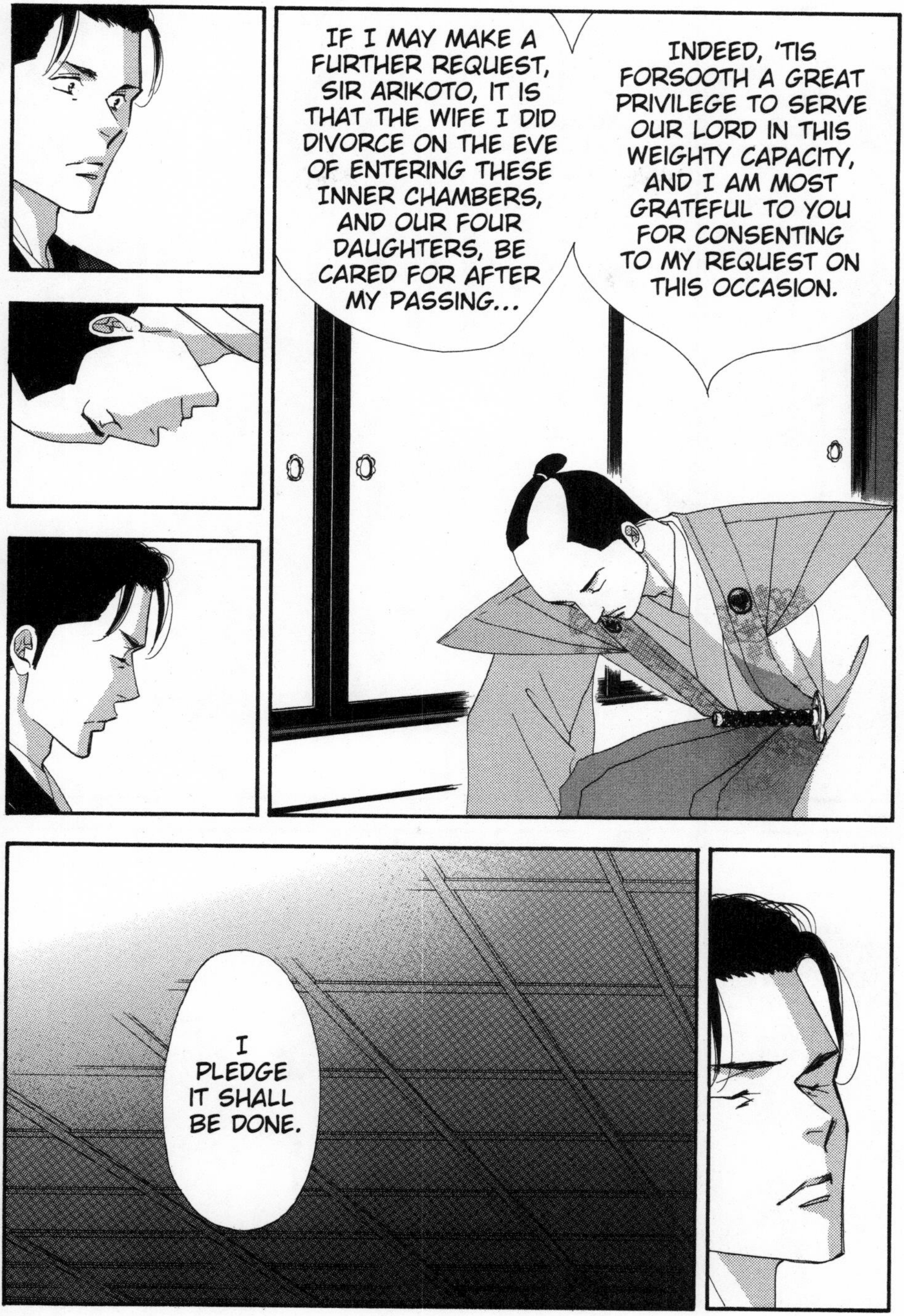
INDEED, 'TIS FORSOOTH A GREAT PRIVILEGE TO SERVE OUR LORD IN THIS WEIGHTY CAPACITY, AND I AM MOST GRATEFUL TO YOU FOR CONSENTING TO MY REQUEST ON THIS OCCASION.
IF I MAY MAKE A FURTHER REQUEST, SIR ARIKOTO, IT IS THAT THE WIFE I DID DIVORCE ON THE EVE OF ENTERING THESE INNER CHAMBERS, AND OUR FOUR DAUGHTERS, BE CARED FOR AFTER MY PASSING...
I PLEDGE IT SHALL BE DONE.

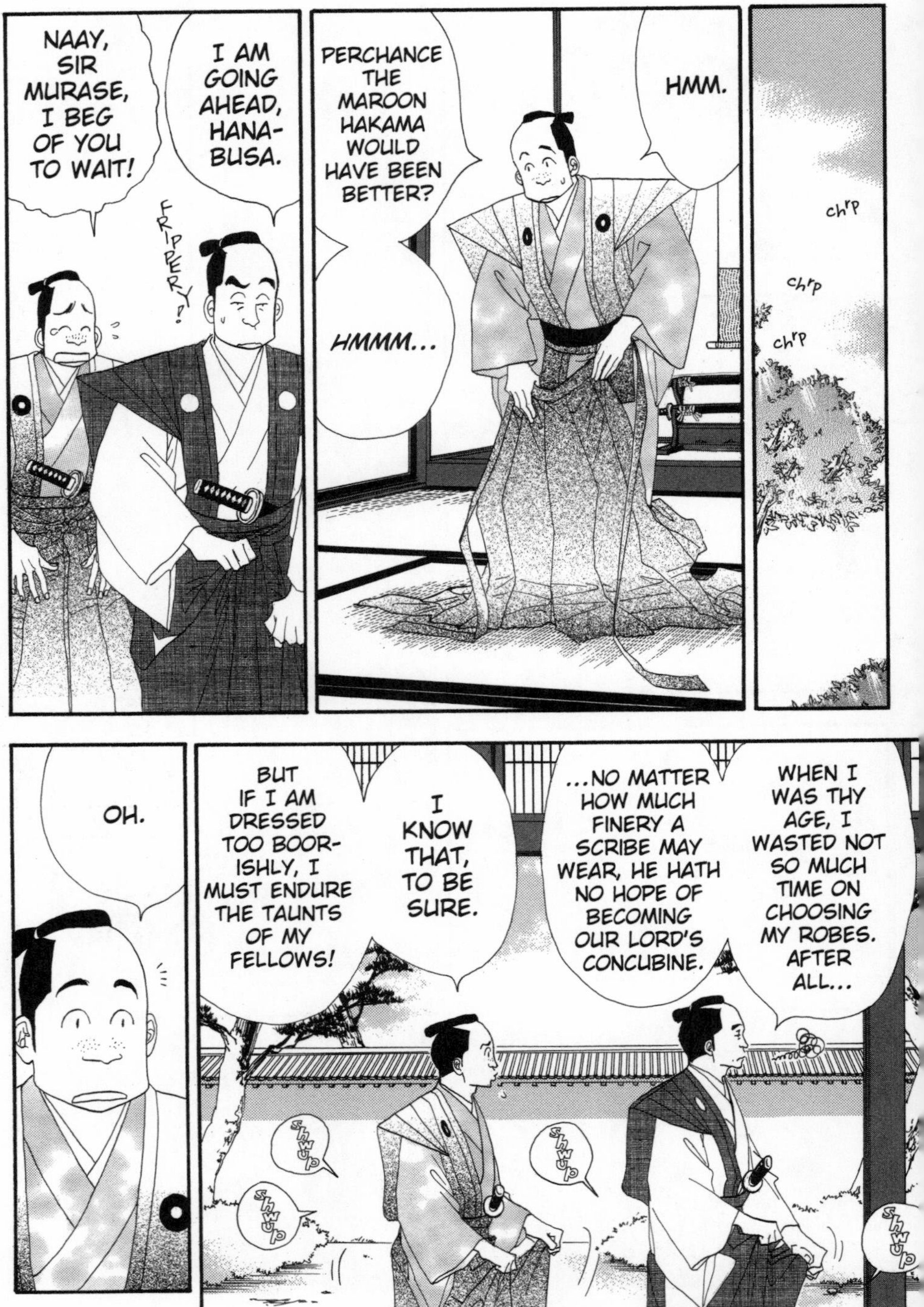
chrp
chrp
chrp
HMM.
PERCHANCE THE MAROON HAKAMA WOULD HAVE BEEN BETTER?
HMMM...
I AM GOING AHEAD, HANA-BUSA.
FRIPPERY!
NAAY, SIR MURASE, I BEG OF YOU TO WAIT!
WHEN I WAS THY AGE, I WASTED NOT SO MUCH TIME ON CHOOSING MY ROBES. AFTER ALL...
...NO MATTER HOW MUCH FINERY A SCRIBE MAY WEAR, HE HATH NO HOPE OF BECOMING OUR LORD'S CONCUBINE.
I KNOW THAT, TO BE SURE.
BUT IF I AM DRESSED TOO BOOR-ISHLY, I MUST ENDURE THE TAUNTS OF MY FELLOWS!
shwup
shwup
shwup
shwup
OH.

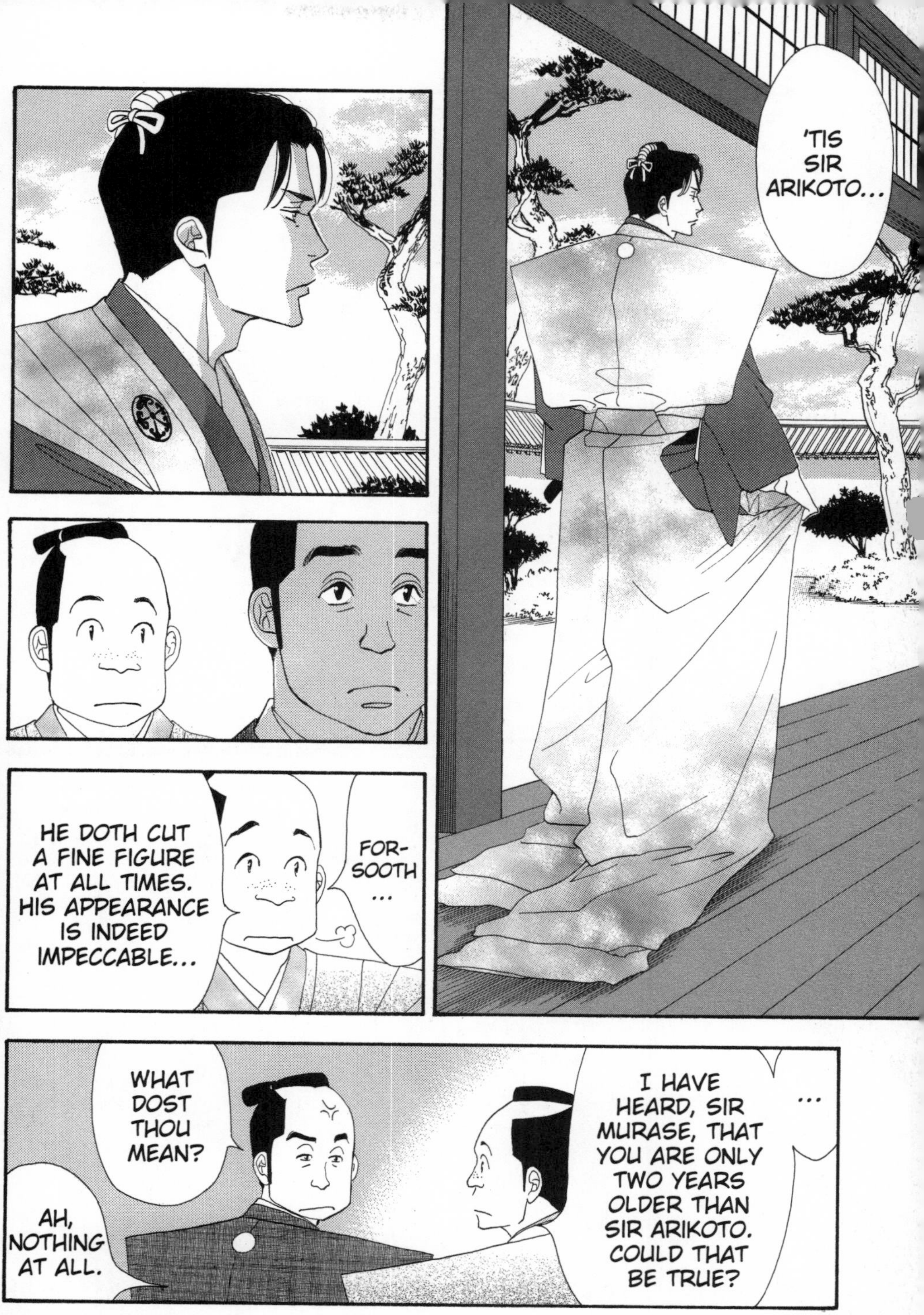
'TIS SIR ARIKOTO...
FOR-SOOTH...
HE DOTH CUT A FINE FIGURE AT ALL TIMES. HIS APPEARANCE IS INDEED IMPECCABLE...
...
I HAVE HEARD, SIR MURASE, THAT YOU ARE ONLY TWO YEARS OLDER THAN SIR ARIKOTO. COULD THAT BE TRUE?
WHAT DOST THOU MEAN?
AH, NOTHING AT ALL.

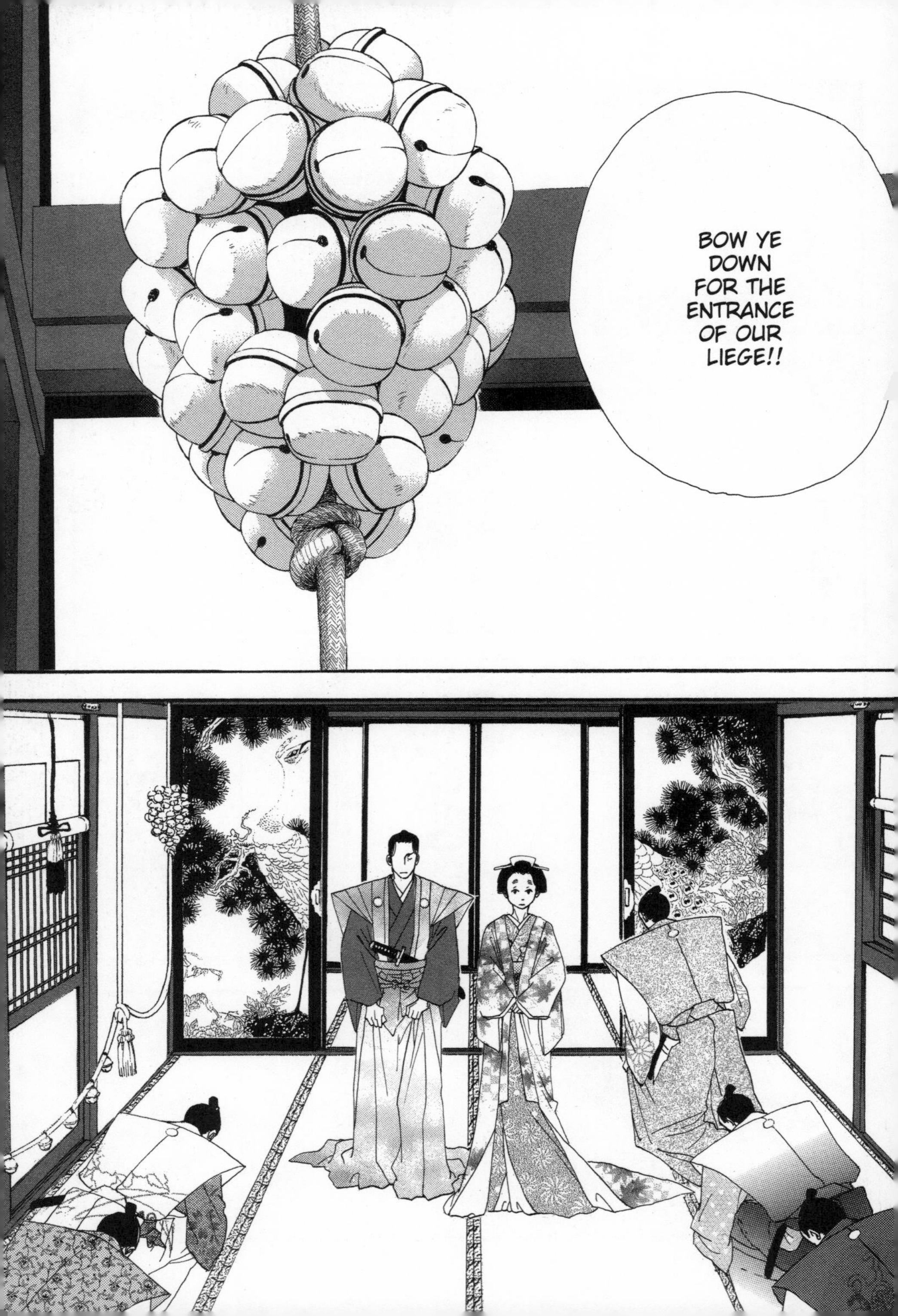
BOW YE DOWN FOR THE ENTRANCE OF OUR LIEGE!!

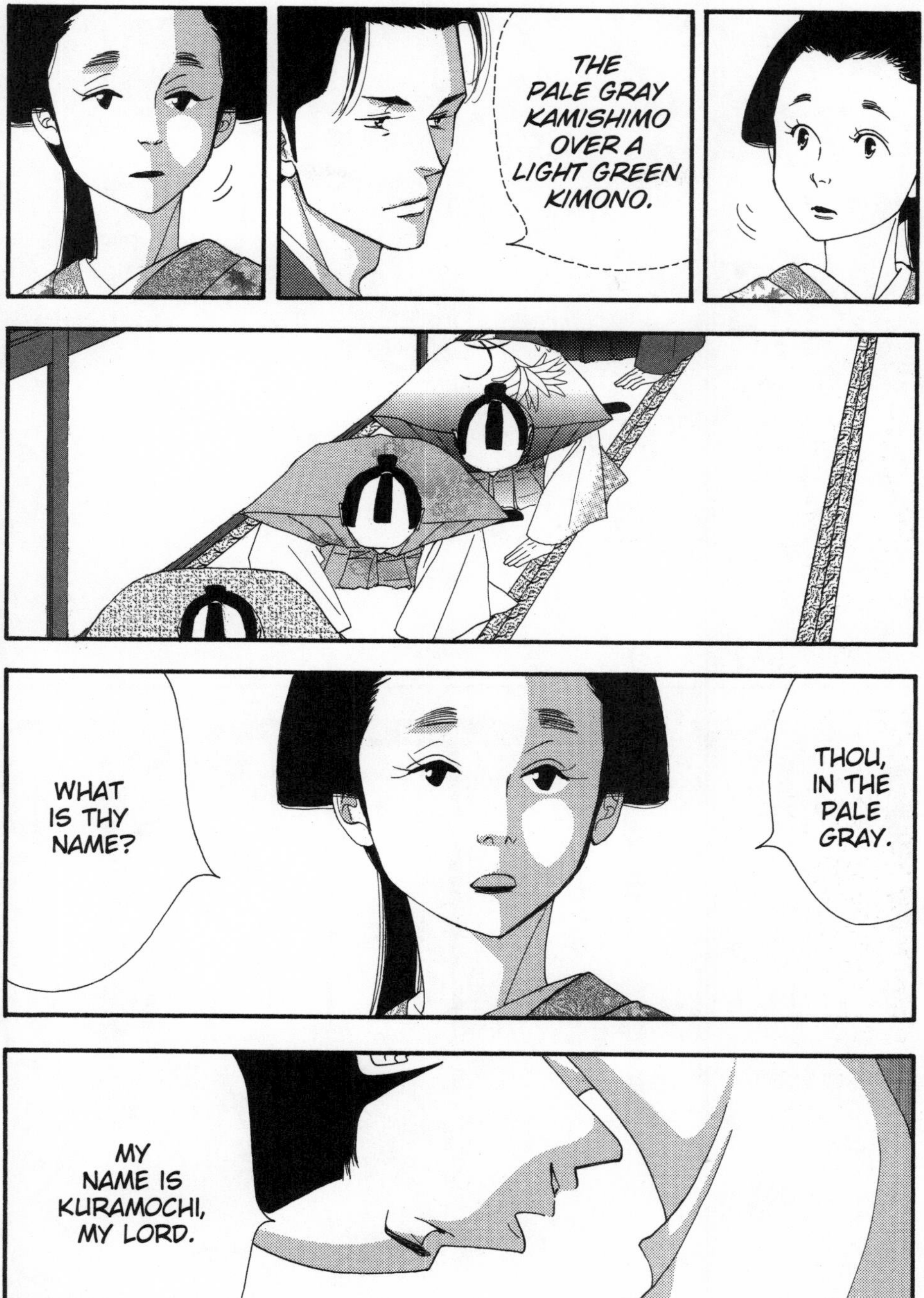
THE PALE GRAY KAMISHIMO OVER A LIGHT GREEN KIMONO.
THOU, IN THE PALE GRAY.
WHAT IS THY NAME?
MY NAME IS KURAMOCHI, MY LORD.

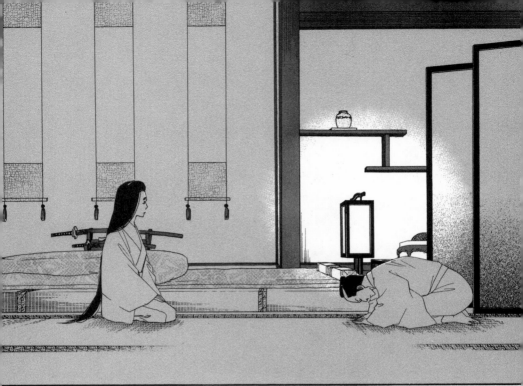

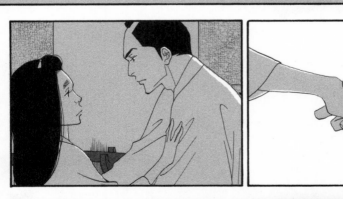

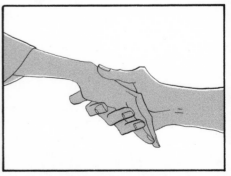

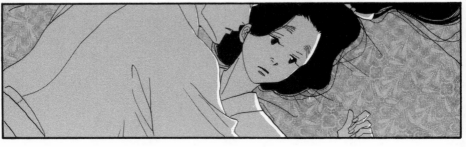

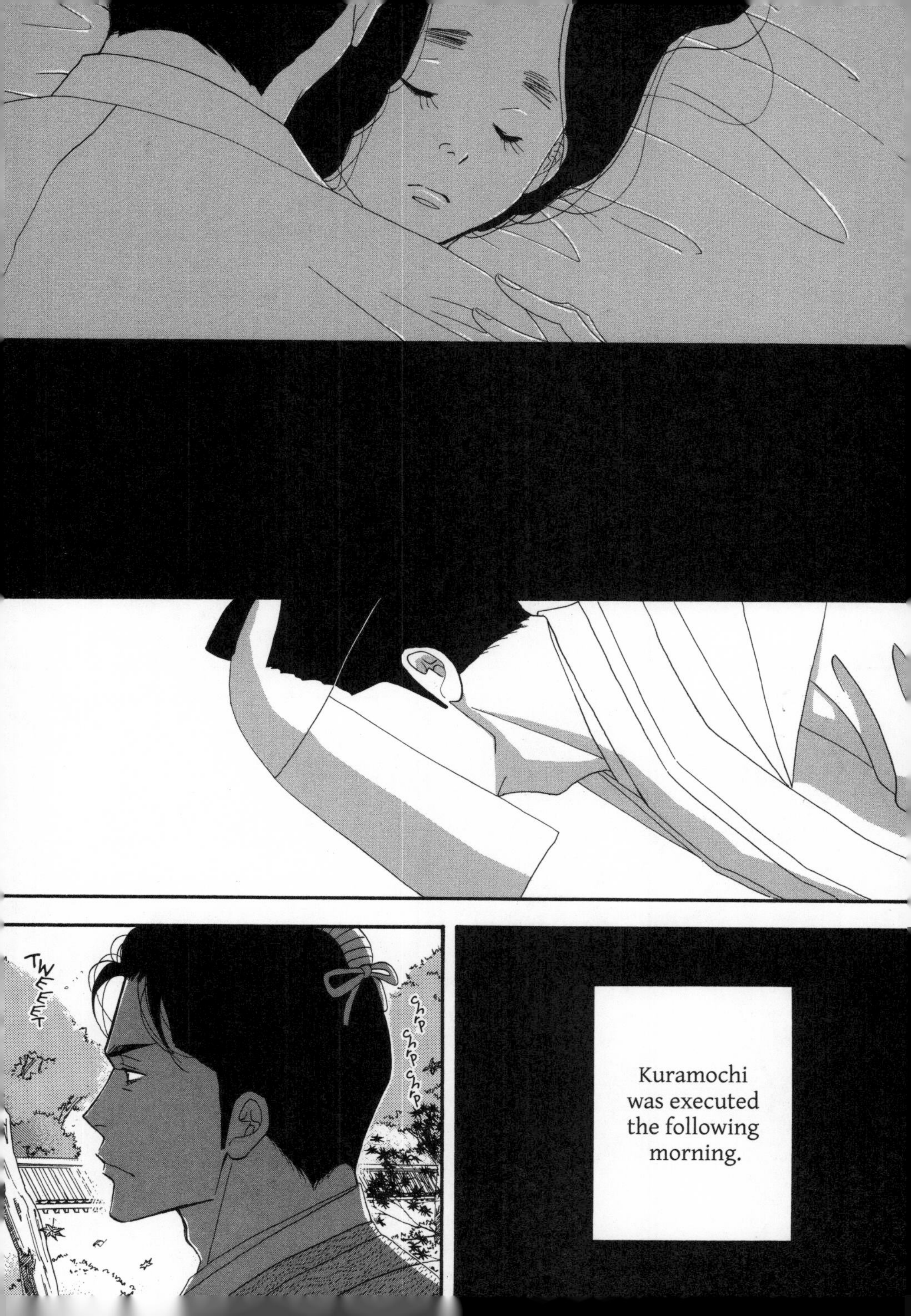
Kuramochi was executed the following morning.
TWEEET
chrp chrp chrp chrp

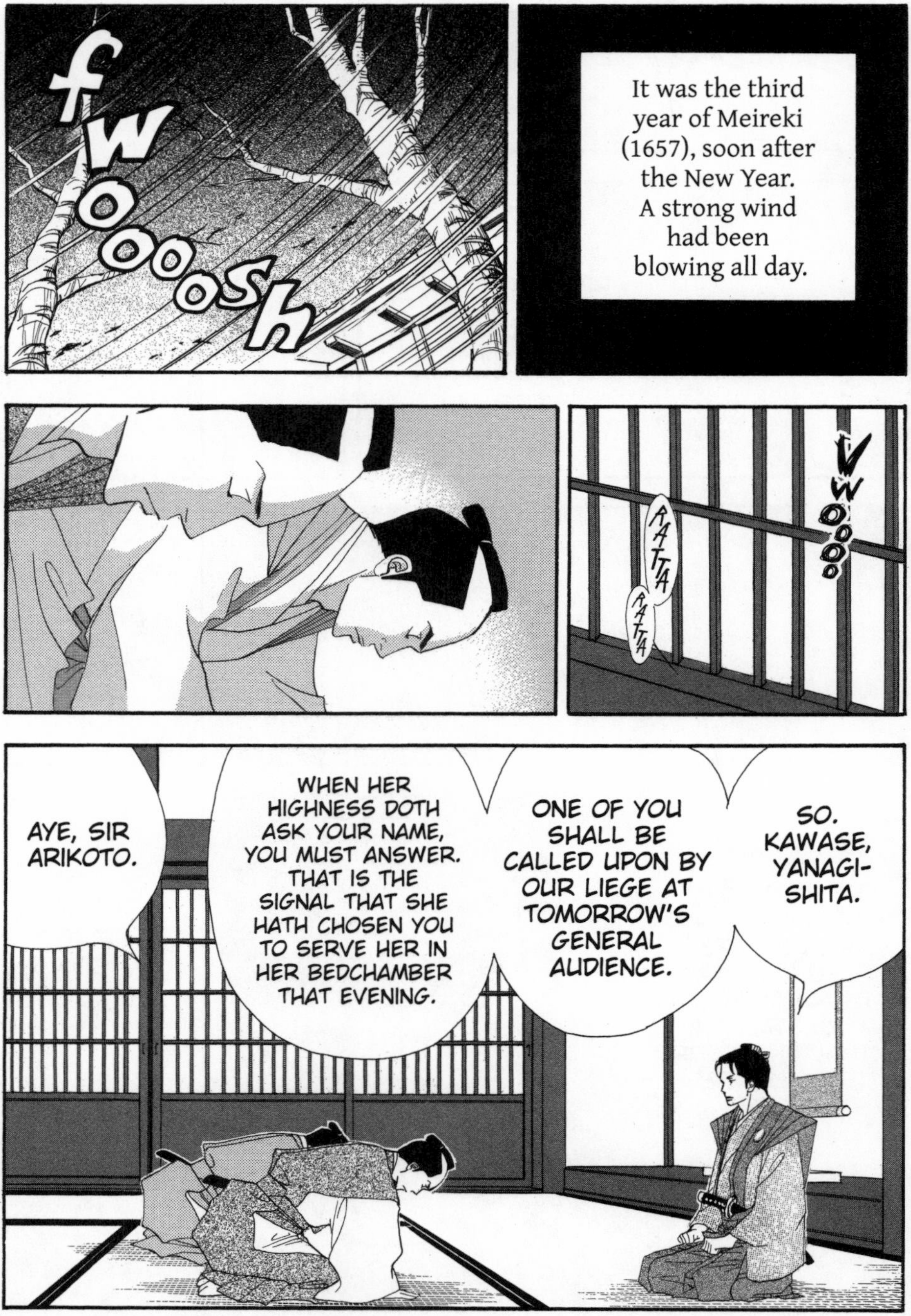
It was the third year of Meireki (1657), soon after the New Year. A strong wind had been blowing all day.
fwooooosh
vwoooo
RATTA
RATTA
SO. KAWASE, YANAGI-SHITA.
ONE OF YOU SHALL BE CALLED UPON BY OUR LIEGE AT TOMORROW'S GENERAL AUDIENCE.
WHEN HER HIGHNESS DOTH ASK YOUR NAME, YOU MUST ANSWER. THAT IS THE SIGNAL THAT SHE HATH CHOSEN YOU TO SERVE HER IN HER BEDCHAMBER THAT EVENING.
AYE, SIR ARIKOTO.

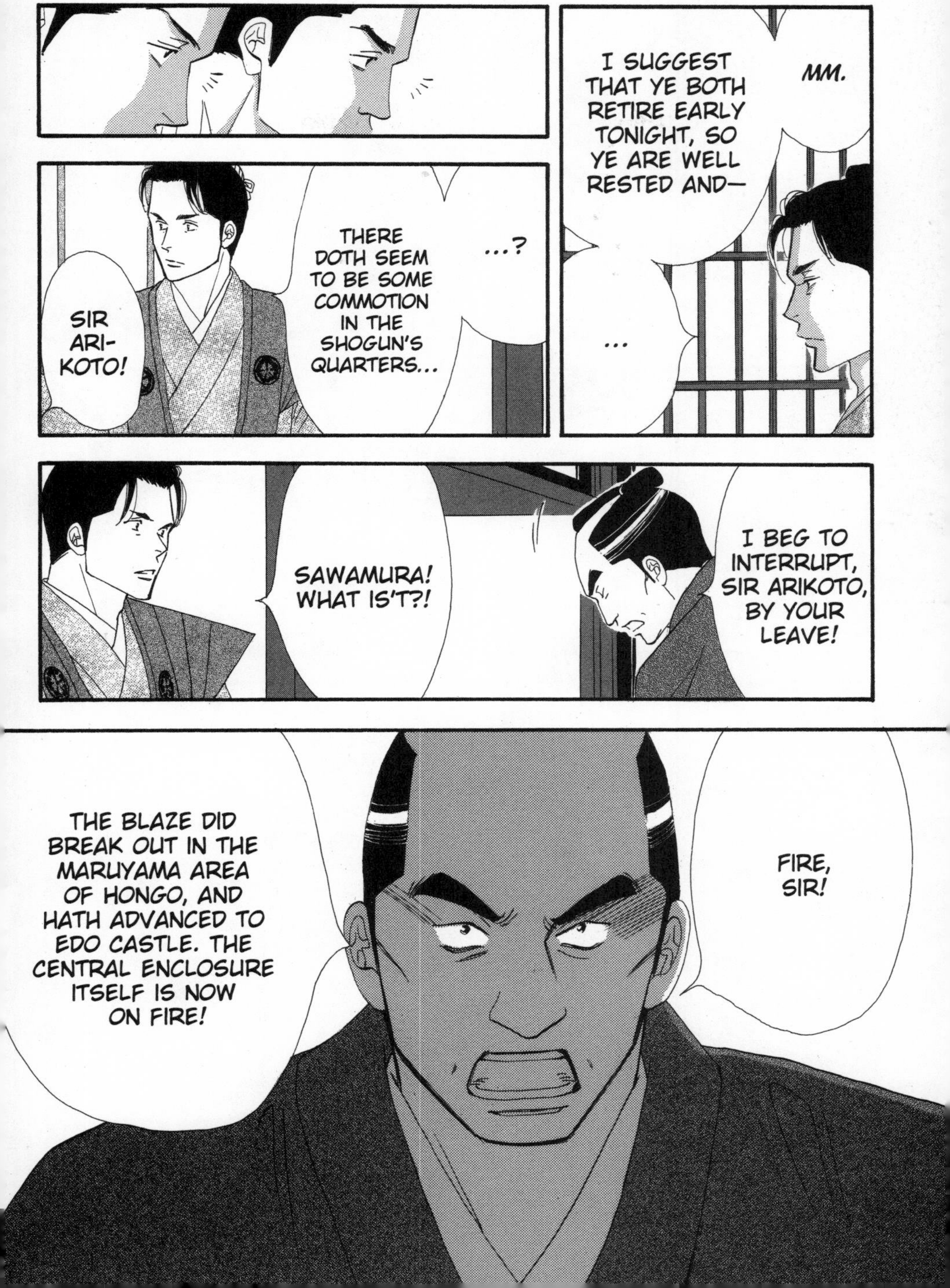
MM.
I SUGGEST THAT YE BOTH RETIRE EARLY TONIGHT, SO YE ARE WELL RESTED AND—
...
...?
THERE DOTH SEEM TO BE SOME COMMOTION IN THE SHOGUN'S QUARTERS...
SIR ARI-KOTO!
I BEG TO INTERRUPT, SIR ARIKOTO, BY YOUR LEAVE!
SAWAMURA! WHAT IS'T?!
FIRE, SIR!
THE BLAZE DID BREAK OUT IN THE MARUYAMA AREA OF HONGO, AND HATH ADVANCED TO EDO CASTLE. THE CENTRAL ENCLOSURE ITSELF IS NOW ON FIRE!

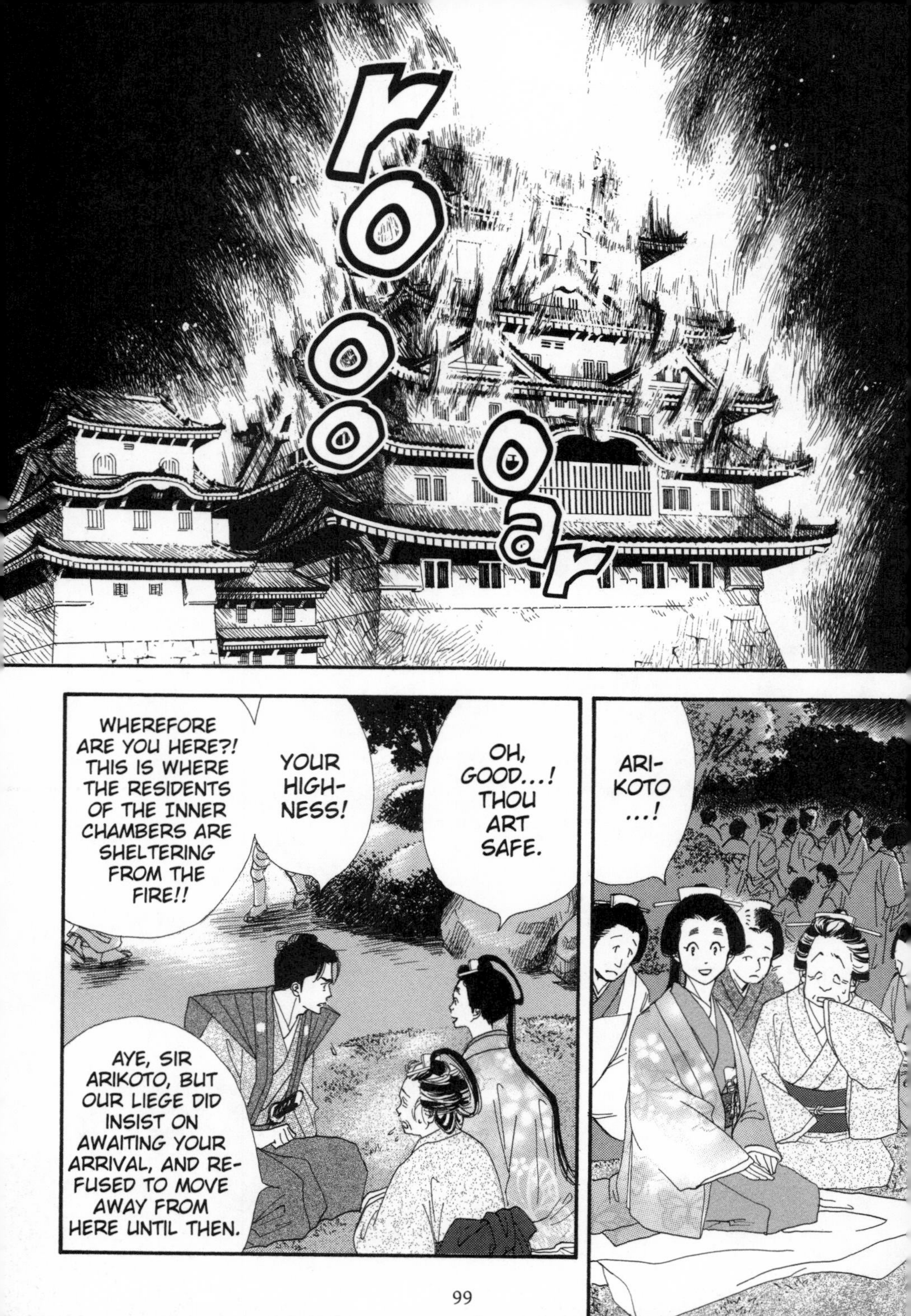
rooooar
ARI-KOTO ...!
OH, GOOD...! THOU ART SAFE.
YOUR HIGHNESS!
WHEREFORE ARE YOU HERE?! THIS IS WHERE THE RESIDENTS OF THE INNER CHAMBERS ARE SHELTERING FROM THE FIRE!!
AYE, SIR ARIKOTO, BUT OUR LIEGE DID INSIST ON AWAITING YOUR ARRIVAL, AND REFUSED TO MOVE AWAY FROM HERE UNTIL THEN.

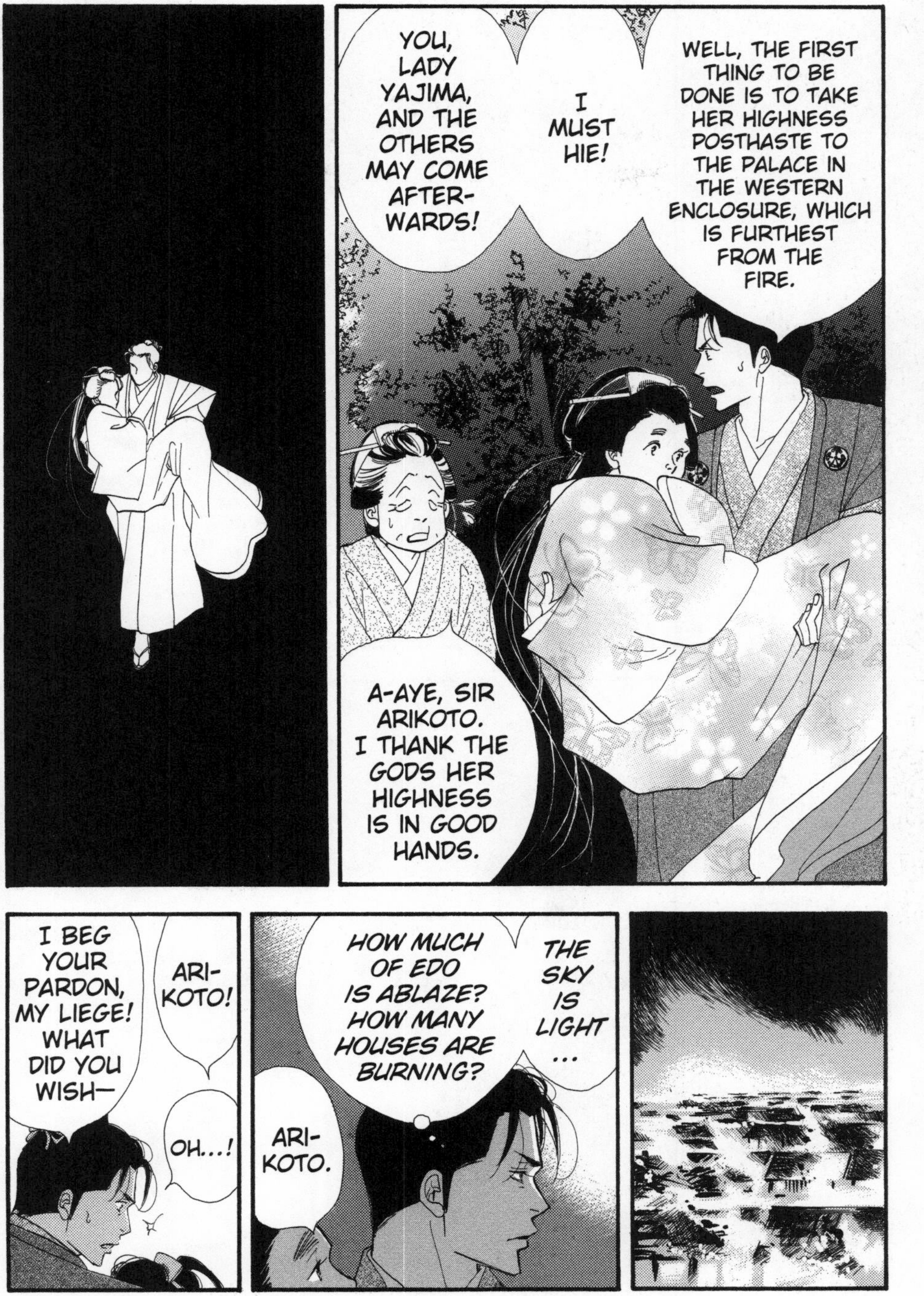
WELL, THE FIRST THING TO BE DONE IS TO TAKE HER HIGHNESS POSTHASTE TO THE PALACE IN THE WESTERN ENCLOSURE, WHICH IS FURTHEST FROM THE FIRE.
I MUST HIE!
YOU, LADY YAJIMA, AND THE OTHERS MAY COME AFTER-WARDS!
A-AYE, SIR ARIKOTO. I THANK THE GODS HER HIGHNESS IS IN GOOD HANDS.
THE SKY IS LIGHT...
HOW MUCH OF EDO IS ABLAZE? HOW MANY HOUSES ARE BURNING?
ARI-KOTO.
ARI-KOTO!
I BEG YOUR PARDON, MY LIEGE! WHAT DID YOU WISH—
OH...!

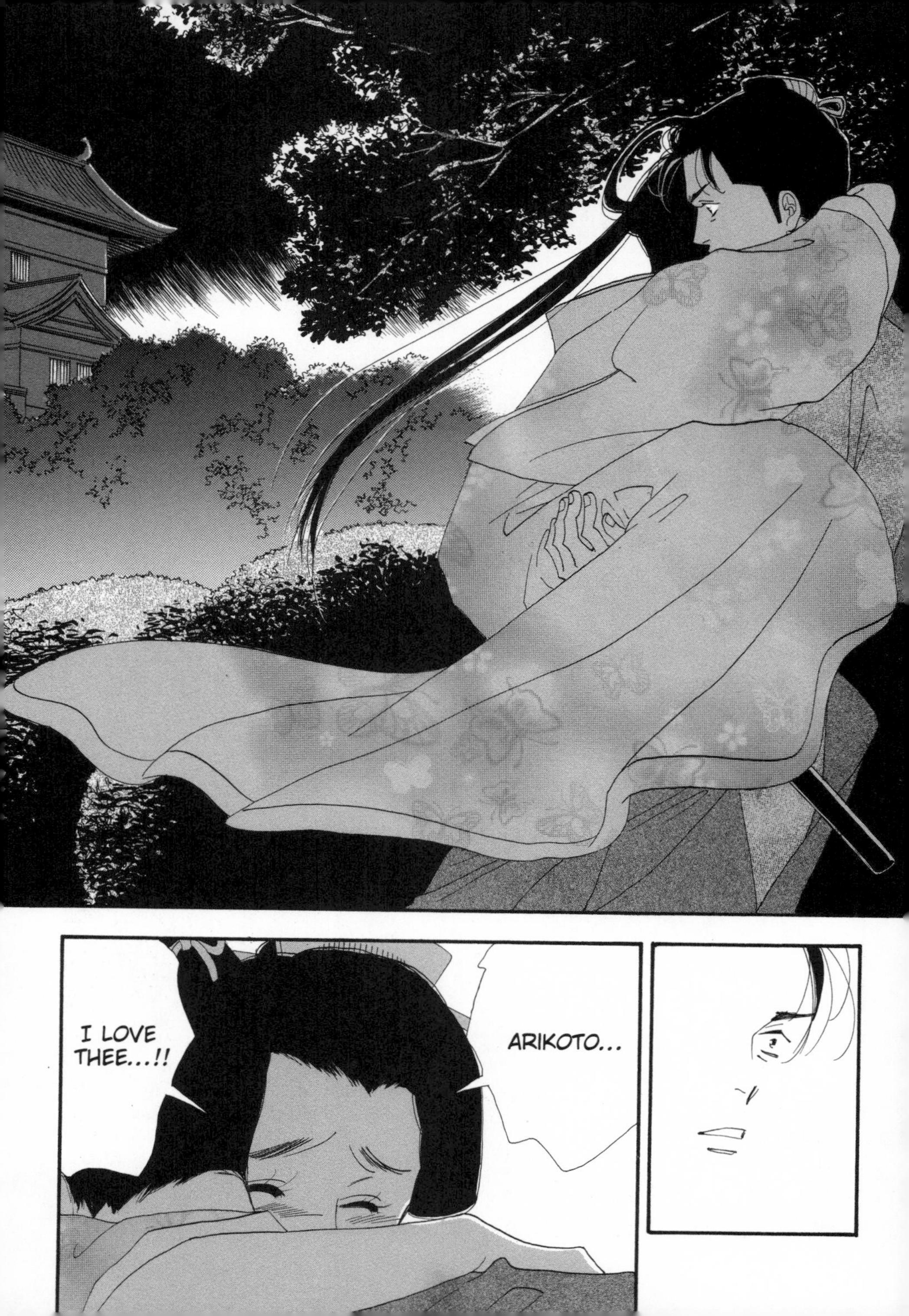
ARIKOTO...
I LOVE THEE...!!

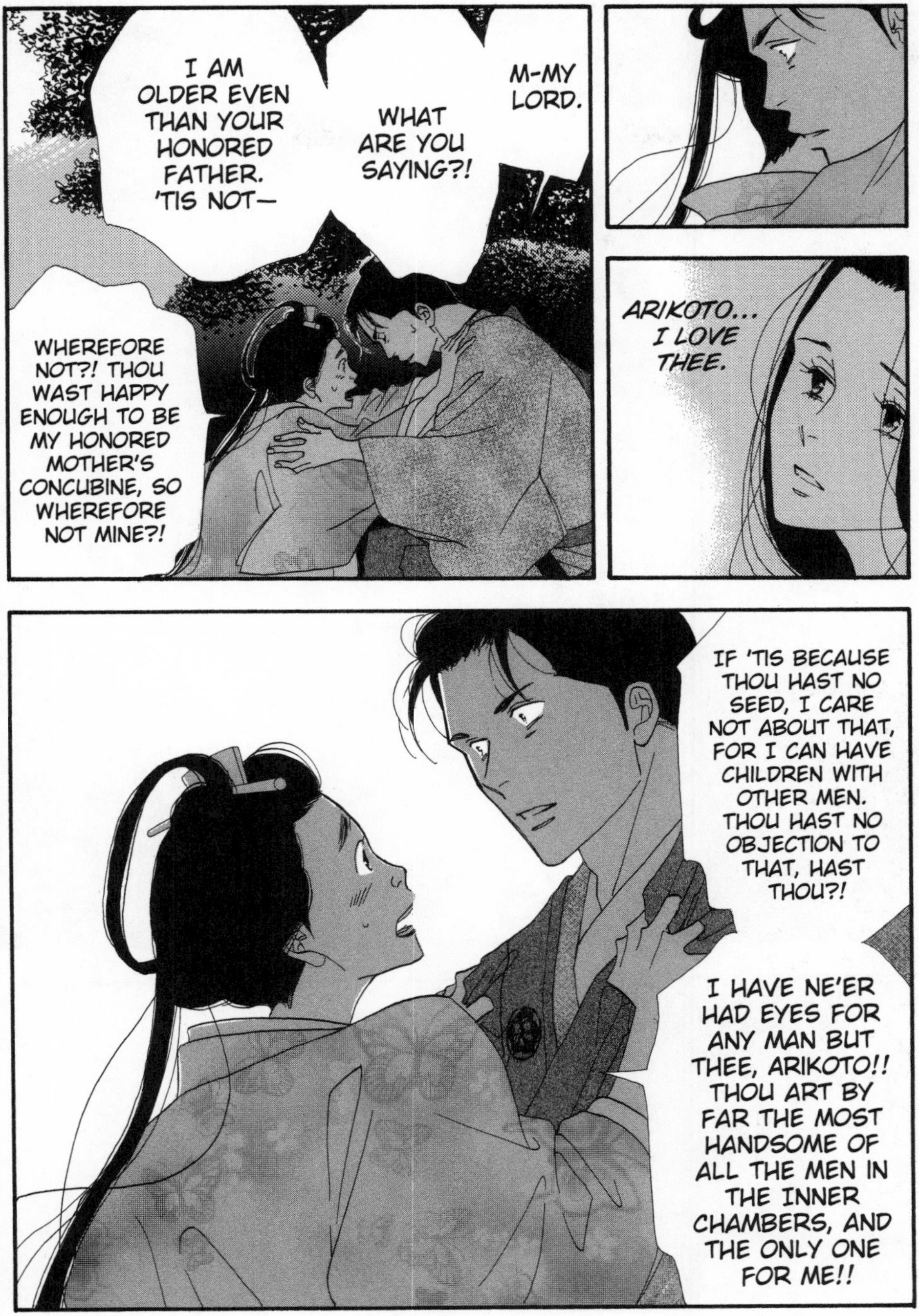
ARIKOTO... I LOVE THEE.
M-MY LORD.
WHAT ARE YOU SAYING?!
I AM OLDER EVEN THAN YOUR HONORED FATHER. 'TIS NOT—
WHEREFORE NOT?! THOU WAST HAPPY ENOUGH TO BE MY HONORED MOTHER'S CONCUBINE, SO WHEREFORE NOT MINE?!
IF 'TIS BECAUSE THOU HAST NO SEED, I CARE NOT ABOUT THAT, FOR I CAN HAVE CHILDREN WITH OTHER MEN. THOU HAST NO OBJECTION TO THAT, HAST THOU?!
I HAVE NE'ER HAD EYES FOR ANY MAN BUT THEE, ARIKOTO!! THOU ART BY FAR THE MOST HANDSOME OF ALL THE MEN IN THE INNER CHAMBERS, AND THE ONLY ONE FOR ME!!

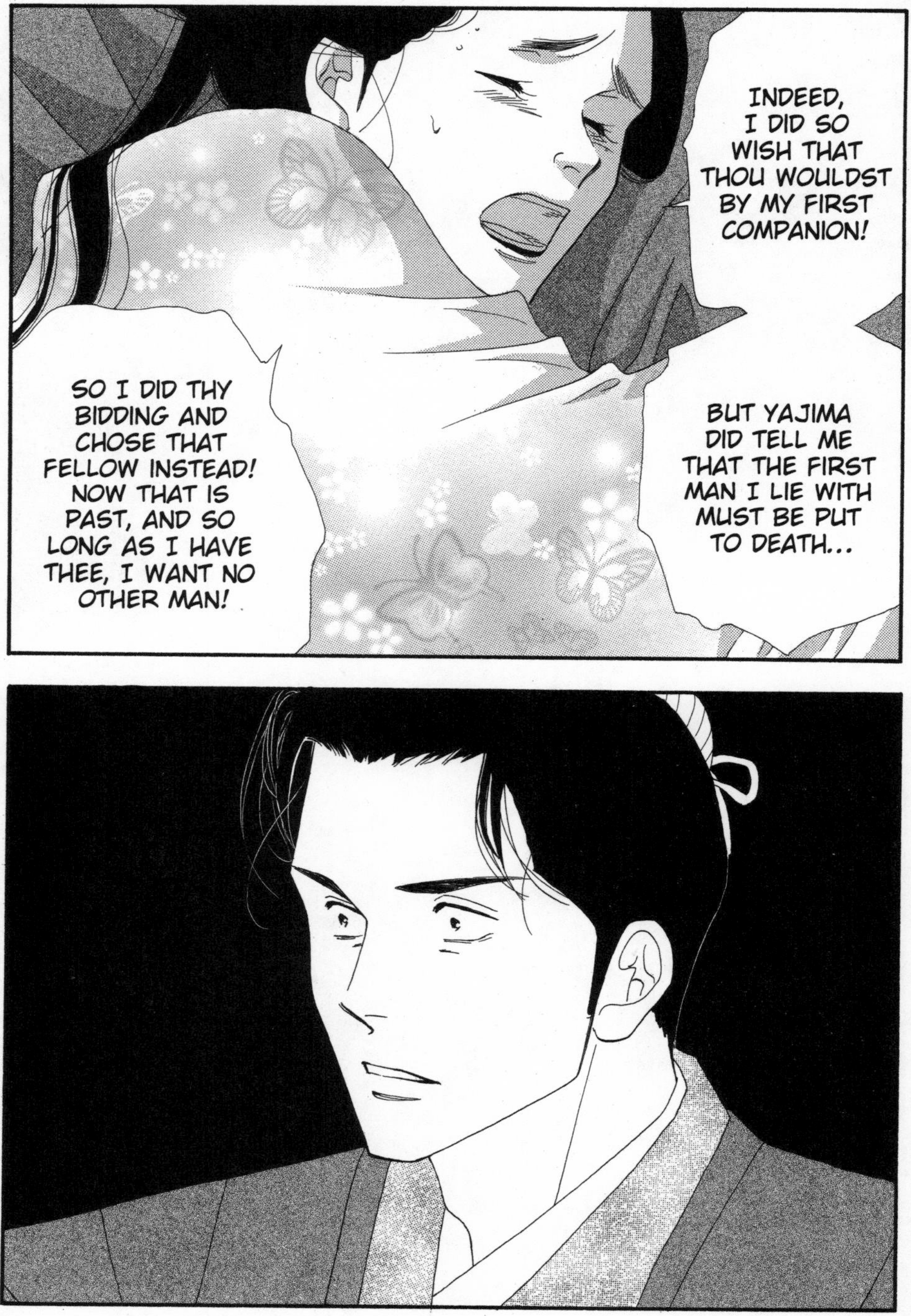
INDEED, I DID SO WISH THAT THOU WOULDST BY MY FIRST COMPANION!
BUT YAJIMA DID TELL ME THAT THE FIRST MAN I LIE WITH MUST BE PUT TO DEATH...
SO I DID THY BIDDING AND CHOSE THAT FELLOW INSTEAD! NOW THAT IS PAST, AND SO LONG AS I HAVE THEE, I WANT NO OTHER MAN!

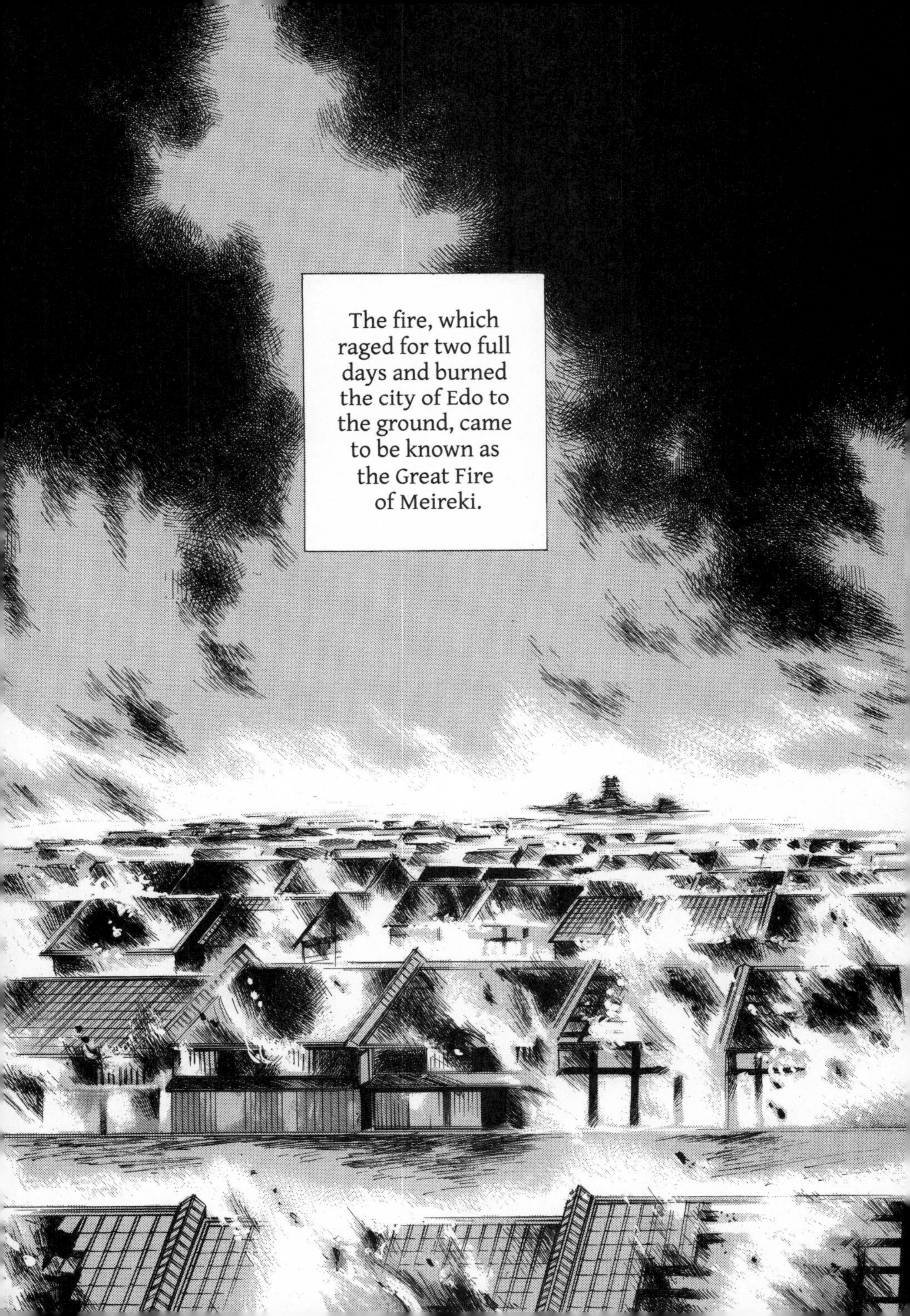
The fire, which raged for two full days and burned the city of Edo to the ground, came to be known as the Great Fire of Meireki.

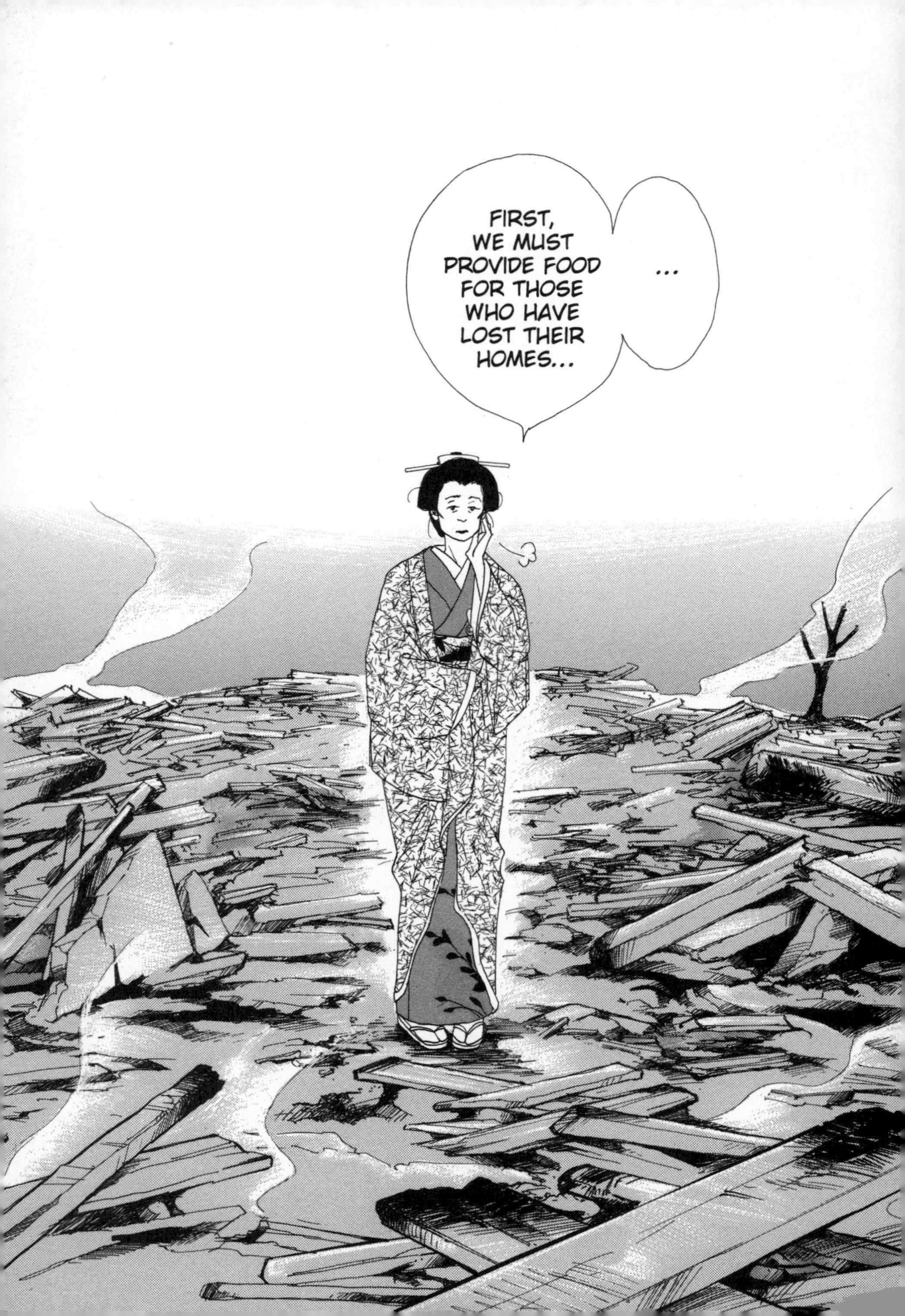
FIRST, WE MUST PROVIDE FOOD FOR THOSE WHO HAVE LOST THEIR HOMES...
...

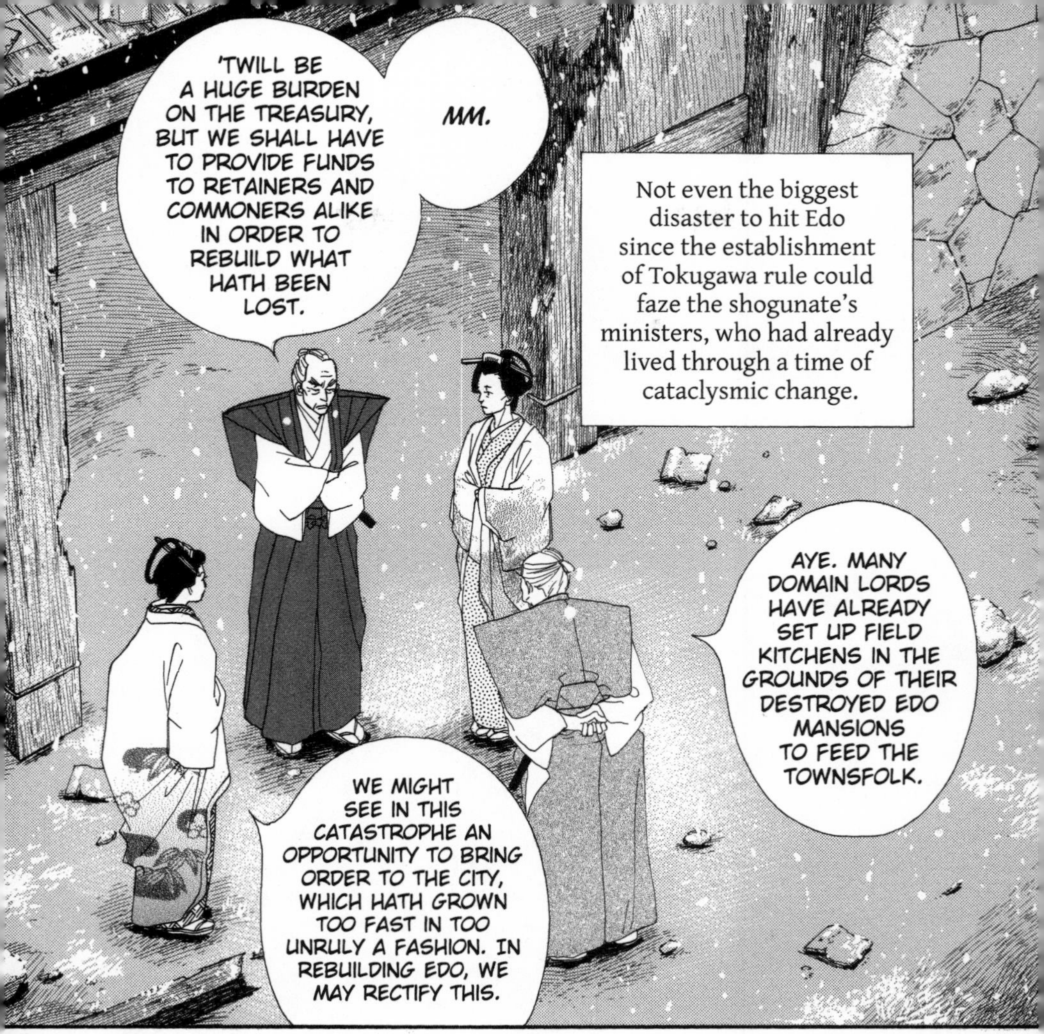
Not even the biggest disaster to hit Edo since the establishment of Tokugawa rule could faze the shogunate's ministers, who had already lived through a time of cataclysmic change.
'TWILL BE A HUGE BURDEN ON THE TREASURY, BUT WE SHALL HAVE TO PROVIDE FUNDS TO RETAINERS AND COMMONERS ALIKE IN ORDER TO REBUILD WHAT HATH BEEN LOST.
MM.
AYE. MANY DOMAIN LORDS HAVE ALREADY SET UP FIELD KITCHENS IN THE GROUNDS OF THEIR DESTROYED EDO MANSIONS TO FEED THE TOWNSFOLK.
WE MIGHT SEE IN THIS CATASTROPHE AN OPPORTUNITY TO BRING ORDER TO THE CITY, WHICH HATH GROWN TOO FAST IN TOO UNRULY A FASHION. IN REBUILDING EDO, WE MAY RECTIFY THIS.
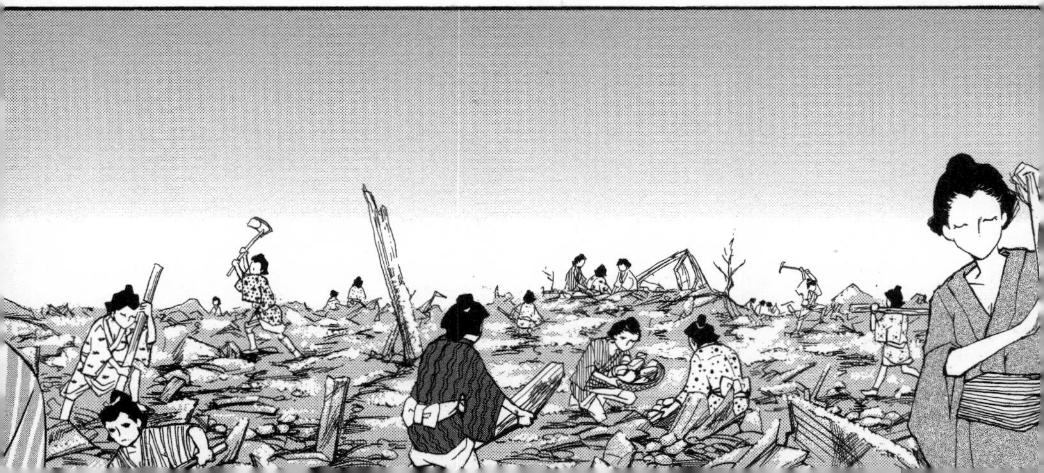

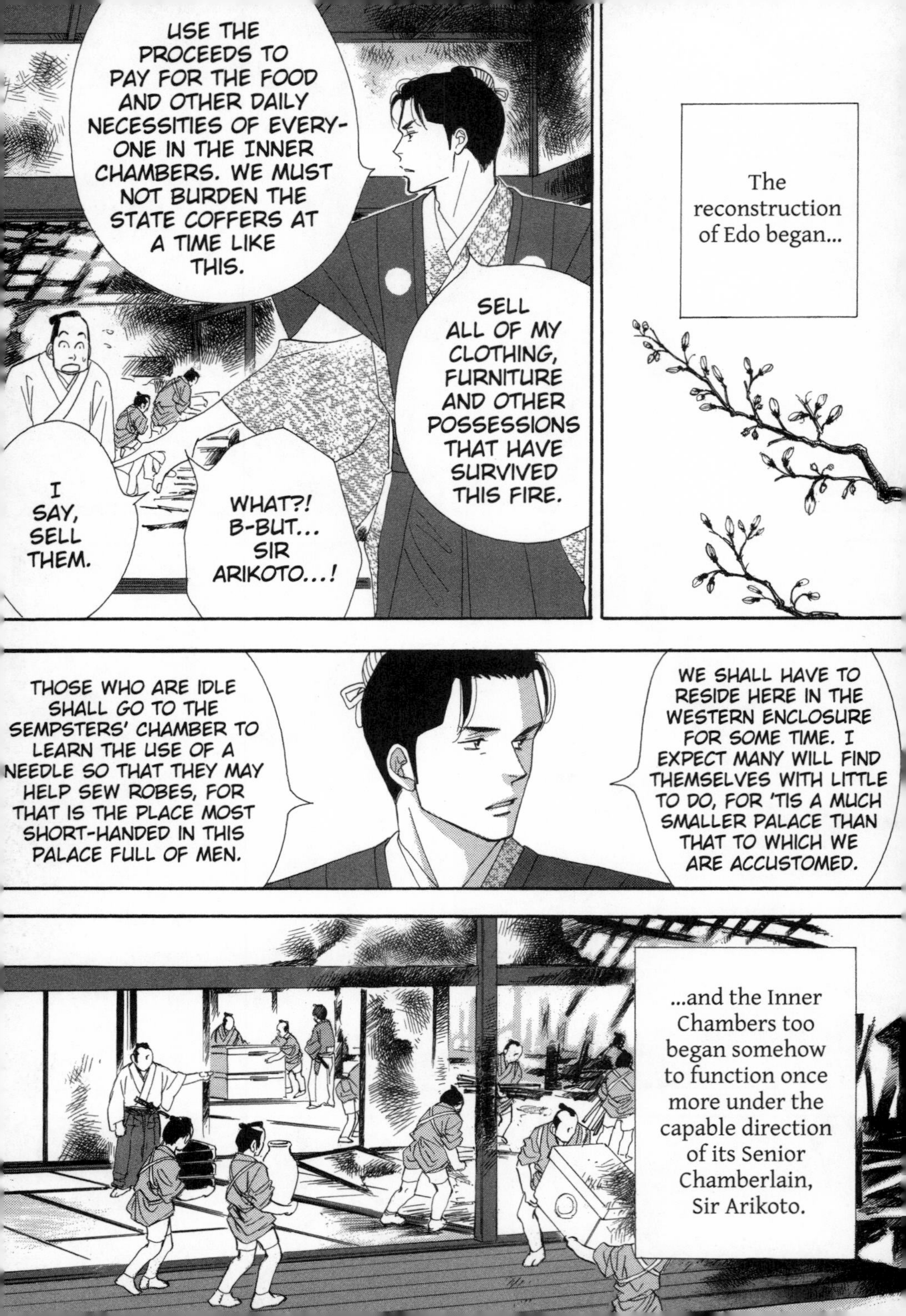
The reconstruction of Edo began...
SELL ALL OF MY CLOTHING, FURNITURE AND OTHER POSSESSIONS THAT HAVE SURVIVED THIS FIRE.
USE THE PROCEEDS TO PAY FOR THE FOOD AND OTHER DAILY NECESSITIES OF EVERY-ONE IN THE INNER CHAMBERS. WE MUST NOT BURDEN THE STATE COFFERS AT A TIME LIKE THIS.
WHAT?! B-BUT... SIR ARIKOTO...!
I SAY, SELL THEM.
WE SHALL HAVE TO RESIDE HERE IN THE WESTERN ENCLOSURE FOR SOME TIME. I EXPECT MANY WILL FIND THEMSELVES WITH LITTLE TO DO, FOR 'TIS A MUCH SMALLER PALACE THAN THAT TO WHICH WE ARE ACCUSTOMED.
THOSE WHO ARE IDLE SHALL GO TO THE SEMPSTERS' CHAMBER TO LEARN THE USE OF A NEEDLE SO THAT THEY MAY HELP SEW ROBES, FOR THAT IS THE PLACE MOST SHORT-HANDED IN THIS PALACE FULL OF MEN.
...and the Inner Chambers too began somehow to function once more under the capable direction of its Senior Chamberlain, Sir Arikoto.

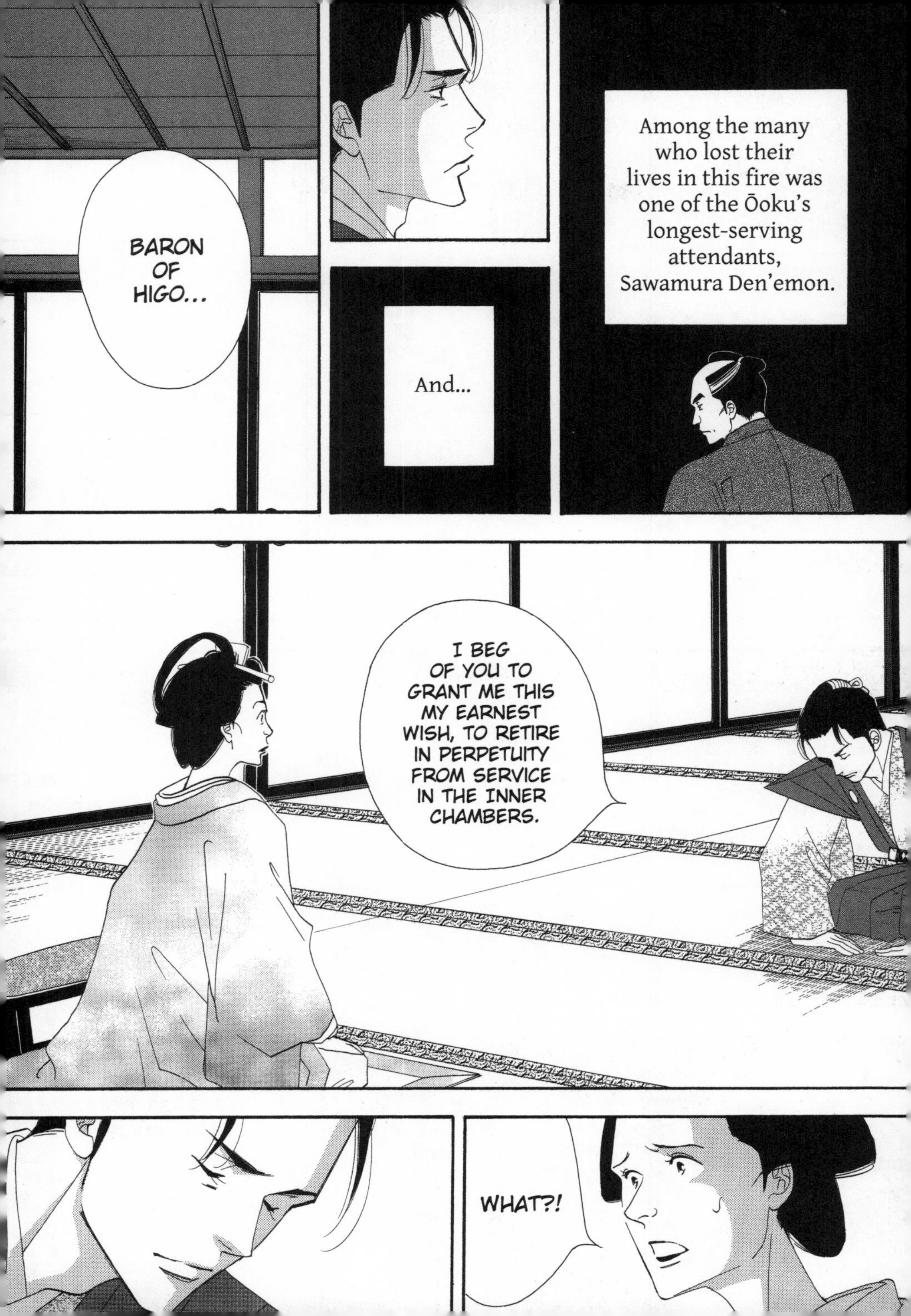
Among the many who lost their lives in this fire was one of the Ōoku's longest-serving attendants, Sawamura Den'emon.
And...
BARON OF HIGO...
I BEG OF YOU TO GRANT ME THIS MY EARNEST WISH, TO RETIRE IN PERPETUITY FROM SERVICE IN THE INNER CHAMBERS.
WHAT?!

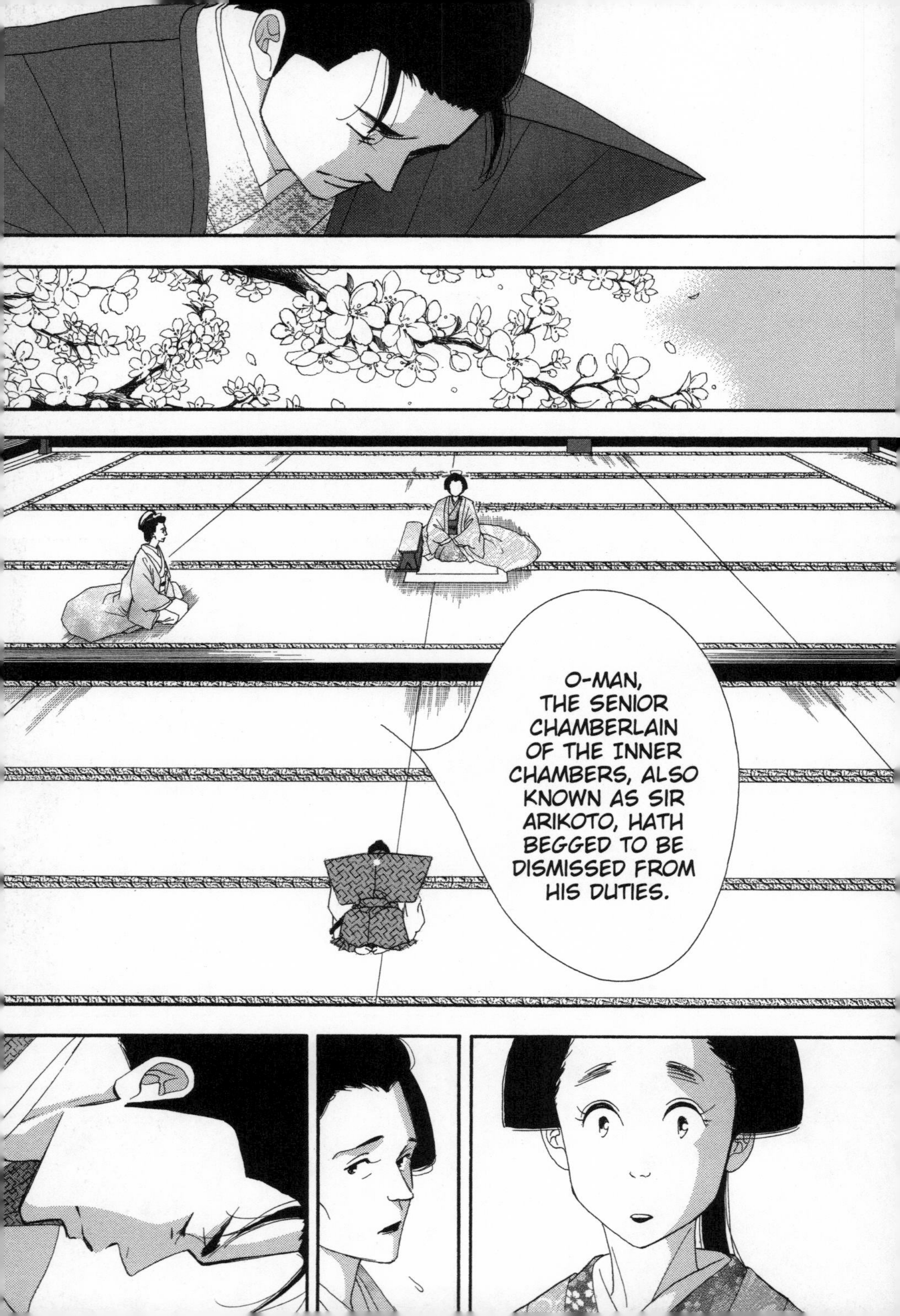
O-MAN, THE SENIOR CHAMBERLAIN OF THE INNER CHAMBERS, ALSO KNOWN AS SIR ARIKOTO, HATH BEGGED TO BE DISMISSED FROM HIS DUTIES.

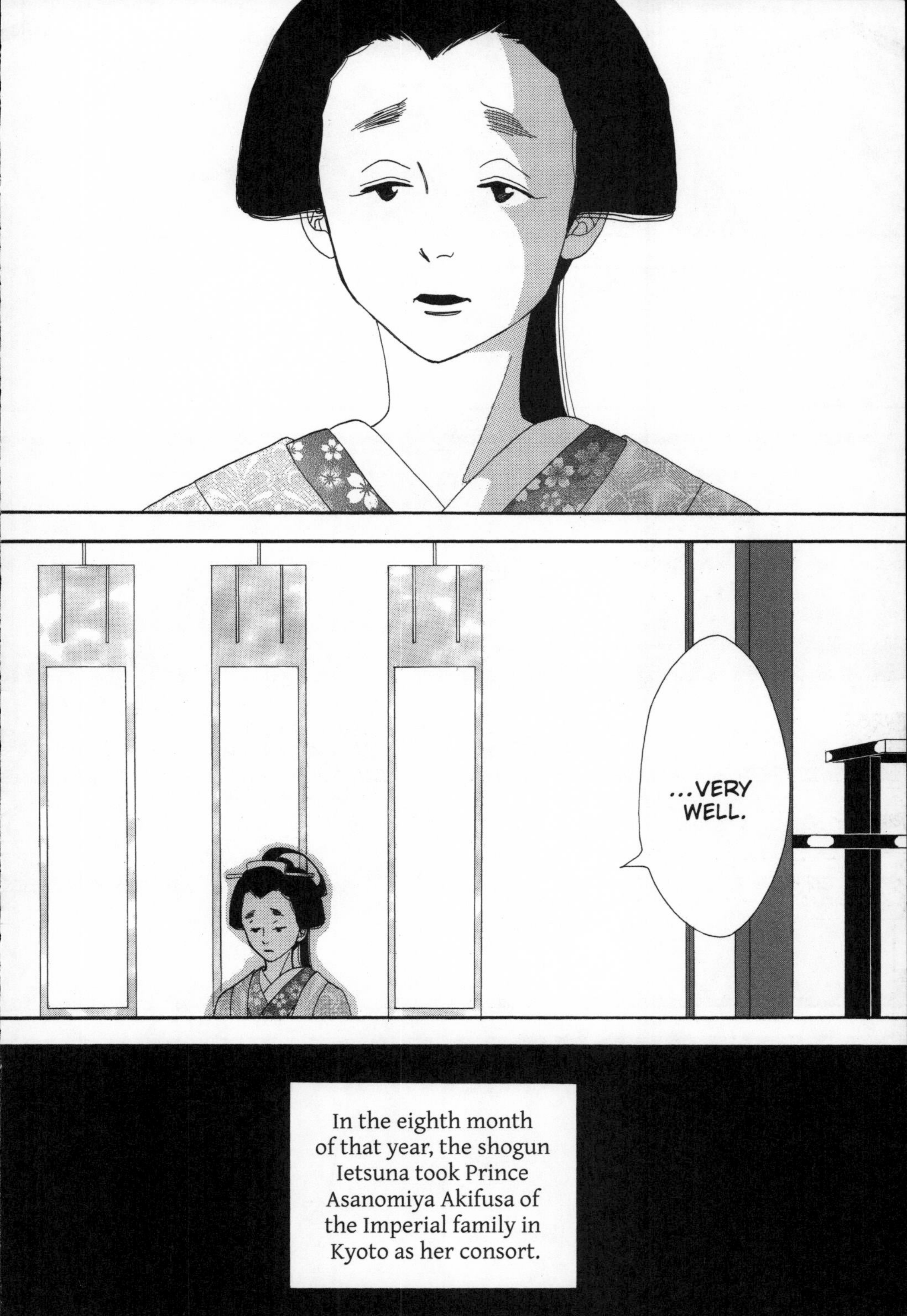
...VERY WELL.
In the eighth month of that year, the shogun Ietsuna took Prince Asanomiya Akifusa of the Imperial family in Kyoto as her consort.

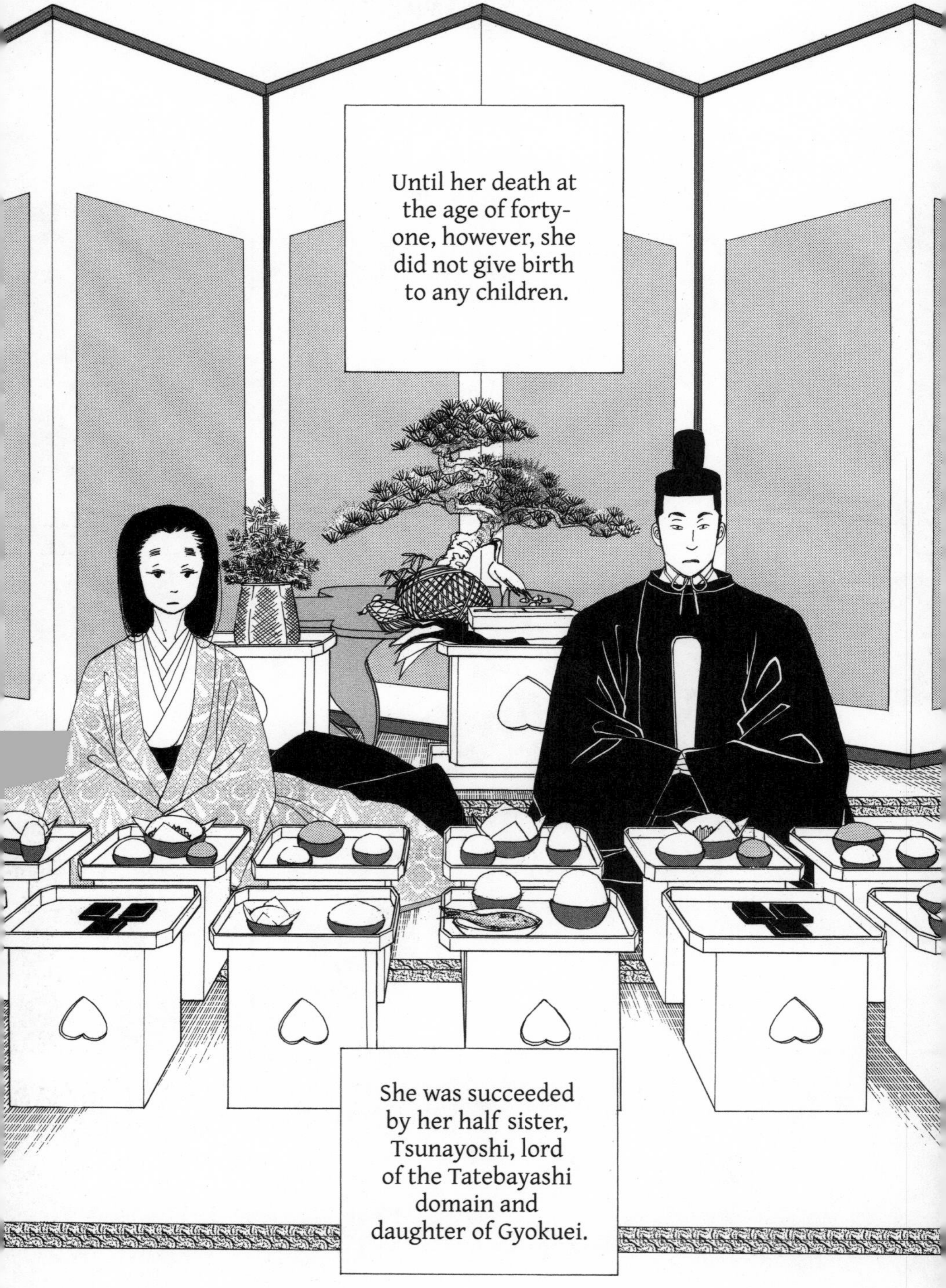
Until her death at the age of forty-one, however, she did not give birth to any children.
She was succeeded by her half sister, Tsunayoshi, lord of the Tatebayashi domain and daughter of Gyokuei.

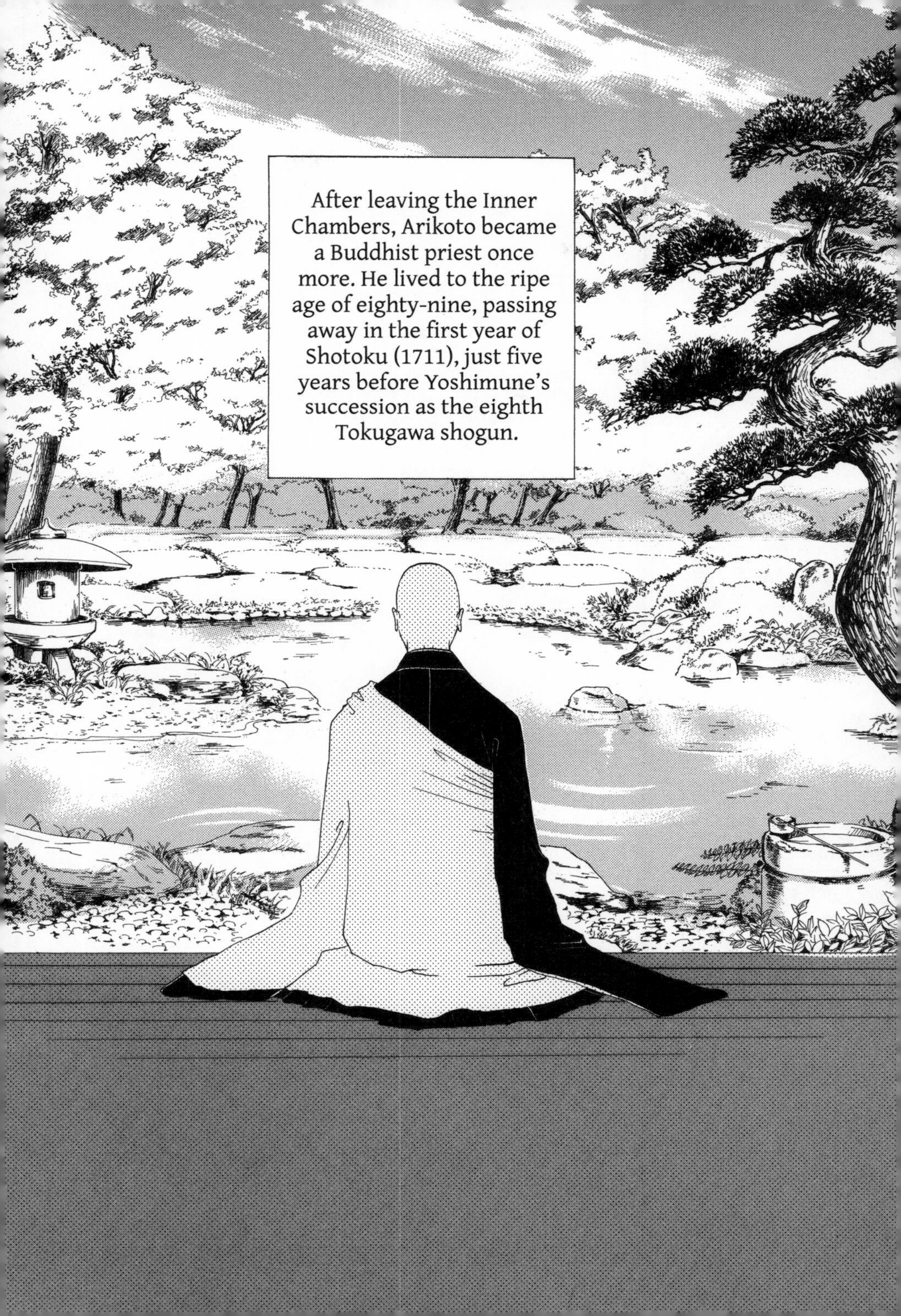
After leaving the Inner Chambers, Arikoto became a Buddhist priest once more. He lived to the ripe age of eighty-nine, passing away in the first year of Shotoku (1711), just five years before Yoshimune's succession as the eighth Tokugawa shogun.

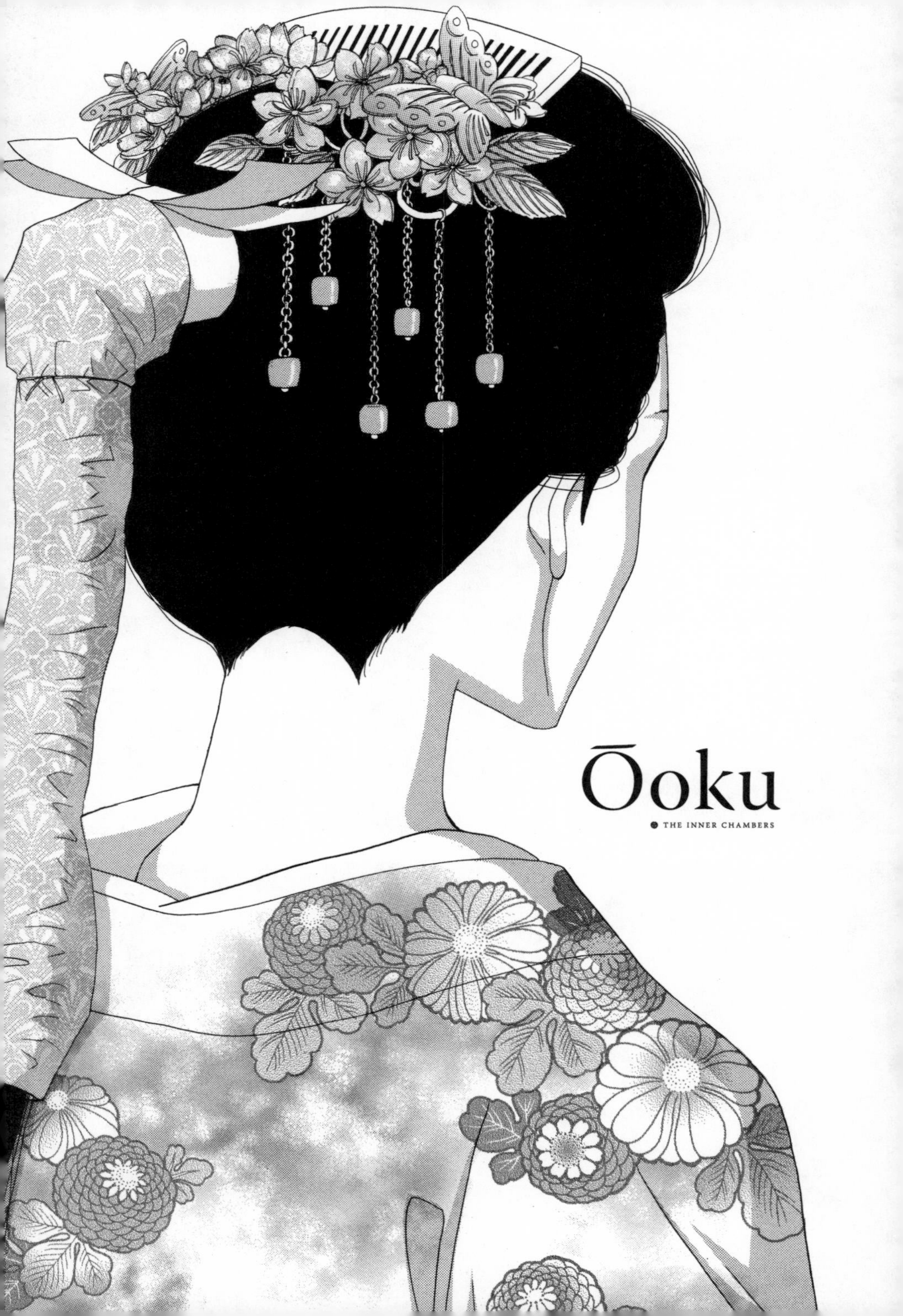
Ōoku
THE INNER CHAMBERS

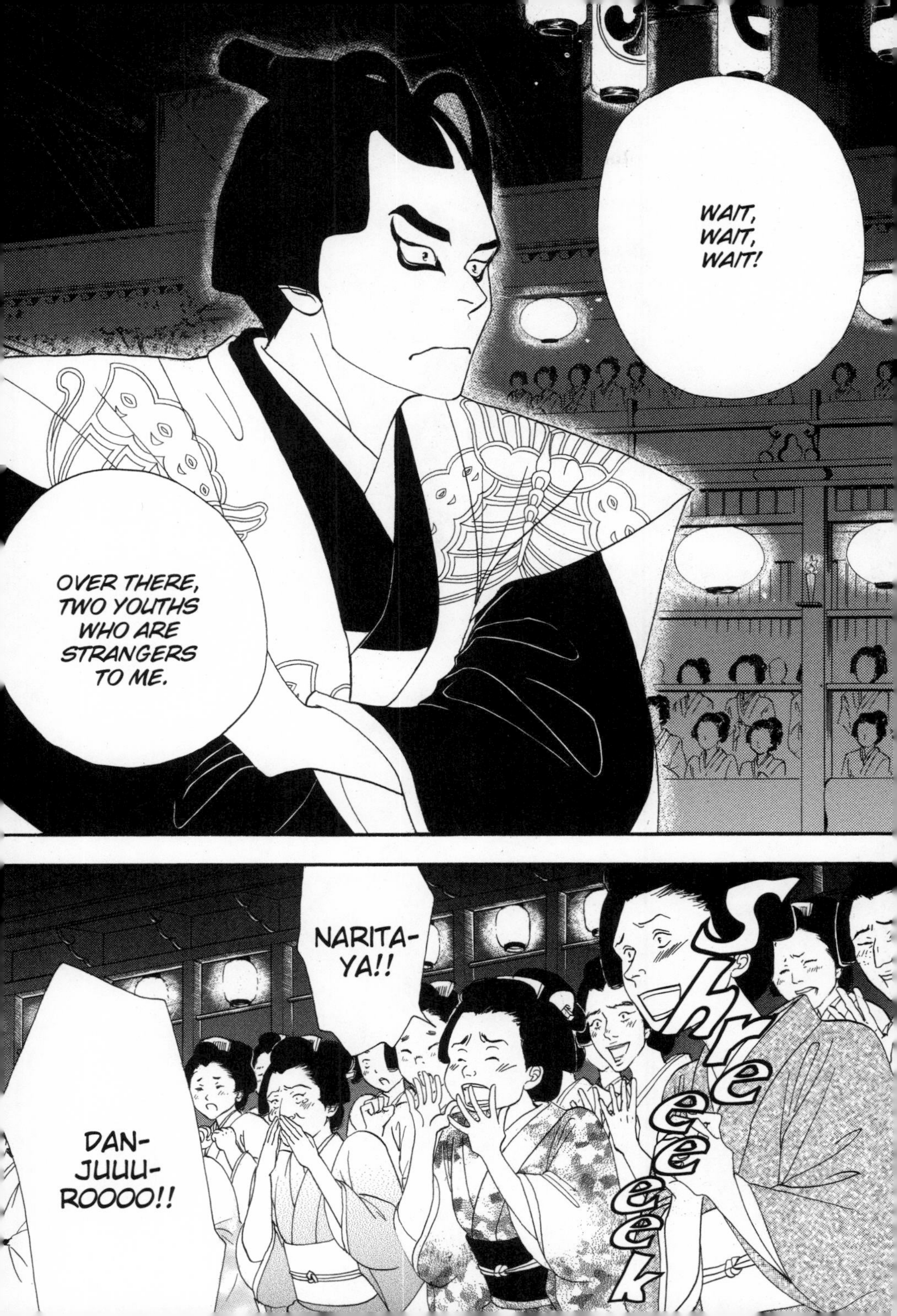
WAIT, WAIT, WAIT!
OVER THERE, TWO YOUTHS WHO ARE STRANGERS TO ME.
Shreeeeek
NARITA-YA!!
DAN-JUUU-ROOOO!!

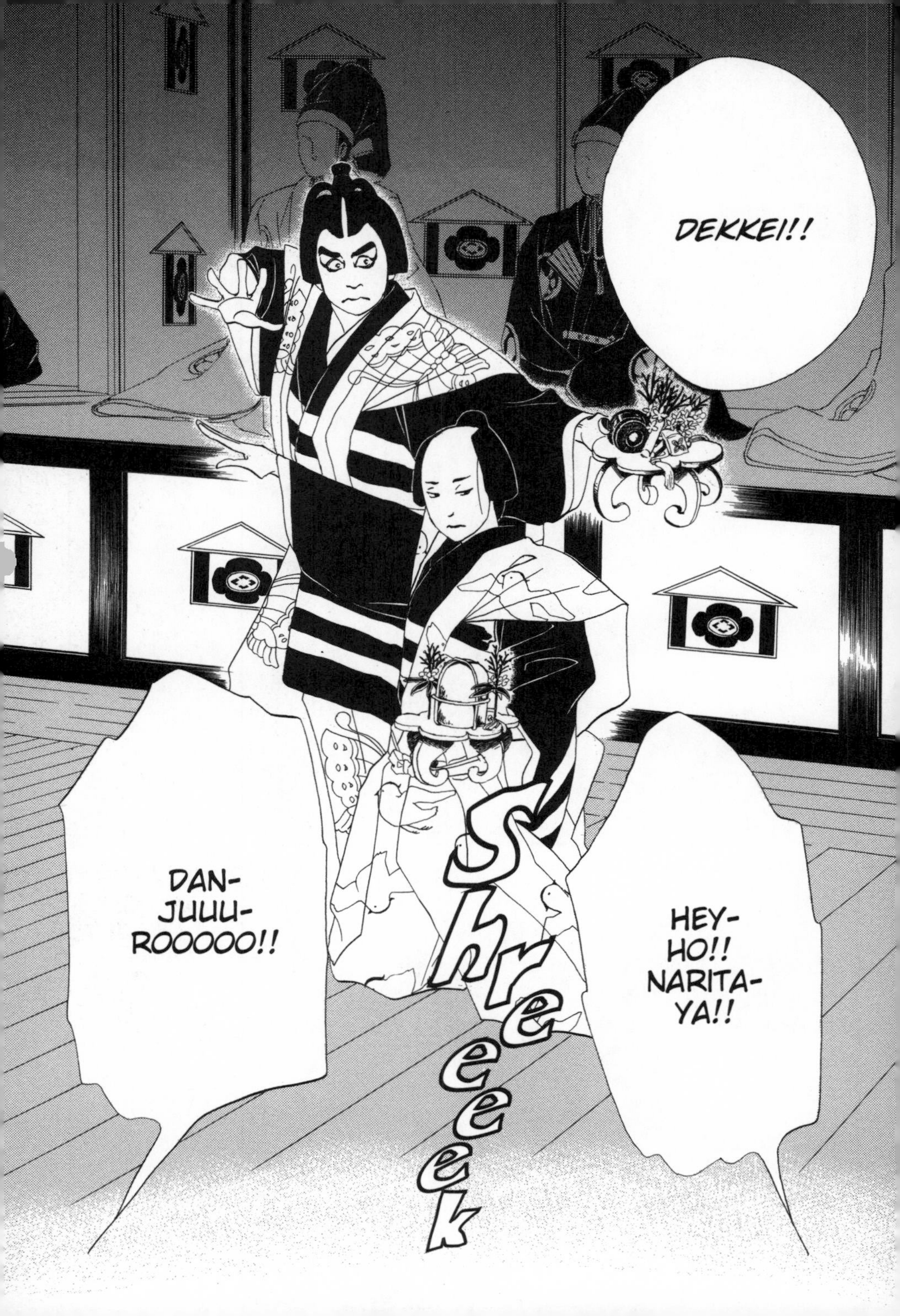
DEKKEI!!
HEY-HO!! NARITA-YA!!
Shreeeek
DAN-JUUU-ROOOOO!!

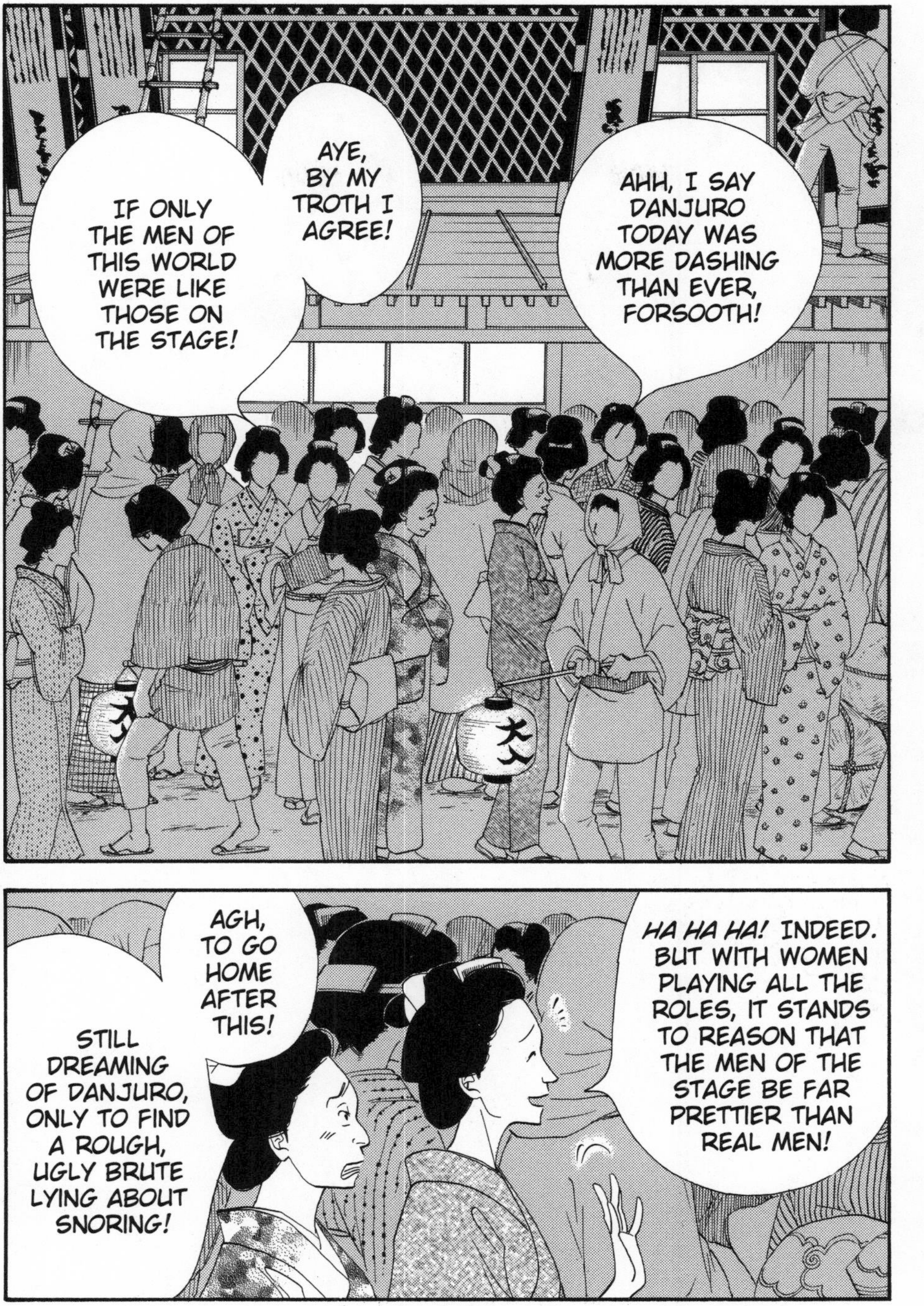

AHH, I SAY DANJURO TODAY WAS MORE DASHING THAN EVER, FORSOOTH!
AYE, BY MY TROTH I AGREE!
IF ONLY THE MEN OF THIS WORLD WERE LIKE THOSE ON THE STAGE!
HA HA HA! INDEED. BUT WITH WOMEN PLAYING ALL THE ROLES, IT STANDS TO REASON THAT THE MEN OF THE STAGE BE FAR PRETTIER THAN REAL MEN!
AGH, TO GO HOME AFTER THIS!
STILL DREAMING OF DANJURO, ONLY TO FIND A ROUGH, UGLY BRUTE LYING ABOUT SNORING!

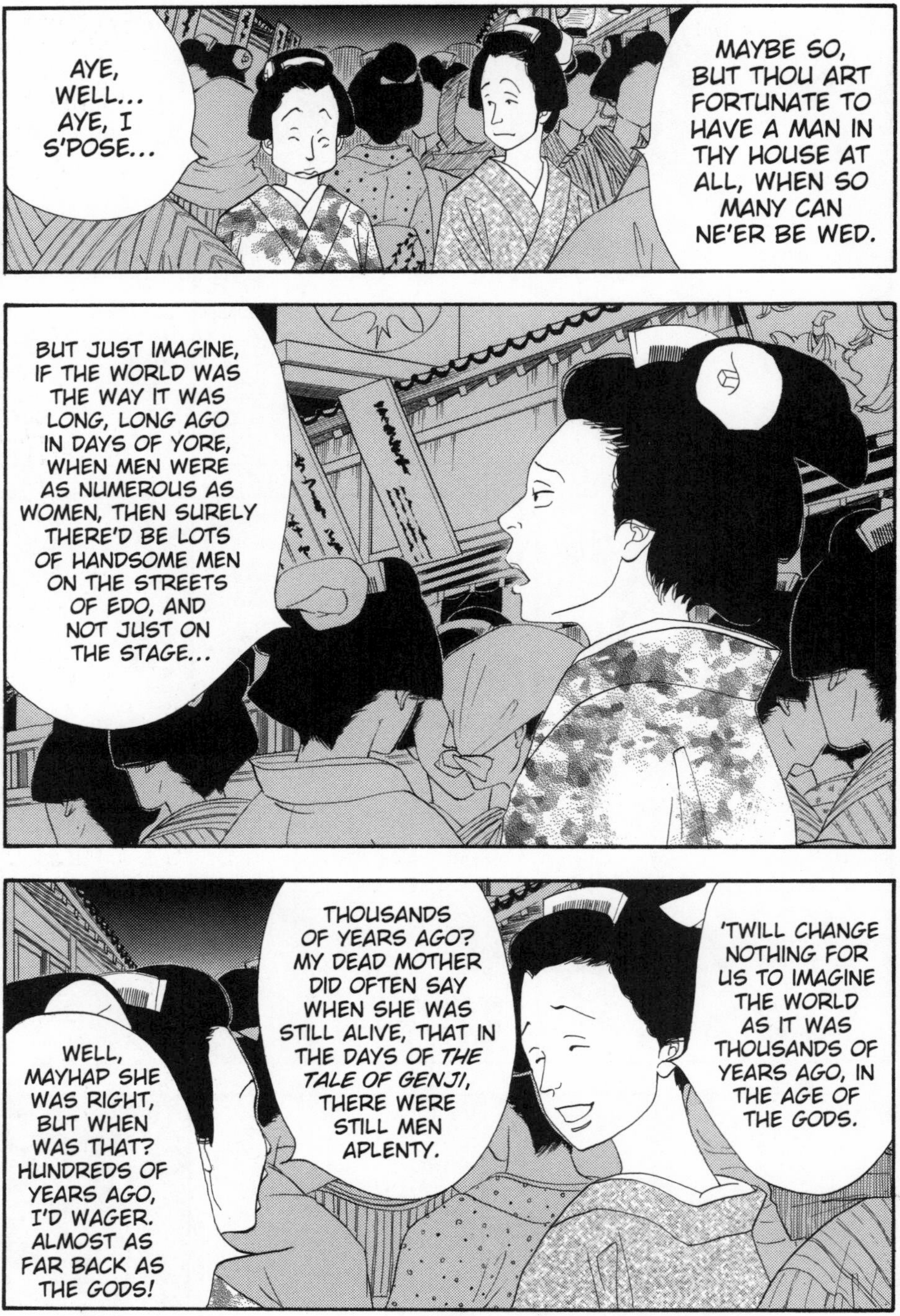
MAYBE SO, BUT THOU ART FORTUNATE TO HAVE A MAN IN THY HOUSE AT ALL, WHEN SO MANY CAN NE'ER BE WED.
AYE, WELL... AYE, I S'POSE...
BUT JUST IMAGINE, IF THE WORLD WAS THE WAY IT WAS LONG, LONG AGO IN DAYS OF YORE, WHEN MEN WERE AS NUMEROUS AS WOMEN, THEN SURELY THERE'D BE LOTS OF HANDSOME MEN ON THE STREETS OF EDO, AND NOT JUST ON THE STAGE...
'TWILL CHANGE NOTHING FOR US TO IMAGINE THE WORLD AS IT WAS THOUSANDS OF YEARS AGO, IN THE AGE OF THE GODS.
THOUSANDS OF YEARS AGO? MY DEAD MOTHER DID OFTEN SAY WHEN SHE WAS STILL ALIVE, THAT IN THE DAYS OF *THE TALE OF GENJI*, THERE WERE STILL MEN APLENTY.
WELL, MAYHAP SHE WAS RIGHT, BUT WHEN WAS THAT? HUNDREDS OF YEARS AGO, I'D WAGER. ALMOST AS FAR BACK AS THE GODS!

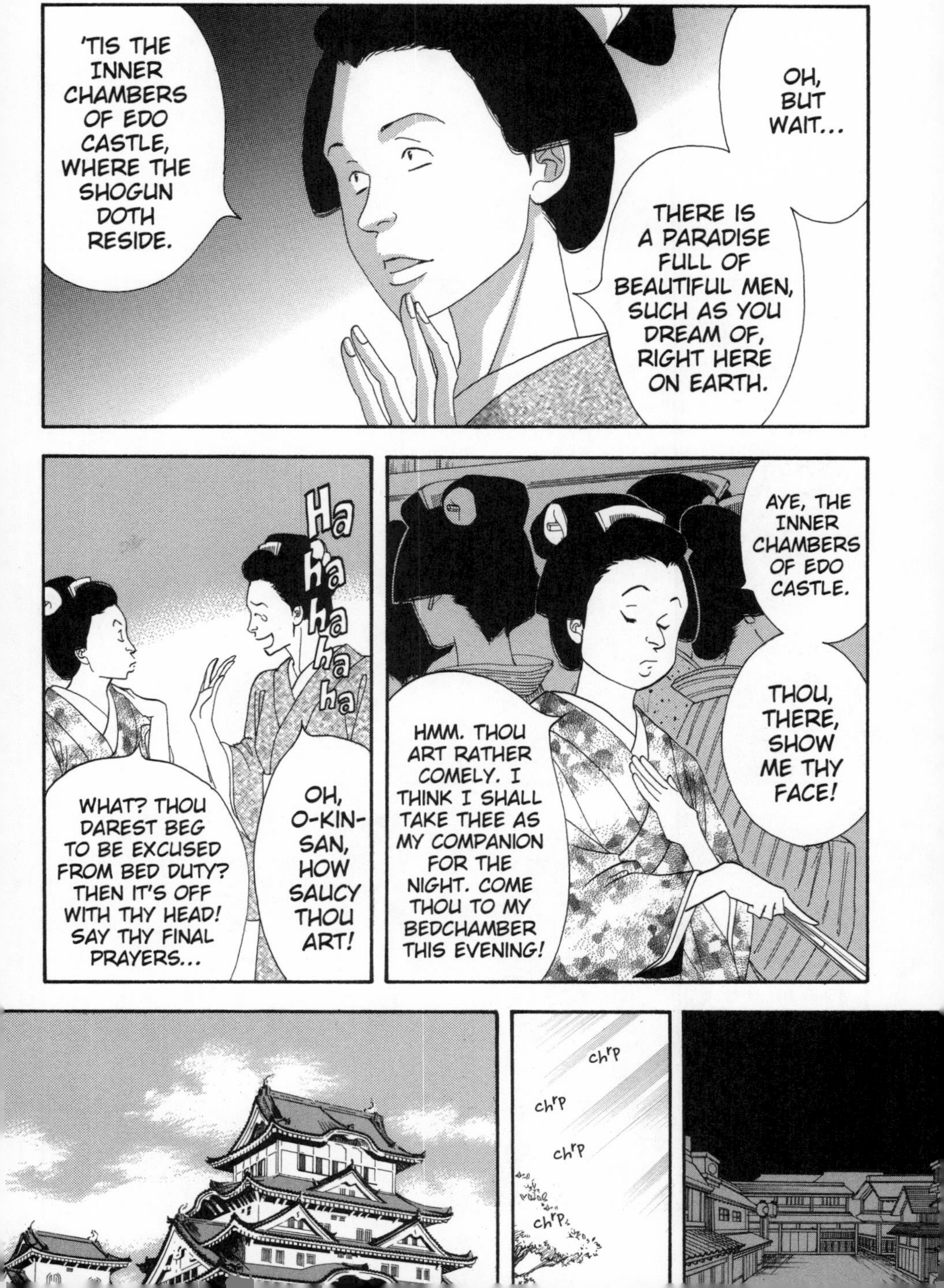
OH, BUT WAIT...
THERE IS A PARADISE FULL OF BEAUTIFUL MEN, SUCH AS YOU DREAM OF, RIGHT HERE ON EARTH.
'TIS THE INNER CHAMBERS OF EDO CASTLE, WHERE THE SHOGUN DOTH RESIDE.
AYE, THE INNER CHAMBERS OF EDO CASTLE.
THOU, THERE, SHOW ME THY FACE!
HMM. THOU ART RATHER COMELY. I THINK I SHALL TAKE THEE AS MY COMPANION FOR THE NIGHT. COME THOU TO MY BEDCHAMBER THIS EVENING!
Ha ha ha ha ha ha
OH, O-KIN-SAN, HOW SAUCY THOU ART!
WHAT? THOU DAREST BEG TO BE EXCUSED FROM BED DUTY? THEN IT'S OFF WITH THY HEAD! SAY THY FINAL PRAYERS...
chrp
chrp
chrp
chrp

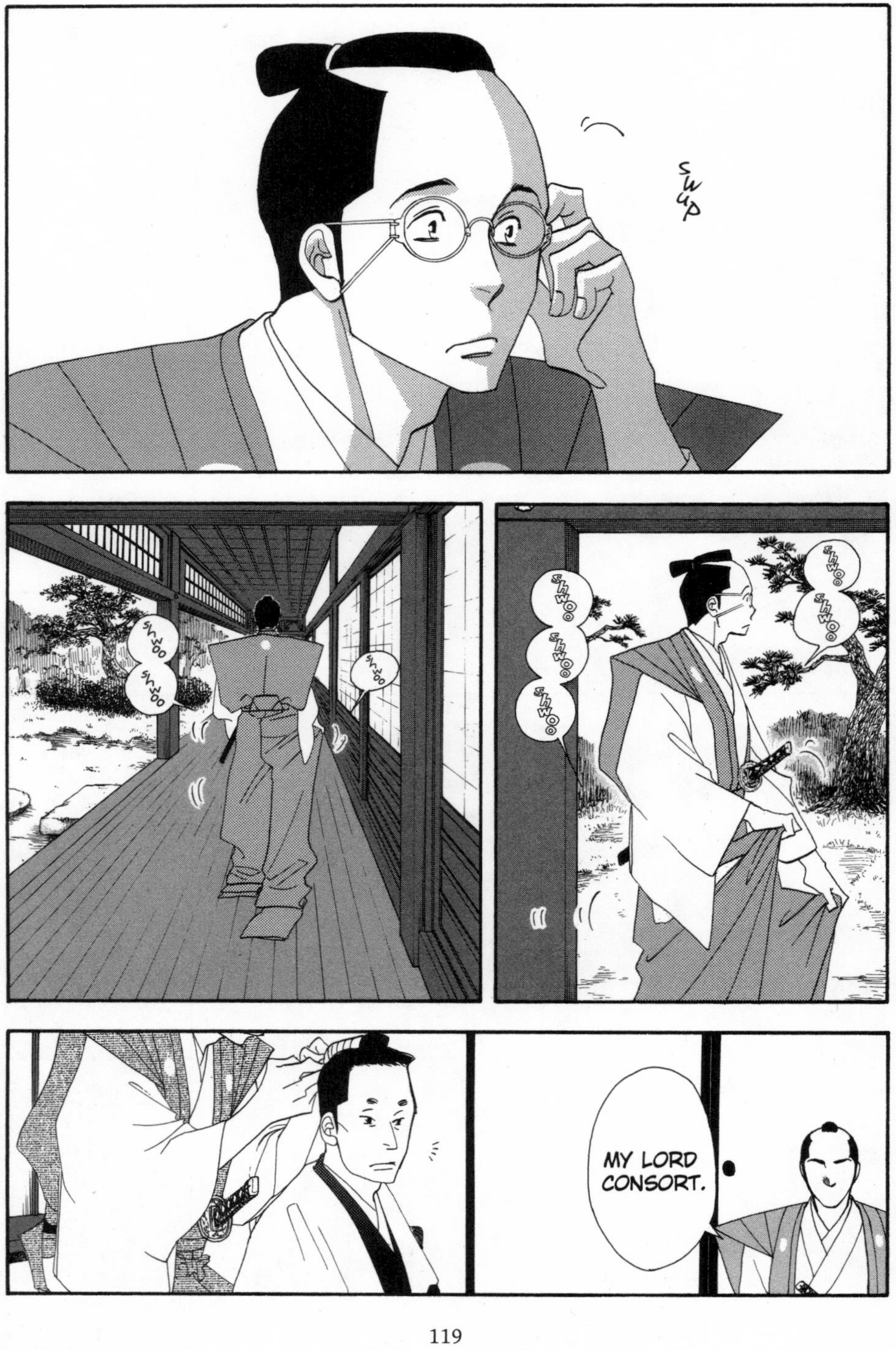
SWUP
SHWOO SHWOO
SHWOO SHWOO SHWOO
SHWOO
SHWOO SHWOO
MY LORD CONSORT.

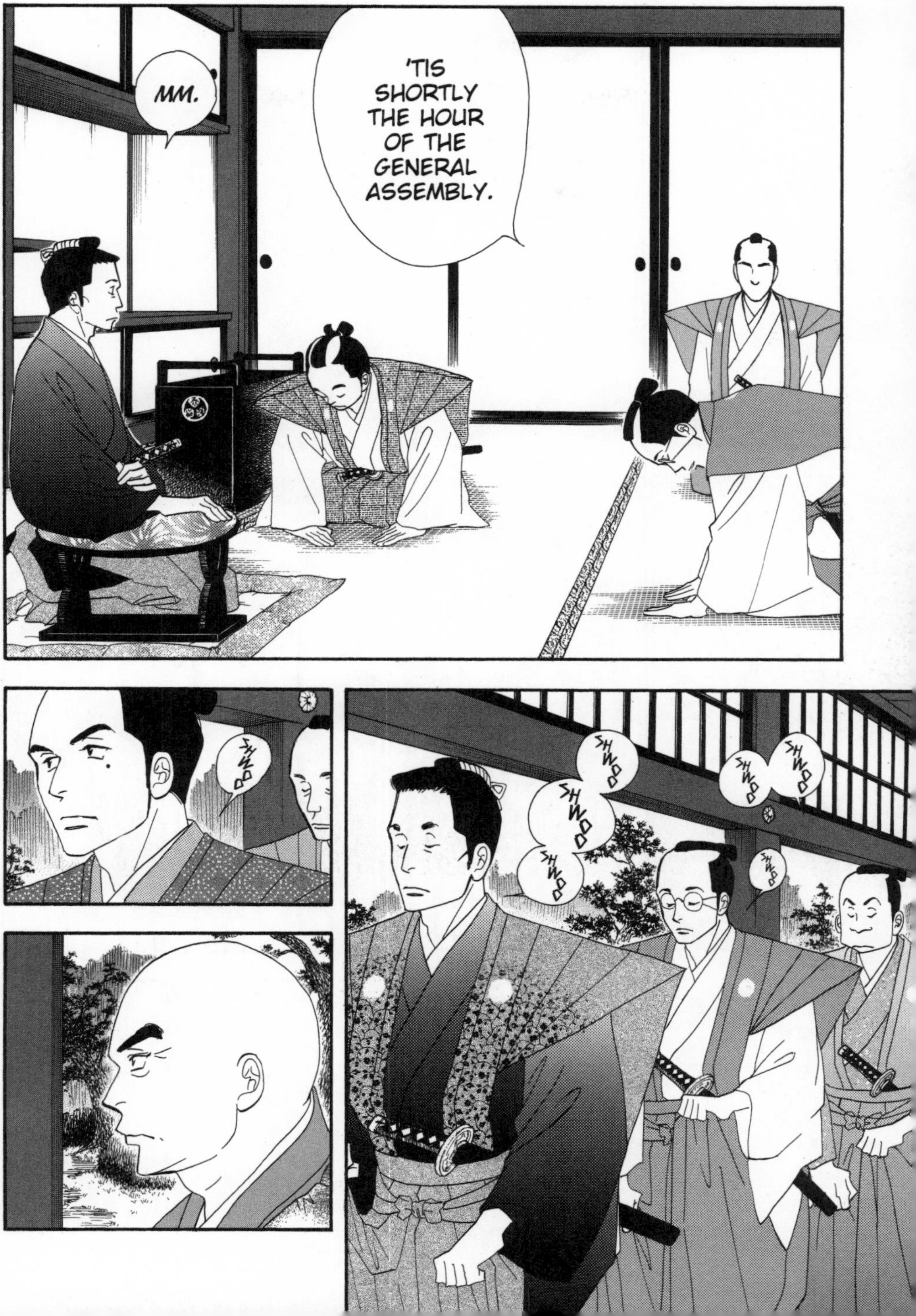
'TIS SHORTLY THE HOUR OF THE GENERAL ASSEMBLY.
MM.
SHWOO
SHWOO
SHWOO
SHWOO
SHWOO
SHWOO
SHWOO

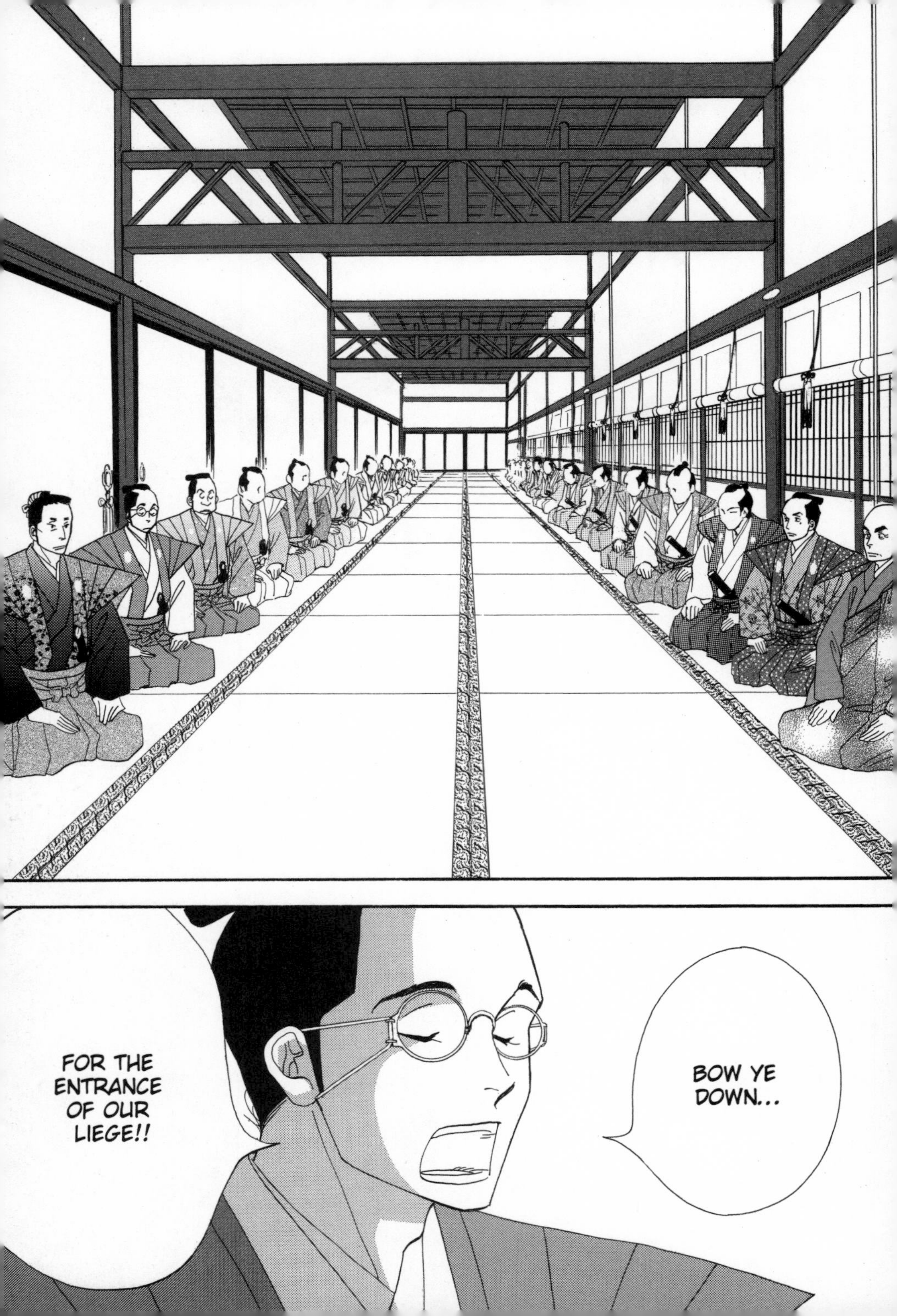
BOW YE DOWN...
FOR THE ENTRANCE OF OUR LIEGE!!

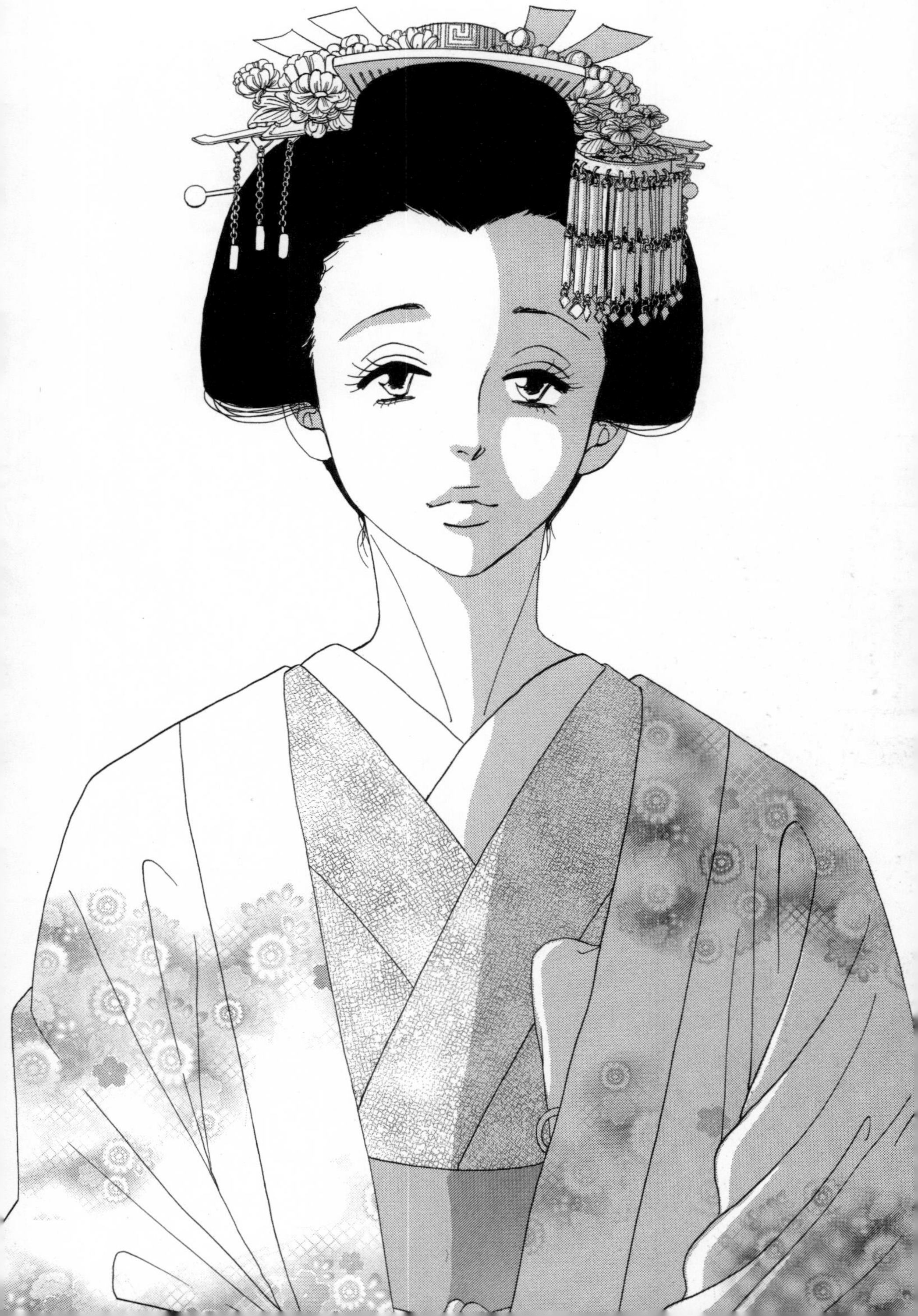

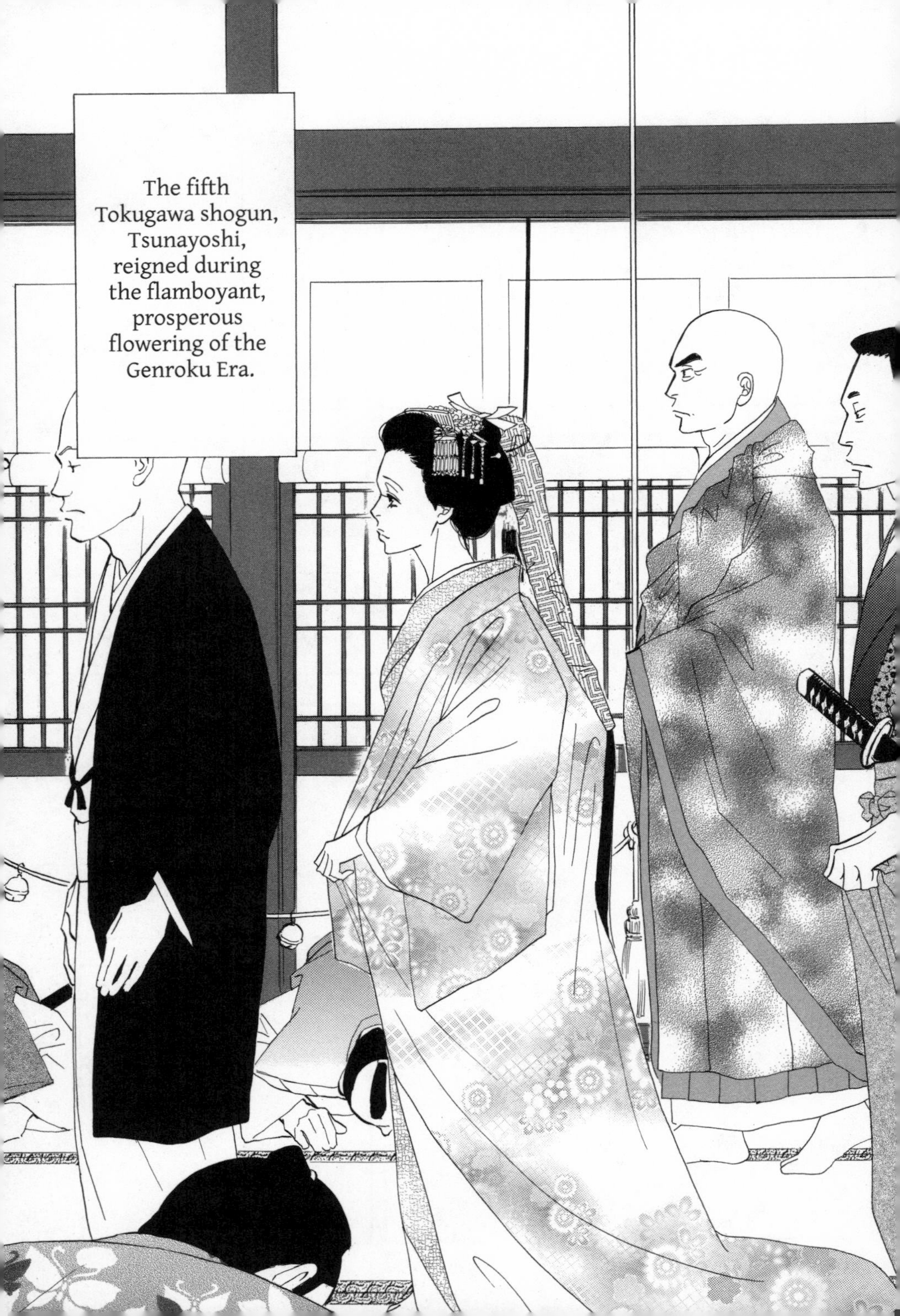
The fifth Tokugawa shogun, Tsunayoshi, reigned during the flamboyant, prosperous flowering of the Genroku Era.

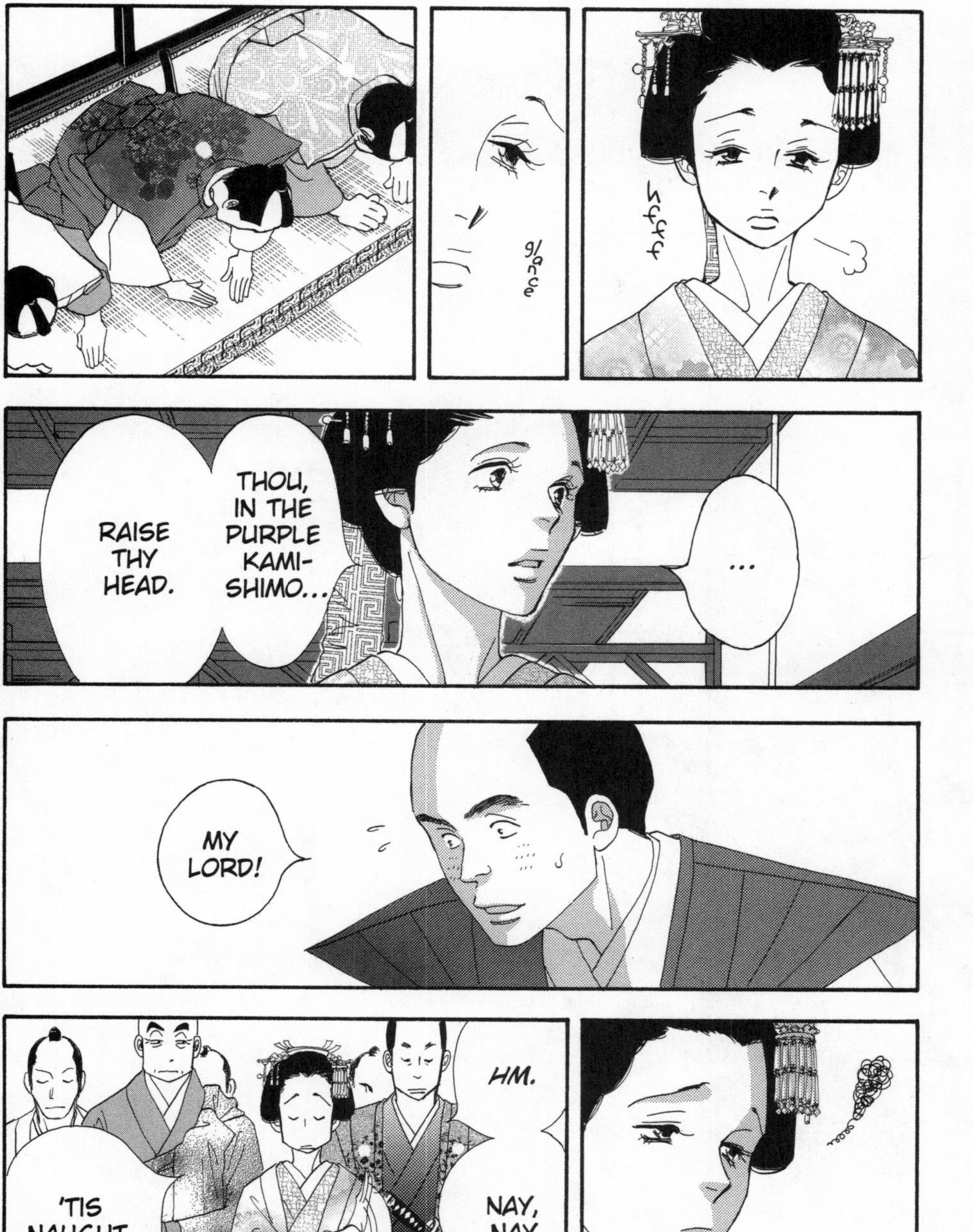
sniff
glance
...
THOU, IN THE PURPLE KAMI-SHIMO...
RAISE THY HEAD.
MY LORD!
HM.
NAY, NAY.
'TIS NAUGHT, 'TIS NAUGHT.

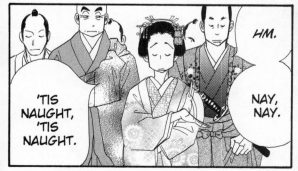

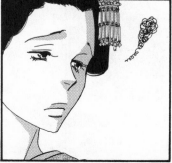

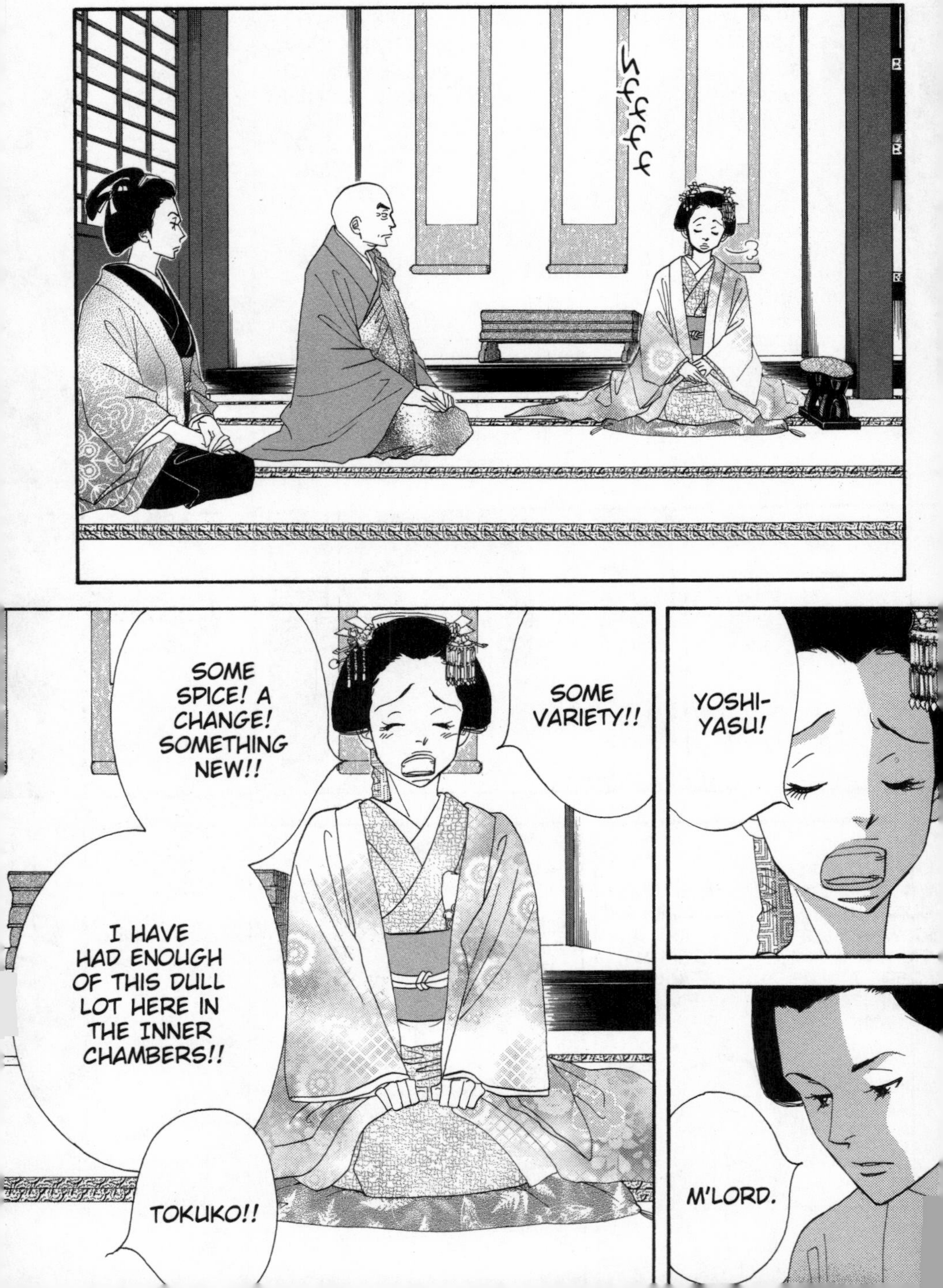
SFFFF
YOSHI-YASU!
M'LORD.
SOME VARIETY!!
SOME SPICE! A CHANGE! SOMETHING NEW!!
I HAVE HAD ENOUGH OF THIS DULL LOT HERE IN THE INNER CHAMBERS!!
TOKUKO!!

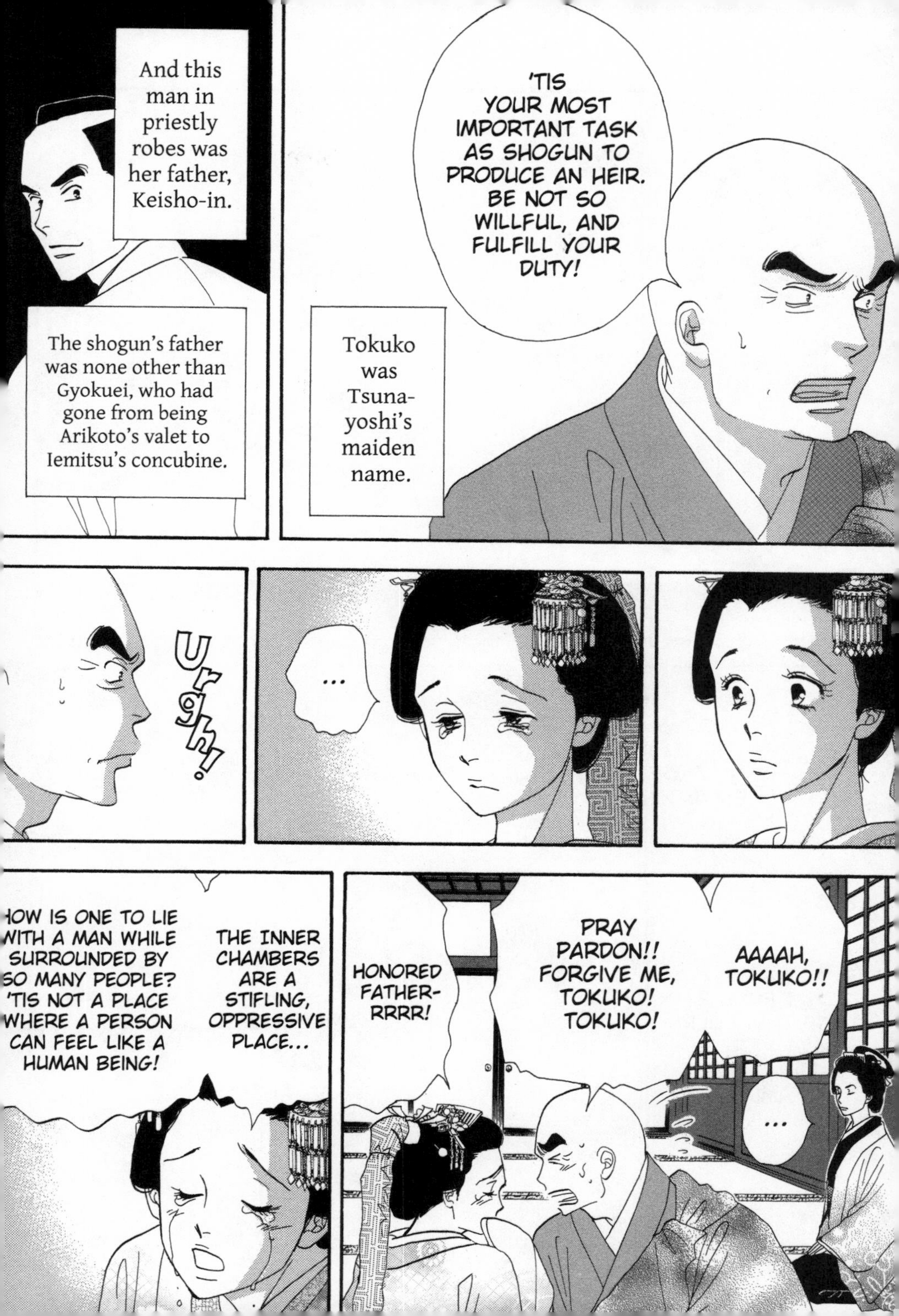
'TIS YOUR MOST IMPORTANT TASK AS SHOGUN TO PRODUCE AN HEIR. BE NOT SO WILLFUL, AND FULFILL YOUR DUTY!
Tokuko was Tsuna-yoshi's maiden name.
And this man in priestly robes was her father, Keisho-in.
The shogun's father was none other than Gyokuei, who had gone from being Arikoto's valet to Iemitsu's concubine.
...
Urgh!
AAAAH, TOKUKO!!
PRAY PARDON!! FORGIVE ME, TOKUKO! TOKUKO!
HONORED FATHER-RRRR!
...
THE INNER CHAMBERS ARE A STIFLING, OPPRESSIVE PLACE...
HOW IS ONE TO LIE WITH A MAN WHILE SURROUNDED BY SO MANY PEOPLE? 'TIS NOT A PLACE WHERE A PERSON CAN FEEL LIKE A HUMAN BEING!

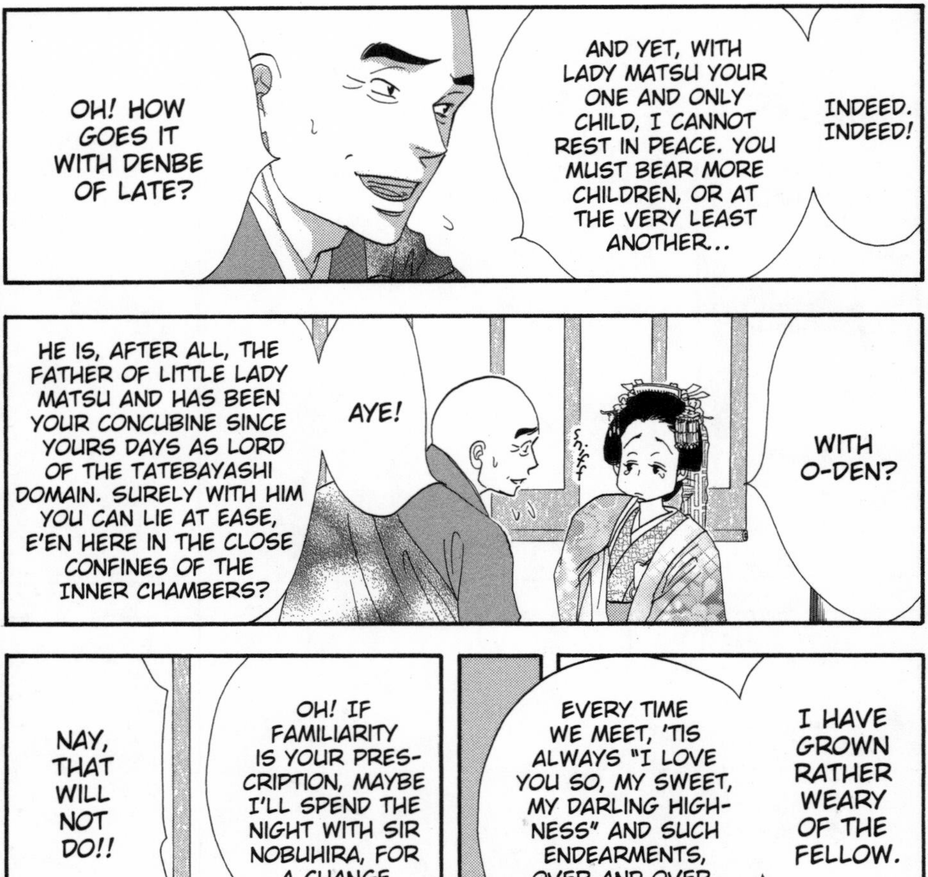
INDEED. INDEED!
AND YET, WITH LADY MATSU YOUR ONE AND ONLY CHILD, I CANNOT REST IN PEACE. YOU MUST BEAR MORE CHILDREN, OR AT THE VERY LEAST ANOTHER...
OH! HOW GOES IT WITH DENBE OF LATE?
WITH O-DEN?
sniff
AYE!
HE IS, AFTER ALL, THE FATHER OF LITTLE LADY MATSU AND HAS BEEN YOUR CONCUBINE SINCE YOURS DAYS AS LORD OF THE TATEBAYASHI DOMAIN. SURELY WITH HIM YOU CAN LIE AT EASE, E'EN HERE IN THE CLOSE CONFINES OF THE INNER CHAMBERS?
I HAVE GROWN RATHER WEARY OF THE FELLOW.
EVERY TIME WE MEET, 'TIS ALWAYS "I LOVE YOU SO, MY SWEET, MY DARLING HIGH-NESS" AND SUCH ENDEARMENTS, OVER AND OVER. WHAT A PRATING BORE!
OH! IF FAMILIARITY IS YOUR PRES-CRIPTION, MAYBE I'LL SPEND THE NIGHT WITH SIR NOBUHIRA, FOR A CHANGE.
NAY, THAT WILL NOT DO!!

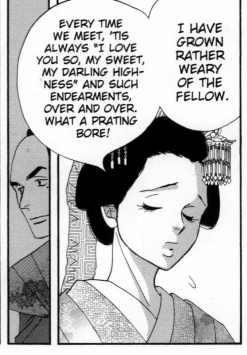

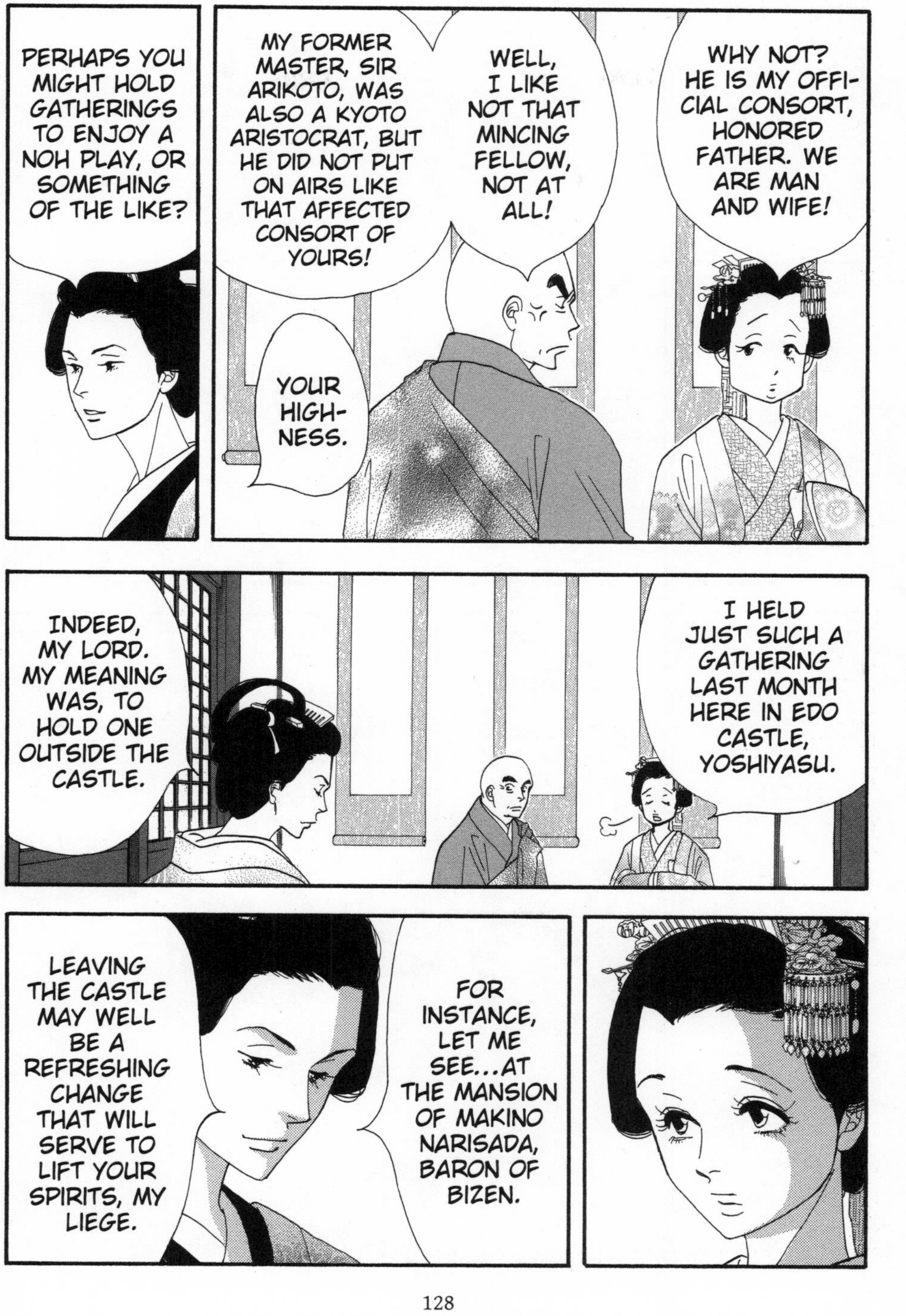
WHY NOT? HE IS MY OFFICIAL CONSORT, HONORED FATHER. WE ARE MAN AND WIFE!
WELL, I LIKE NOT THAT MINCING FELLOW, NOT AT ALL!
MY FORMER MASTER, SIR ARIKOTO, WAS ALSO A KYOTO ARISTOCRAT, BUT HE DID NOT PUT ON AIRS LIKE THAT AFFECTED CONSORT OF YOURS!
YOUR HIGHNESS.
PERHAPS YOU MIGHT HOLD GATHERINGS TO ENJOY A NOH PLAY, OR SOMETHING OF THE LIKE?
I HELD JUST SUCH A GATHERING LAST MONTH HERE IN EDO CASTLE, YOSHIYASU.
INDEED, MY LORD. MY MEANING WAS, TO HOLD ONE OUTSIDE THE CASTLE.
FOR INSTANCE, LET ME SEE...AT THE MANSION OF MAKINO NARISADA, BARON OF BIZEN.
LEAVING THE CASTLE MAY WELL BE A REFRESHING CHANGE THAT WILL SERVE TO LIFT YOUR SPIRITS, MY LIEGE.

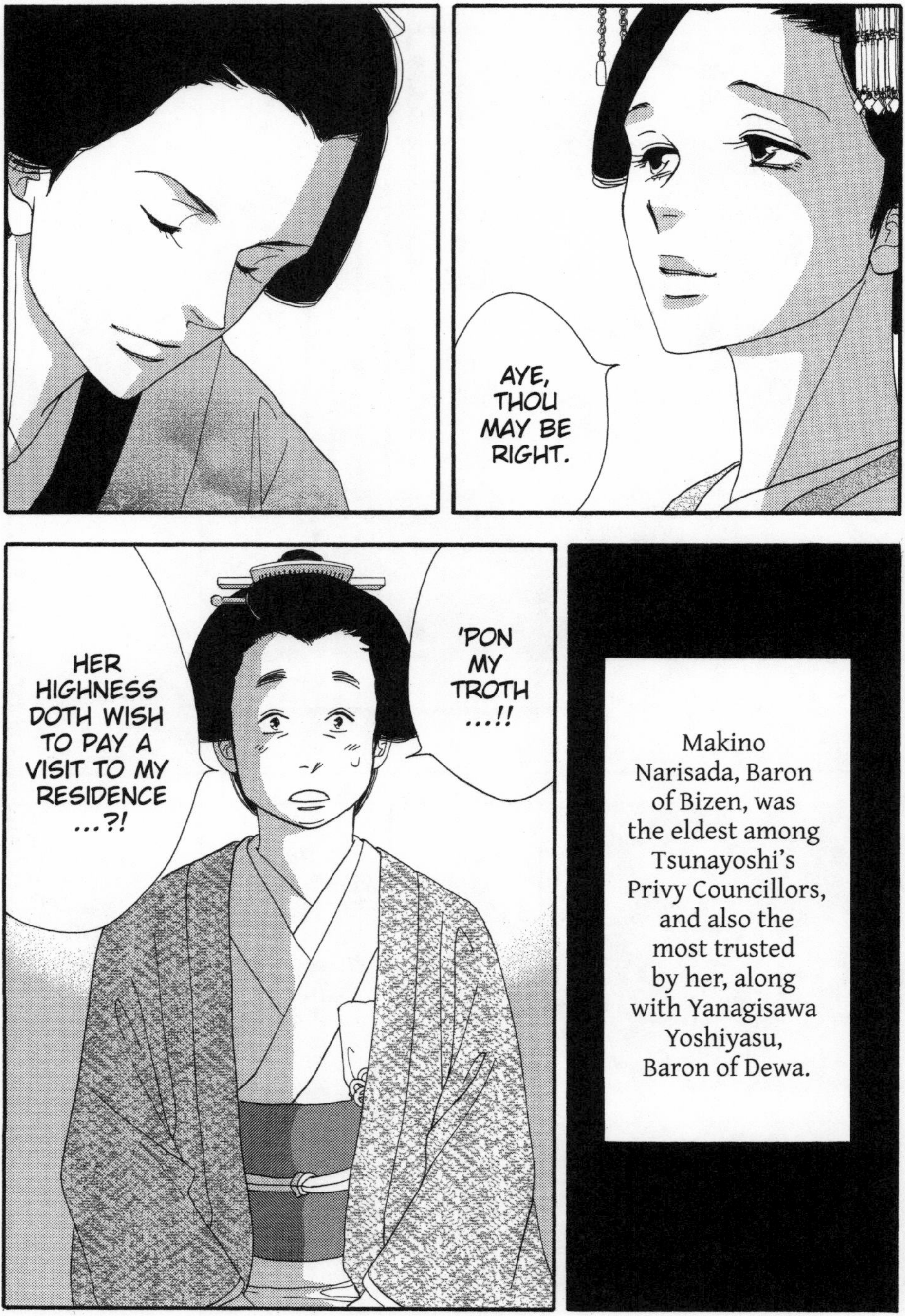
AYE, THOU MAY BE RIGHT.
Makino Narisada, Baron of Bizen, was the eldest among Tsunayoshi's Privy Councillors, and also the most trusted by her, along with Yanagisawa Yoshiyasu, Baron of Dewa.
'PON MY TROTH ...!!
HER HIGHNESS DOTH WISH TO PAY A VISIT TO MY RESIDENCE ...?!

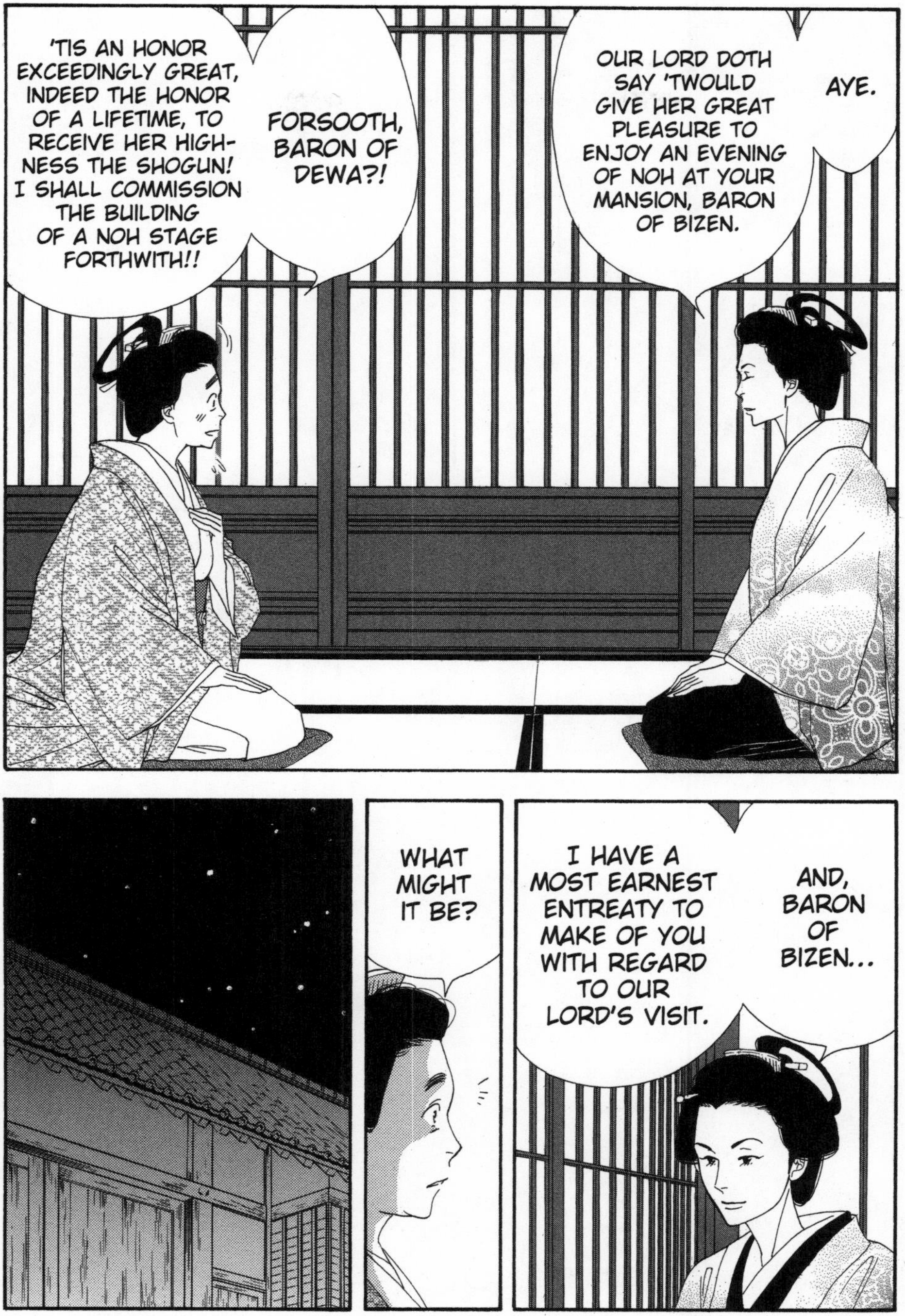
AYE.
OUR LORD DOTH SAY 'TWOULD GIVE HER GREAT PLEASURE TO ENJOY AN EVENING OF NOH AT YOUR MANSION, BARON OF BIZEN.
FORSOOTH, BARON OF DEWA?!
'TIS AN HONOR EXCEEDINGLY GREAT, INDEED THE HONOR OF A LIFETIME, TO RECEIVE HER HIGH-NESS THE SHOGUN! I SHALL COMMISSION THE BUILDING OF A NOH STAGE FORTHWITH!!
AND, BARON OF BIZEN...
I HAVE A MOST EARNEST ENTREATY TO MAKE OF YOU WITH REGARD TO OUR LORD'S VISIT.
WHAT MIGHT IT BE?

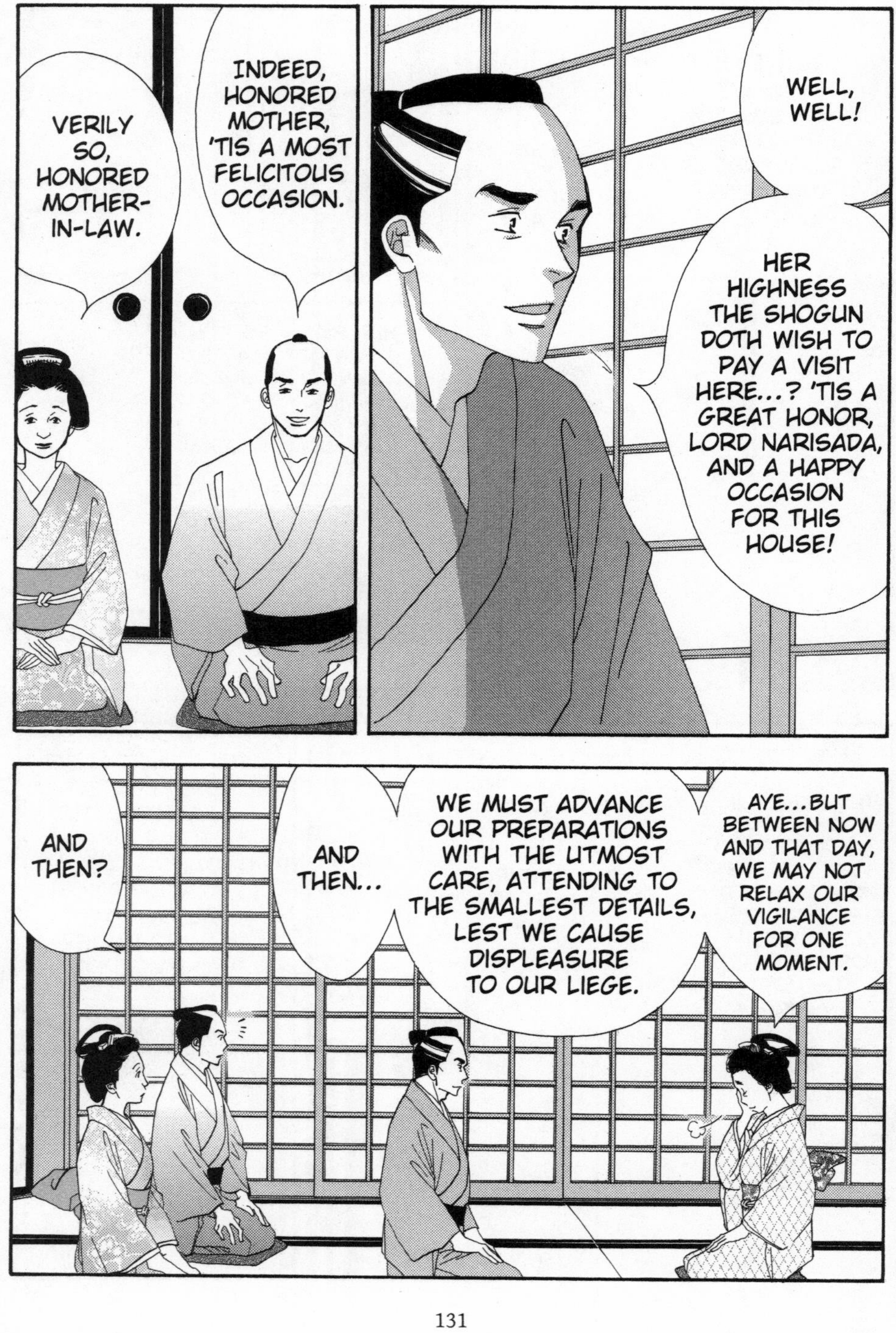
WELL, WELL!
HER HIGHNESS THE SHOGUN DOTH WISH TO PAY A VISIT HERE...? 'TIS A GREAT HONOR, LORD NARISADA, AND A HAPPY OCCASION FOR THIS HOUSE!
INDEED, HONORED MOTHER, 'TIS A MOST FELICITOUS OCCASION.
VERILY SO, HONORED MOTHER-IN-LAW.
AYE...BUT BETWEEN NOW AND THAT DAY, WE MAY NOT RELAX OUR VIGILANCE FOR ONE MOMENT.
WE MUST ADVANCE OUR PREPARATIONS WITH THE UTMOST CARE, ATTENDING TO THE SMALLEST DETAILS, LEST WE CAUSE DISPLEASURE TO OUR LIEGE.
AND THEN...
AND THEN?

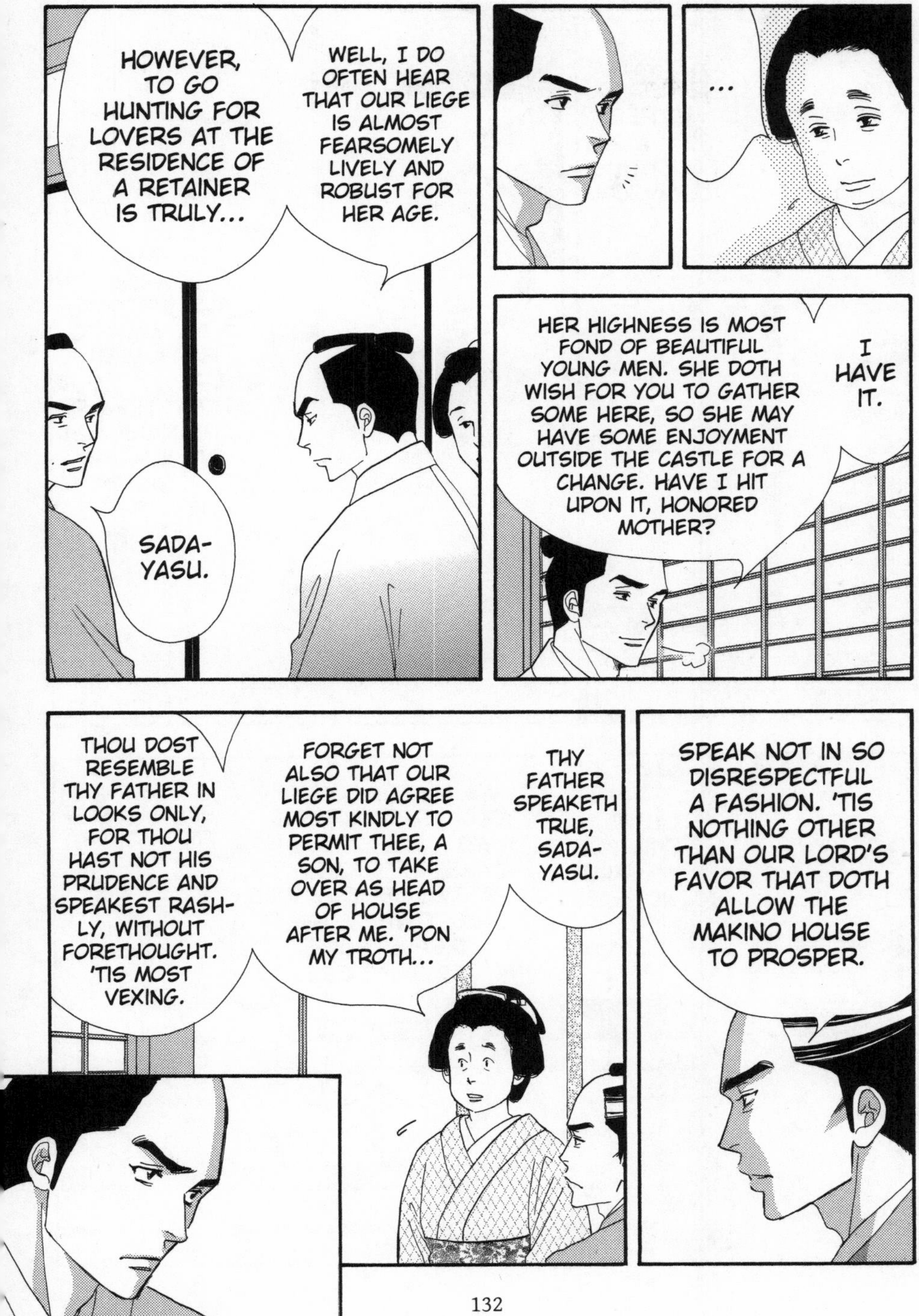
...
I HAVE IT.
HER HIGHNESS IS MOST FOND OF BEAUTIFUL YOUNG MEN. SHE DOTH WISH FOR YOU TO GATHER SOME HERE, SO SHE MAY HAVE SOME ENJOYMENT OUTSIDE THE CASTLE FOR A CHANGE. HAVE I HIT UPON IT, HONORED MOTHER?
WELL, I DO OFTEN HEAR THAT OUR LIEGE IS ALMOST FEARSOMELY LIVELY AND ROBUST FOR HER AGE.
HOWEVER, TO GO HUNTING FOR LOVERS AT THE RESIDENCE OF A RETAINER IS TRULY...
SADA-YASU.
SPEAK NOT IN SO DISRESPECTFUL A FASHION. 'TIS NOTHING OTHER THAN OUR LORD'S FAVOR THAT DOTH ALLOW THE MAKINO HOUSE TO PROSPER.
THY FATHER SPEAKETH TRUE, SADA-YASU.
FORGET NOT ALSO THAT OUR LIEGE DID AGREE MOST KINDLY TO PERMIT THEE, A SON, TO TAKE OVER AS HEAD OF HOUSE AFTER ME. 'PON MY TROTH...
THOU DOST RESEMBLE THY FATHER IN LOOKS ONLY, FOR THOU HAST NOT HIS PRUDENCE AND SPEAKEST RASH-LY, WITHOUT FORETHOUGHT. 'TIS MOST VEXING.

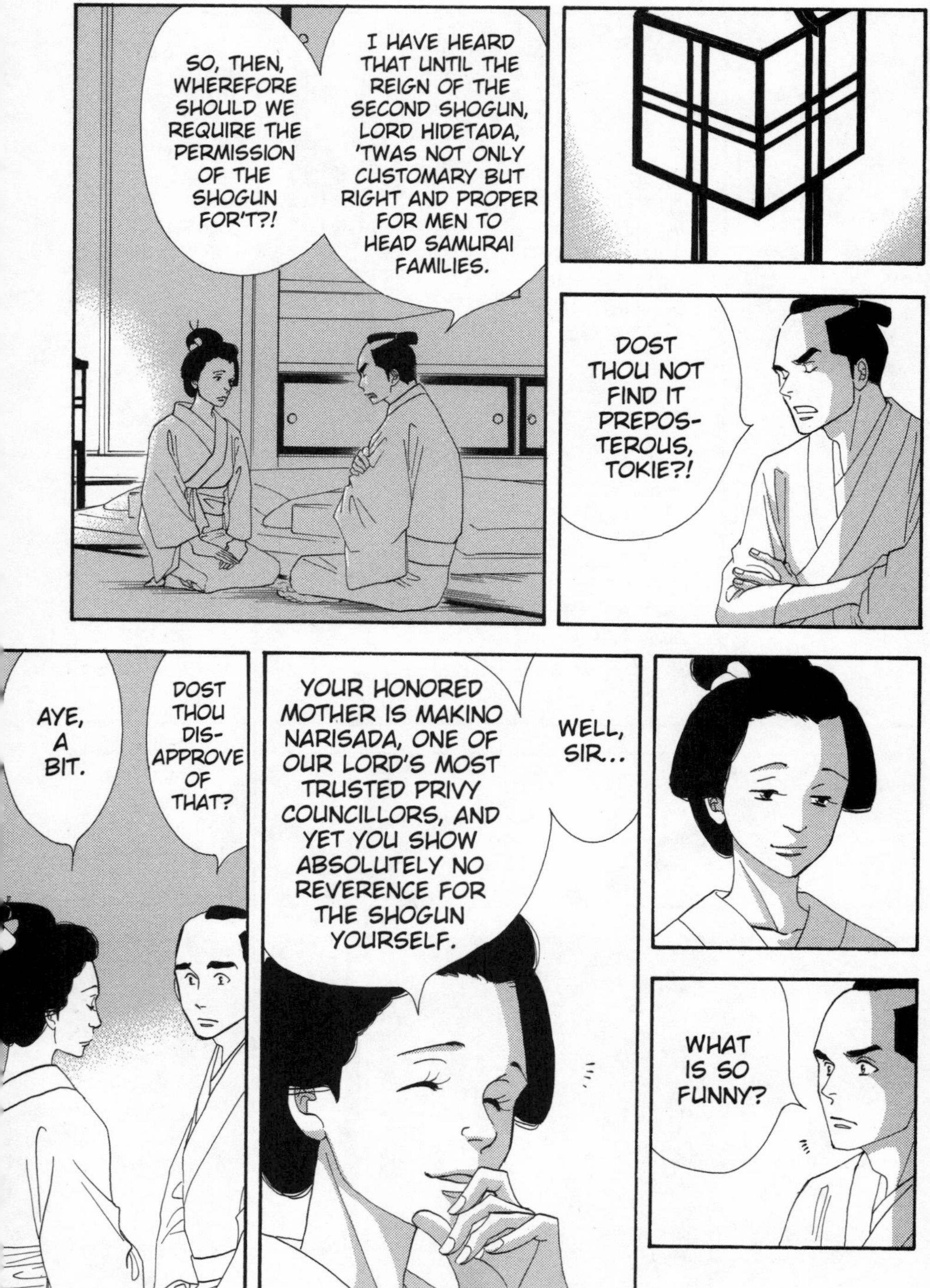
DOST THOU NOT FIND IT PREPOSTEROUS, TOKIE?!
I HAVE HEARD THAT UNTIL THE REIGN OF THE SECOND SHOGUN, LORD HIDETADA, 'TWAS NOT ONLY CUSTOMARY BUT RIGHT AND PROPER FOR MEN TO HEAD SAMURAI FAMILIES.
SO, THEN, WHEREFORE SHOULD WE REQUIRE THE PERMISSION OF THE SHOGUN FOR'T?!
WHAT IS SO FUNNY?
WELL, SIR...
YOUR HONORED MOTHER IS MAKINO NARISADA, ONE OF OUR LORD'S MOST TRUSTED PRIVY COUNCILLORS, AND YET YOU SHOW ABSOLUTELY NO REVERENCE FOR THE SHOGUN YOURSELF.
DOST THOU DIS-APPROVE OF THAT?
AYE, A BIT.

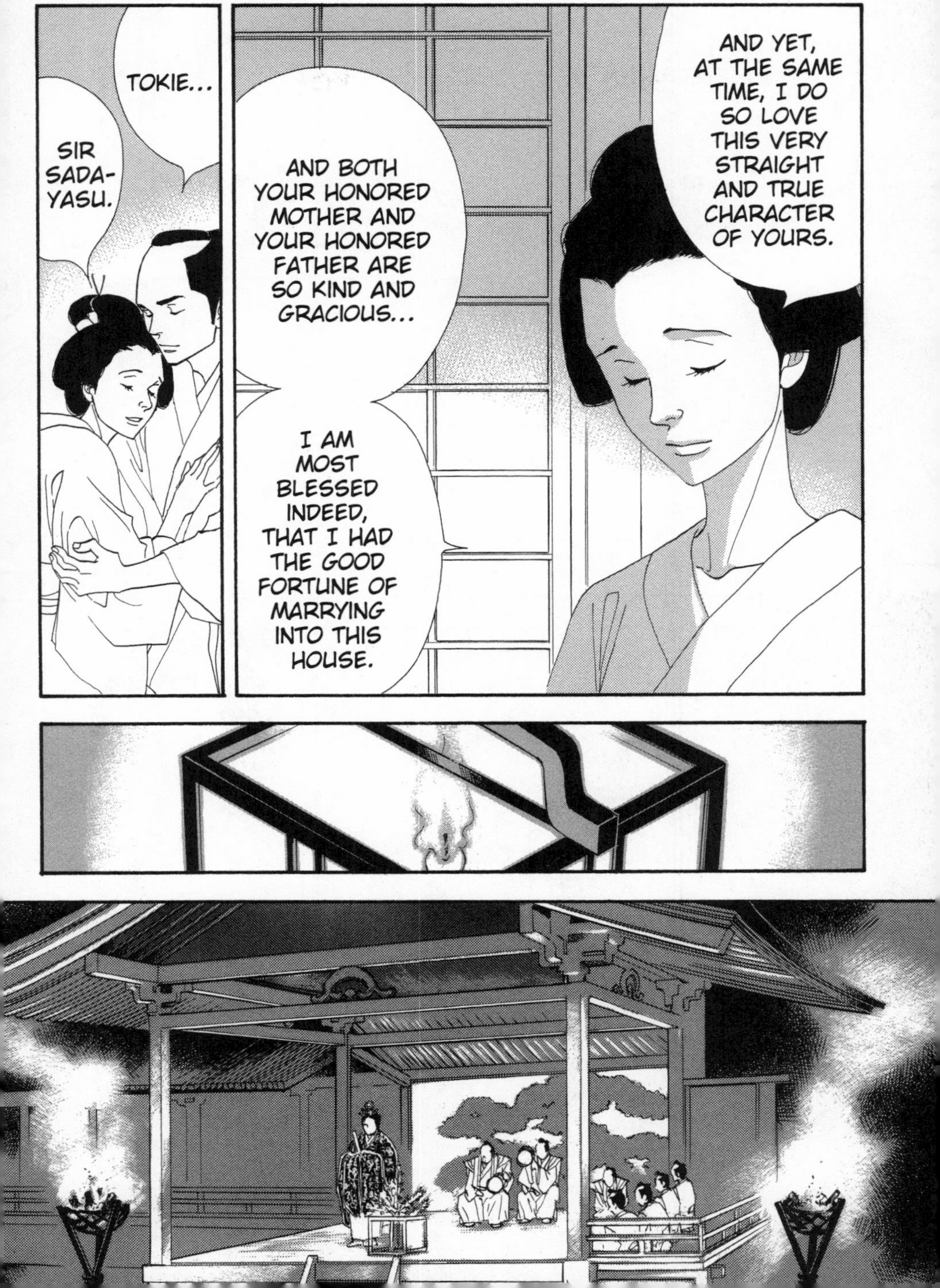
AND YET, AT THE SAME TIME, I DO SO LOVE THIS VERY STRAIGHT AND TRUE CHARACTER OF YOURS.
AND BOTH YOUR HONORED MOTHER AND YOUR HONORED FATHER ARE SO KIND AND GRACIOUS...
I AM MOST BLESSED INDEED, THAT I HAD THE GOOD FORTUNE OF MARRYING INTO THIS HOUSE.
TOKIE...
SIR SADA-YASU.

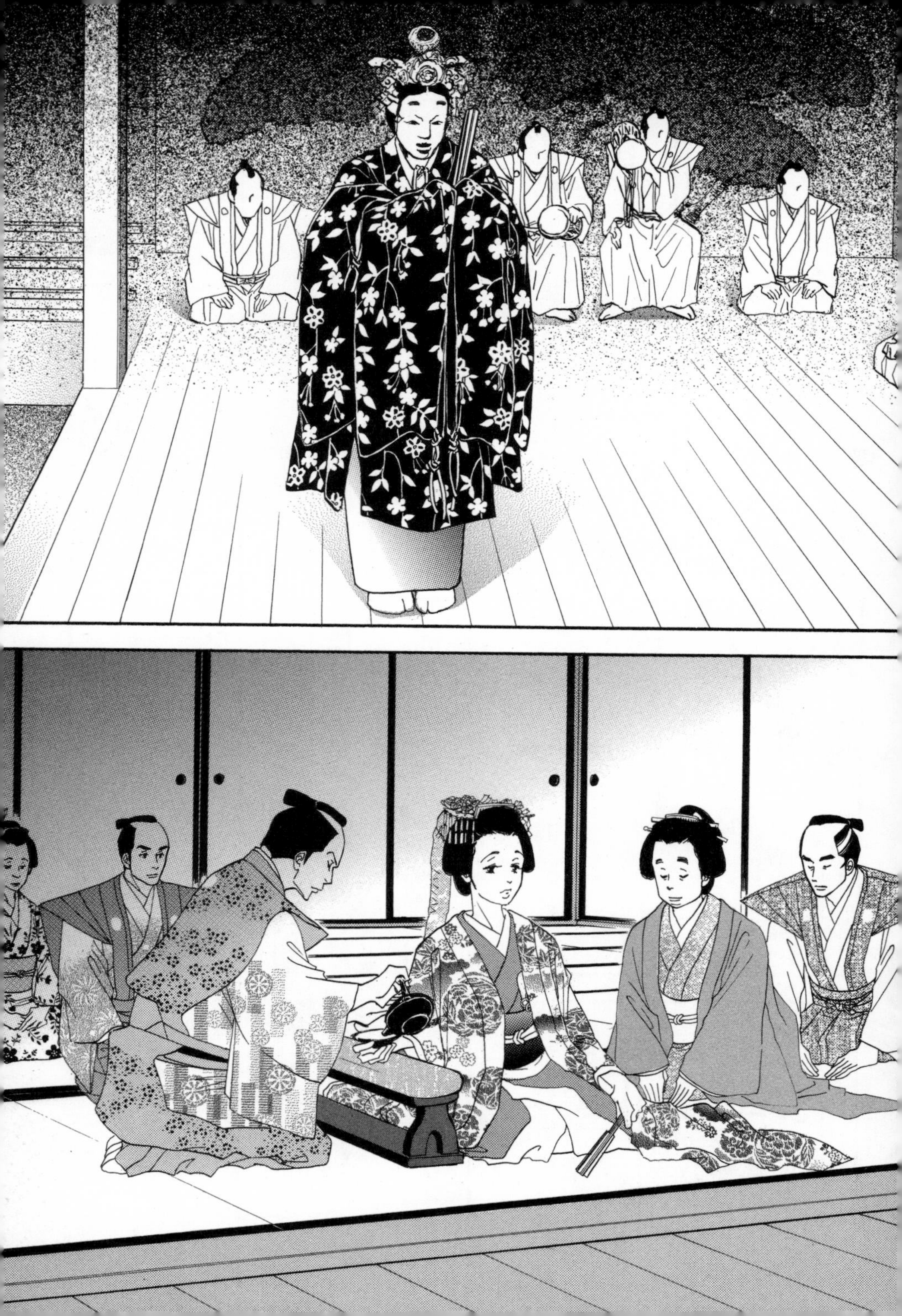

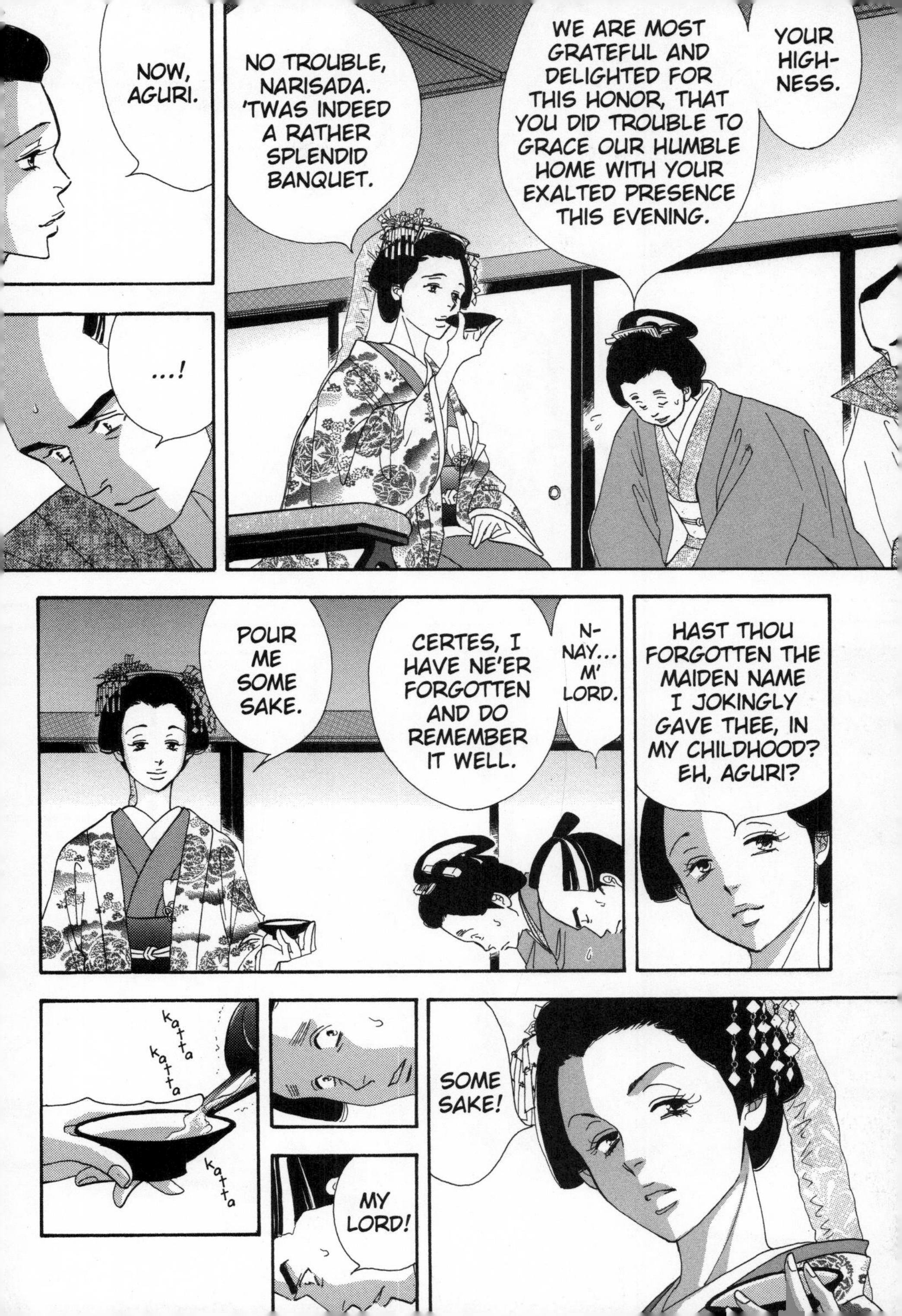
YOUR HIGHNESS.
WE ARE MOST GRATEFUL AND DELIGHTED FOR THIS HONOR, THAT YOU DID TROUBLE TO GRACE OUR HUMBLE HOME WITH YOUR EXALTED PRESENCE THIS EVENING.
NO TROUBLE, NARISADA. 'TWAS INDEED A RATHER SPLENDID BANQUET.
NOW, AGURI.
...!
HAST THOU FORGOTTEN THE MAIDEN NAME I JOKINGLY GAVE THEE, IN MY CHILDHOOD? EH, AGURI?
N-NAY... M' LORD.
CERTES, I HAVE NE'ER FORGOTTEN AND DO REMEMBER IT WELL.
POUR ME SOME SAKE.
SOME SAKE!
MY LORD!
katta
katta
katta

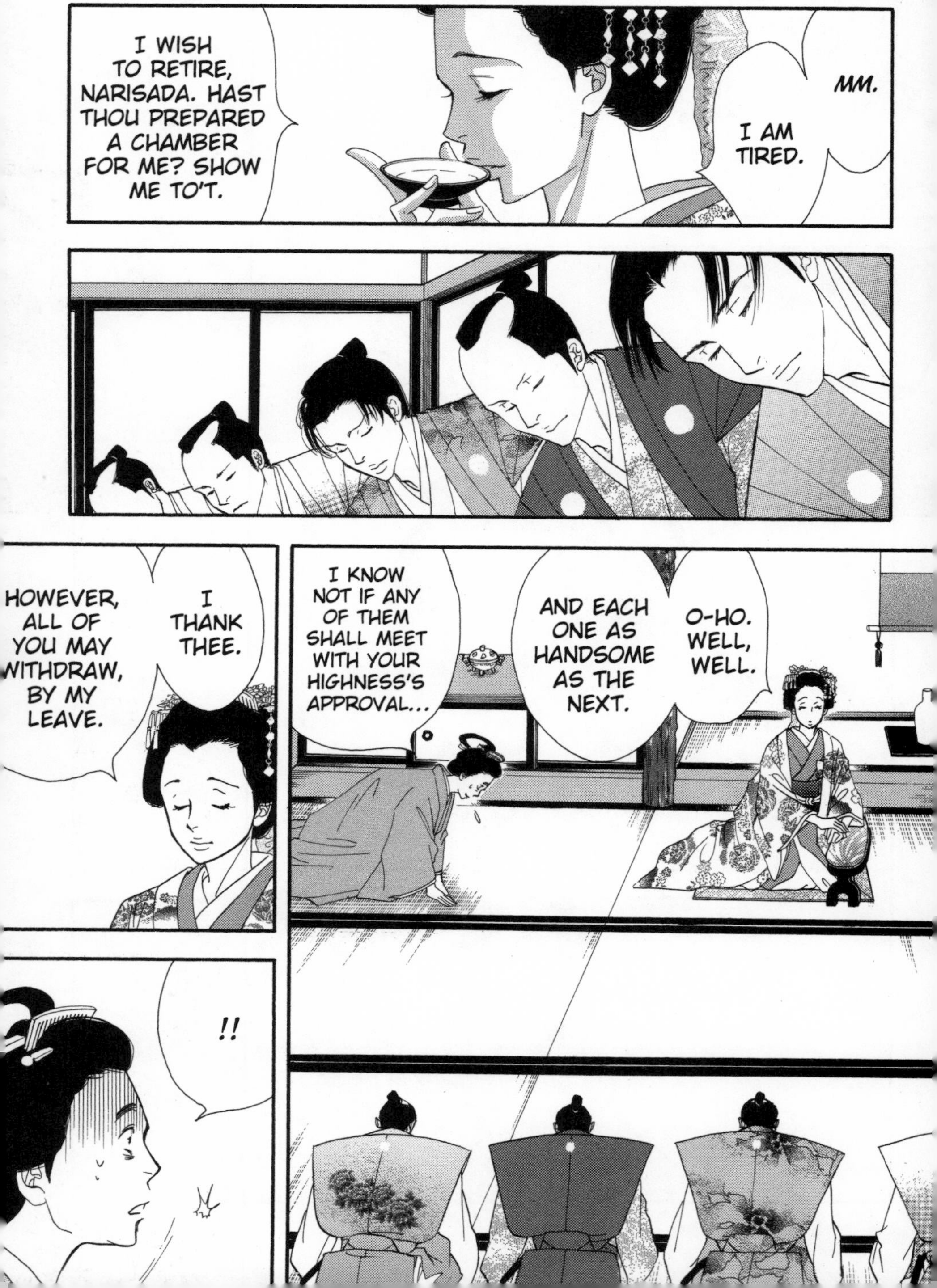
MM.
I AM TIRED.
I WISH TO RETIRE, NARISADA. HAST THOU PREPARED A CHAMBER FOR ME? SHOW ME TO'T.
O-HO. WELL, WELL.
AND EACH ONE AS HANDSOME AS THE NEXT.
I KNOW NOT IF ANY OF THEM SHALL MEET WITH YOUR HIGHNESS'S APPROVAL...
I THANK THEE.
HOWEVER, ALL OF YOU MAY WITHDRAW, BY MY LEAVE.
!!

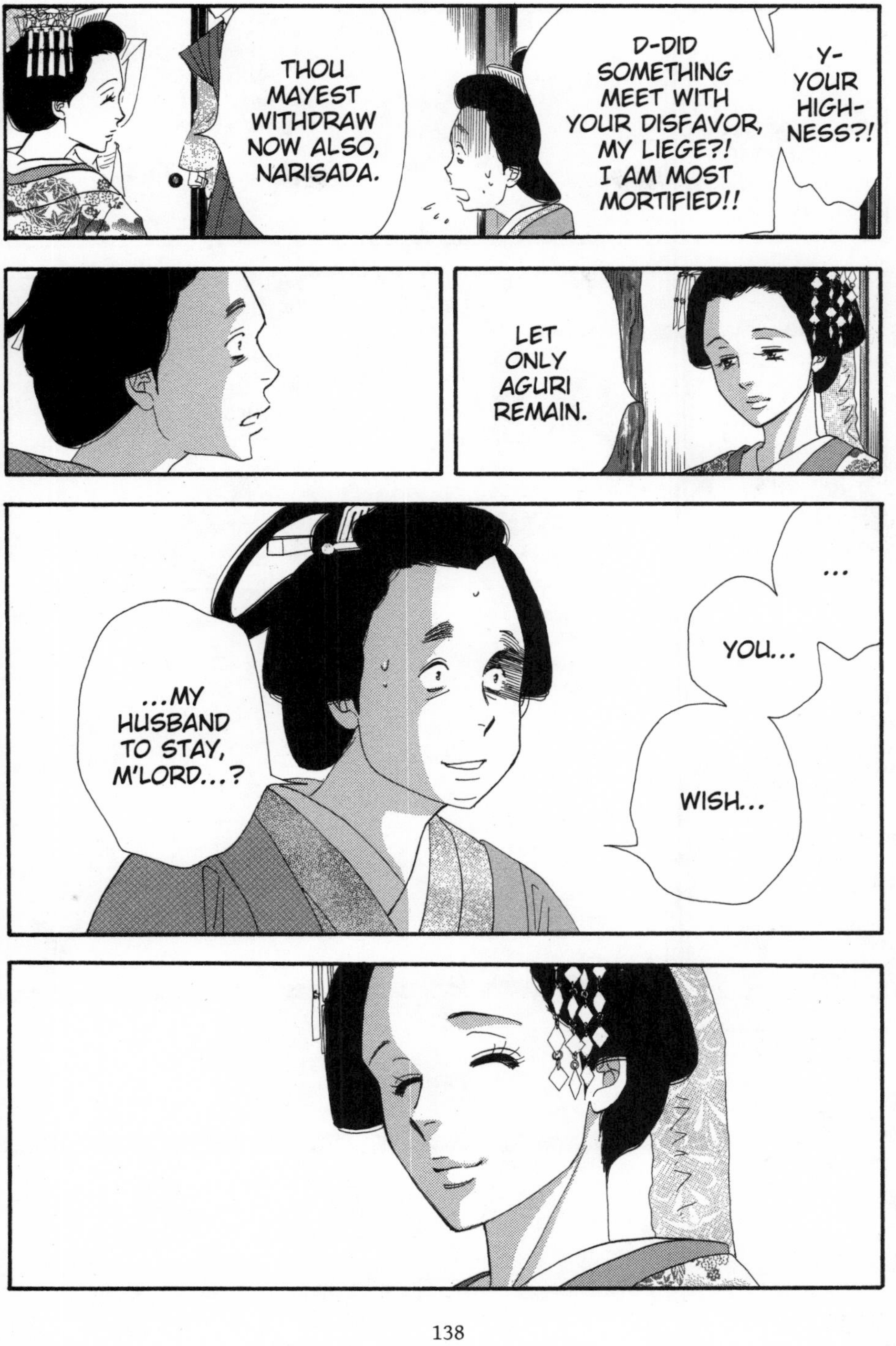
Y- YOUR HIGH- NESS?!
D-DID SOMETHING MEET WITH YOUR DISFAVOR, MY LIEGE?! I AM MOST MORTIFIED!!
THOU MAYEST WITHDRAW NOW ALSO, NARISADA.
LET ONLY AGURI REMAIN.
...
YOU...
WISH...
...MY HUSBAND TO STAY, M'LORD...?

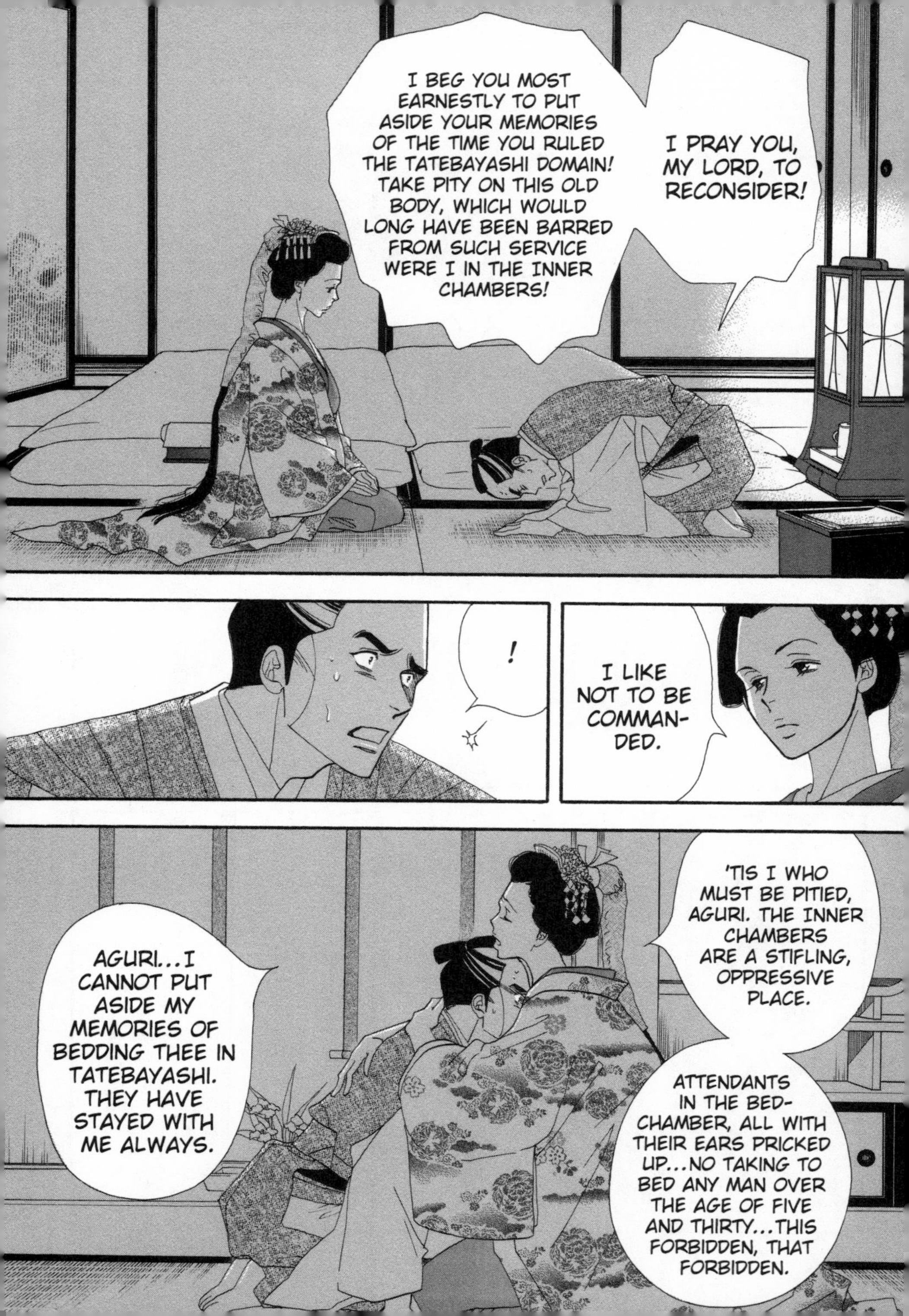
I PRAY YOU, MY LORD, TO RECONSIDER!
I BEG YOU MOST EARNESTLY TO PUT ASIDE YOUR MEMORIES OF THE TIME YOU RULED THE TATEBAYASHI DOMAIN! TAKE PITY ON THIS OLD BODY, WHICH WOULD LONG HAVE BEEN BARRED FROM SUCH SERVICE WERE I IN THE INNER CHAMBERS!
I LIKE NOT TO BE COMMAN-DED.
!
'TIS I WHO MUST BE PITIED, AGURI. THE INNER CHAMBERS ARE A STIFLING, OPPRESSIVE PLACE.
ATTENDANTS IN THE BED-CHAMBER, ALL WITH THEIR EARS PRICKED UP...NO TAKING TO BED ANY MAN OVER THE AGE OF FIVE AND THIRTY...THIS FORBIDDEN, THAT FORBIDDEN.
AGURI...I CANNOT PUT ASIDE MY MEMORIES OF BEDDING THEE IN TATEBAYASHI. THEY HAVE STAYED WITH ME ALWAYS.

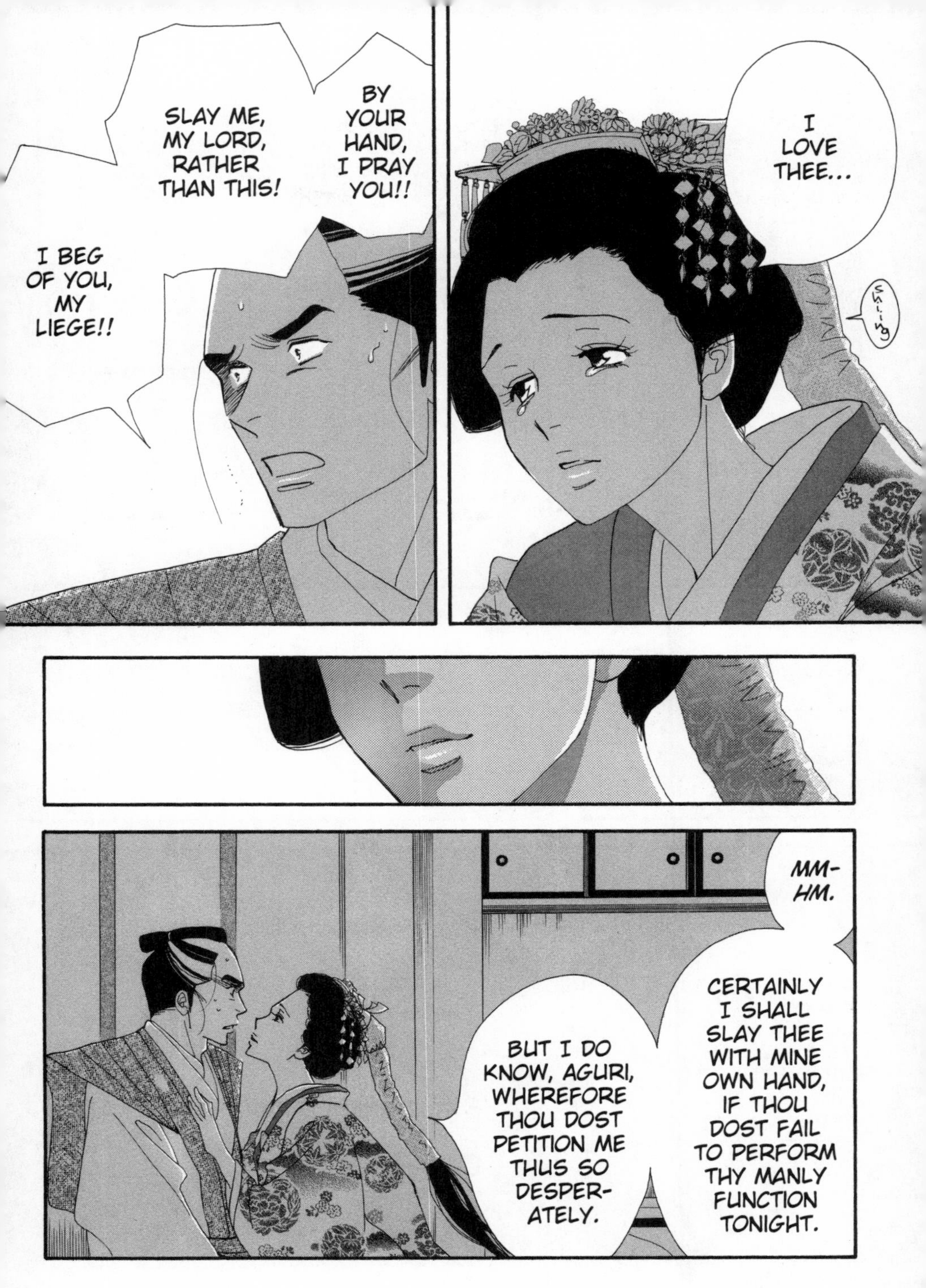
I LOVE THEE...
shi-i-ing
BY YOUR HAND, I PRAY YOU!!
SLAY ME, MY LORD, RATHER THAN THIS!
I BEG OF YOU, MY LIEGE!!
MM-HM.
CERTAINLY I SHALL SLAY THEE WITH MINE OWN HAND, IF THOU DOST FAIL TO PERFORM THY MANLY FUNCTION TONIGHT.
BUT I DO KNOW, AGURI, WHEREFORE THOU DOST PETITION ME THUS SO DESPER-ATELY.

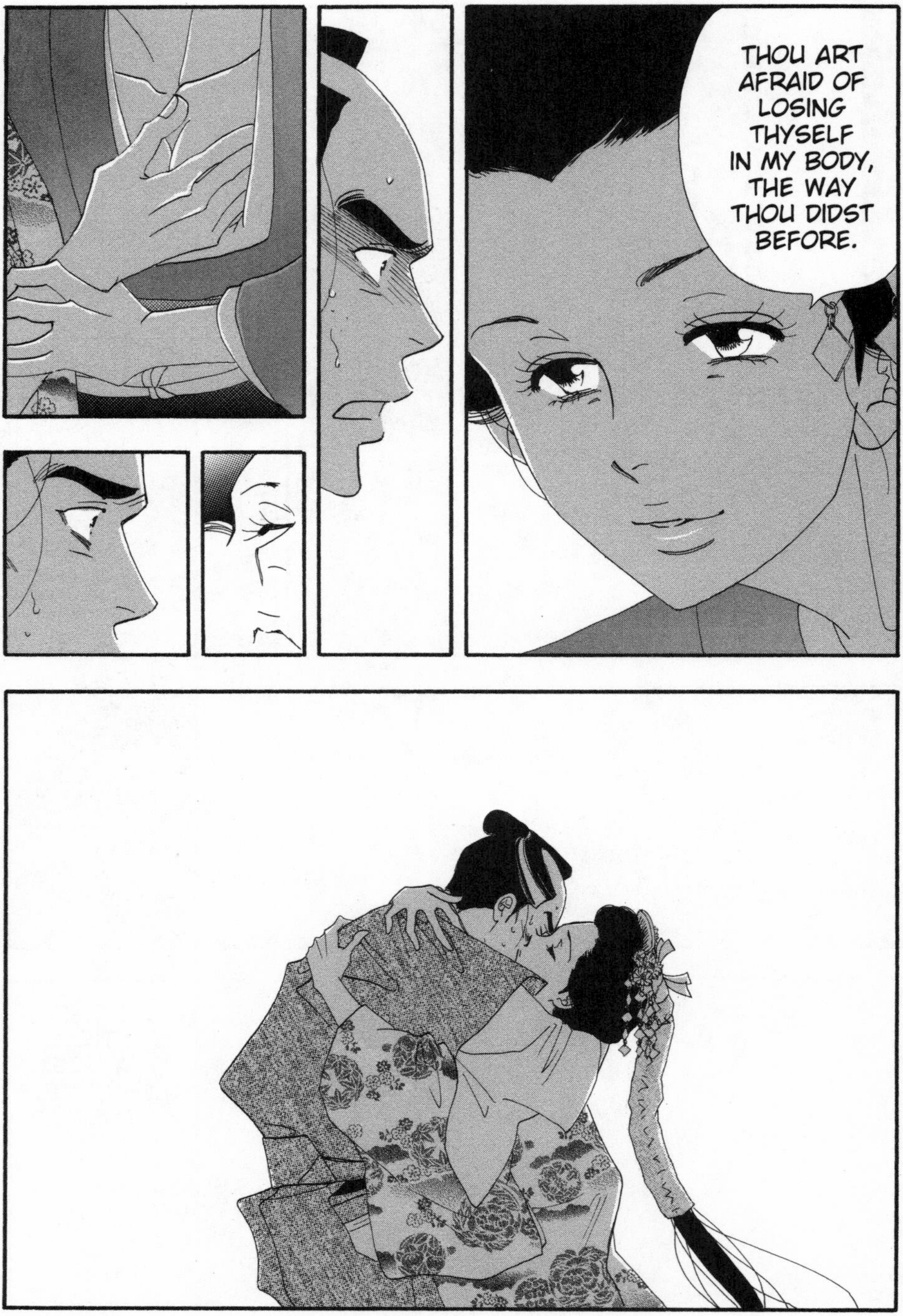
THOU ART AFRAID OF LOSING THYSELF IN MY BODY, THE WAY THOU DIDST BEFORE.

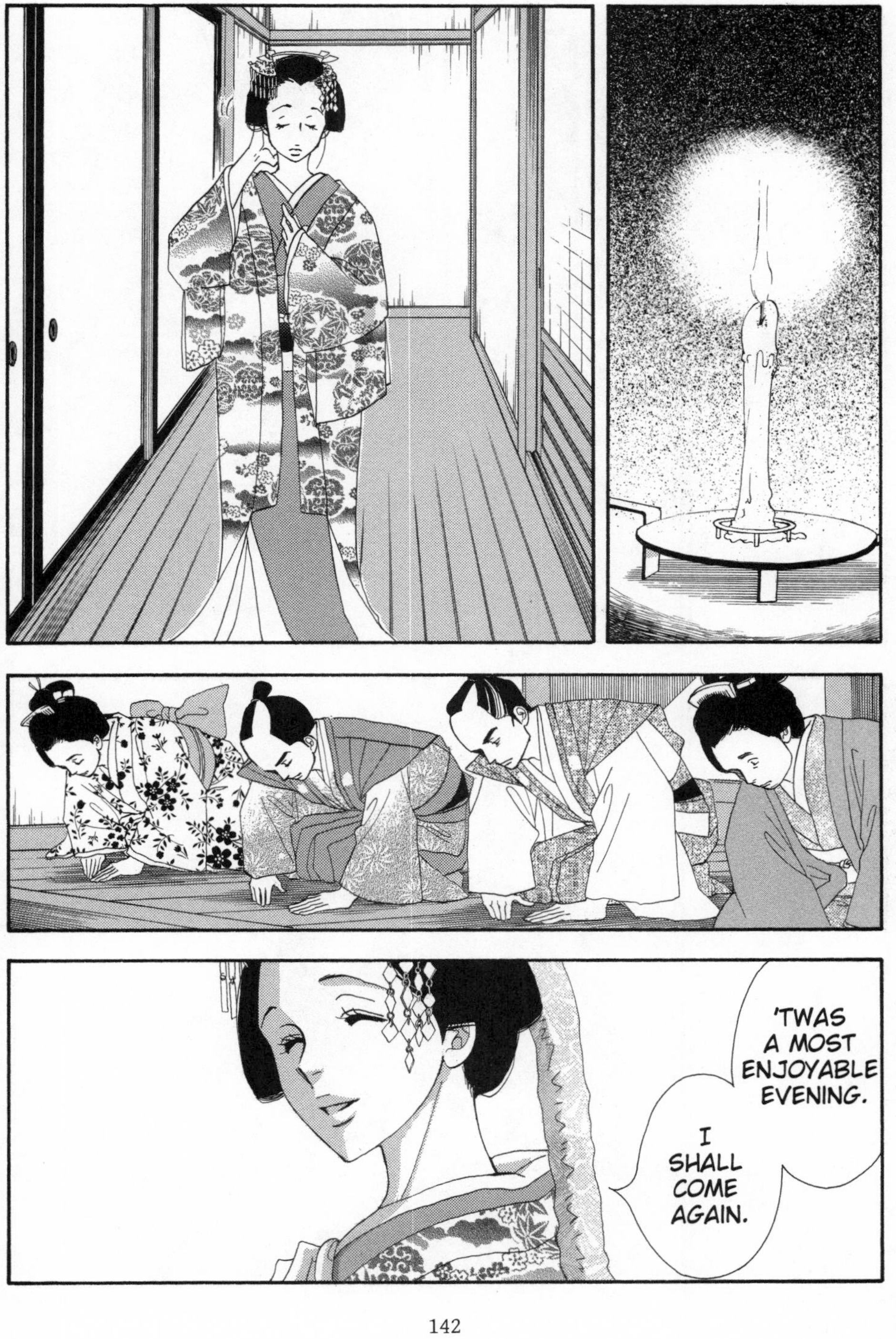
'TWAS A MOST ENJOYABLE EVENING.
I SHALL COME AGAIN.

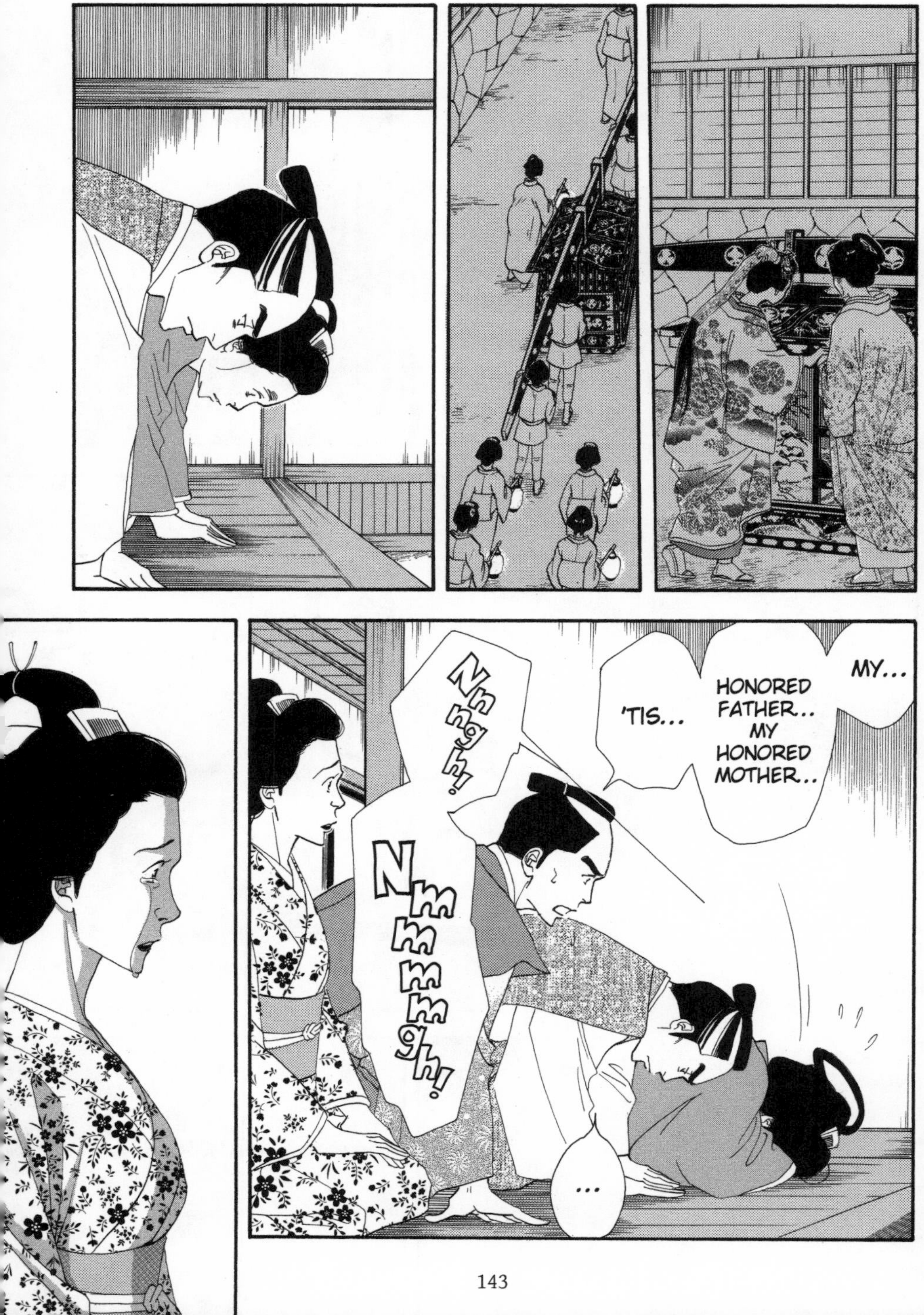
MY...
HONORED FATHER... MY HONORED MOTHER...
'TIS...
Nnngh!
Nmmmmmgh!
...

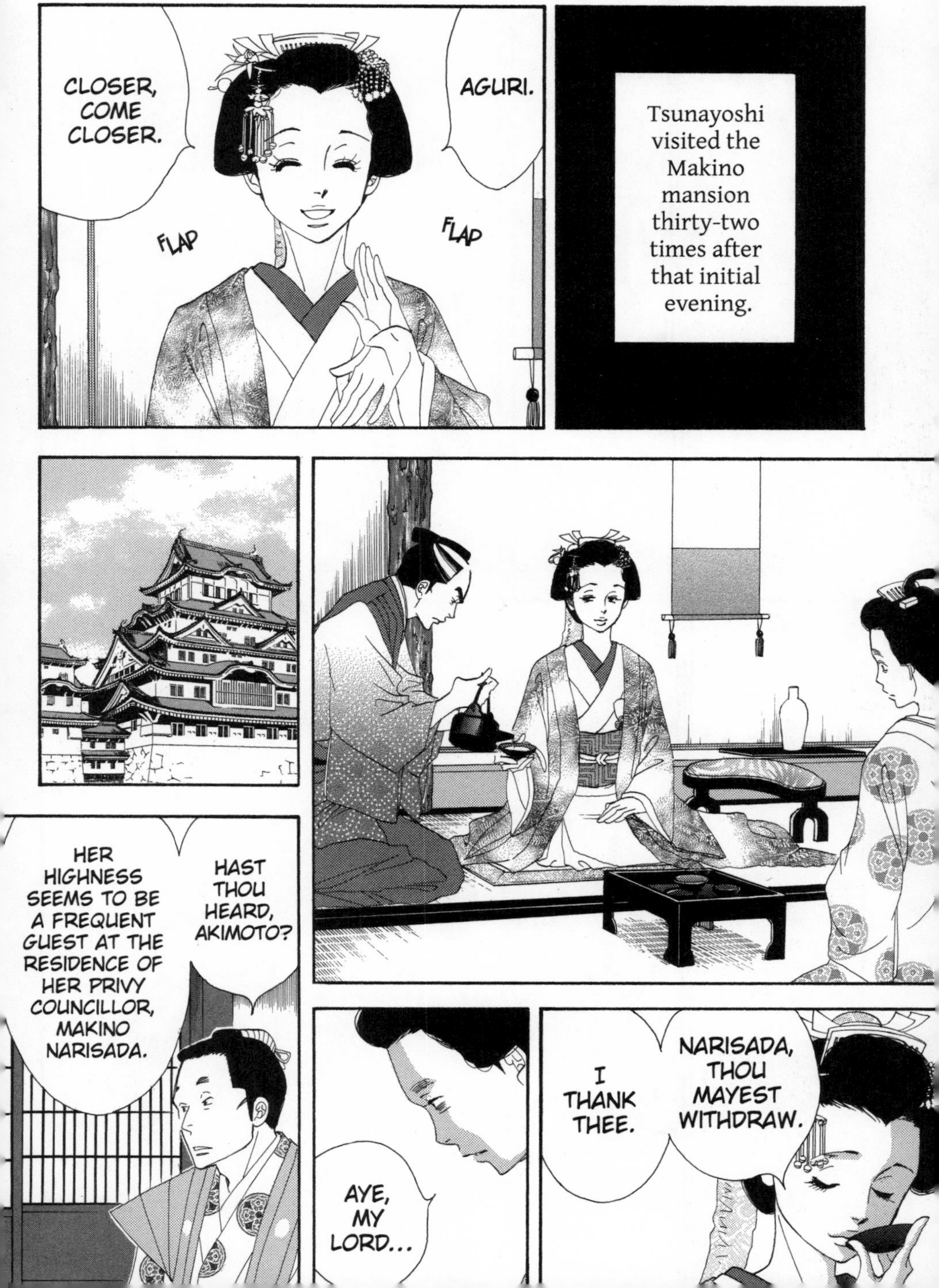
Tsunayoshi visited the Makino mansion thirty-two times after that initial evening.
AGURI.
CLOSER, COME CLOSER.
FLAP
FLAP
NARISADA, THOU MAYEST WITHDRAW.
I THANK THEE.
AYE, MY LORD...
HAST THOU HEARD, AKIMOTO?
HER HIGHNESS SEEMS TO BE A FREQUENT GUEST AT THE RESIDENCE OF HER PRIVY COUNCILLOR, MAKINO NARISADA.

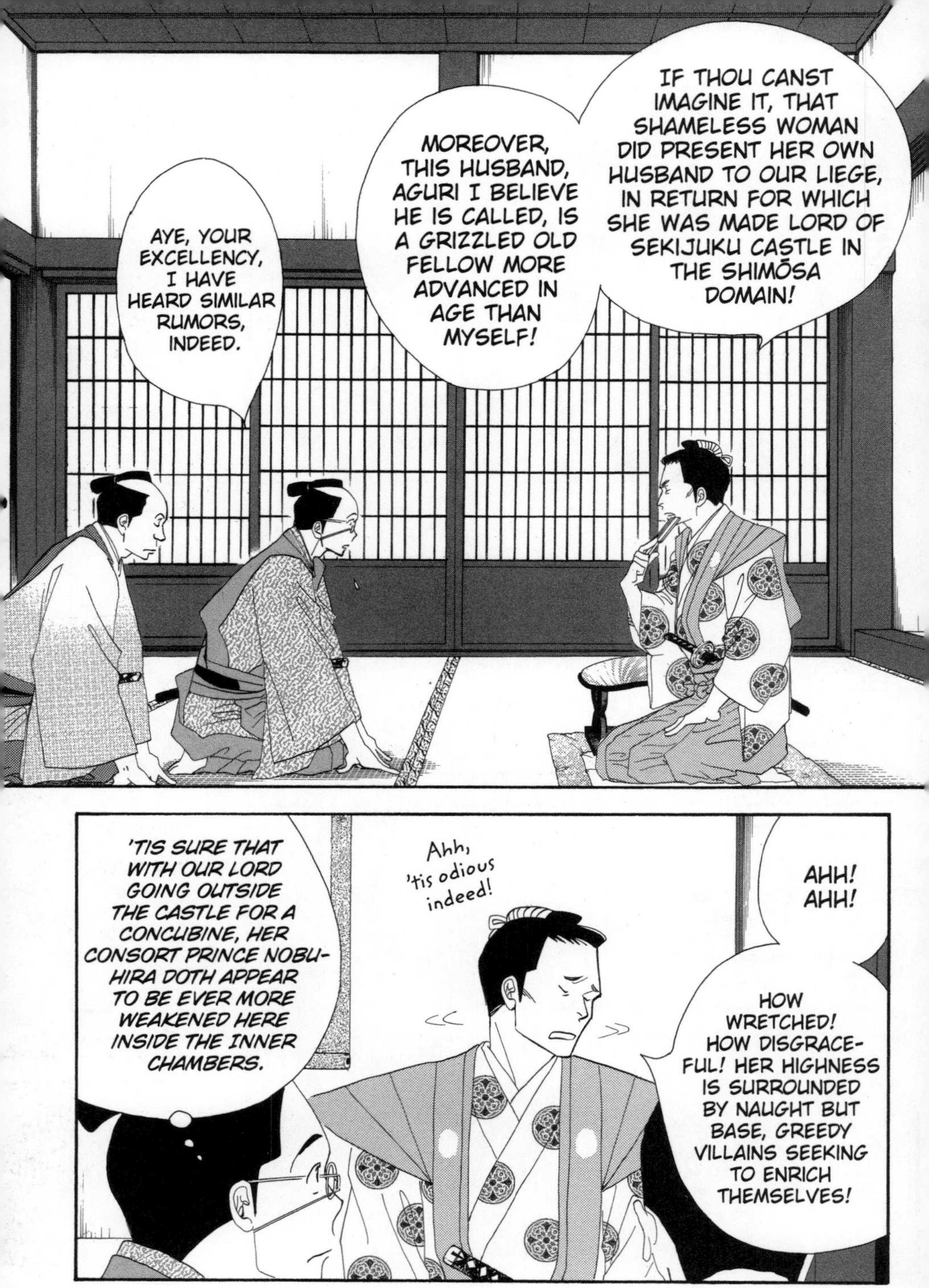
IF THOU CANST IMAGINE IT, THAT SHAMELESS WOMAN DID PRESENT HER OWN HUSBAND TO OUR LIEGE, IN RETURN FOR WHICH SHE WAS MADE LORD OF SEKIJUKU CASTLE IN THE SHIMŌSA DOMAIN!
MOREOVER, THIS HUSBAND, AGURI I BELIEVE HE IS CALLED, IS A GRIZZLED OLD FELLOW MORE ADVANCED IN AGE THAN MYSELF!
AYE, YOUR EXCELLENCY, I HAVE HEARD SIMILAR RUMORS, INDEED.
AHH! AHH!
HOW WRETCHED! HOW DISGRACEFUL! HER HIGHNESS IS SURROUNDED BY NAUGHT BUT BASE, GREEDY VILLAINS SEEKING TO ENRICH THEMSELVES!
Ahh, 'tis odious indeed!
'TIS SURE THAT WITH OUR LORD GOING OUTSIDE THE CASTLE FOR A CONCUBINE, HER CONSORT PRINCE NOBUHIRA DOTH APPEAR TO BE EVER MORE WEAKENED HERE INSIDE THE INNER CHAMBERS.

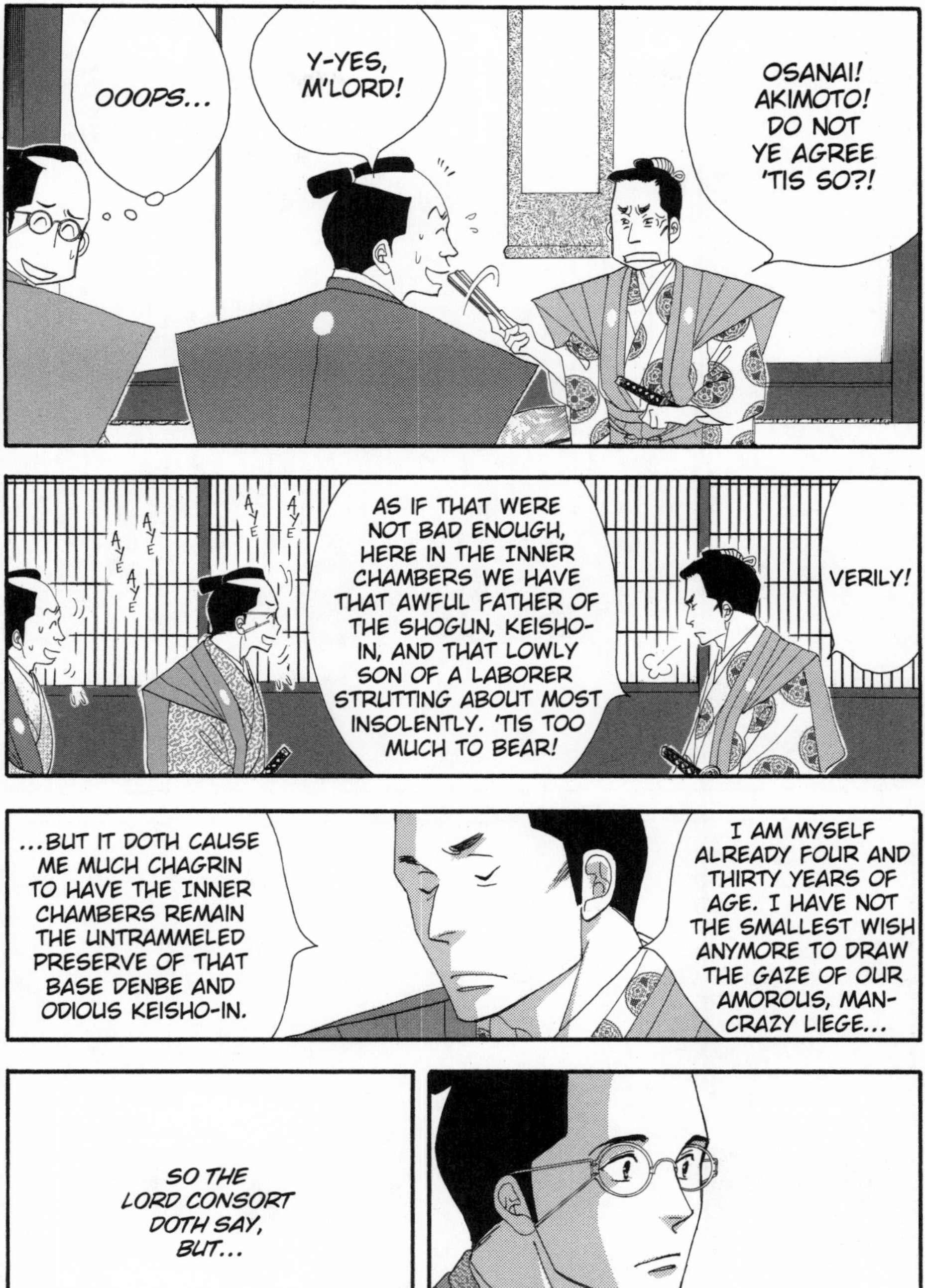
OSANAI! AKIMOTO! DO NOT YE AGREE 'TIS SO?!
Y-YES, M'LORD!
OOOPS...
VERILY!
AS IF THAT WERE NOT BAD ENOUGH, HERE IN THE INNER CHAMBERS WE HAVE THAT AWFUL FATHER OF THE SHOGUN, KEISHO-IN, AND THAT LOWLY SON OF A LABORER STRUTTING ABOUT MOST INSOLENTLY. 'TIS TOO MUCH TO BEAR!
AYE AYE AYE AYE
I AM MYSELF ALREADY FOUR AND THIRTY YEARS OF AGE. I HAVE NOT THE SMALLEST WISH ANYMORE TO DRAW THE GAZE OF OUR AMOROUS, MAN-CRAZY LIEGE...
...BUT IT DOTH CAUSE ME MUCH CHAGRIN TO HAVE THE INNER CHAMBERS REMAIN THE UNTRAMMELED PRESERVE OF THAT BASE DENBE AND ODIOUS KEISHO-IN.
SO THE LORD CONSORT DOTH SAY, BUT...

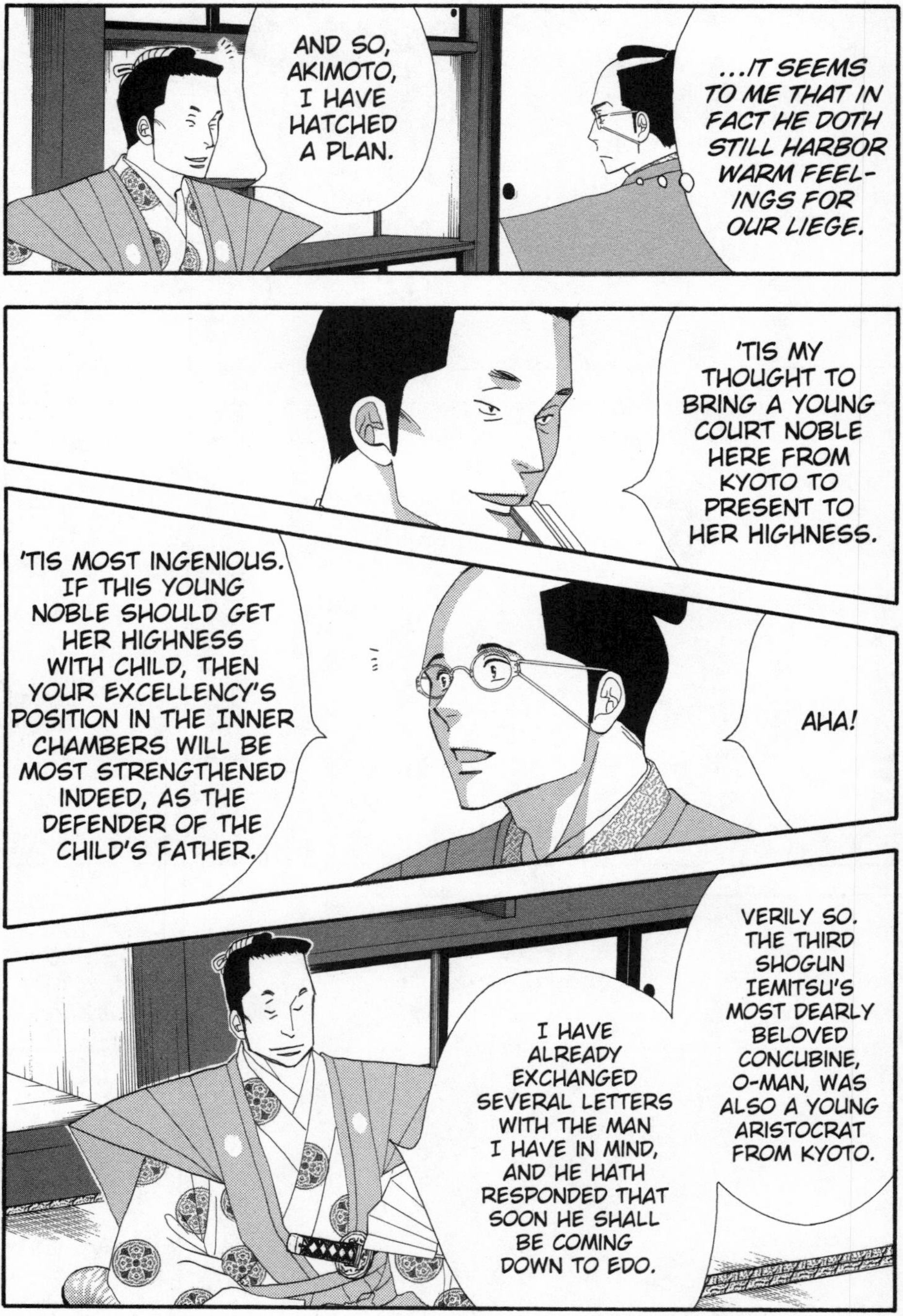
...IT SEEMS TO ME THAT IN FACT HE DOTH STILL HARBOR WARM FEELINGS FOR OUR LIEGE.
AND SO, AKIMOTO, I HAVE HATCHED A PLAN.
'TIS MY THOUGHT TO BRING A YOUNG COURT NOBLE HERE FROM KYOTO TO PRESENT TO HER HIGHNESS.
AHA!
'TIS MOST INGENIOUS. IF THIS YOUNG NOBLE SHOULD GET HER HIGHNESS WITH CHILD, THEN YOUR EXCELLENCY'S POSITION IN THE INNER CHAMBERS WILL BE MOST STRENGTHENED INDEED, AS THE DEFENDER OF THE CHILD'S FATHER.
VERILY SO. THE THIRD SHOGUN IEMITSU'S MOST DEARLY BELOVED CONCUBINE, O-MAN, WAS ALSO A YOUNG ARISTOCRAT FROM KYOTO.
I HAVE ALREADY EXCHANGED SEVERAL LETTERS WITH THE MAN I HAVE IN MIND, AND HE HATH RESPONDED THAT SOON HE SHALL BE COMING DOWN TO EDO.

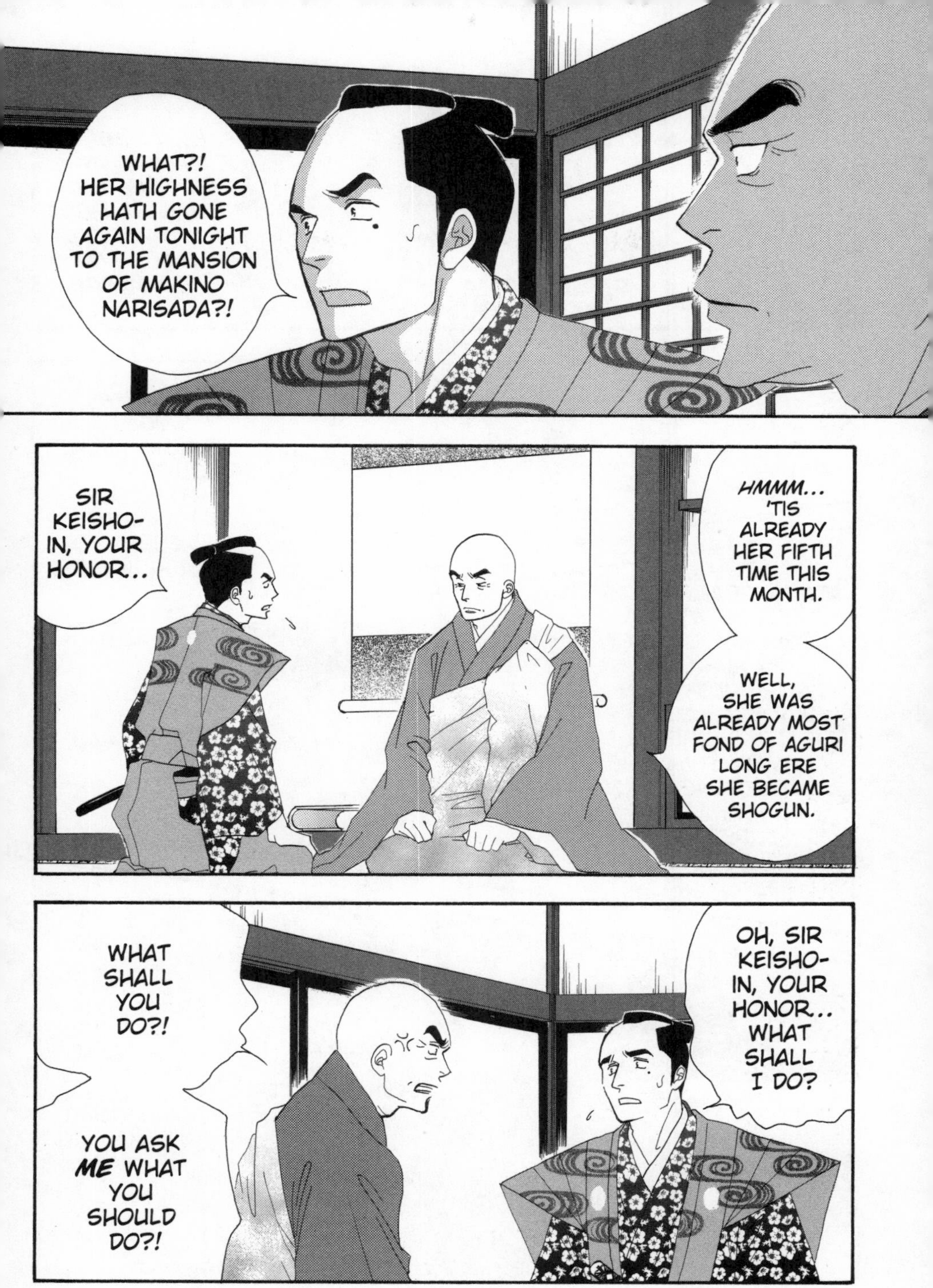
WHAT?! HER HIGHNESS HATH GONE AGAIN TONIGHT TO THE MANSION OF MAKINO NARISADA?!
HMMM... 'TIS ALREADY HER FIFTH TIME THIS MONTH.
SIR KEISHO-IN, YOUR HONOR...
WELL, SHE WAS ALREADY MOST FOND OF AGURI LONG ERE SHE BECAME SHOGUN.
OH, SIR KEISHO-IN, YOUR HONOR... WHAT SHALL I DO?
WHAT SHALL YOU DO?!
YOU ASK *ME* WHAT YOU SHOULD DO?!

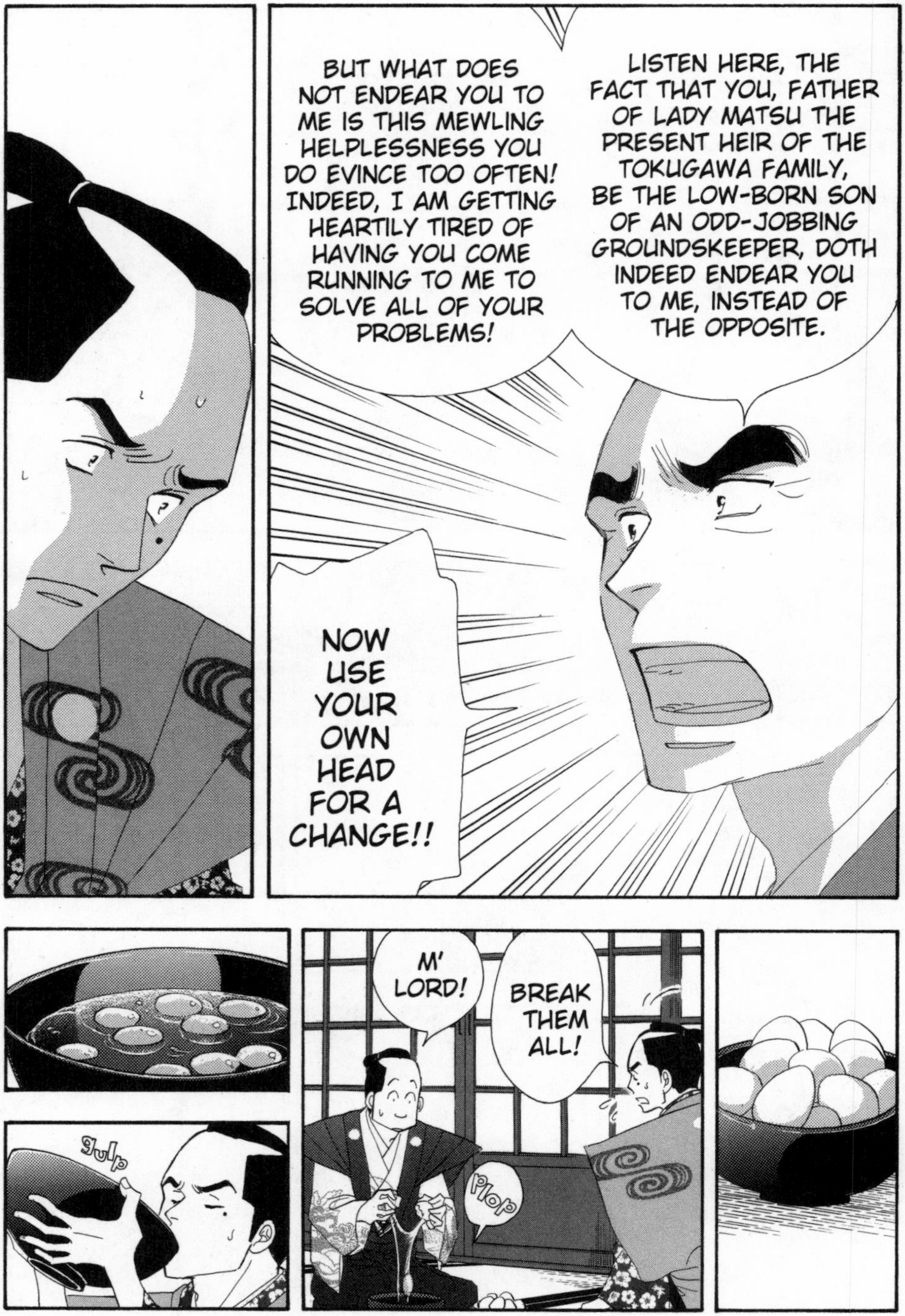
LISTEN HERE, THE FACT THAT YOU, FATHER OF LADY MATSU THE PRESENT HEIR OF THE TOKUGAWA FAMILY, BE THE LOW-BORN SON OF AN ODD-JOBBING GROUNDSKEEPER, DOTH INDEED ENDEAR YOU TO ME, INSTEAD OF THE OPPOSITE.
BUT WHAT DOES NOT ENDEAR YOU TO ME IS THIS MEWLING HELPLESSNESS YOU DO EVINCE TOO OFTEN! INDEED, I AM GETTING HEARTILY TIRED OF HAVING YOU COME RUNNING TO ME TO SOLVE ALL OF YOUR PROBLEMS!
NOW USE YOUR OWN HEAD FOR A CHANGE!!
BREAK THEM ALL!
M' LORD!
Plop
gulp

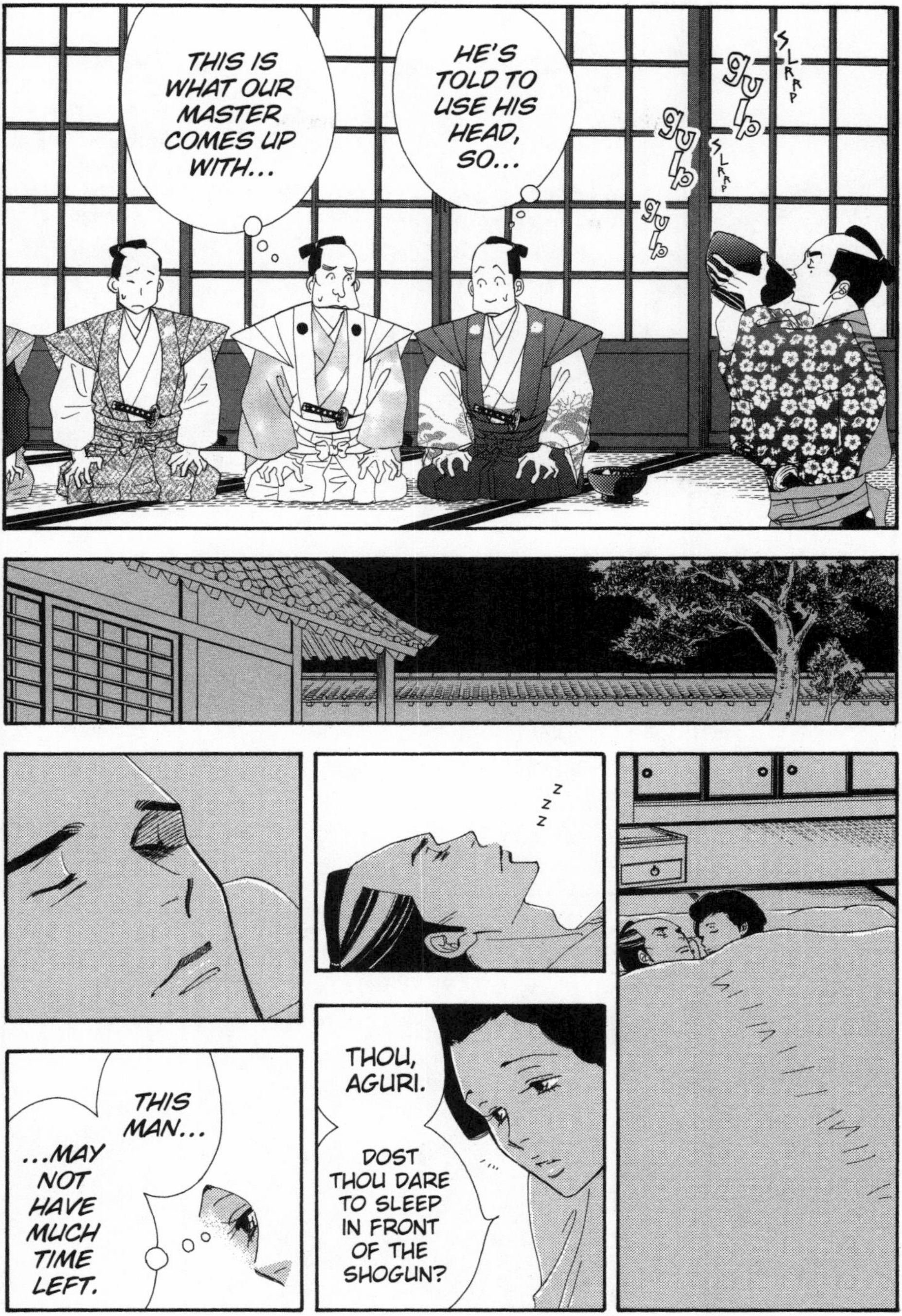
SLRRP
gulp
gulp
SLRRP
gulp
HE'S TOLD TO USE HIS HEAD, SO...
THIS IS WHAT OUR MASTER COMES UP WITH...
ZZZ
THOU, AGURI.
DOST THOU DARE TO SLEEP IN FRONT OF THE SHOGUN?
THIS MAN...
...MAY NOT HAVE MUCH TIME LEFT.

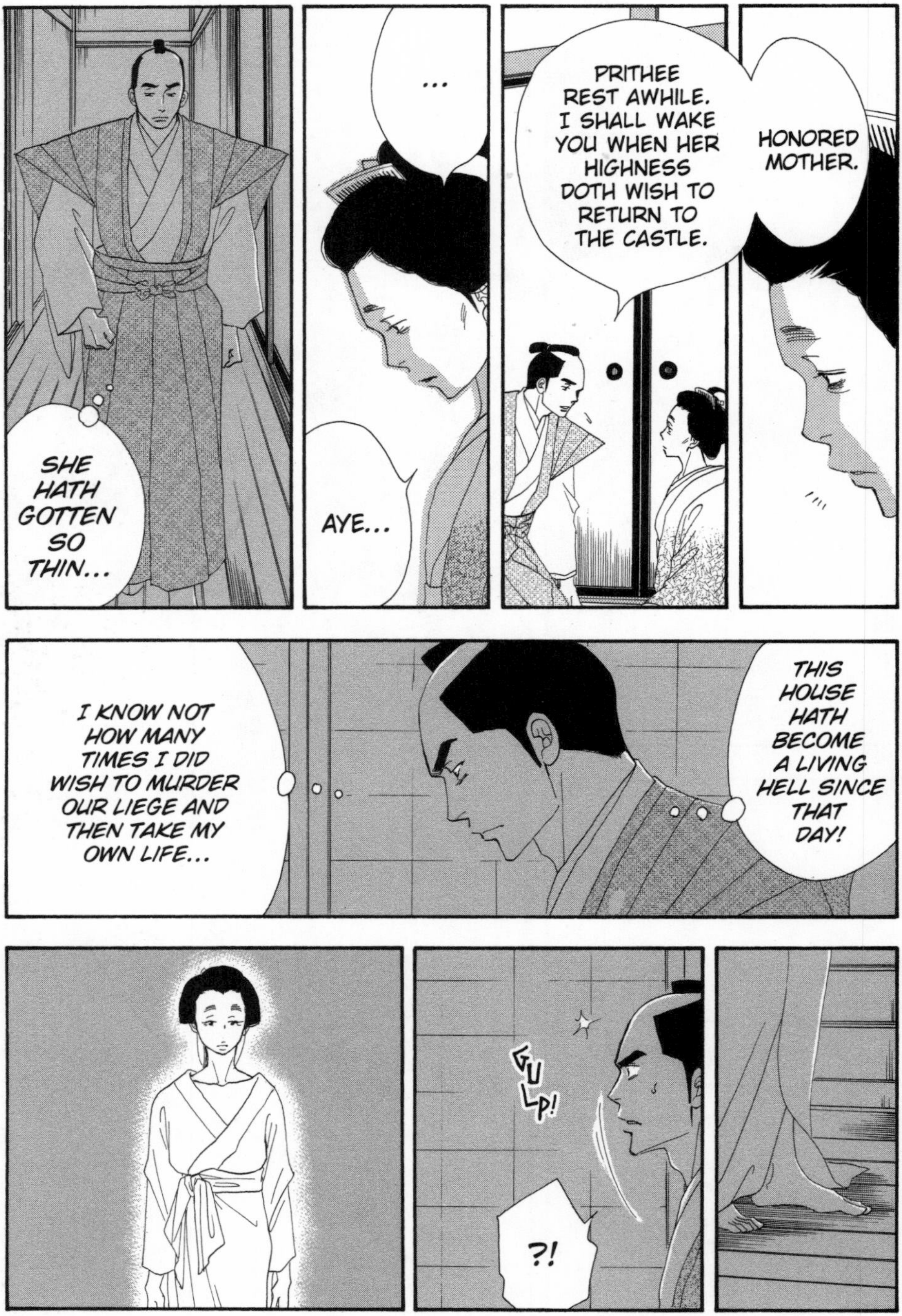
HONORED MOTHER.
PRITHEE REST AWHILE. I SHALL WAKE YOU WHEN HER HIGHNESS DOTH WISH TO RETURN TO THE CASTLE.
...
AYE...
SHE HATH GOTTEN SO THIN...
THIS HOUSE HATH BECOME A LIVING HELL SINCE THAT DAY!
I KNOW NOT HOW MANY TIMES I DID WISH TO MURDER OUR LIEGE AND THEN TAKE MY OWN LIFE...
GULP!
?!

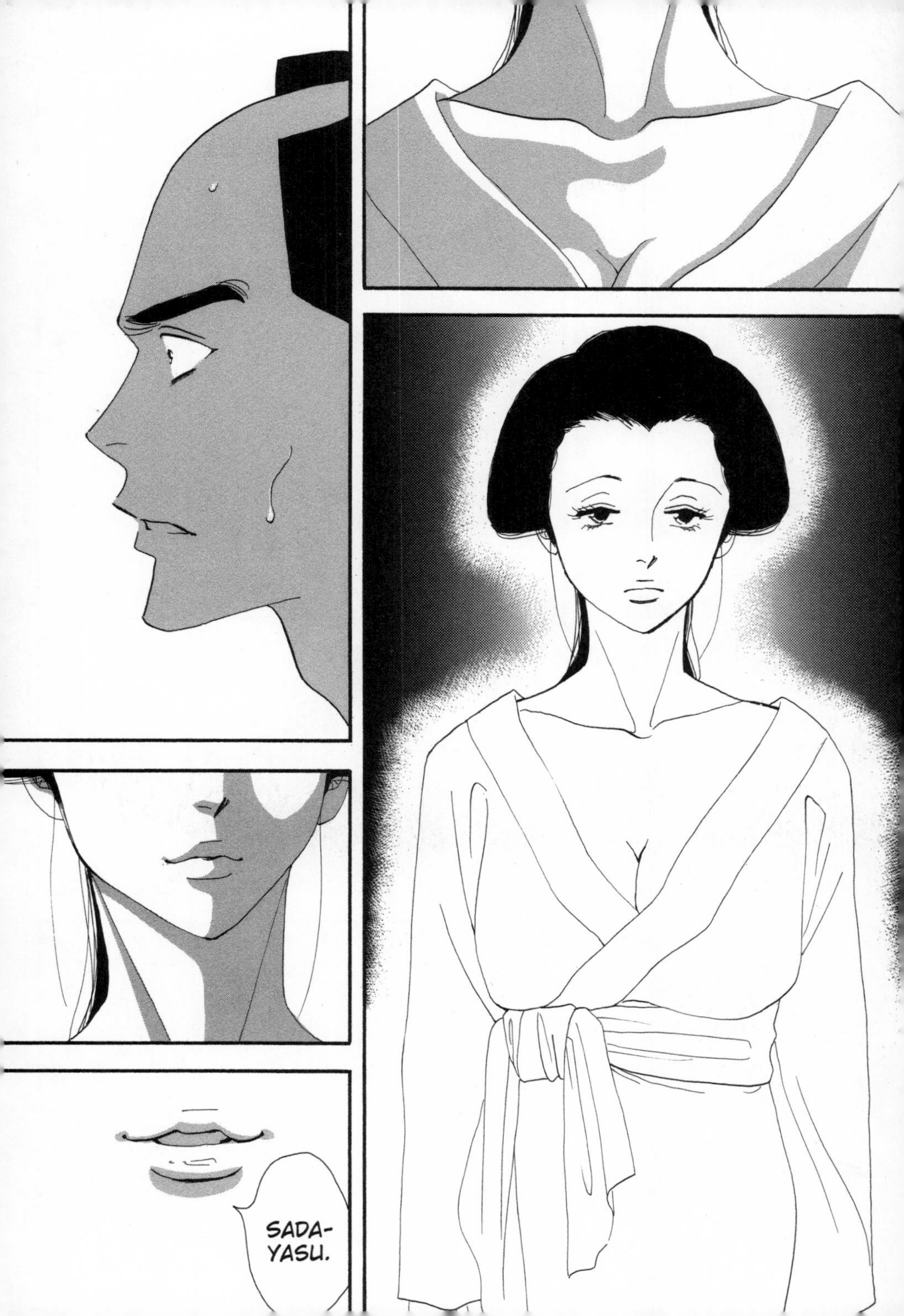
SADA-YASU.

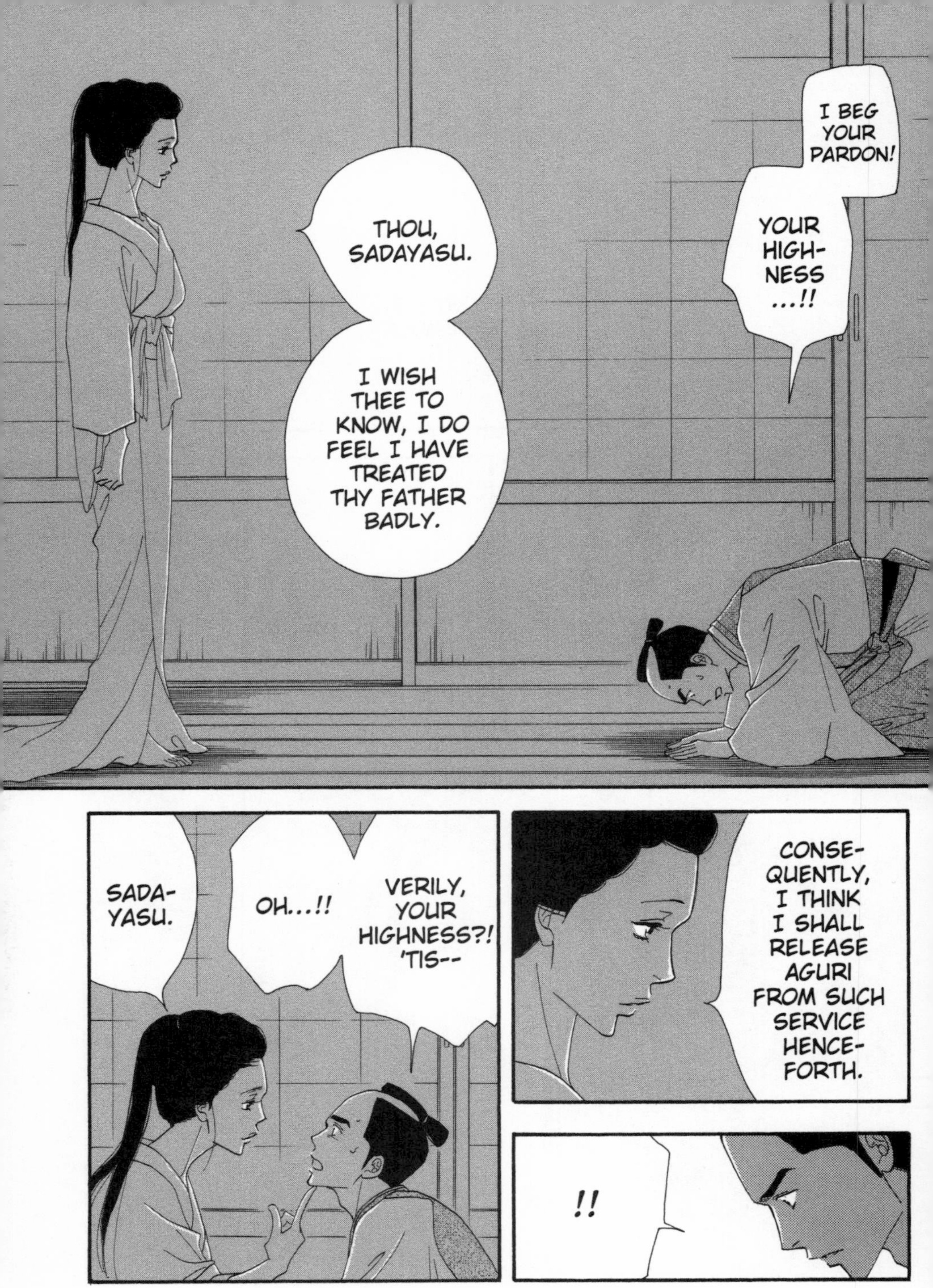
I BEG YOUR PARDON!
YOUR HIGHNESS...!!
THOU, SADAYASU.
I WISH THEE TO KNOW, I DO FEEL I HAVE TREATED THY FATHER BADLY.
CONSE-QUENTLY, I THINK I SHALL RELEASE AGURI FROM SUCH SERVICE HENCE-FORTH.
!!
VERILY, YOUR HIGHNESS?! 'TIS--
OH...!!
SADA-YASU.

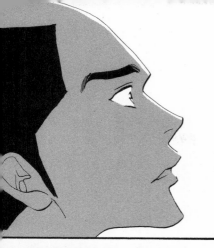
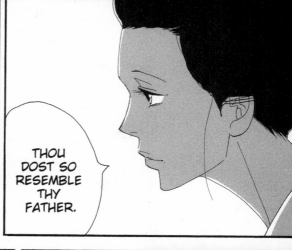

THOU
DOST SO
RESEMBLE
THY
FATHER.

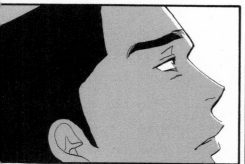
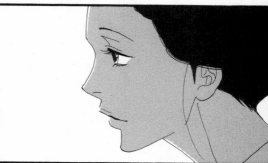

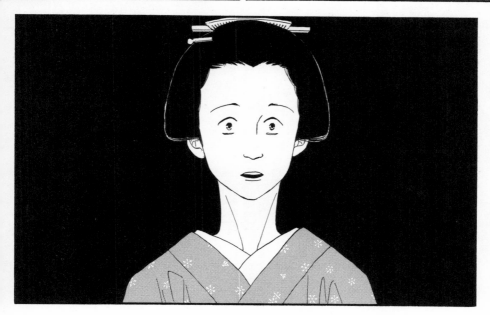

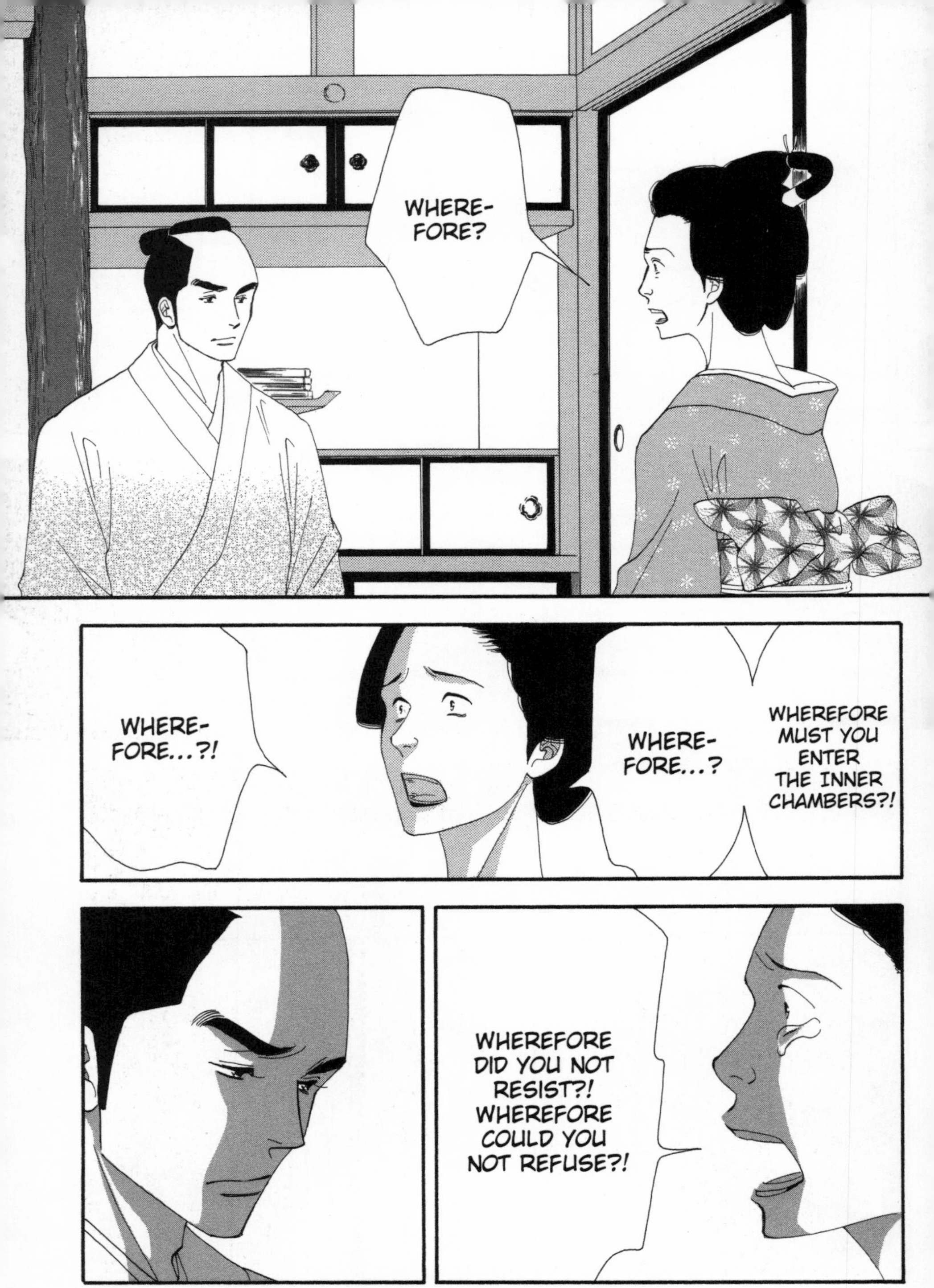
WHERE-FORE?
WHEREFORE MUST YOU ENTER THE INNER CHAMBERS?!
WHERE-FORE...?
WHERE-FORE...?!
WHEREFORE DID YOU NOT RESIST?! WHEREFORE COULD YOU NOT REFUSE?!

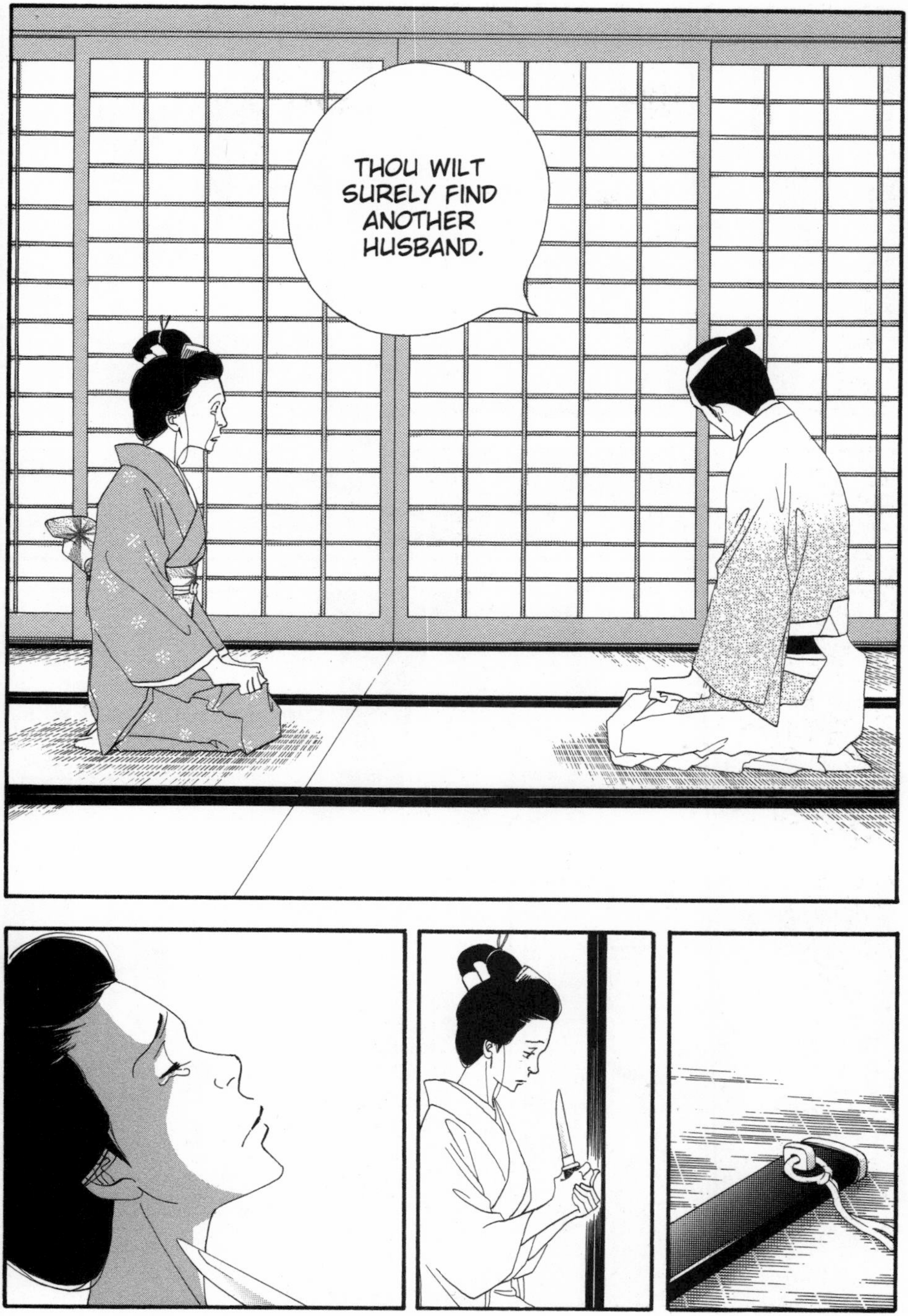
THOU WILT SURELY FIND ANOTHER HUSBAND.

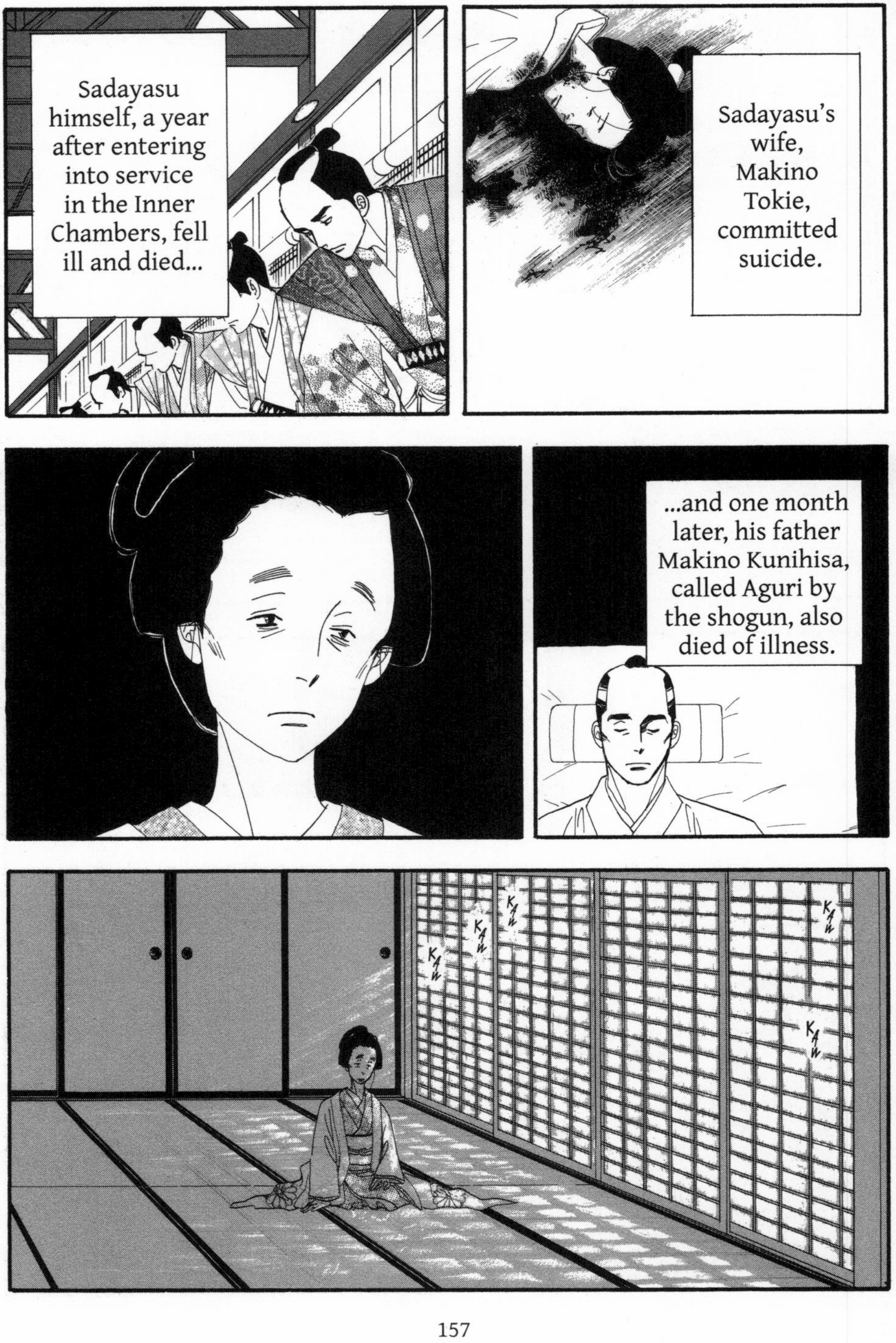
Sadayasu's wife, Makino Tokie, committed suicide.
Sadayasu himself, a year after entering into service in the Inner Chambers, fell ill and died...
...and one month later, his father Makino Kunihisa, called Aguri by the shogun, also died of illness.
KAW
KAW
KAW
KAW
KAW

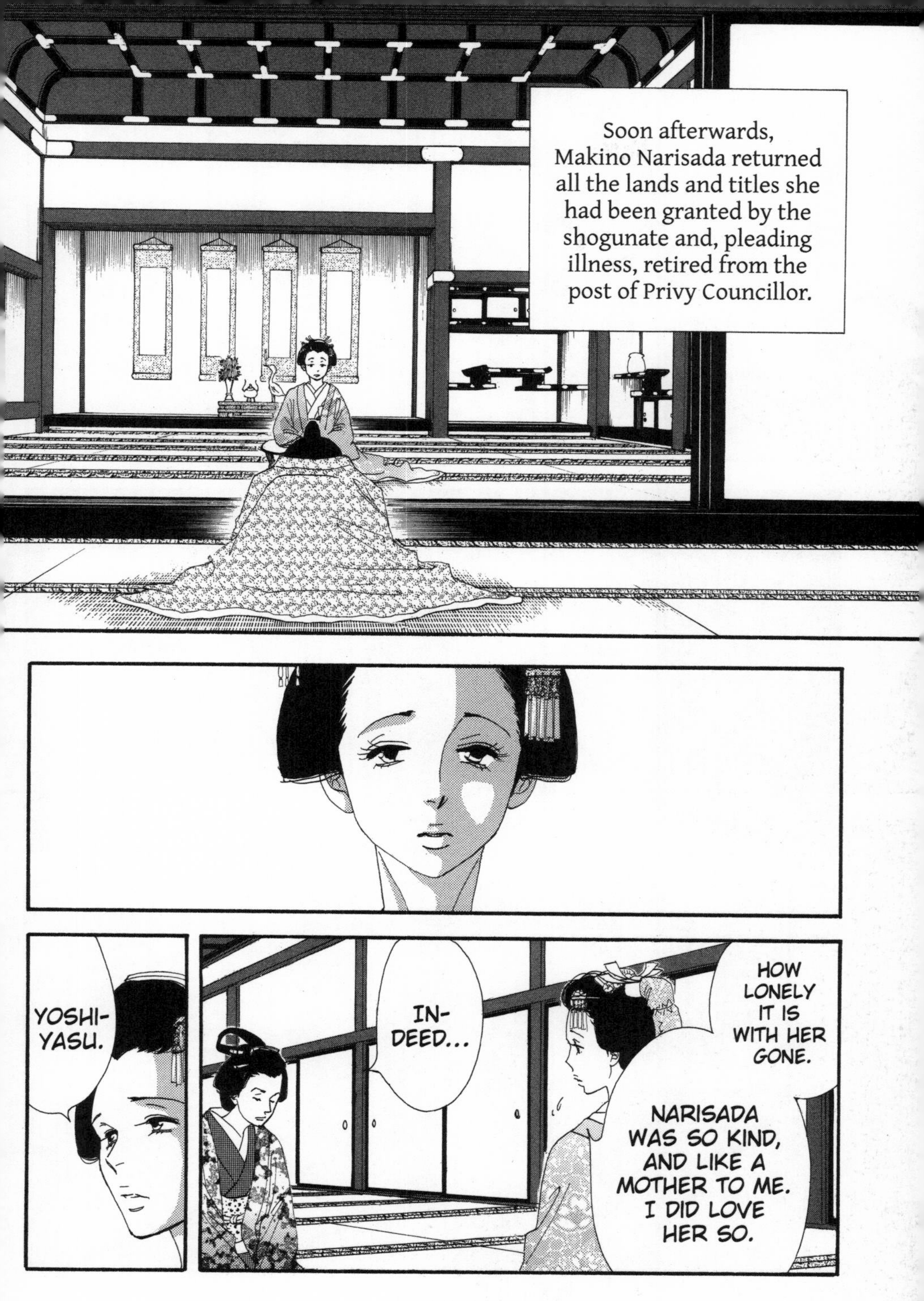
Soon afterwards, Makino Narisada returned all the lands and titles she had been granted by the shogunate and, pleading illness, retired from the post of Privy Councillor.
HOW LONELY IT IS WITH HER GONE.
NARISADA WAS SO KIND, AND LIKE A MOTHER TO ME. I DID LOVE HER SO.
IN-DEED...
YOSHI-YASU.

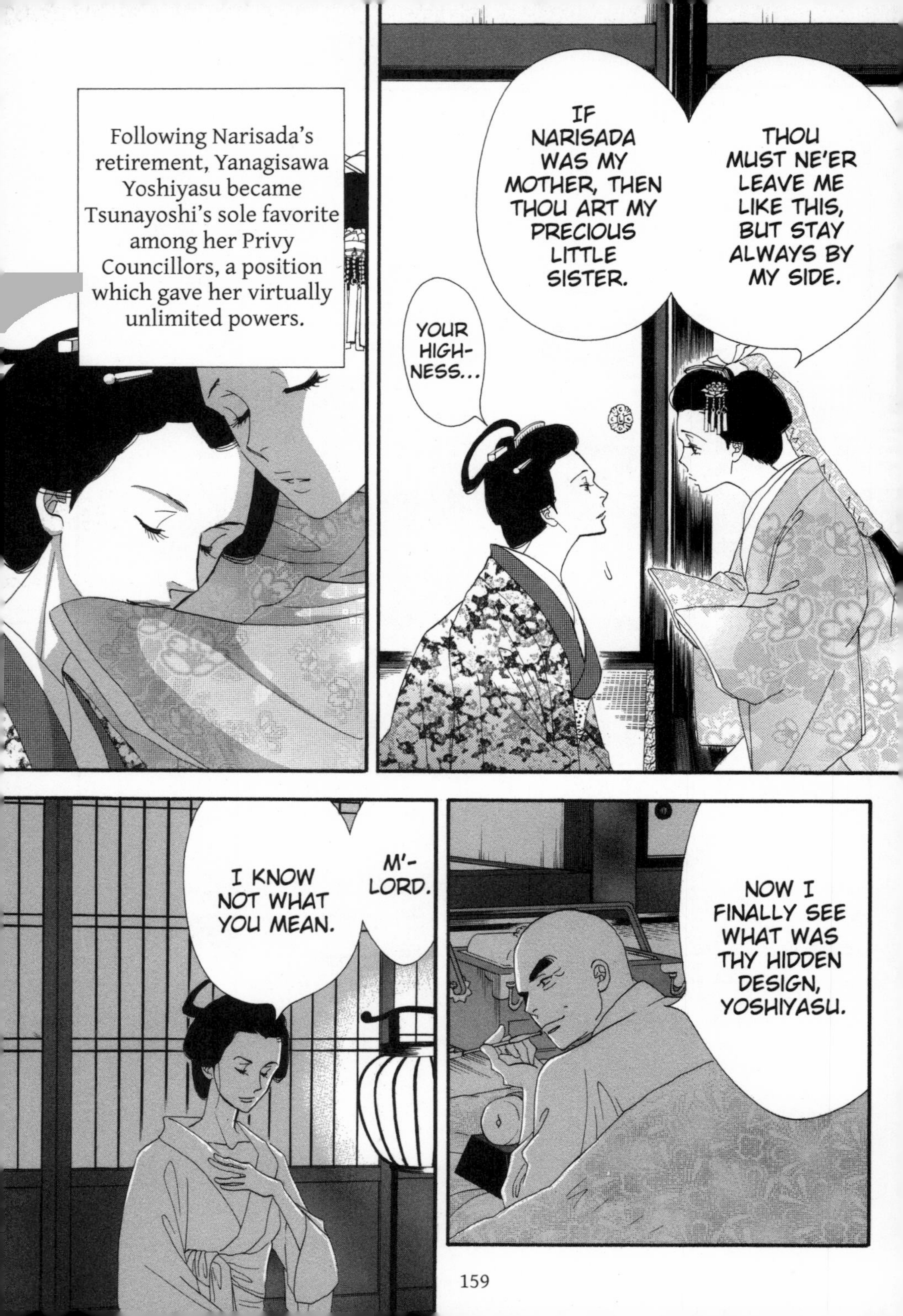
IF NARISADA WAS MY MOTHER, THEN THOU ART MY PRECIOUS LITTLE SISTER.
THOU MUST NE'ER LEAVE ME LIKE THIS, BUT STAY ALWAYS BY MY SIDE.
YOUR HIGH-NESS...
Following Narisada's retirement, Yanagisawa Yoshiyasu became Tsunayoshi's sole favorite among her Privy Councillors, a position which gave her virtually unlimited powers.
NOW I FINALLY SEE WHAT WAS THY HIDDEN DESIGN, YOSHIYASU.
M'-LORD.
I KNOW NOT WHAT YOU MEAN.

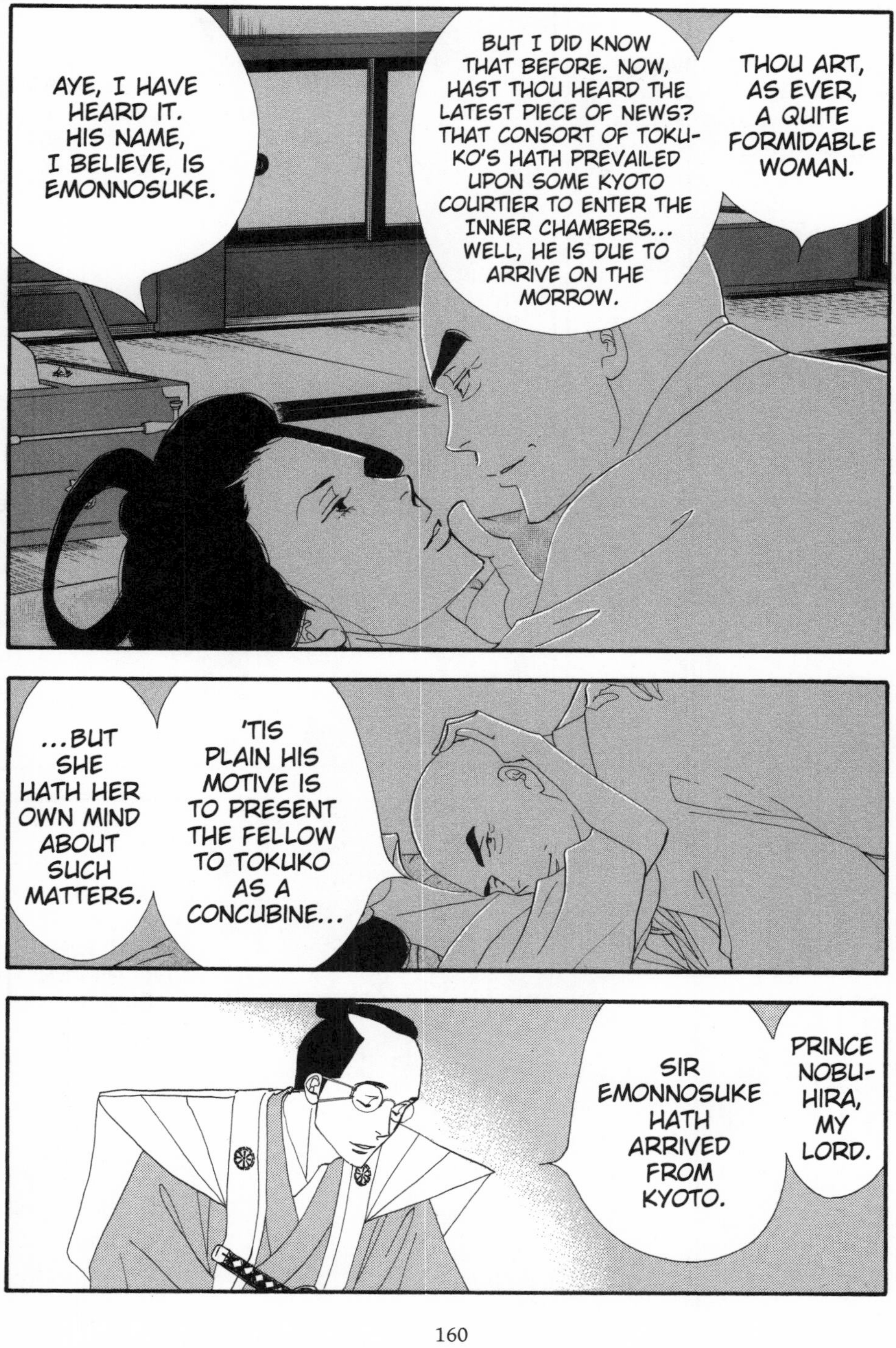
THOU ART, AS EVER, A QUITE FORMIDABLE WOMAN.
BUT I DID KNOW THAT BEFORE. NOW, HAST THOU HEARD THE LATEST PIECE OF NEWS? THAT CONSORT OF TOKU-KO'S HATH PREVAILED UPON SOME KYOTO COURTIER TO ENTER THE INNER CHAMBERS... WELL, HE IS DUE TO ARRIVE ON THE MORROW.
AYE, I HAVE HEARD IT. HIS NAME, I BELIEVE, IS EMONNOSUKE.
'TIS PLAIN HIS MOTIVE IS TO PRESENT THE FELLOW TO TOKUKO AS A CONCUBINE...
...BUT SHE HATH HER OWN MIND ABOUT SUCH MATTERS.
PRINCE NOBU-HIRA, MY LORD.
SIR EMONNOSUKE HATH ARRIVED FROM KYOTO.

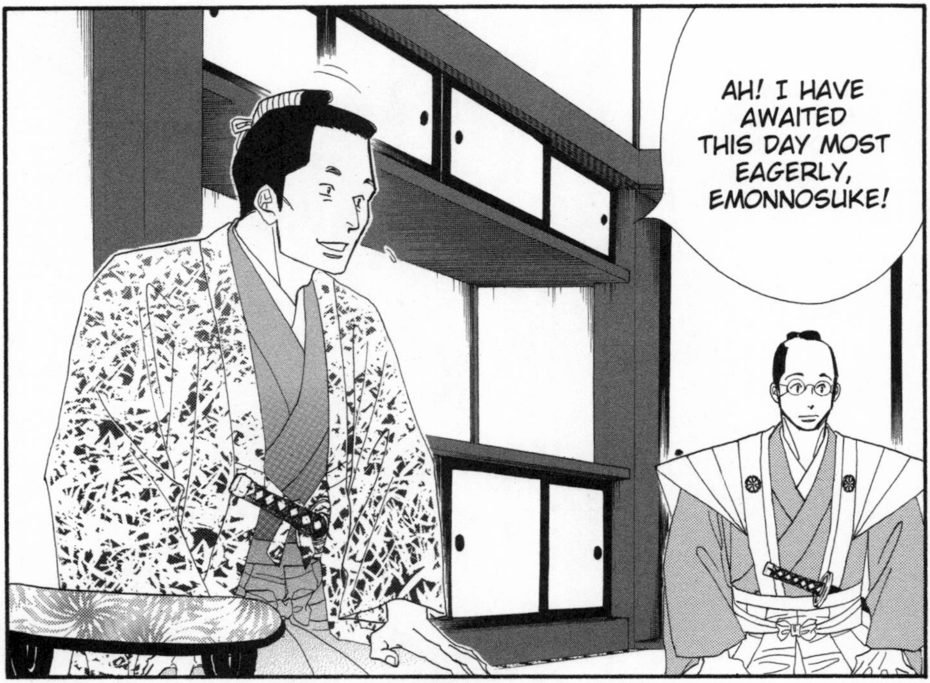
AH! I HAVE AWAITED THIS DAY MOST EAGERLY, EMONNOSUKE!

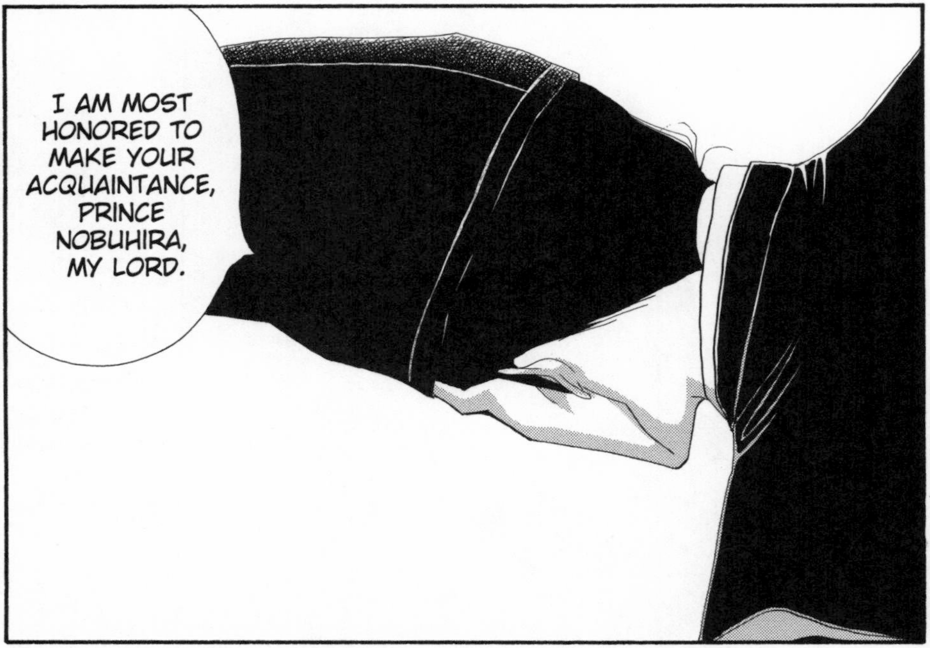
I AM MOST HONORED TO MAKE YOUR ACQUAINTANCE, PRINCE NOBUHIRA, MY LORD.

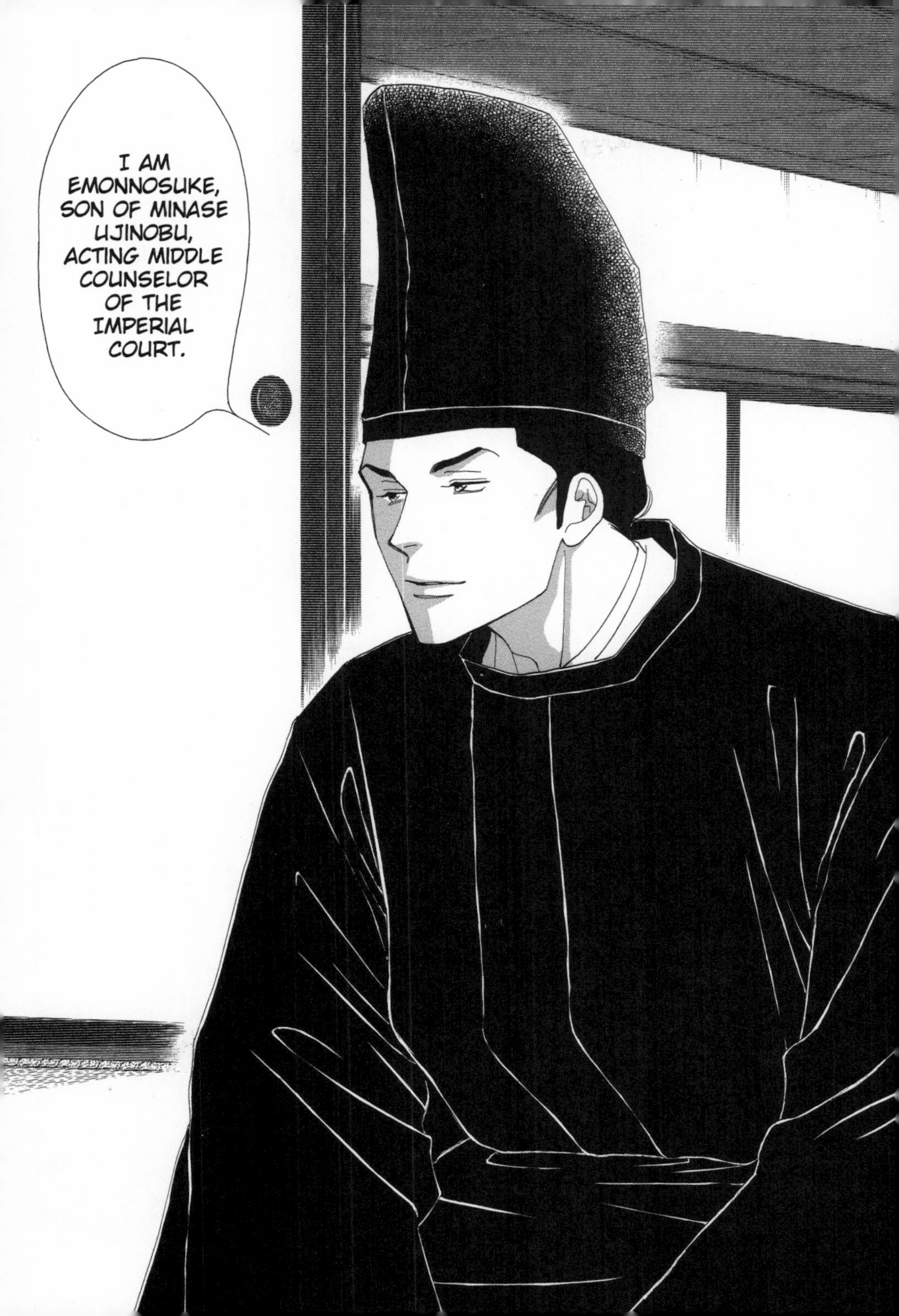
I AM EMONNOSUKE, SON OF MINASE UJINOBU, ACTING MIDDLE COUNSELOR OF THE IMPERIAL COURT.

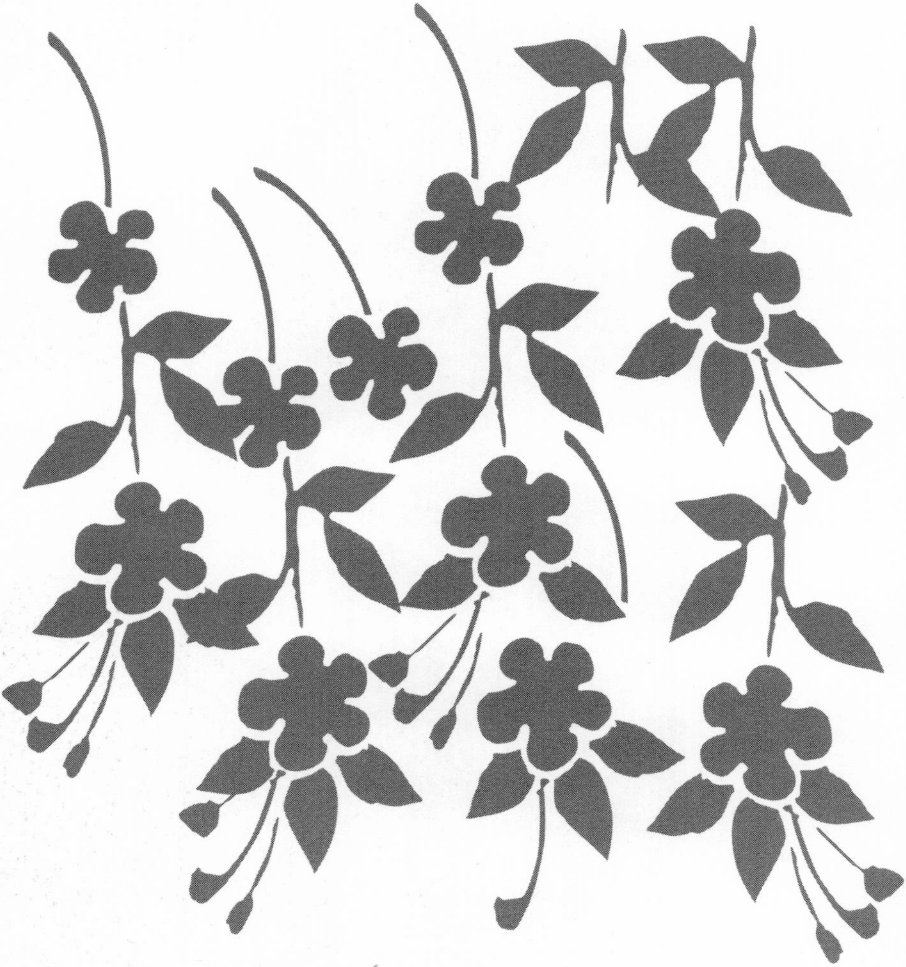

Ōoku

THE INNER CHAMBERS

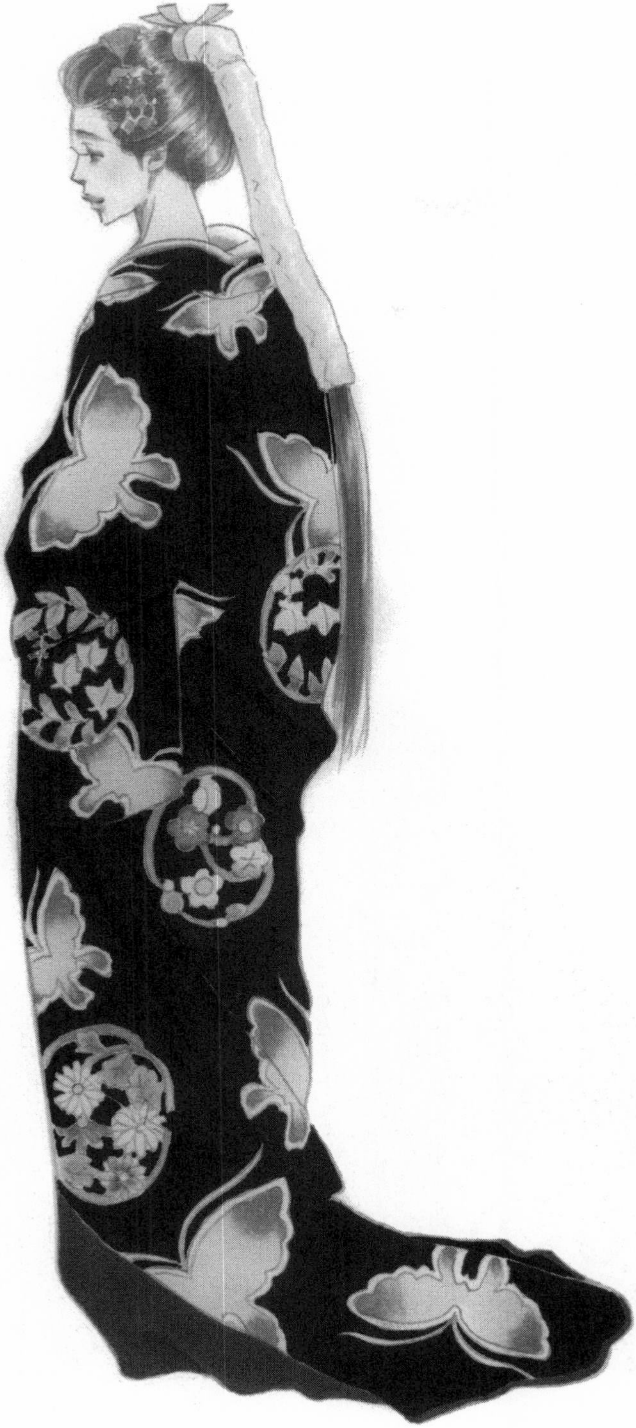

Ōoku

THE INNER CHAMBERS

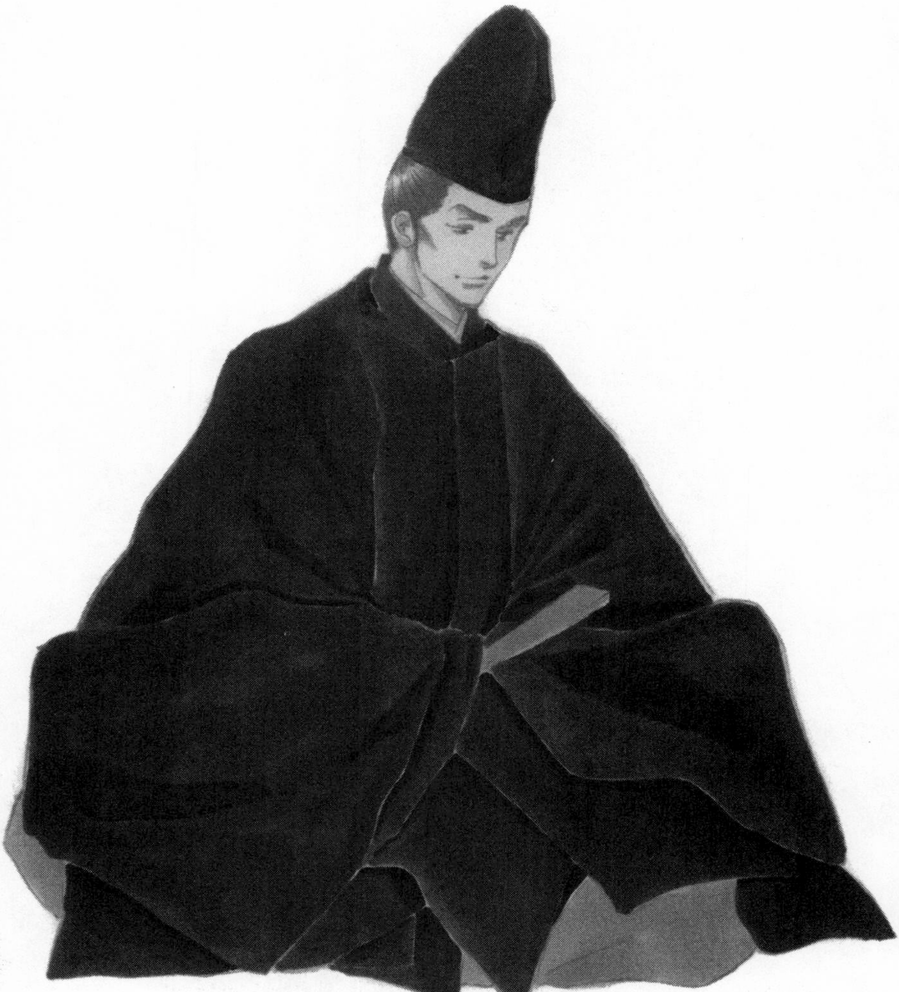

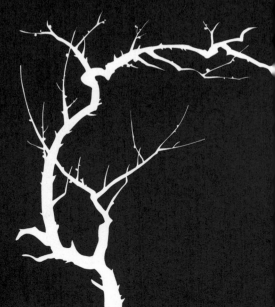

Ōoku

THE INNER CHAMBERS

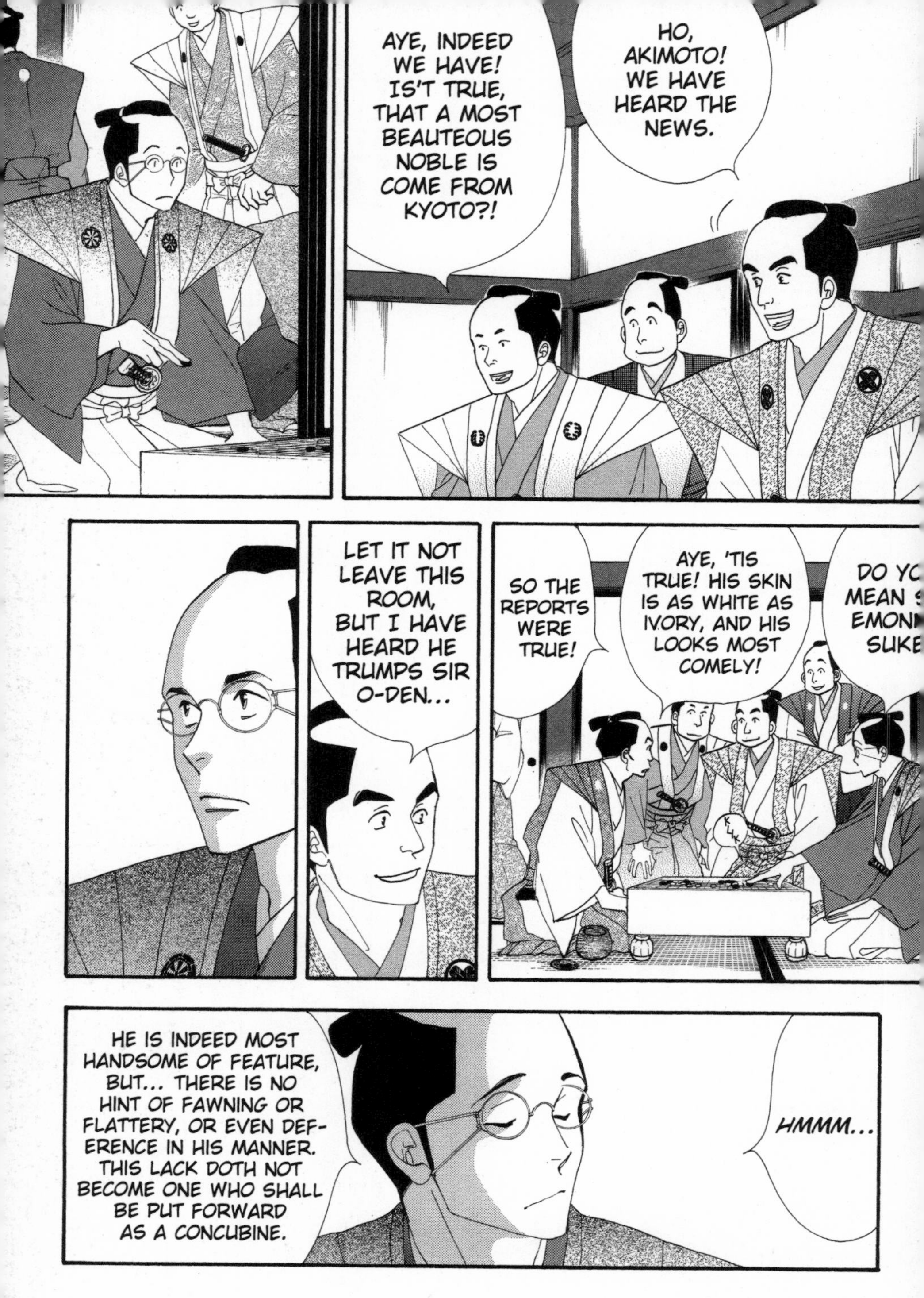
HO, AKIMOTO! WE HAVE HEARD THE NEWS.
AYE, INDEED WE HAVE! IS'T TRUE, THAT A MOST BEAUTEOUS NOBLE IS COME FROM KYOTO?!
DO YO MEAN S EMON SUKE
AYE, 'TIS TRUE! HIS SKIN IS AS WHITE AS IVORY, AND HIS LOOKS MOST COMELY!
SO THE REPORTS WERE TRUE!
LET IT NOT LEAVE THIS ROOM, BUT I HAVE HEARD HE TRUMPS SIR O-DEN...
HMMM...
HE IS INDEED MOST HANDSOME OF FEATURE, BUT... THERE IS NO HINT OF FAWNING OR FLATTERY, OR EVEN DEFERENCE IN HIS MANNER. THIS LACK DOTH NOT BECOME ONE WHO SHALL BE PUT FORWARD AS A CONCUBINE.

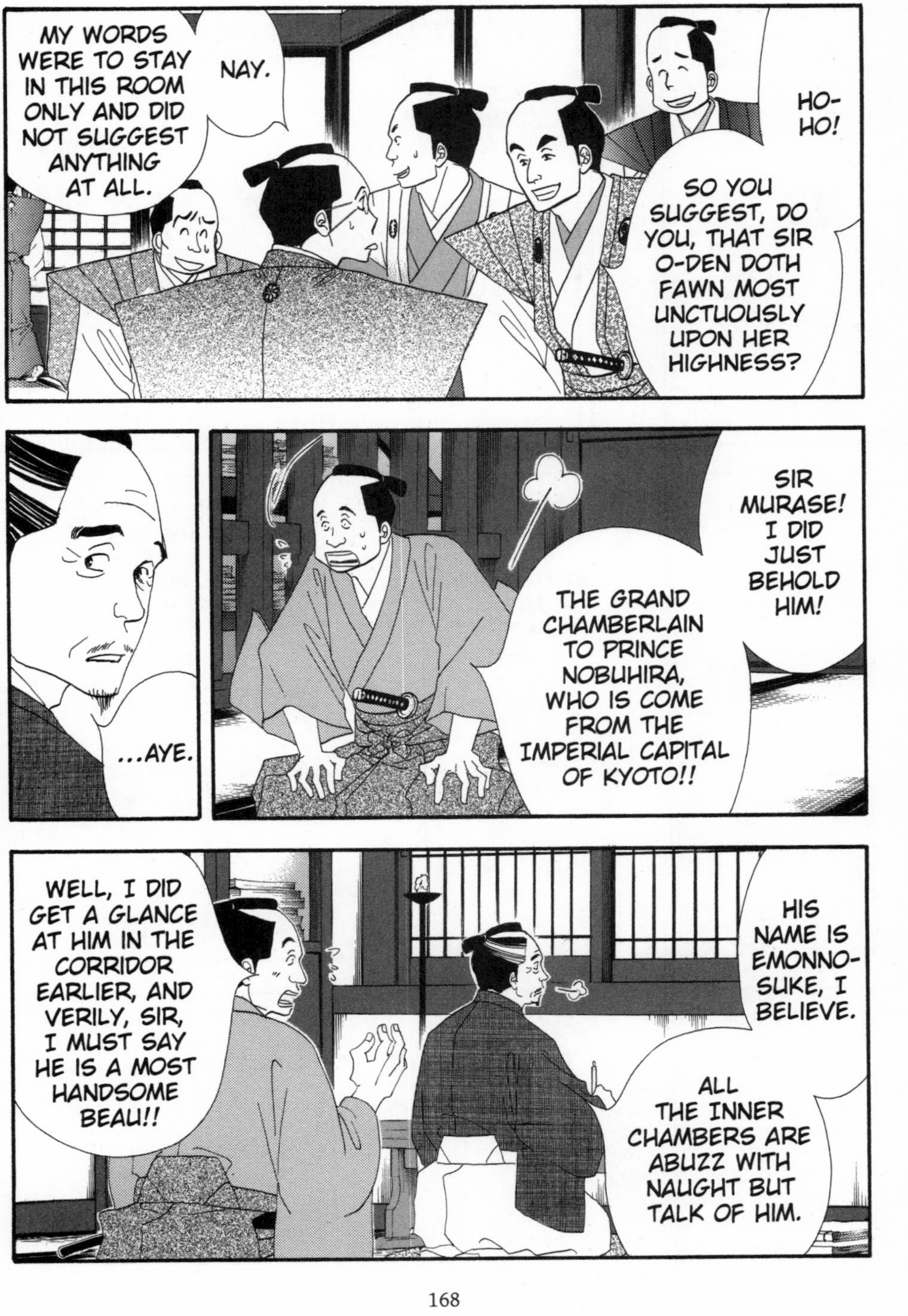
HO-HO!
SO YOU SUGGEST, DO YOU, THAT SIR O-DEN DOTH FAWN MOST UNCTUOUSLY UPON HER HIGHNESS?
NAY.
MY WORDS WERE TO STAY IN THIS ROOM ONLY AND DID NOT SUGGEST ANYTHING AT ALL.
SIR MURASE! I DID JUST BEHOLD HIM!
THE GRAND CHAMBERLAIN TO PRINCE NOBUHIRA, WHO IS COME FROM THE IMPERIAL CAPITAL OF KYOTO!!
...AYE.
HIS NAME IS EMONNO-SUKE, I BELIEVE.
ALL THE INNER CHAMBERS ARE ABUZZ WITH NAUGHT BUT TALK OF HIM.
WELL, I DID GET A GLANCE AT HIM IN THE CORRIDOR EARLIER, AND VERILY, SIR, I MUST SAY HE IS A MOST HANDSOME BEAU!!

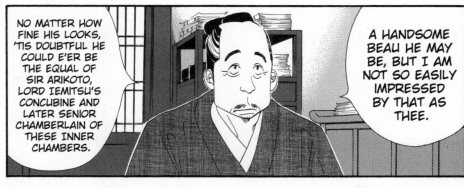

A HANDSOME BEAU HE MAY BE, BUT I AM NOT SO EASILY IMPRESSED BY THAT AS THEE.
NO MATTER HOW FINE HIS LOOKS, 'TIS DOUBTFUL HE COULD E'ER BE THE EQUAL OF SIR ARIKOTO, LORD IEMITSU'S CONCUBINE AND LATER SENIOR CHAMBERLAIN OF THESE INNER CHAMBERS.
SIR KEISHO-IN, SIR KEISHO-IN!!
'TIS REPORTED THAT A KYOTO NOBLE BY THE NAME OF EMONNOSUKE IS COME TO THE INNER CHAMBERS, AND THAT HE BE FEARSOMELY BEAUTEOUS!!
'TIS HARDLY NEWS YOU BRING ME—I HAVE HEARD IT LONG AGO!!
HMPH...
I HAVE HEARD ALSO THAT THE FELLOW DID NOT CHANGE HIS ATTIRE TO ENTER EDO CASTLE BUT DID ARRIVE IN HIS COURTIER'S ROBES.
FROM THIS WE MAY ASSUME HE IS JUST ANOTHER IMPOVERISHED ARISTOCRAT'S SON, TOO DESTITUTE EVEN TO HAVE AN EDO-STYLE KAMISHIMO MADE FOR THE OCCASION. I LOOK FORWARD TO RECEIVING HIM.

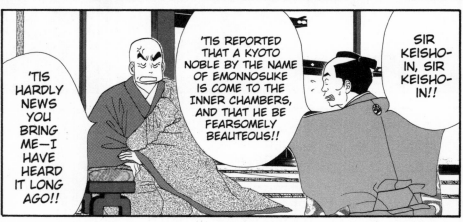

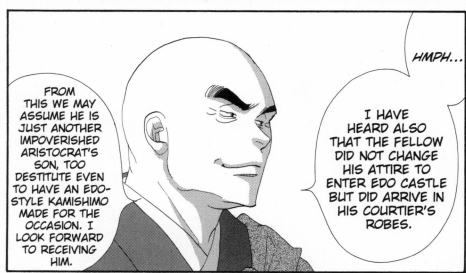

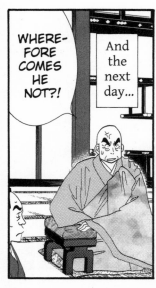

How-ever...
...
WHERE IS HE?
And the next day...
WHERE-FORE COMES HE NOT?!
And still, on the third day...
HOW DARE THIS FELLOW NEGLECT ME LIKE THIS?!
I AM THE FATHER OF THE SHOGUN! 'TIS A GROTESQUE BREACH OF COURTESY THAT HE DOTH NOT CALL ON ME!
SIR KEISHO-IN!!
JUST NOW! JUST NOW EMONNOSUKE IS COME BEGGING TO BE ALLOWED THE HONOR OF PAYING HIS RESPECTS TO YOUR EXCELLENCY!

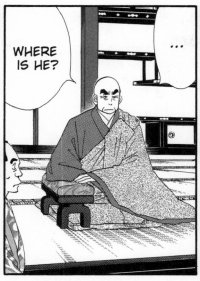

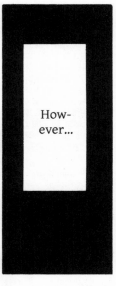

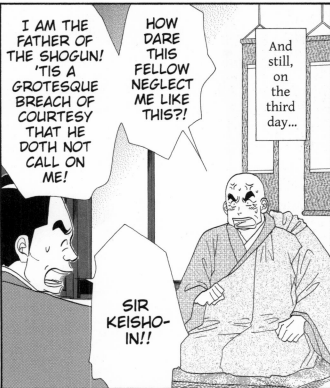

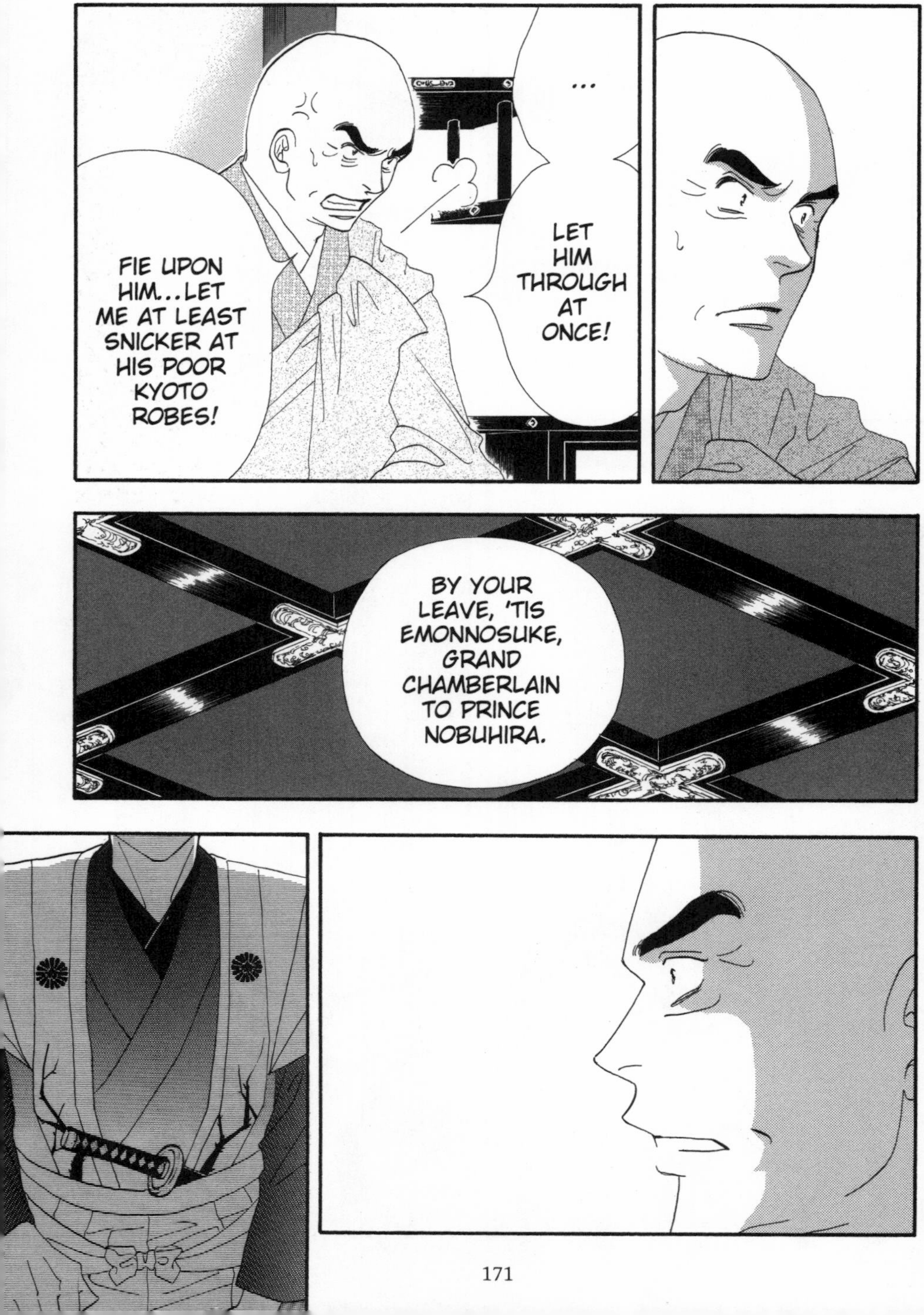
...
LET HIM THROUGH AT ONCE!
FIE UPON HIM...LET ME AT LEAST SNICKER AT HIS POOR KYOTO ROBES!
BY YOUR LEAVE, 'TIS EMONNOSUKE, GRAND CHAMBERLAIN TO PRINCE NOBUHIRA.

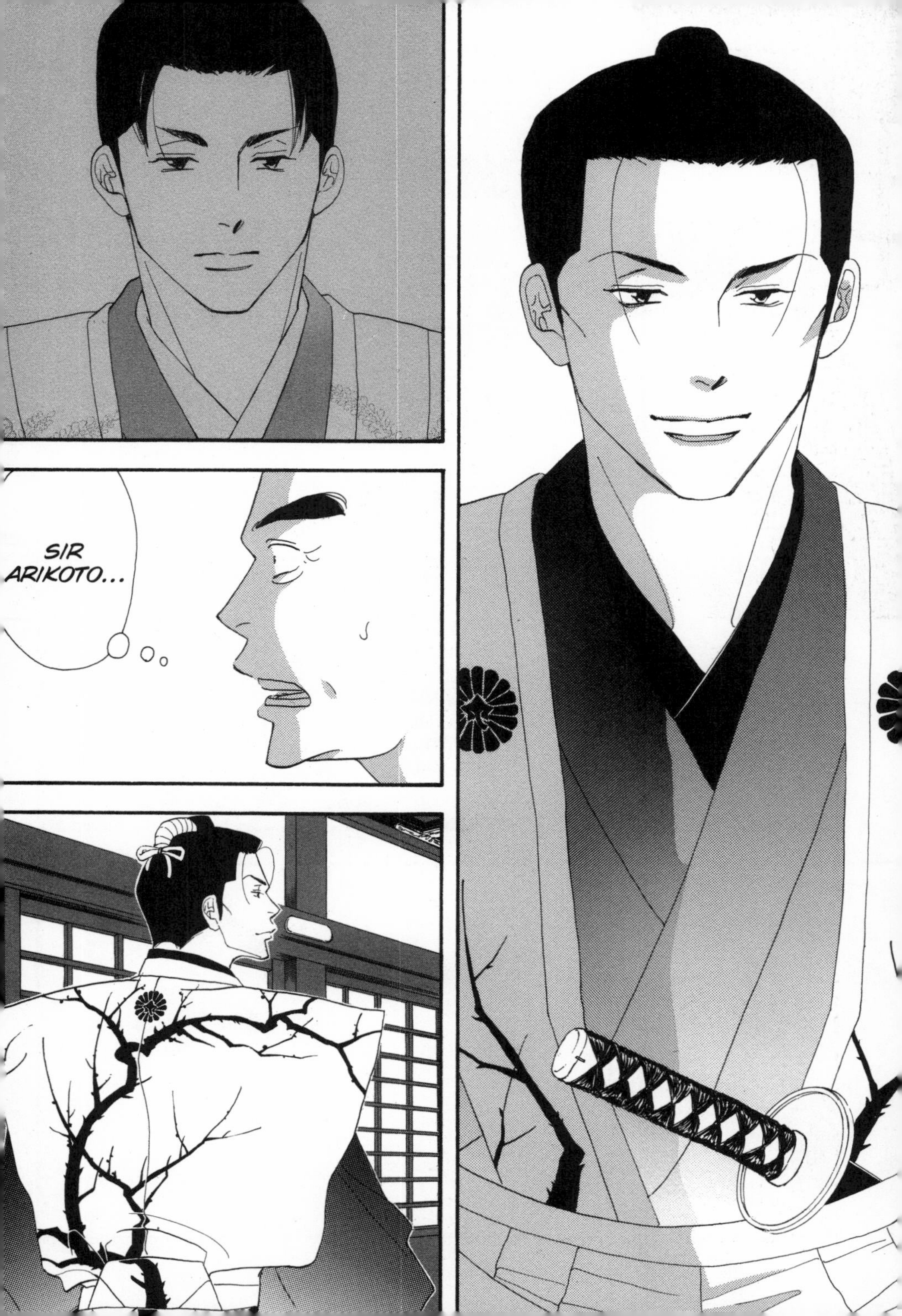
SIR ARIKOTO...

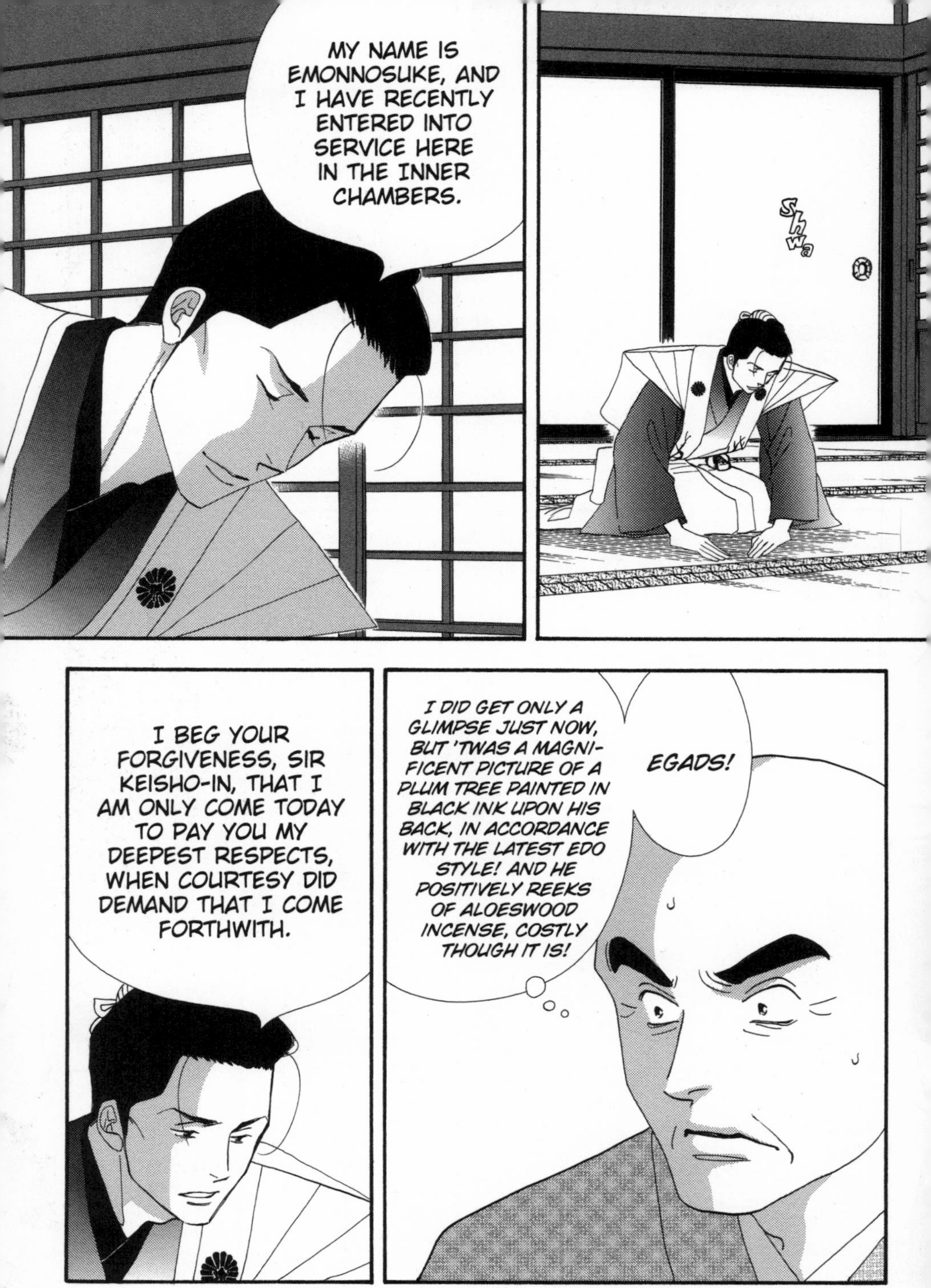
Shwa
MY NAME IS EMONNOSUKE, AND I HAVE RECENTLY ENTERED INTO SERVICE HERE IN THE INNER CHAMBERS.
EGADS!
I DID GET ONLY A GLIMPSE JUST NOW, BUT 'TWAS A MAGNIFICENT PICTURE OF A PLUM TREE PAINTED IN BLACK INK UPON HIS BACK, IN ACCORDANCE WITH THE LATEST EDO STYLE! AND HE POSITIVELY REEKS OF ALOESWOOD INCENSE, COSTLY THOUGH IT IS!
I BEG YOUR FORGIVENESS, SIR KEISHO-IN, THAT I AM ONLY COME TODAY TO PAY YOU MY DEEPEST RESPECTS, WHEN COURTESY DID DEMAND THAT I COME FORTHWITH.

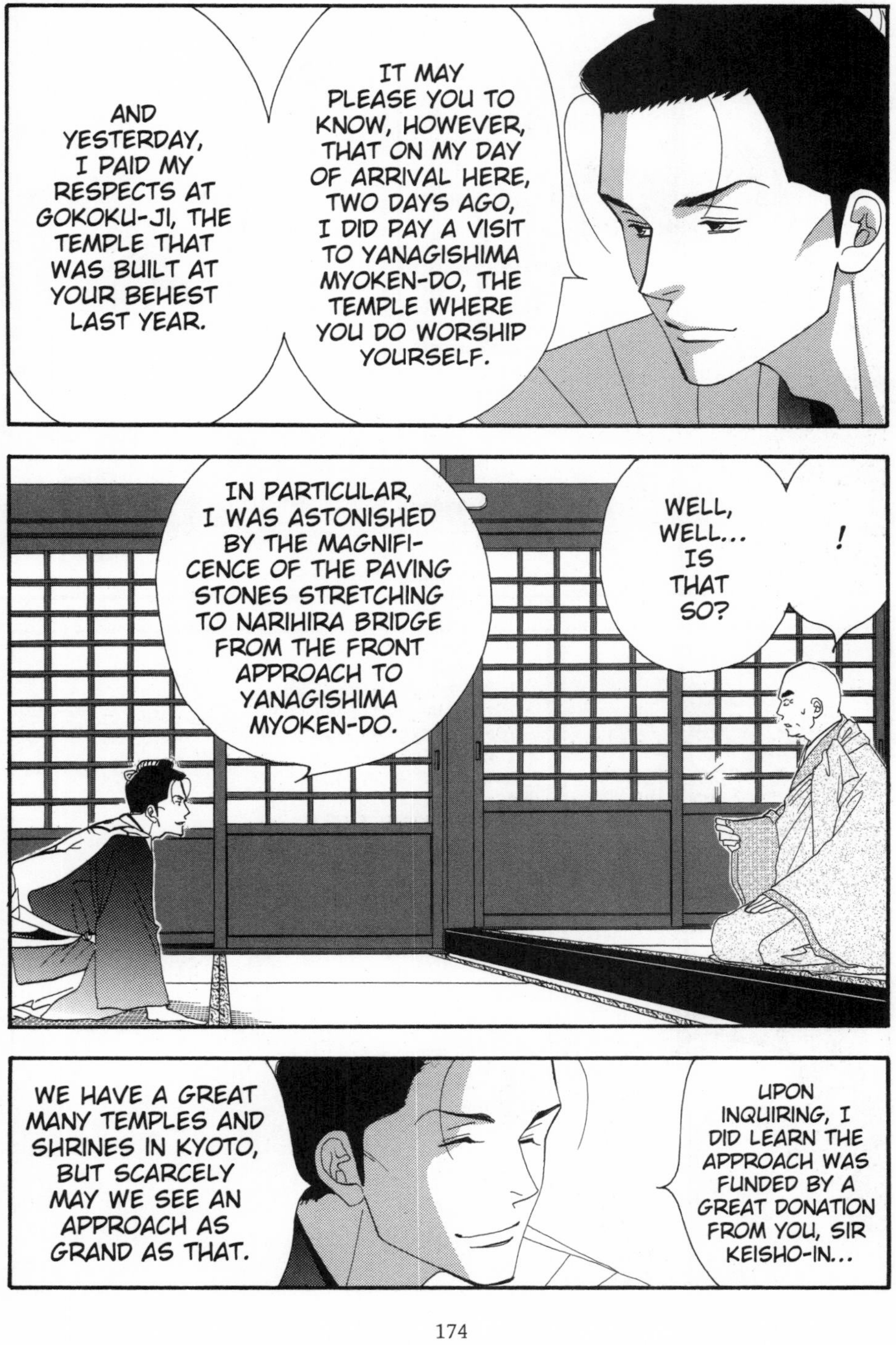
IT MAY PLEASE YOU TO KNOW, HOWEVER, THAT ON MY DAY OF ARRIVAL HERE, TWO DAYS AGO, I DID PAY A VISIT TO YANAGISHIMA MYOKEN-DO, THE TEMPLE WHERE YOU DO WORSHIP YOURSELF.
AND YESTERDAY, I PAID MY RESPECTS AT GOKOKU-JI, THE TEMPLE THAT WAS BUILT AT YOUR BEHEST LAST YEAR.
WELL, WELL... IS THAT SO?
!
IN PARTICULAR, I WAS ASTONISHED BY THE MAGNIFICENCE OF THE PAVING STONES STRETCHING TO NARIHIRA BRIDGE FROM THE FRONT APPROACH TO YANAGISHIMA MYOKEN-DO.
UPON INQUIRING, I DID LEARN THE APPROACH WAS FUNDED BY A GREAT DONATION FROM YOU, SIR KEISHO-IN...
WE HAVE A GREAT MANY TEMPLES AND SHRINES IN KYOTO, BUT SCARCELY MAY WE SEE AN APPROACH AS GRAND AS THAT.

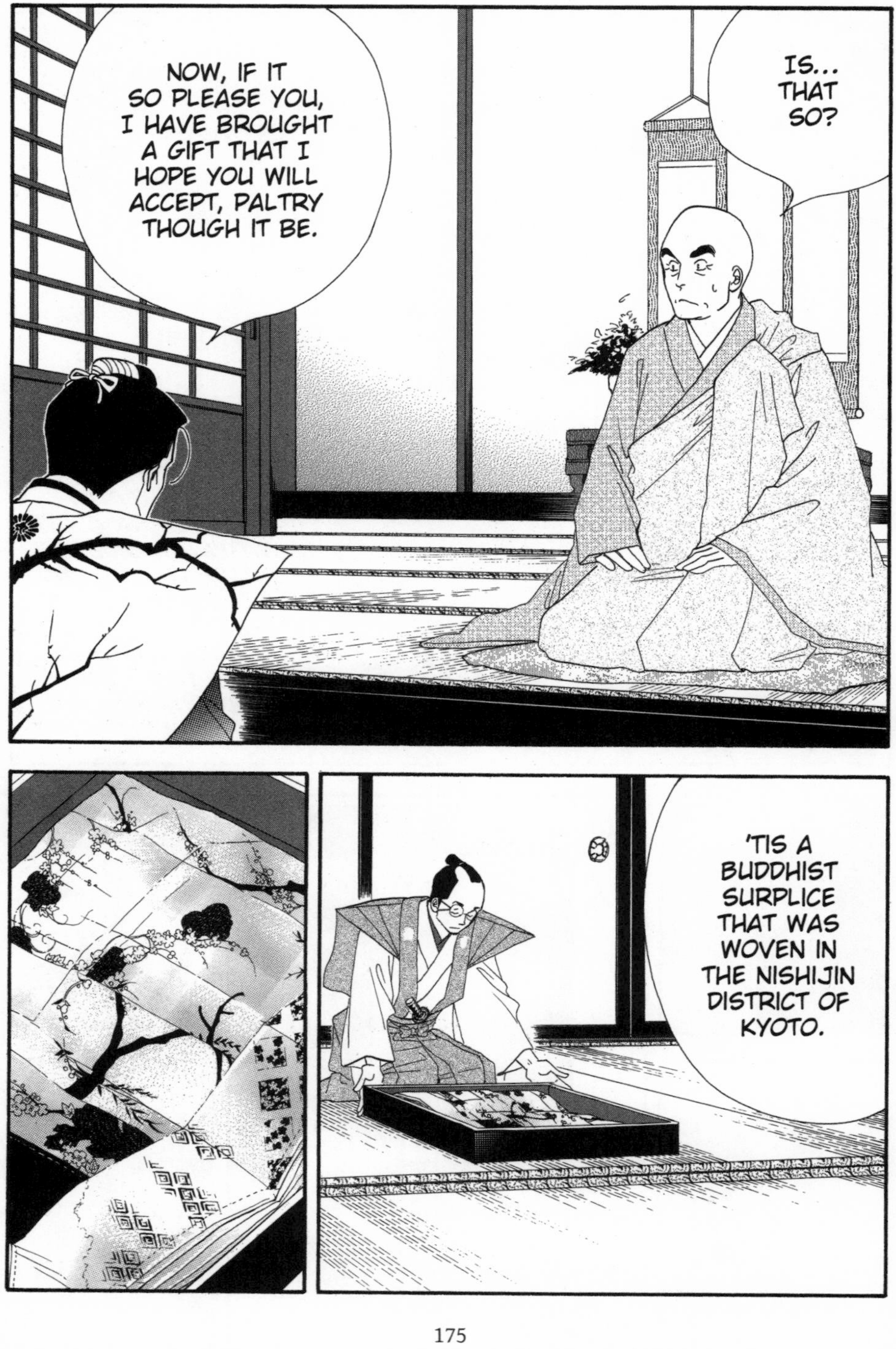
IS... THAT SO?
NOW, IF IT SO PLEASE YOU, I HAVE BROUGHT A GIFT THAT I HOPE YOU WILL ACCEPT, PALTRY THOUGH IT BE.
'TIS A BUDDHIST SURPLICE THAT WAS WOVEN IN THE NISHIJIN DISTRICT OF KYOTO.

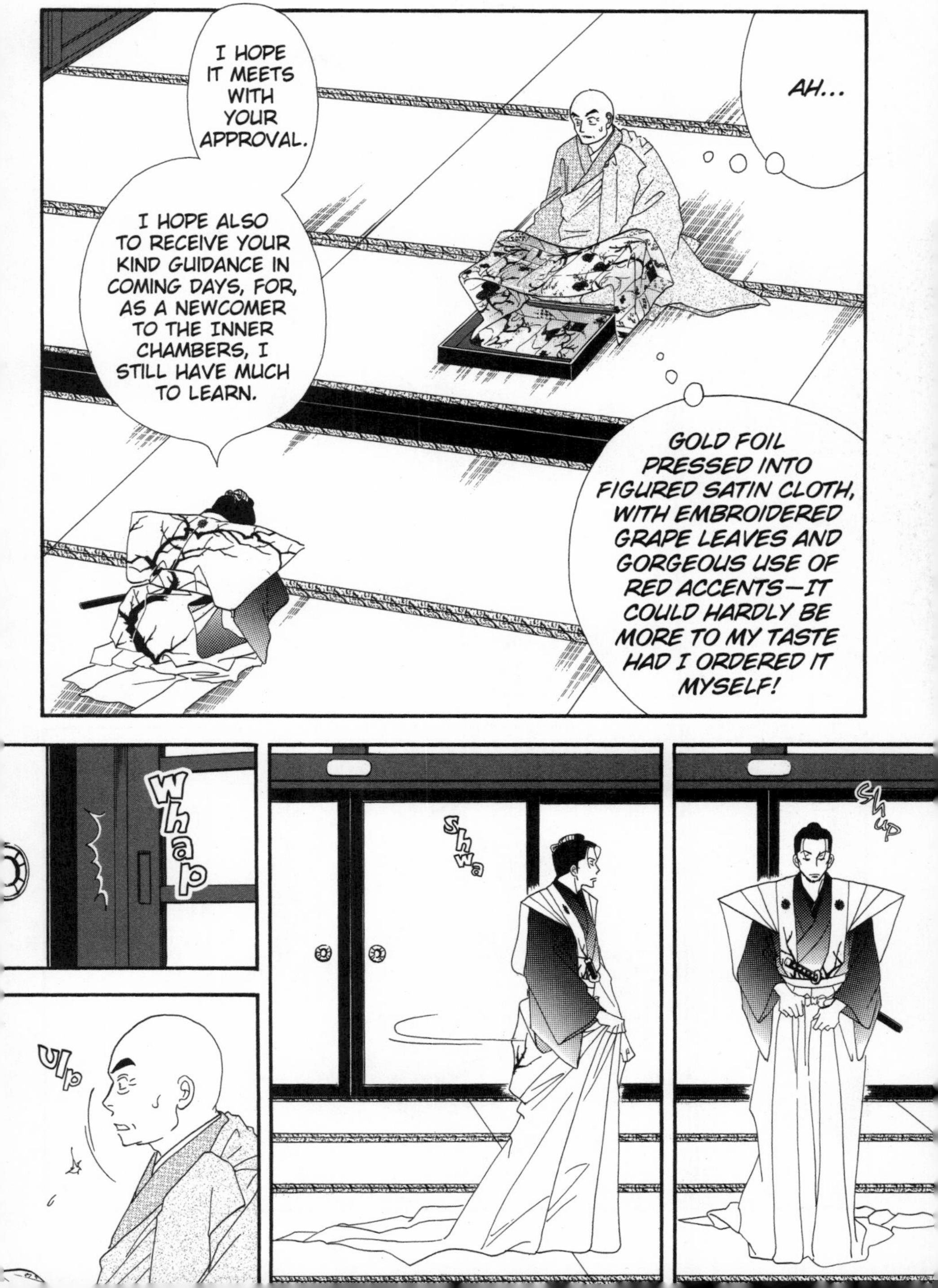
AH...
I HOPE IT MEETS WITH YOUR APPROVAL.
I HOPE ALSO TO RECEIVE YOUR KIND GUIDANCE IN COMING DAYS, FOR, AS A NEWCOMER TO THE INNER CHAMBERS, I STILL HAVE MUCH TO LEARN.
GOLD FOIL PRESSED INTO FIGURED SATIN CLOTH, WITH EMBROIDERED GRAPE LEAVES AND GORGEOUS USE OF RED ACCENTS—IT COULD HARDLY BE MORE TO MY TASTE HAD I ORDERED IT MYSELF!
Shup
Shwa
Whap
Ulp

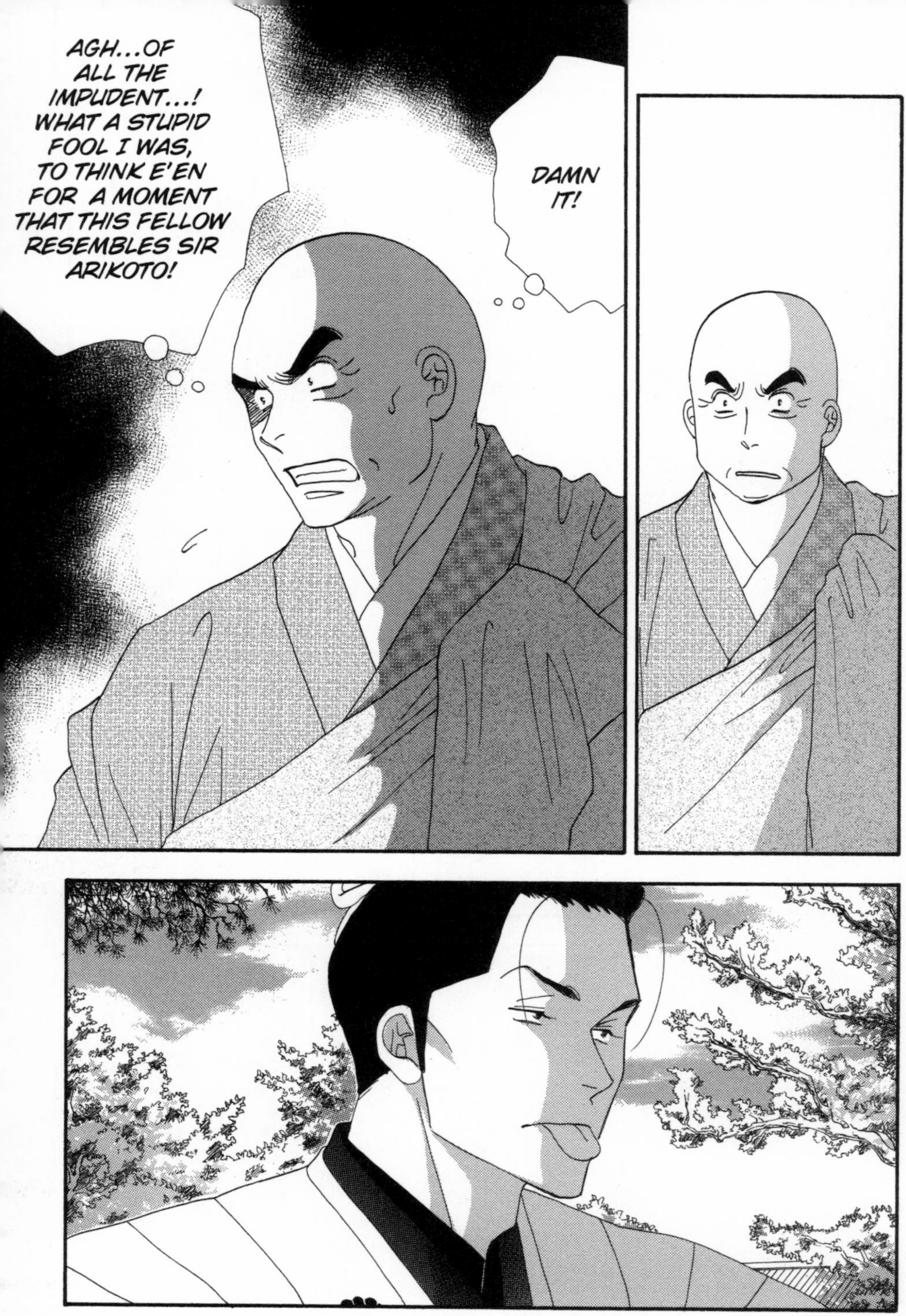
DAMN IT!
AGH...OF ALL THE IMPUDENT...! WHAT A STUPID FOOL I WAS, TO THINK E'EN FOR A MOMENT THAT THIS FELLOW RESEMBLES SIR ARIKOTO!

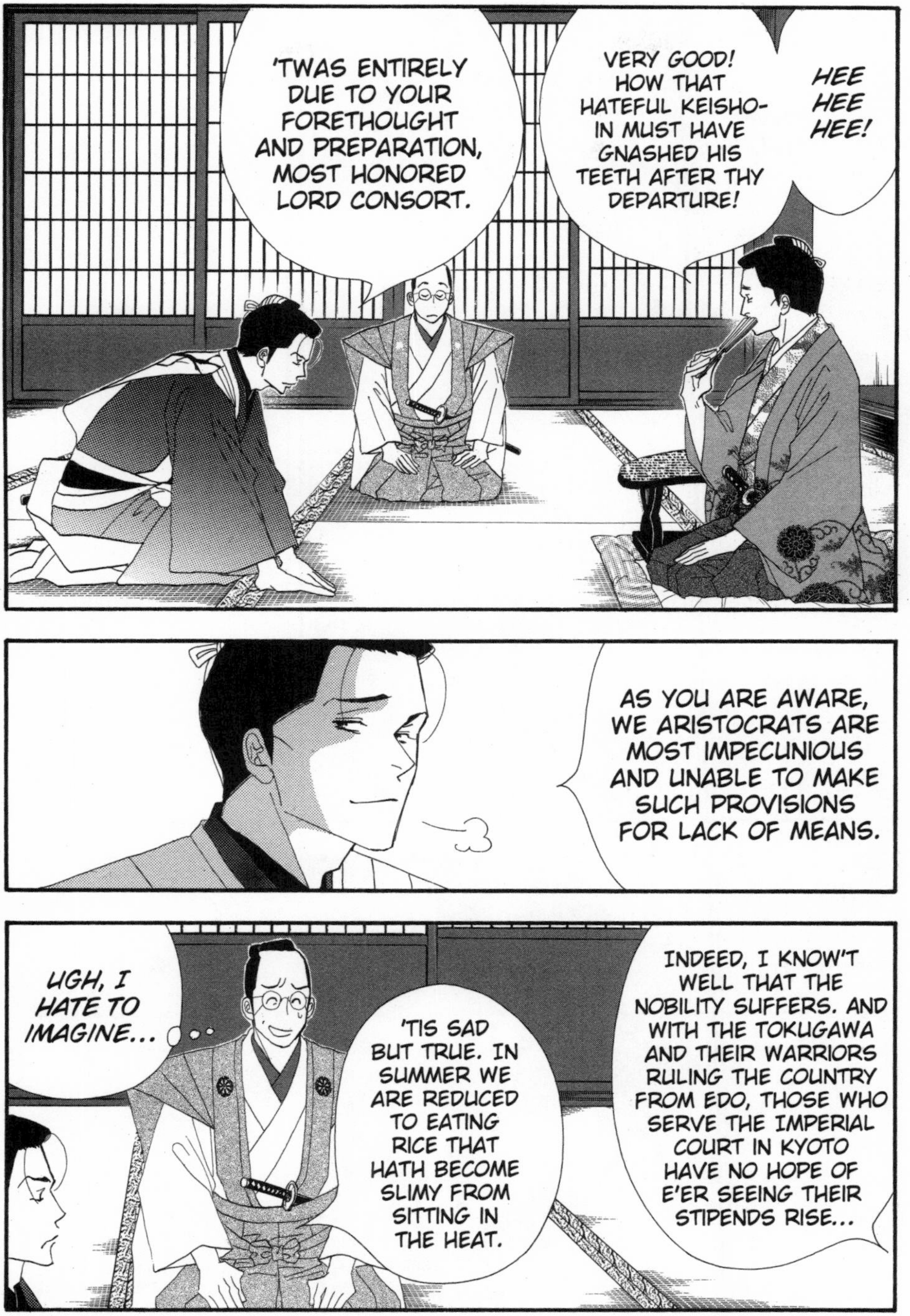
VERY GOOD! HOW THAT HATEFUL KEISHO-IN MUST HAVE GNASHED HIS TEETH AFTER THY DEPARTURE!
HEE HEE HEE!
'TWAS ENTIRELY DUE TO YOUR FORETHOUGHT AND PREPARATION, MOST HONORED LORD CONSORT.
AS YOU ARE AWARE, WE ARISTOCRATS ARE MOST IMPECUNIOUS AND UNABLE TO MAKE SUCH PROVISIONS FOR LACK OF MEANS.
INDEED, I KNOW'T WELL THAT THE NOBILITY SUFFERS. AND WITH THE TOKUGAWA AND THEIR WARRIORS RULING THE COUNTRY FROM EDO, THOSE WHO SERVE THE IMPERIAL COURT IN KYOTO HAVE NO HOPE OF E'ER SEEING THEIR STIPENDS RISE...
'TIS SAD BUT TRUE. IN SUMMER WE ARE REDUCED TO EATING RICE THAT HATH BECOME SLIMY FROM SITTING IN THE HEAT.
UGH, I HATE TO IMAGINE...

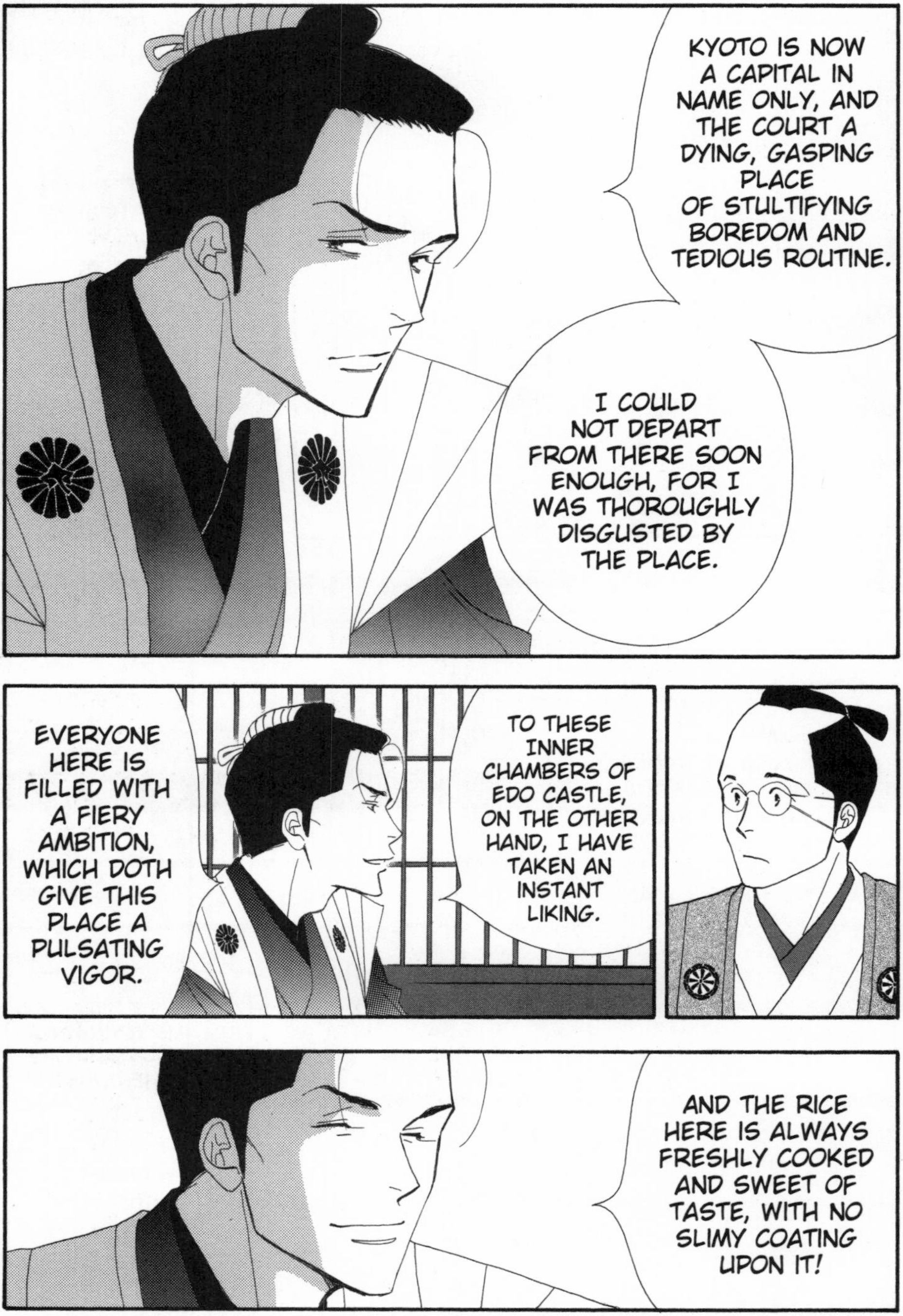
KYOTO IS NOW A CAPITAL IN NAME ONLY, AND THE COURT A DYING, GASPING PLACE OF STULTIFYING BOREDOM AND TEDIOUS ROUTINE.
I COULD NOT DEPART FROM THERE SOON ENOUGH, FOR I WAS THOROUGHLY DISGUSTED BY THE PLACE.
TO THESE INNER CHAMBERS OF EDO CASTLE, ON THE OTHER HAND, I HAVE TAKEN AN INSTANT LIKING.
EVERYONE HERE IS FILLED WITH A FIERY AMBITION, WHICH DOTH GIVE THIS PLACE A PULSATING VIGOR.
AND THE RICE HERE IS ALWAYS FRESHLY COOKED AND SWEET OF TASTE, WITH NO SLIMY COATING UPON IT!

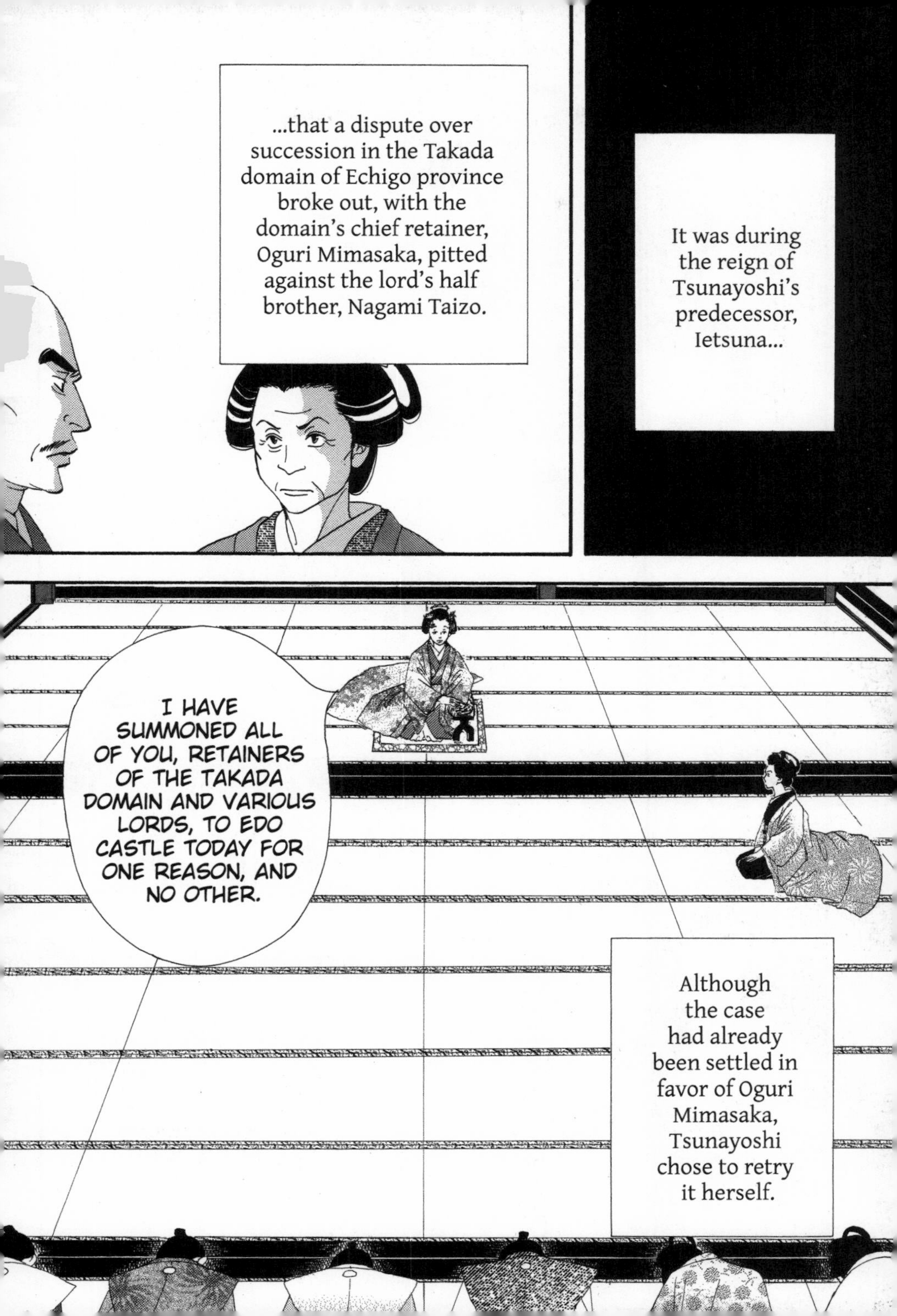
It was during the reign of Tsunayoshi's predecessor, Ietsuna...
...that a dispute over succession in the Takada domain of Echigo province broke out, with the domain's chief retainer, Oguri Mimasaka, pitted against the lord's half brother, Nagami Taizo.
I HAVE SUMMONED ALL OF YOU, RETAINERS OF THE TAKADA DOMAIN AND VARIOUS LORDS, TO EDO CASTLE TODAY FOR ONE REASON, AND NO OTHER.
Although the case had already been settled in favor of Oguri Mimasaka, Tsunayoshi chose to retry it herself.

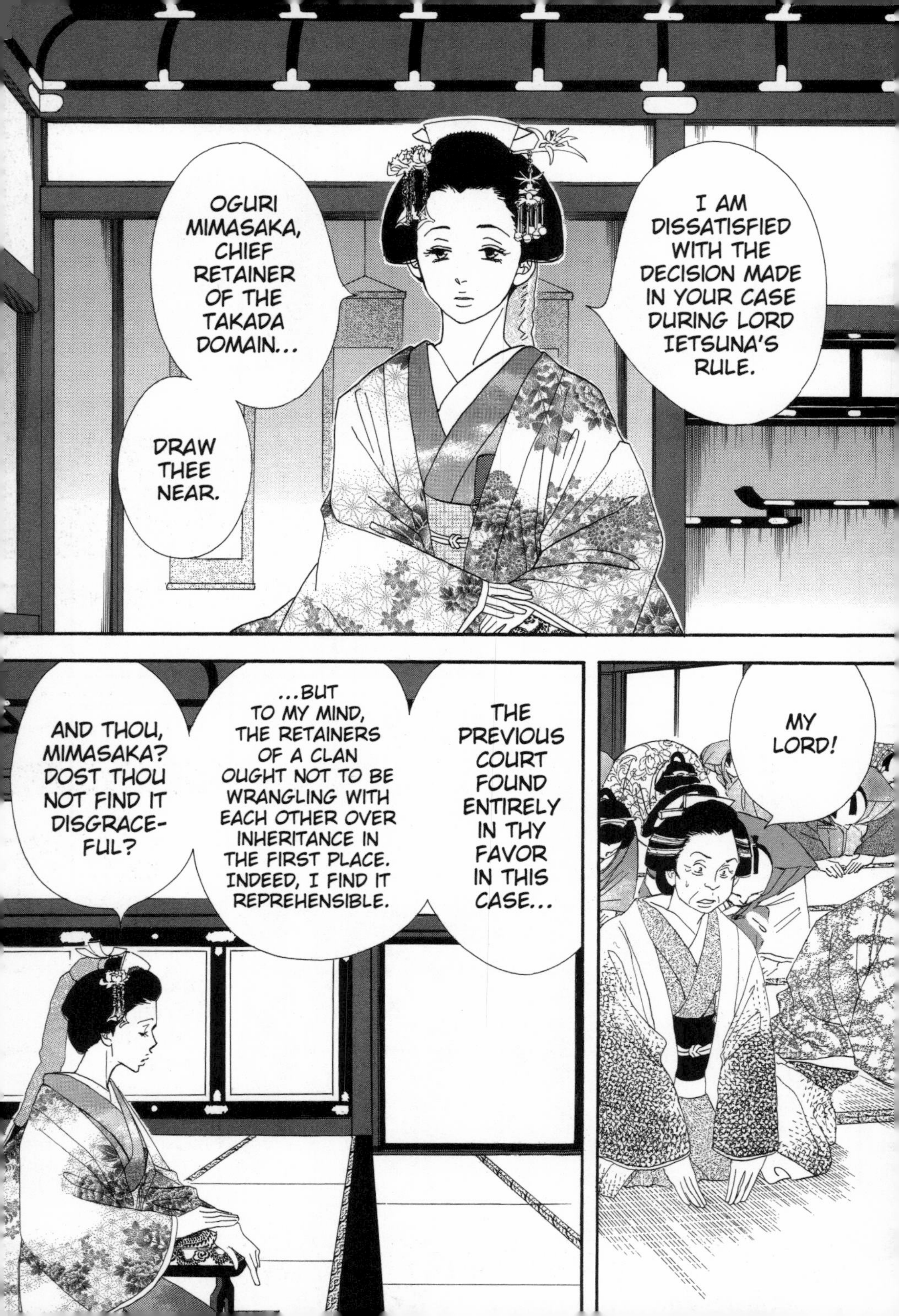
OGURI MIMASAKA, CHIEF RETAINER OF THE TAKADA DOMAIN...
DRAW THEE NEAR.
I AM DISSATISFIED WITH THE DECISION MADE IN YOUR CASE DURING LORD IETSUNA'S RULE.
MY LORD!
THE PREVIOUS COURT FOUND ENTIRELY IN THY FAVOR IN THIS CASE...
...BUT TO MY MIND, THE RETAINERS OF A CLAN OUGHT NOT TO BE WRANGLING WITH EACH OTHER OVER INHERITANCE IN THE FIRST PLACE. INDEED, I FIND IT REPREHENSIBLE.
AND THOU, MIMASAKA? DOST THOU NOT FIND IT DISGRACE-FUL?

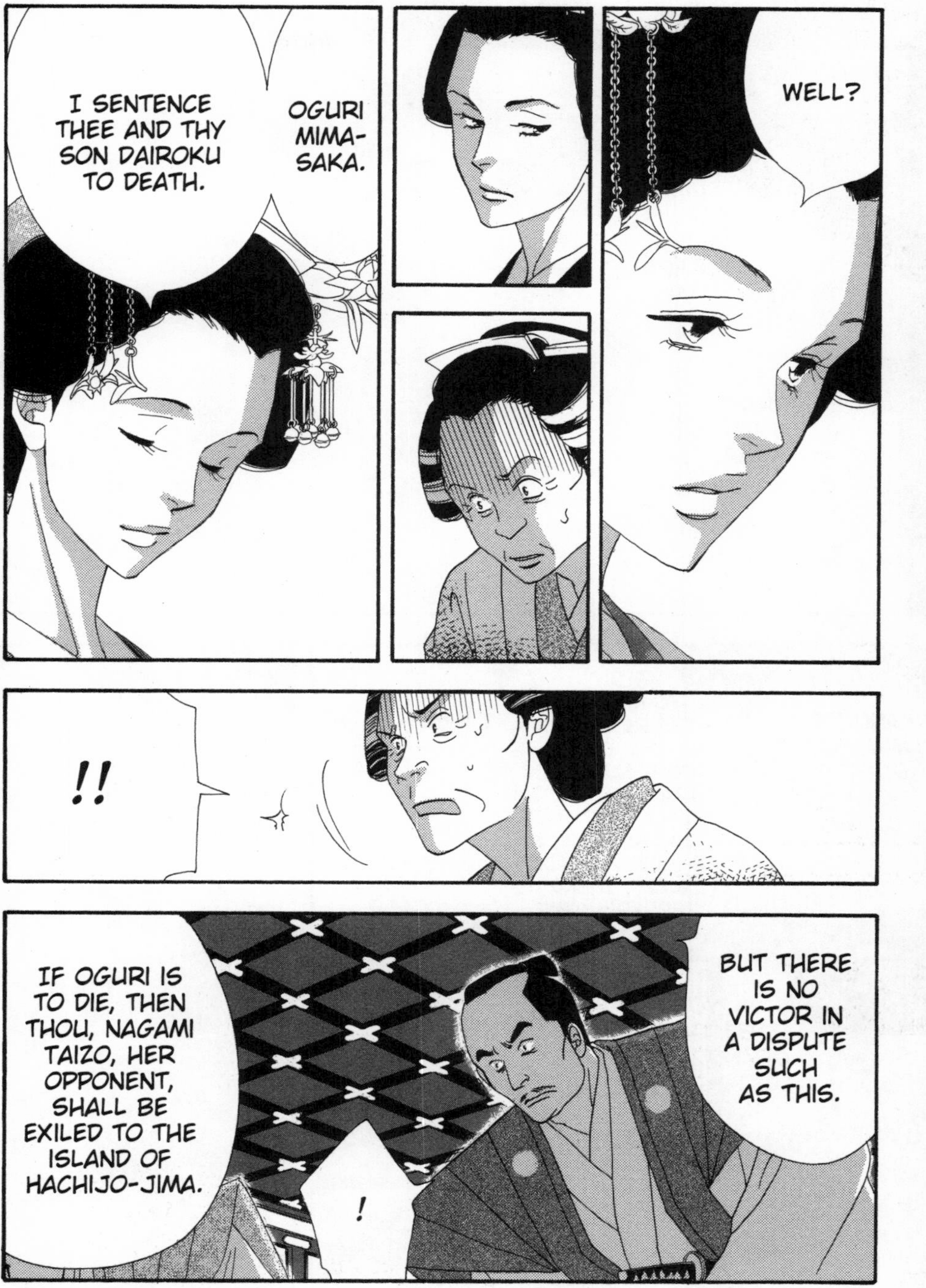
WELL?
OGURI MIMASAKA.
I SENTENCE THEE AND THY SON DAIROKU TO DEATH.
!!
BUT THERE IS NO VICTOR IN A DISPUTE SUCH AS THIS.
IF OGURI IS TO DIE, THEN THOU, NAGAMI TAIZO, HER OPPONENT, SHALL BE EXILED TO THE ISLAND OF HACHIJO-JIMA.
!

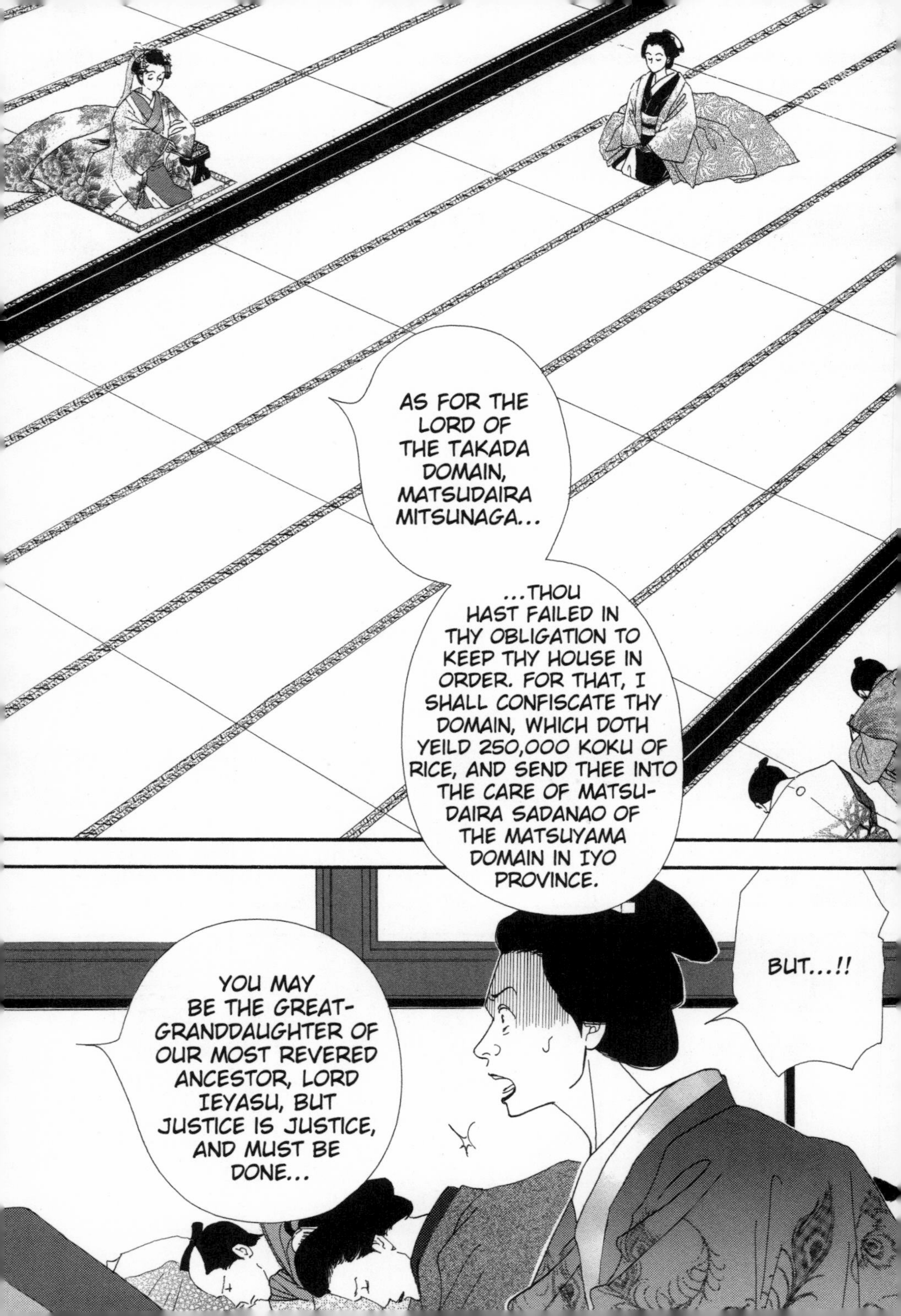
AS FOR THE LORD OF THE TAKADA DOMAIN, MATSUDAIRA MITSUNAGA...
...THOU HAST FAILED IN THY OBLIGATION TO KEEP THY HOUSE IN ORDER. FOR THAT, I SHALL CONFISCATE THY DOMAIN, WHICH DOTH YEILD 250,000 KOKU OF RICE, AND SEND THEE INTO THE CARE OF MATSU-DAIRA SADANAO OF THE MATSUYAMA DOMAIN IN IYO PROVINCE.
BUT...!!
YOU MAY BE THE GREAT-GRANDDAUGHTER OF OUR MOST REVERED ANCESTOR, LORD IEYASU, BUT JUSTICE IS JUSTICE, AND MUST BE DONE...

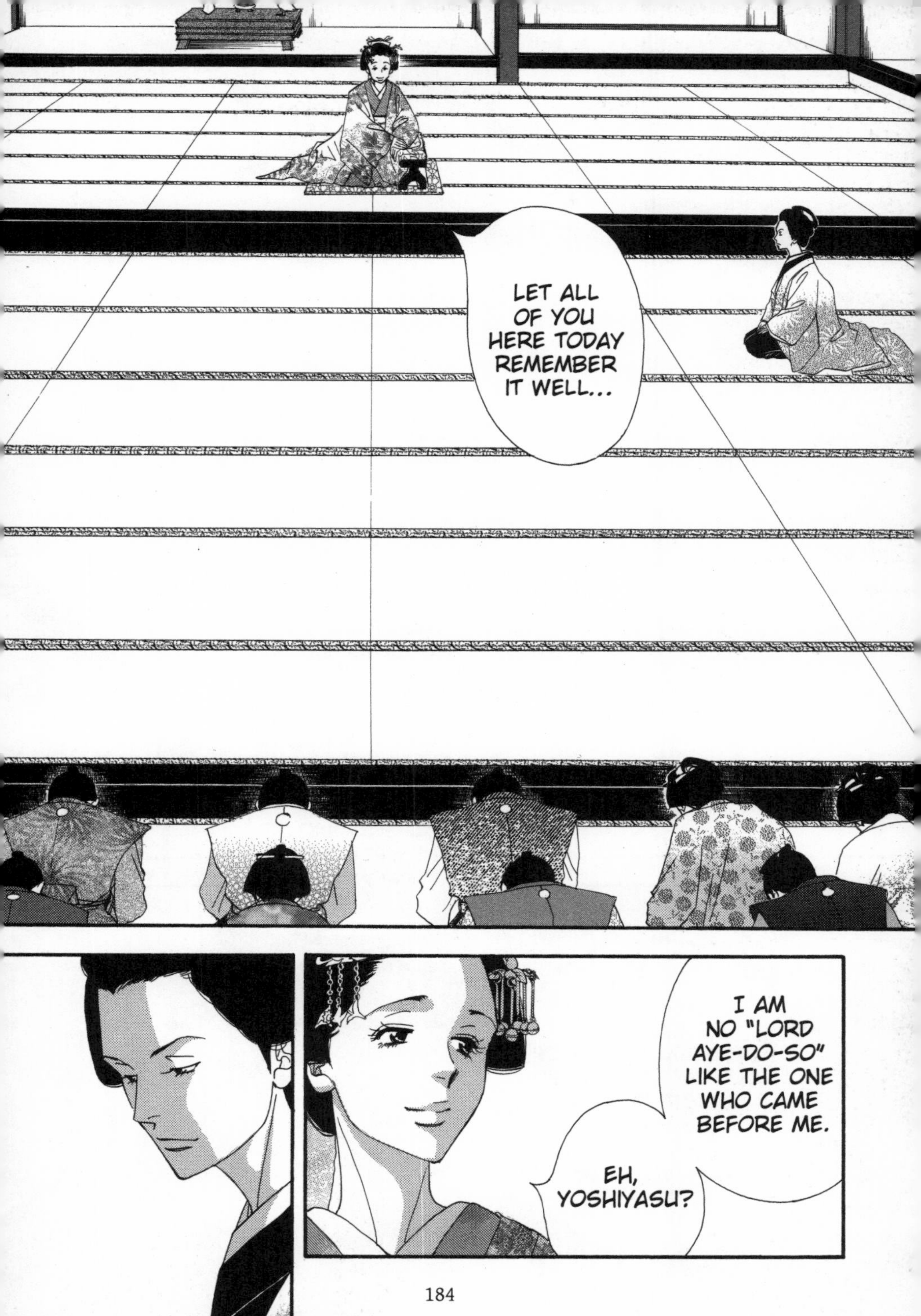
LET ALL OF YOU HERE TODAY REMEMBER IT WELL...
I AM NO "LORD AYE-DO-SO" LIKE THE ONE WHO CAME BEFORE ME.
EH, YOSHIYASU?

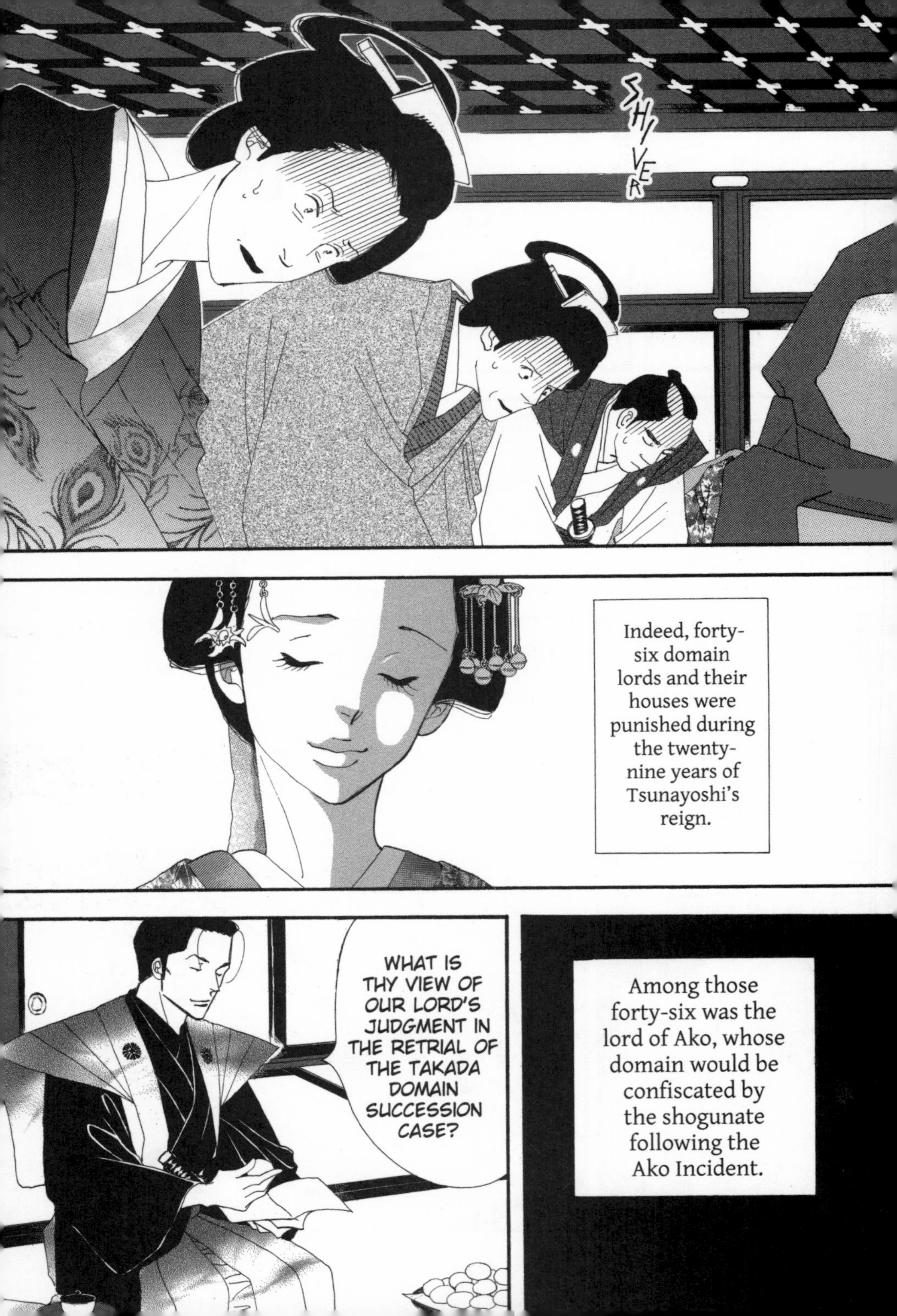
SHIVER
Indeed, forty-six domain lords and their houses were punished during the twenty-nine years of Tsunayoshi's reign.
Among those forty-six was the lord of Ako, whose domain would be confiscated by the shogunate following the Ako Incident.
WHAT IS THY VIEW OF OUR LORD'S JUDGMENT IN THE RETRIAL OF THE TAKADA DOMAIN SUCCESSION CASE?

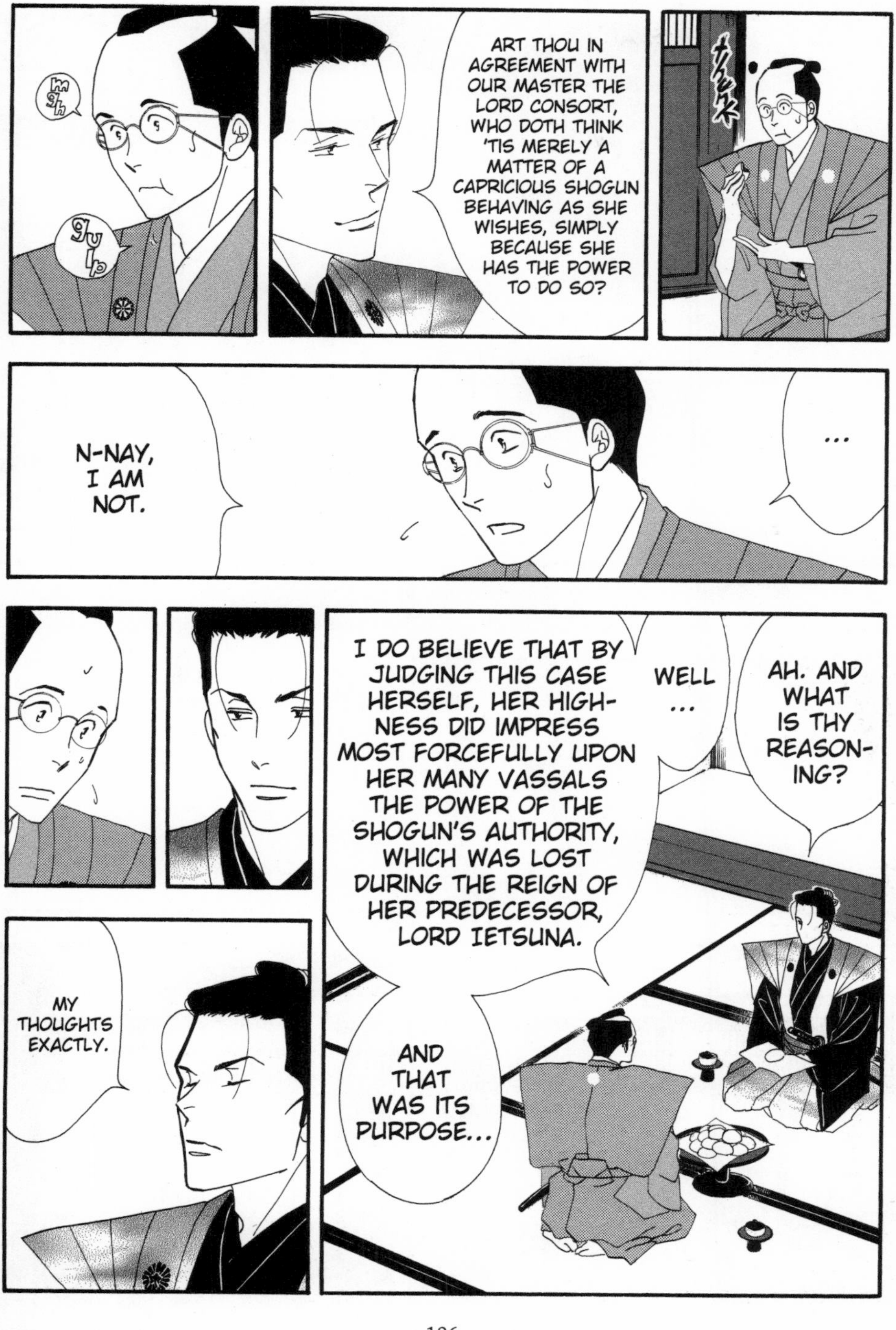
ART THOU IN AGREEMENT WITH OUR MASTER THE LORD CONSORT, WHO DOTH THINK 'TIS MERELY A MATTER OF A CAPRICIOUS SHOGUN BEHAVING AS SHE WISHES, SIMPLY BECAUSE SHE HAS THE POWER TO DO SO?
mgh
gulp
...
N-NAY, I AM NOT.
AH. AND WHAT IS THY REASONING?
WELL...
I DO BELIEVE THAT BY JUDGING THIS CASE HERSELF, HER HIGHNESS DID IMPRESS MOST FORCEFULLY UPON HER MANY VASSALS THE POWER OF THE SHOGUN'S AUTHORITY, WHICH WAS LOST DURING THE REIGN OF HER PREDECESSOR, LORD IETSUNA.
AND THAT WAS ITS PURPOSE...
MY THOUGHTS EXACTLY.

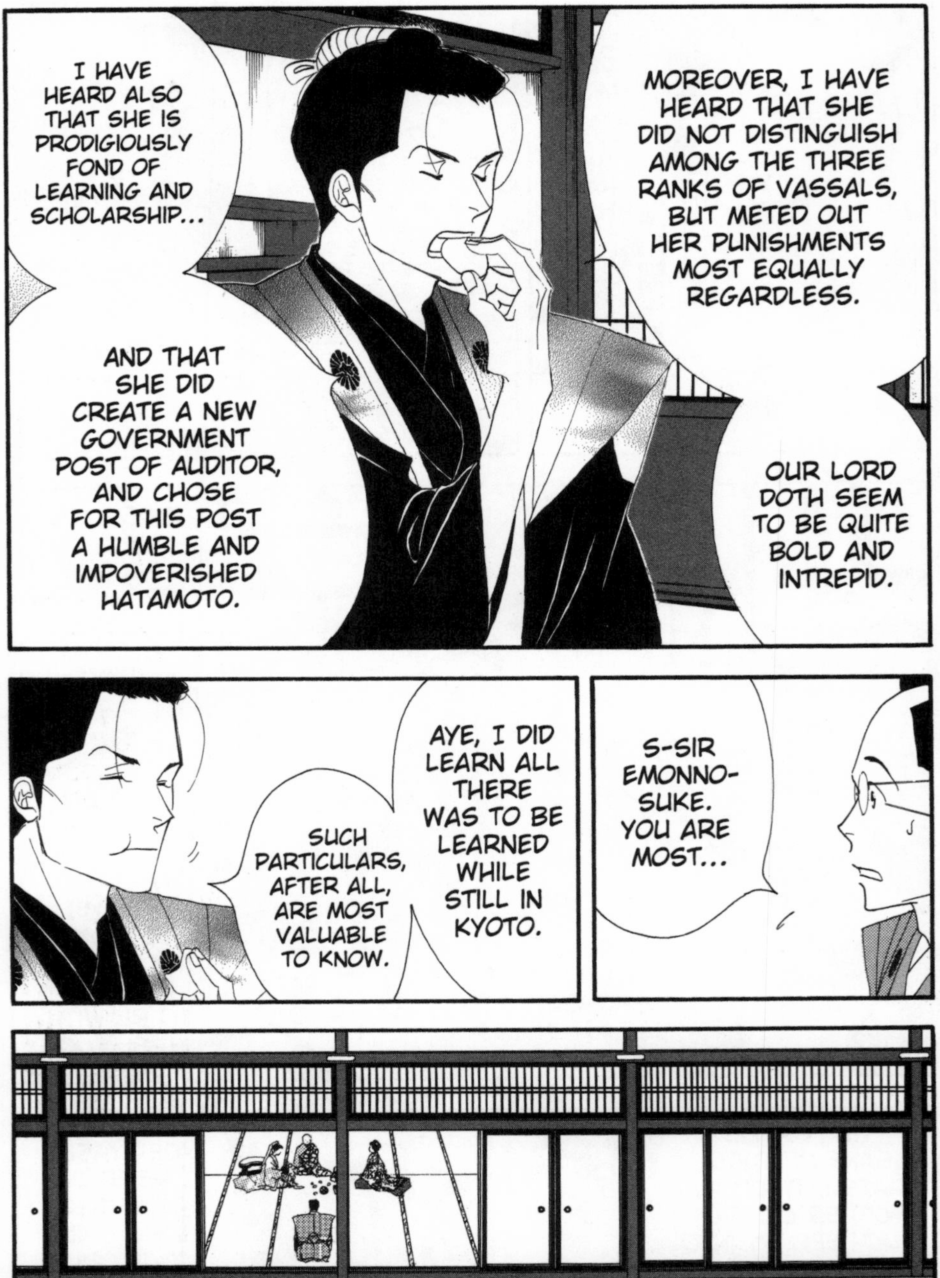
MOREOVER, I HAVE HEARD THAT SHE DID NOT DISTINGUISH AMONG THE THREE RANKS OF VASSALS, BUT METED OUT HER PUNISHMENTS MOST EQUALLY REGARDLESS.
OUR LORD DOTH SEEM TO BE QUITE BOLD AND INTREPID.
I HAVE HEARD ALSO THAT SHE IS PRODIGIOUSLY FOND OF LEARNING AND SCHOLARSHIP...
AND THAT SHE DID CREATE A NEW GOVERNMENT POST OF AUDITOR, AND CHOSE FOR THIS POST A HUMBLE AND IMPOVERISHED HATAMOTO.
S-SIR EMONNO-SUKE. YOU ARE MOST...
AYE, I DID LEARN ALL THERE WAS TO BE LEARNED WHILE STILL IN KYOTO.
SUCH PARTICULARS, AFTER ALL, ARE MOST VALUABLE TO KNOW.

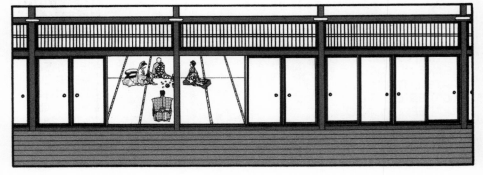

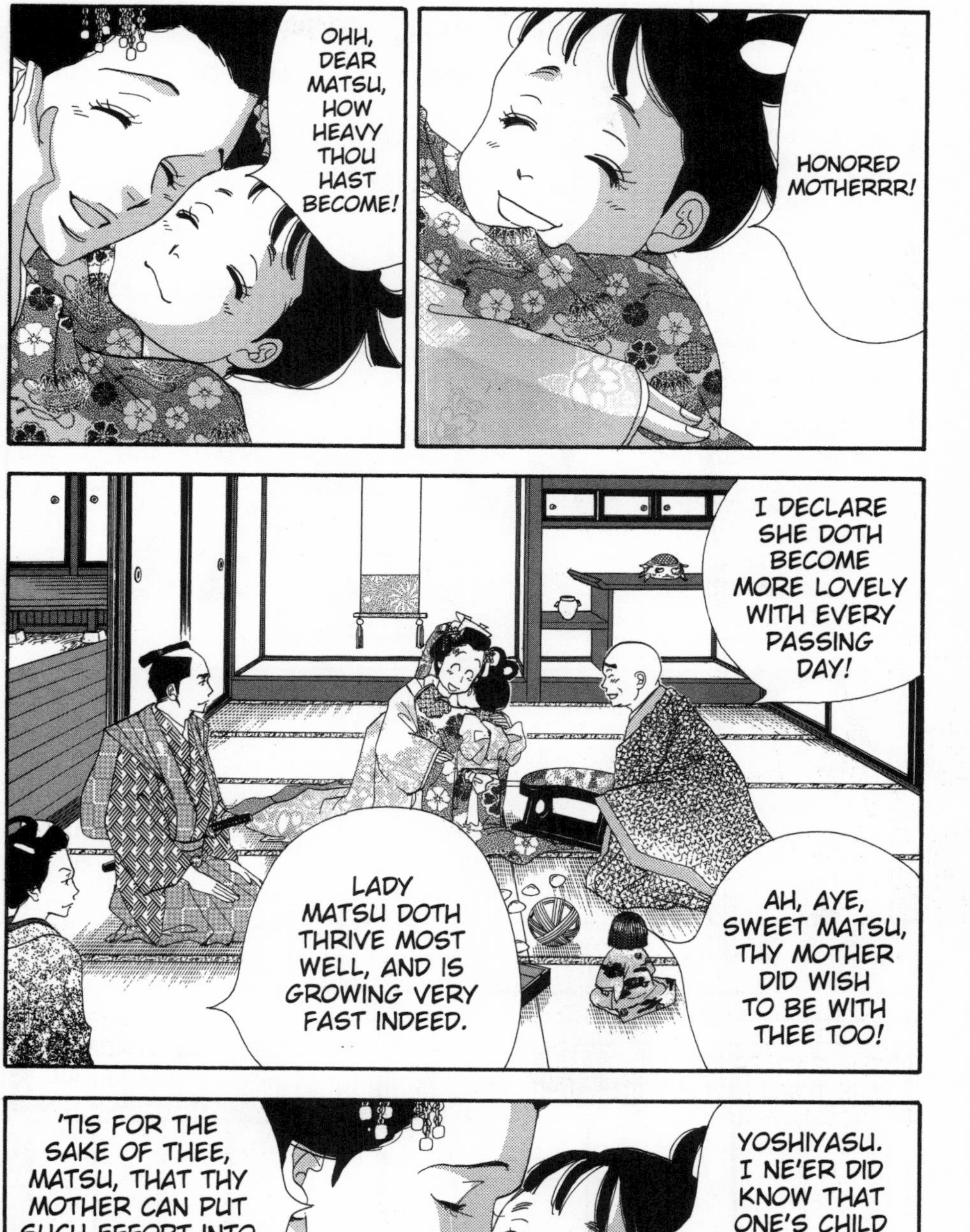
HONORED MOTHERRR!
OHH, DEAR MATSU, HOW HEAVY THOU HAST BECOME!
I DECLARE SHE DOTH BECOME MORE LOVELY WITH EVERY PASSING DAY!
AH, AYE, SWEET MATSU, THY MOTHER DID WISH TO BE WITH THEE TOO!
LADY MATSU DOTH THRIVE MOST WELL, AND IS GROWING VERY FAST INDEED.
YOSHIYASU. I NE'ER DID KNOW THAT ONE'S CHILD COULD FILL ONE WITH SO MUCH LOVE.
'TIS FOR THE SAKE OF THEE, MATSU, THAT THY MOTHER CAN PUT SUCH EFFORT INTO GOVERNMENT. 'TIS THE THOUGHT OF SEEING THEE!

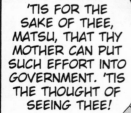

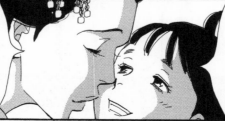

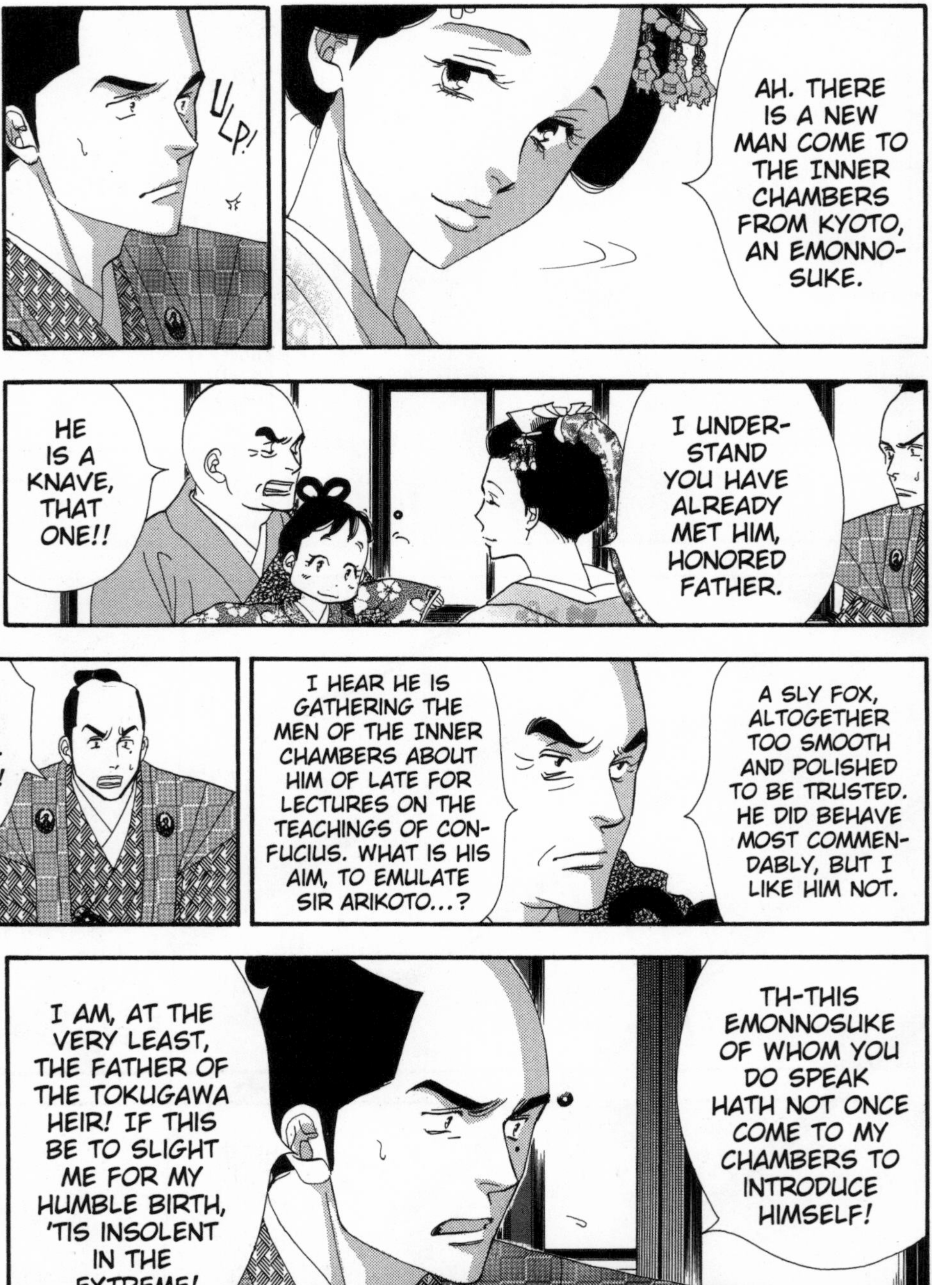
AH. THERE IS A NEW MAN COME TO THE INNER CHAMBERS FROM KYOTO, AN EMONNOSUKE.
ULP!
I UNDERSTAND YOU HAVE ALREADY MET HIM, HONORED FATHER.
HE IS A KNAVE, THAT ONE!!
A SLY FOX, ALTOGETHER TOO SMOOTH AND POLISHED TO BE TRUSTED. HE DID BEHAVE MOST COMMENDABLY, BUT I LIKE HIM NOT.
I HEAR HE IS GATHERING THE MEN OF THE INNER CHAMBERS ABOUT HIM OF LATE FOR LECTURES ON THE TEACHINGS OF CONFUCIUS. WHAT IS HIS AIM, TO EMULATE SIR ARIKOTO...?
Y-YOUR HIGHNESS!
TH-THIS EMONNOSUKE OF WHOM YOU DO SPEAK HATH NOT ONCE COME TO MY CHAMBERS TO INTRODUCE HIMSELF!
I AM, AT THE VERY LEAST, THE FATHER OF THE TOKUGAWA HEIR! IF THIS BE TO SLIGHT ME FOR MY HUMBLE BIRTH, 'TIS INSOLENT IN THE EXTREME!

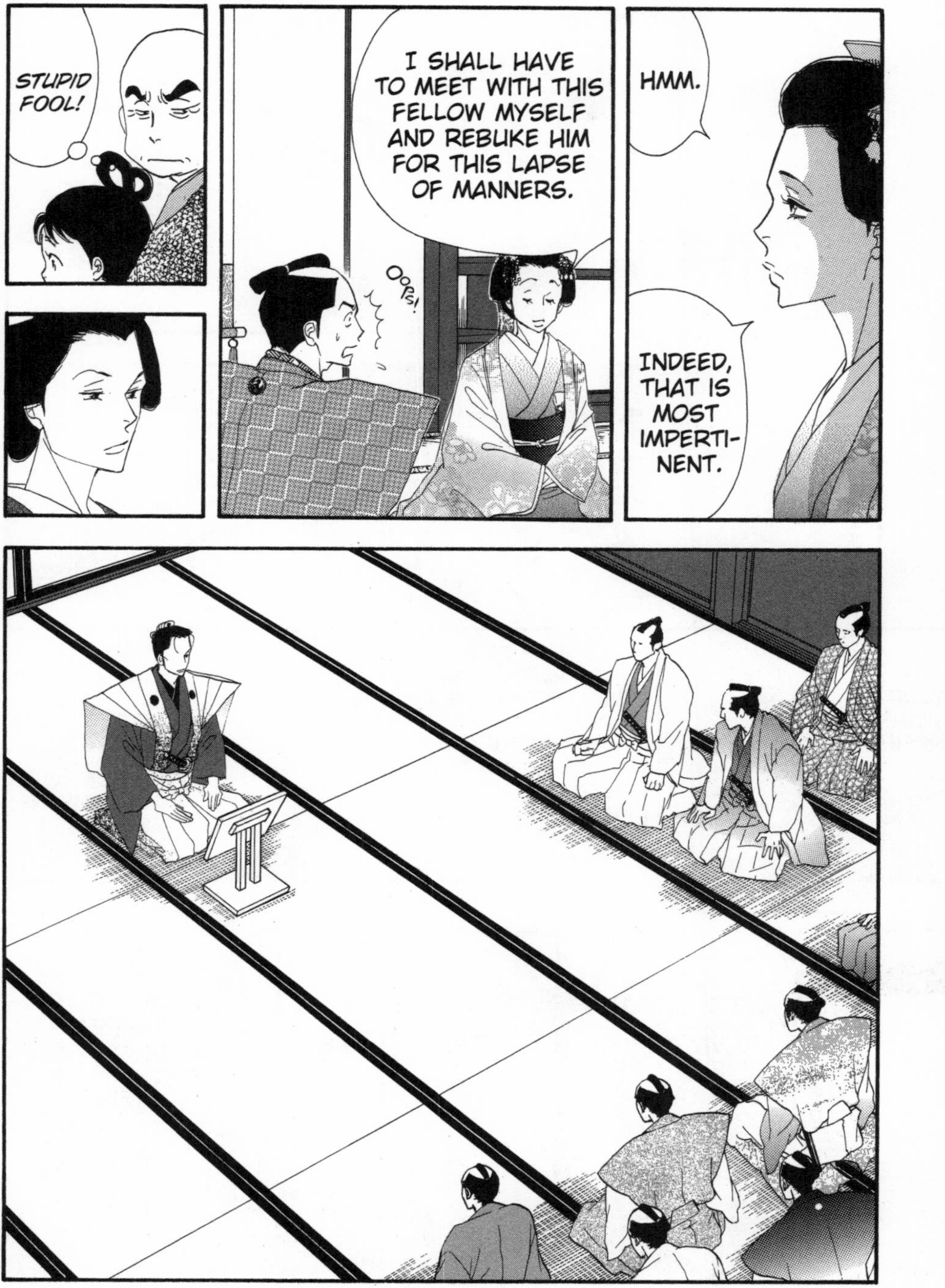
HMM.
INDEED, THAT IS MOST IMPERTI-NENT.
I SHALL HAVE TO MEET WITH THIS FELLOW MYSELF AND REBUKE HIM FOR THIS LAPSE OF MANNERS.
OOPS!
STUPID FOOL!

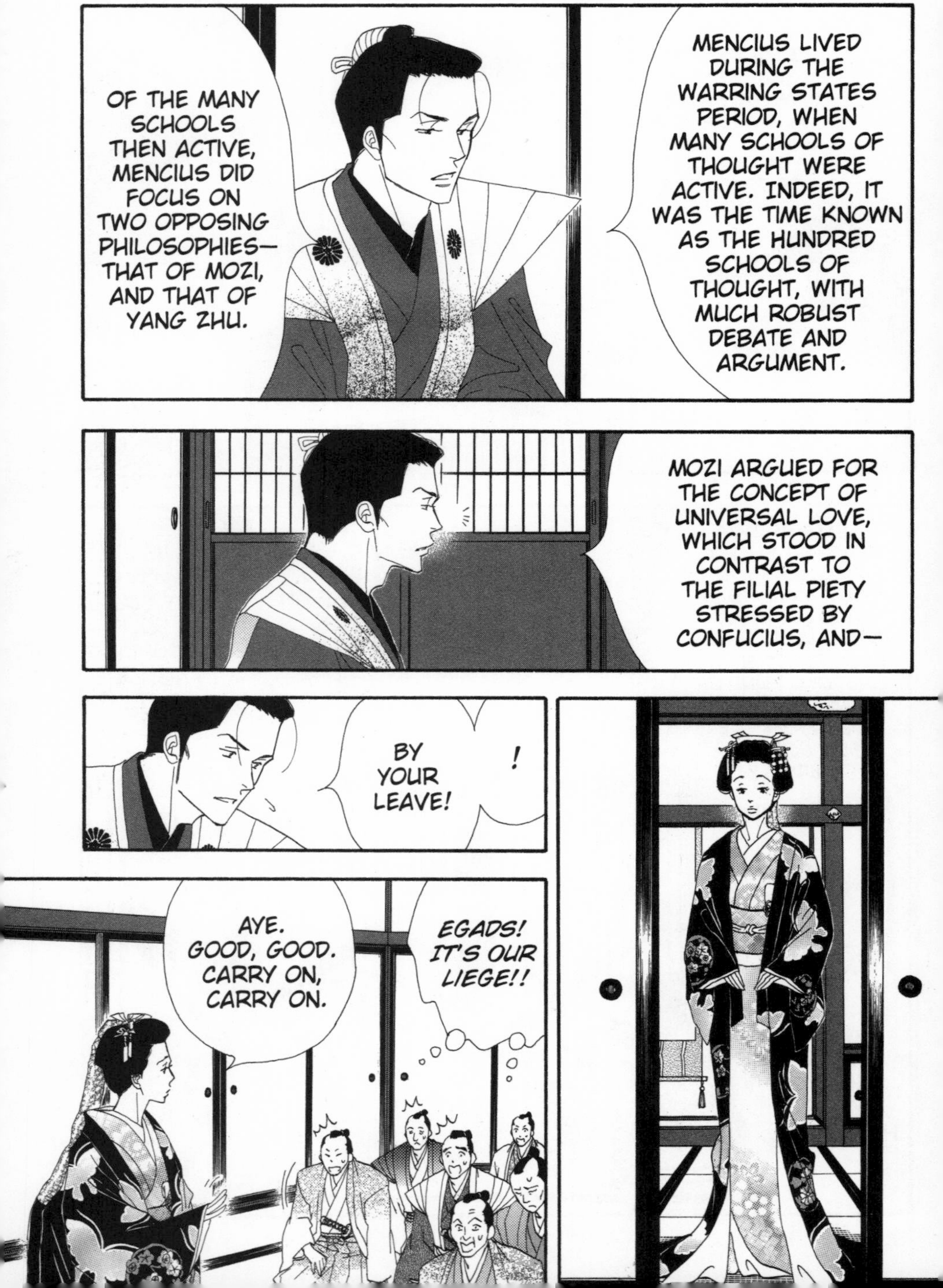
MENCIUS LIVED DURING THE WARRING STATES PERIOD, WHEN MANY SCHOOLS OF THOUGHT WERE ACTIVE. INDEED, IT WAS THE TIME KNOWN AS THE HUNDRED SCHOOLS OF THOUGHT, WITH MUCH ROBUST DEBATE AND ARGUMENT.
OF THE MANY SCHOOLS THEN ACTIVE, MENCIUS DID FOCUS ON TWO OPPOSING PHILOSOPHIES—THAT OF MOZI, AND THAT OF YANG ZHU.
MOZI ARGUED FOR THE CONCEPT OF UNIVERSAL LOVE, WHICH STOOD IN CONTRAST TO THE FILIAL PIETY STRESSED BY CONFUCIUS, AND—
!
BY YOUR LEAVE!
EGADS! IT'S OUR LIEGE!!
AYE. GOOD, GOOD. CARRY ON, CARRY ON.

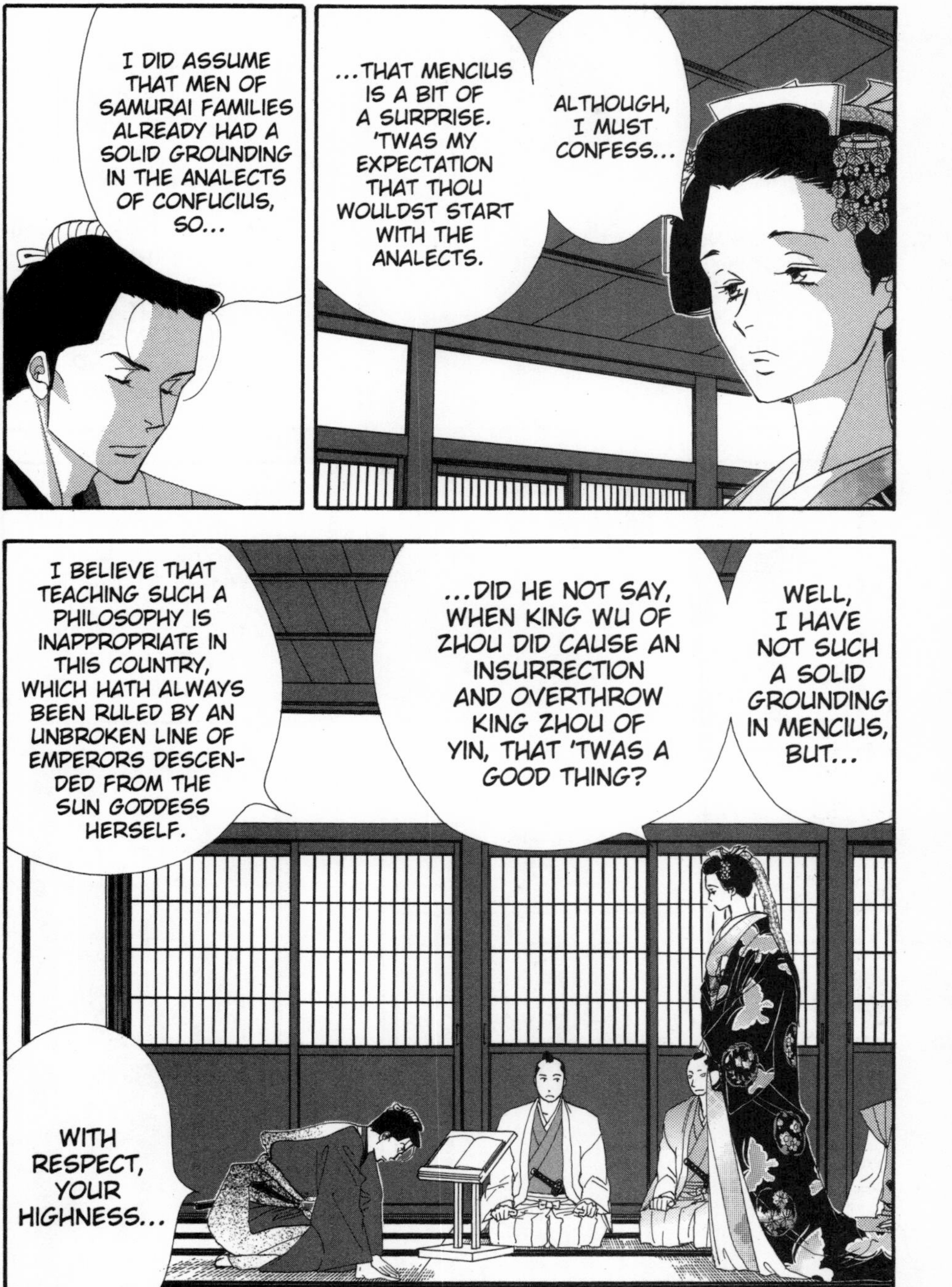
ALTHOUGH, I MUST CONFESS...
...THAT MENCIUS IS A BIT OF A SURPRISE. 'TWAS MY EXPECTATION THAT THOU WOULDST START WITH THE ANALECTS.
I DID ASSUME THAT MEN OF SAMURAI FAMILIES ALREADY HAD A SOLID GROUNDING IN THE ANALECTS OF CONFUCIUS, SO...
WELL, I HAVE NOT SUCH A SOLID GROUNDING IN MENCIUS, BUT...
...DID HE NOT SAY, WHEN KING WU OF ZHOU DID CAUSE AN INSURRECTION AND OVERTHROW KING ZHOU OF YIN, THAT 'TWAS A GOOD THING?
I BELIEVE THAT TEACHING SUCH A PHILOSOPHY IS INAPPROPRIATE IN THIS COUNTRY, WHICH HATH ALWAYS BEEN RULED BY AN UNBROKEN LINE OF EMPERORS DESCENDED FROM THE SUN GODDESS HERSELF.
WITH RESPECT, YOUR HIGHNESS...

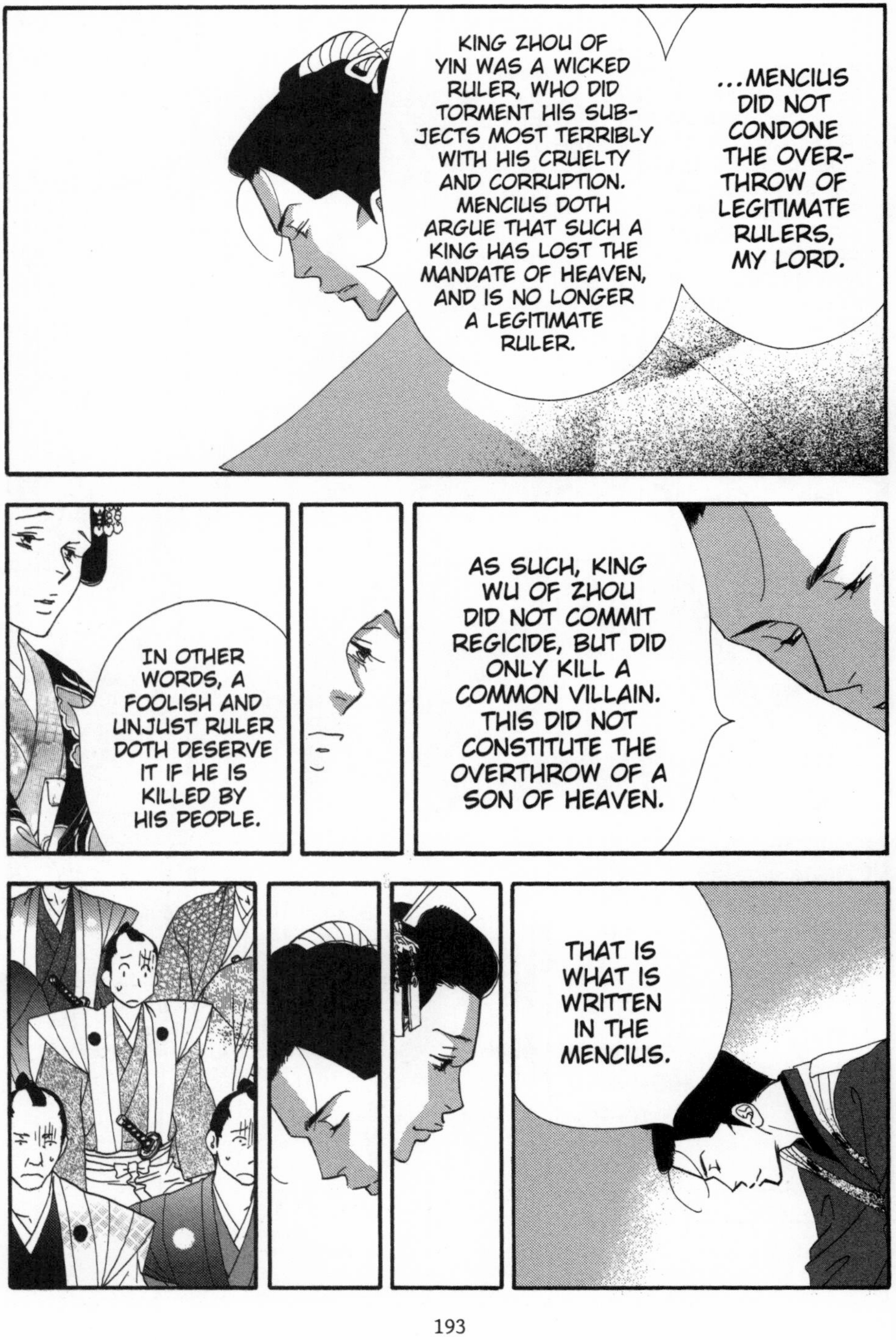
...MENCIUS DID NOT CONDONE THE OVERTHROW OF LEGITIMATE RULERS, MY LORD.
KING ZHOU OF YIN WAS A WICKED RULER, WHO DID TORMENT HIS SUBJECTS MOST TERRIBLY WITH HIS CRUELTY AND CORRUPTION. MENCIUS DOTH ARGUE THAT SUCH A KING HAS LOST THE MANDATE OF HEAVEN, AND IS NO LONGER A LEGITIMATE RULER.
AS SUCH, KING WU OF ZHOU DID NOT COMMIT REGICIDE, BUT DID ONLY KILL A COMMON VILLAIN. THIS DID NOT CONSTITUTE THE OVERTHROW OF A SON OF HEAVEN.
IN OTHER WORDS, A FOOLISH AND UNJUST RULER DOTH DESERVE IT IF HE IS KILLED BY HIS PEOPLE.
THAT IS WHAT IS WRITTEN IN THE MENCIUS.

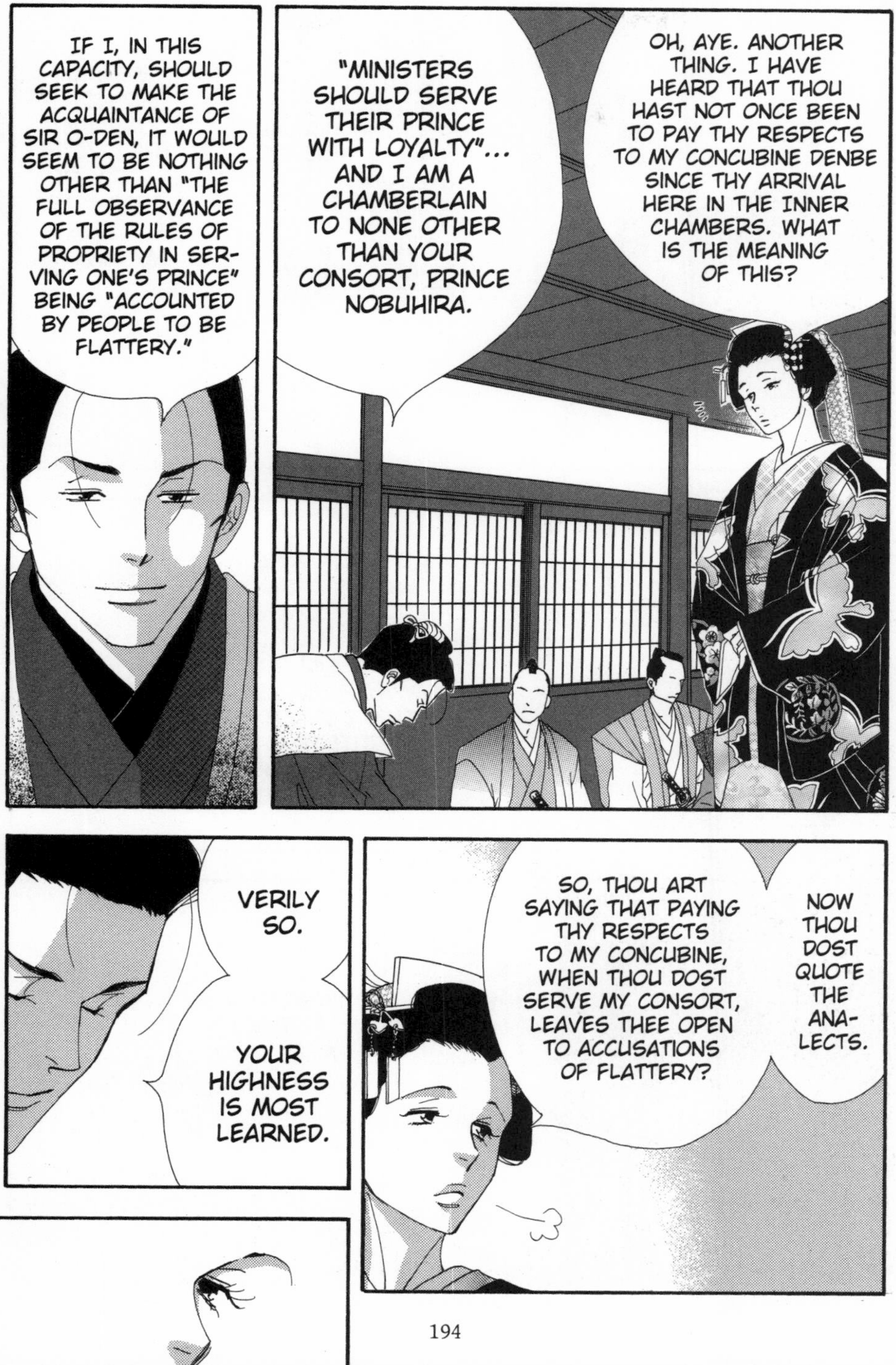
OH, AYE. ANOTHER THING. I HAVE HEARD THAT THOU HAST NOT ONCE BEEN TO PAY THY RESPECTS TO MY CONCUBINE DENBE SINCE THY ARRIVAL HERE IN THE INNER CHAMBERS. WHAT IS THE MEANING OF THIS?
"MINISTERS SHOULD SERVE THEIR PRINCE WITH LOYALTY"... AND I AM A CHAMBERLAIN TO NONE OTHER THAN YOUR CONSORT, PRINCE NOBUHIRA.
IF I, IN THIS CAPACITY, SHOULD SEEK TO MAKE THE ACQUAINTANCE OF SIR O-DEN, IT WOULD SEEM TO BE NOTHING OTHER THAN "THE FULL OBSERVANCE OF THE RULES OF PROPRIETY IN SER-VING ONE'S PRINCE" BEING "ACCOUNTED BY PEOPLE TO BE FLATTERY."
NOW THOU DOST QUOTE THE ANA-LECTS.
SO, THOU ART SAYING THAT PAYING THY RESPECTS TO MY CONCUBINE, WHEN THOU DOST SERVE MY CONSORT, LEAVES THEE OPEN TO ACCUSATIONS OF FLATTERY?
VERILY SO.
YOUR HIGHNESS IS MOST LEARNED.

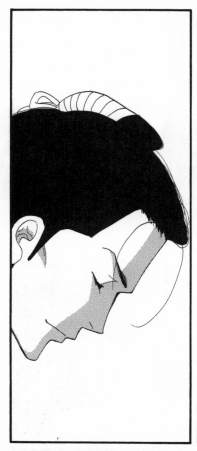

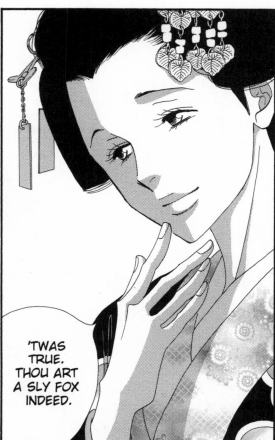

'TWAS TRUE. THOU ART A SLY FOX INDEED.

It happened quite often that the shogun came to the Inner Chambers to take her midday meal in the private chambers of her consort.

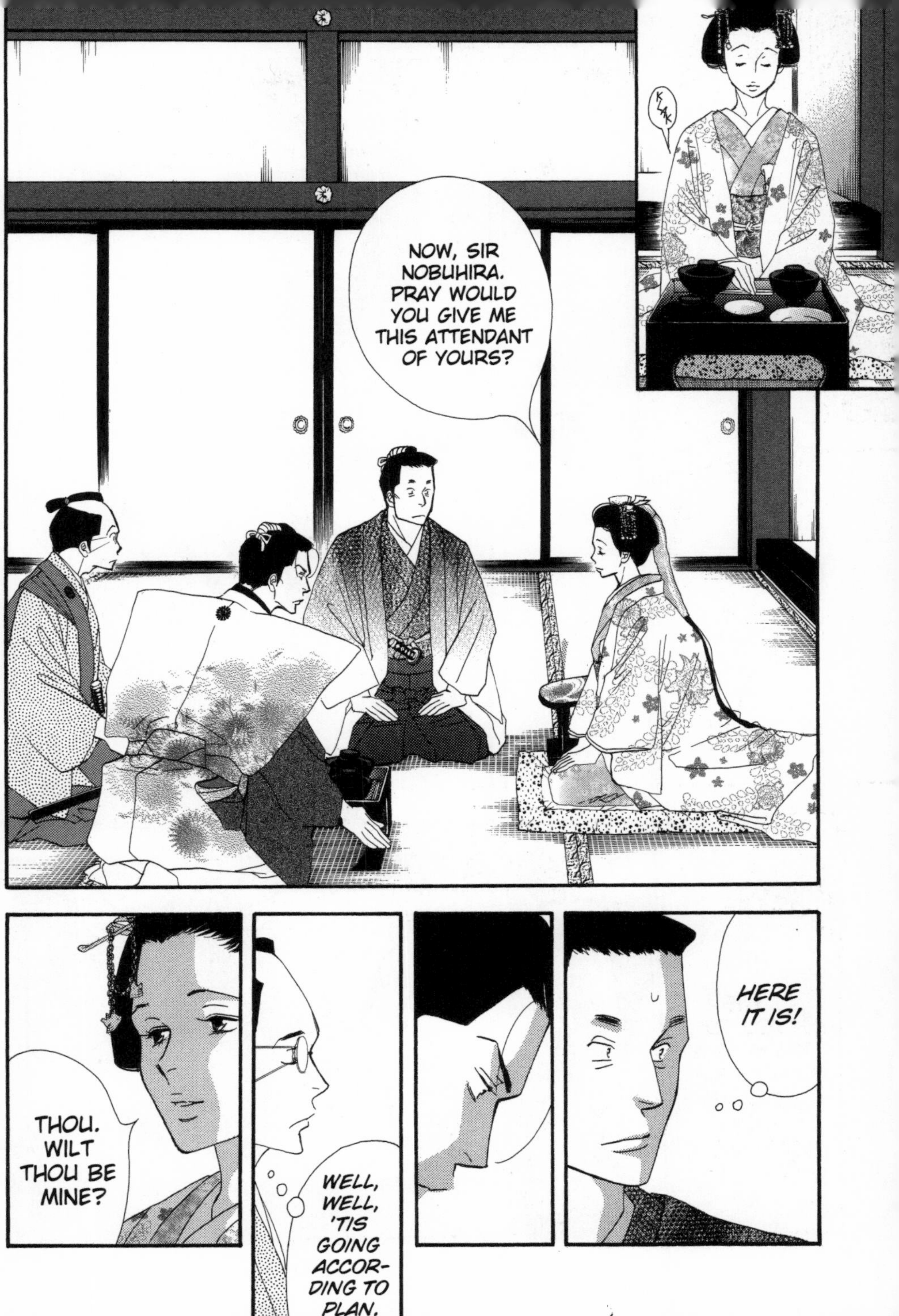
KLAK
NOW, SIR NOBUHIRA. PRAY WOULD YOU GIVE ME THIS ATTENDANT OF YOURS?
HERE IT IS!
WELL, WELL, 'TIS GOING ACCORD-DING TO PLAN.
THOU. WILT THOU BE MINE?

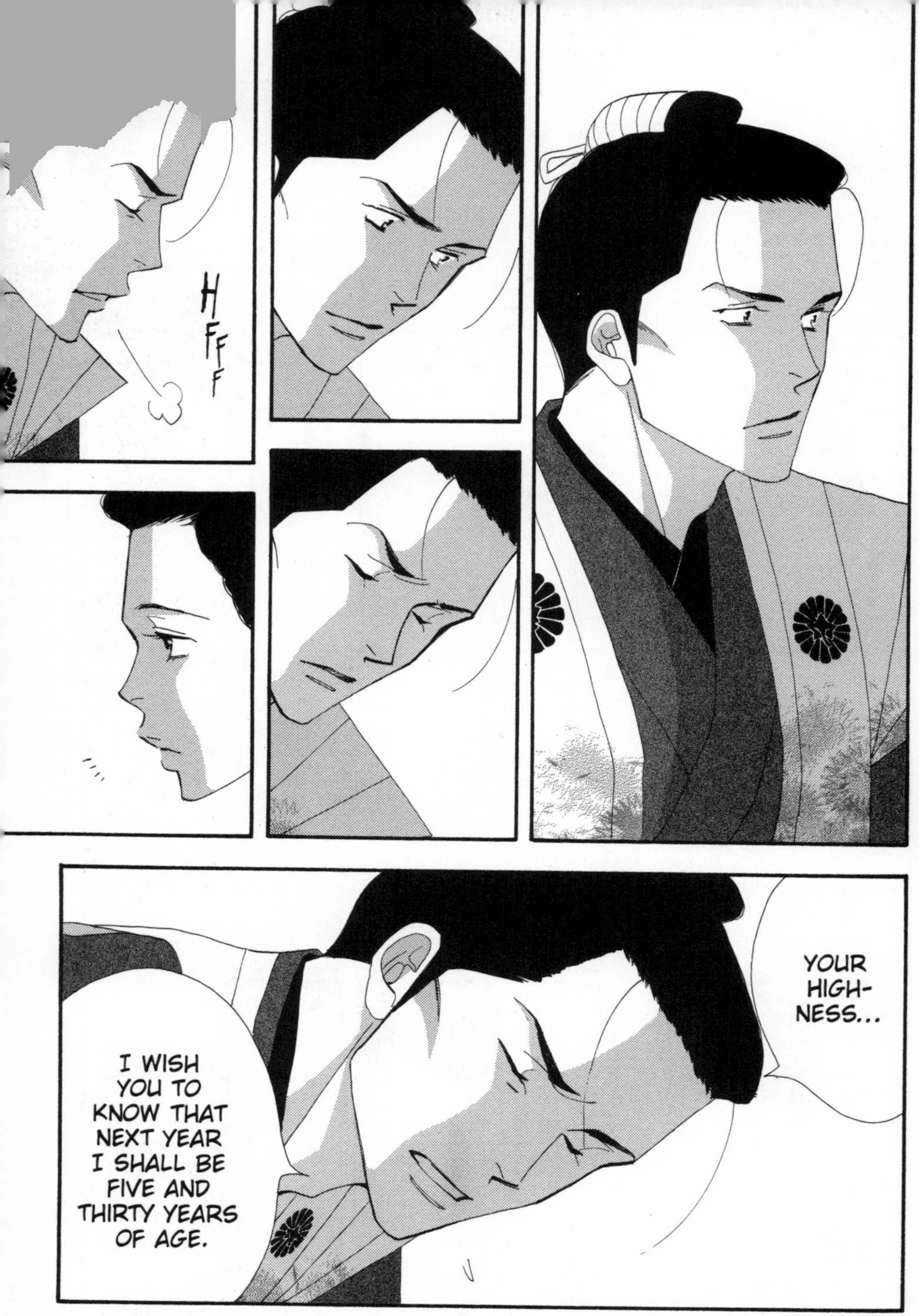
HFFF
YOUR HIGH-NESS...
I WISH YOU TO KNOW THAT NEXT YEAR I SHALL BE FIVE AND THIRTY YEARS OF AGE.

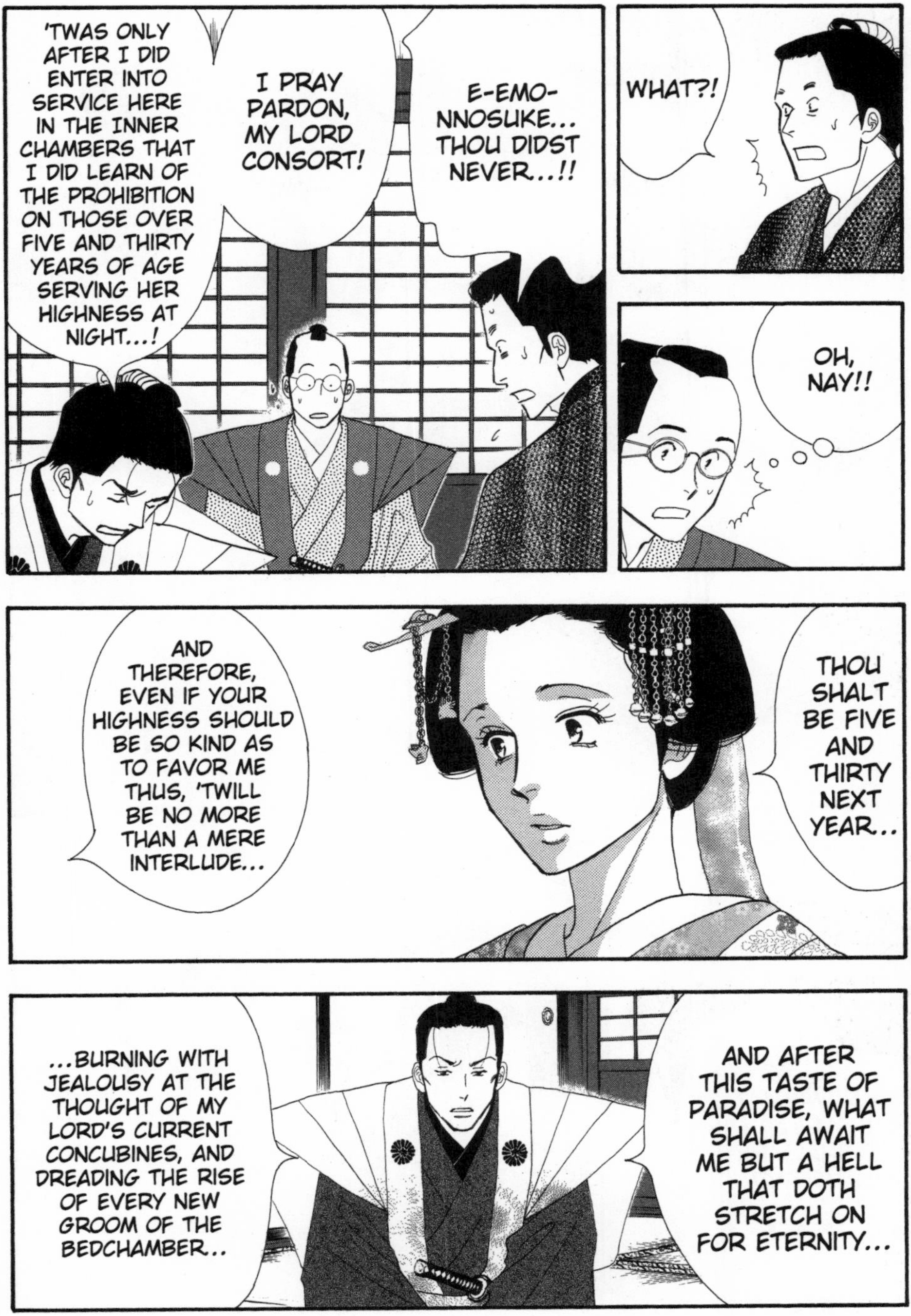
WHAT?!
OH, NAY!!
E-EMO-NNOSUKE... THOU DIDST NEVER...!!
I PRAY PARDON, MY LORD CONSORT!
'TWAS ONLY AFTER I DID ENTER INTO SERVICE HERE IN THE INNER CHAMBERS THAT I DID LEARN OF THE PROHIBITION ON THOSE OVER FIVE AND THIRTY YEARS OF AGE SERVING HER HIGHNESS AT NIGHT...!
THOU SHALT BE FIVE AND THIRTY NEXT YEAR...
AND THEREFORE, EVEN IF YOUR HIGHNESS SHOULD BE SO KIND AS TO FAVOR ME THUS, 'TWILL BE NO MORE THAN A MERE INTERLUDE...
AND AFTER THIS TASTE OF PARADISE, WHAT SHALL AWAIT ME BUT A HELL THAT DOTH STRETCH ON FOR ETERNITY...
...BURNING WITH JEALOUSY AT THE THOUGHT OF MY LORD'S CURRENT CONCUBINES, AND DREADING THE RISE OF EVERY NEW GROOM OF THE BEDCHAMBER...

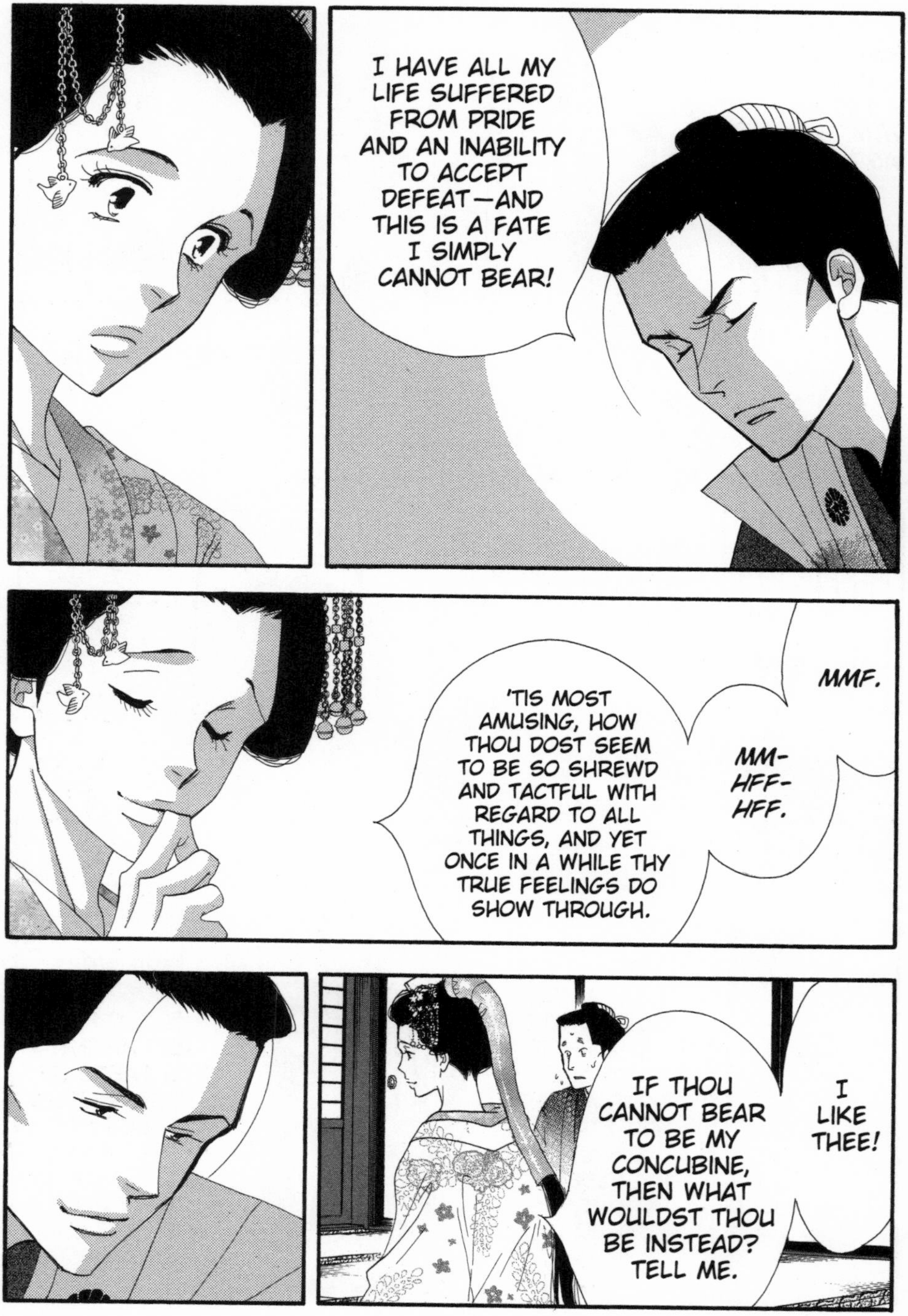
I HAVE ALL MY LIFE SUFFERED FROM PRIDE AND AN INABILITY TO ACCEPT DEFEAT—AND THIS IS A FATE I SIMPLY CANNOT BEAR!
MMF.
MM-HFF-HFF.
'TIS MOST AMUSING, HOW THOU DOST SEEM TO BE SO SHREWD AND TACTFUL WITH REGARD TO ALL THINGS, AND YET ONCE IN A WHILE THY TRUE FEELINGS DO SHOW THROUGH.
I LIKE THEE!
IF THOU CANNOT BEAR TO BE MY CONCUBINE, THEN WHAT WOULDST THOU BE INSTEAD? TELL ME.

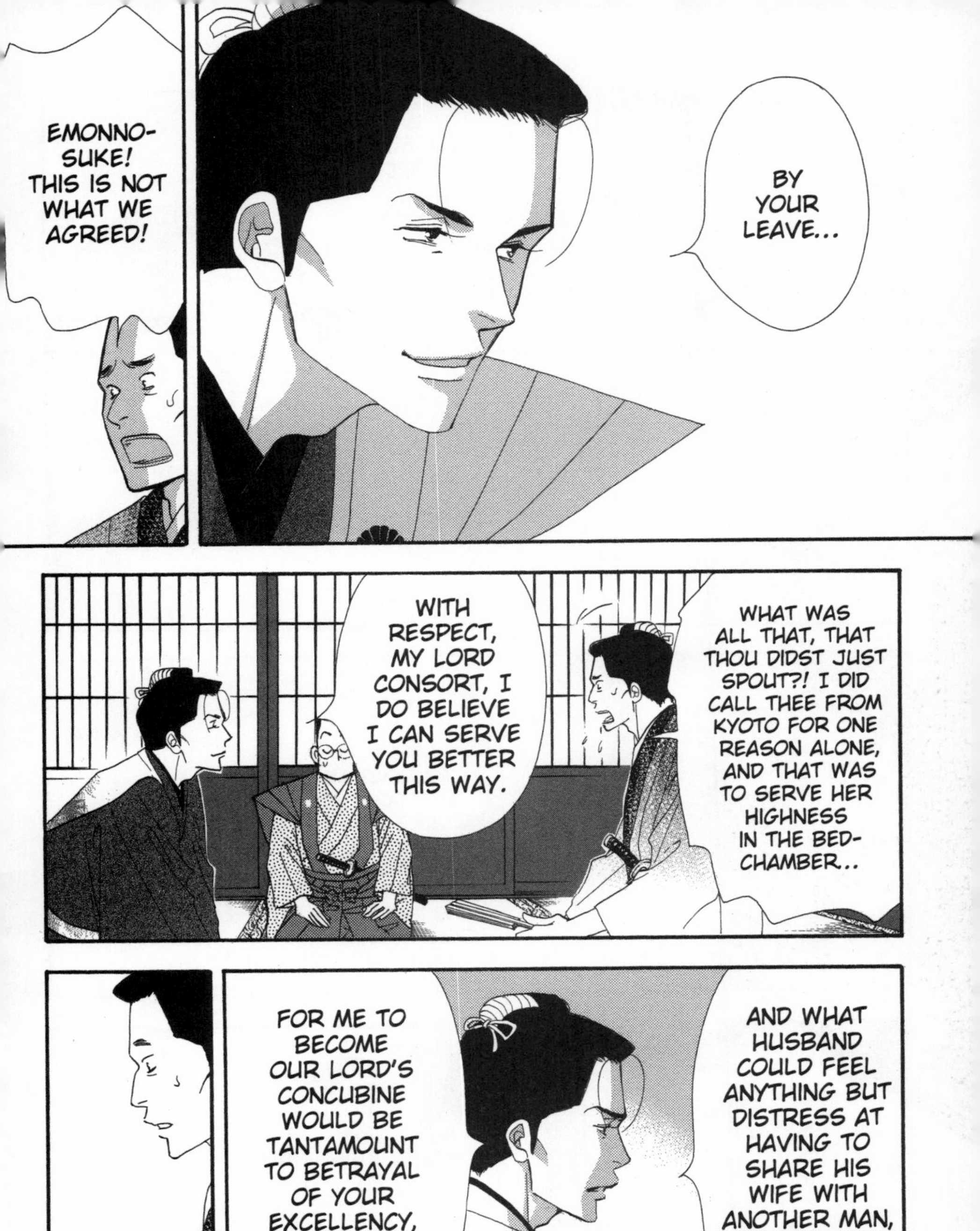
BY YOUR LEAVE...
EMONNO-SUKE! THIS IS NOT WHAT WE AGREED!
WHAT WAS ALL THAT, THAT THOU DIDST JUST SPOUT?! I DID CALL THEE FROM KYOTO FOR ONE REASON ALONE, AND THAT WAS TO SERVE HER HIGHNESS IN THE BED-CHAMBER..
WITH RESPECT, MY LORD CONSORT, I DO BELIEVE I CAN SERVE YOU BETTER THIS WAY.
AND WHAT HUSBAND COULD FEEL ANYTHING BUT DISTRESS AT HAVING TO SHARE HIS WIFE WITH ANOTHER MAN, REGARDLESS OF THE CIR-CUMSTANCES?
FOR ME TO BECOME OUR LORD'S CONCUBINE WOULD BE TANTAMOUNT TO BETRAYAL OF YOUR EXCELLENCY, AND 'TWAS INTOLERABLE TO ME.

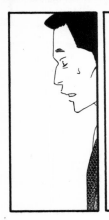

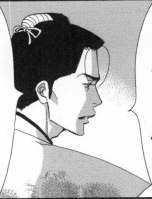

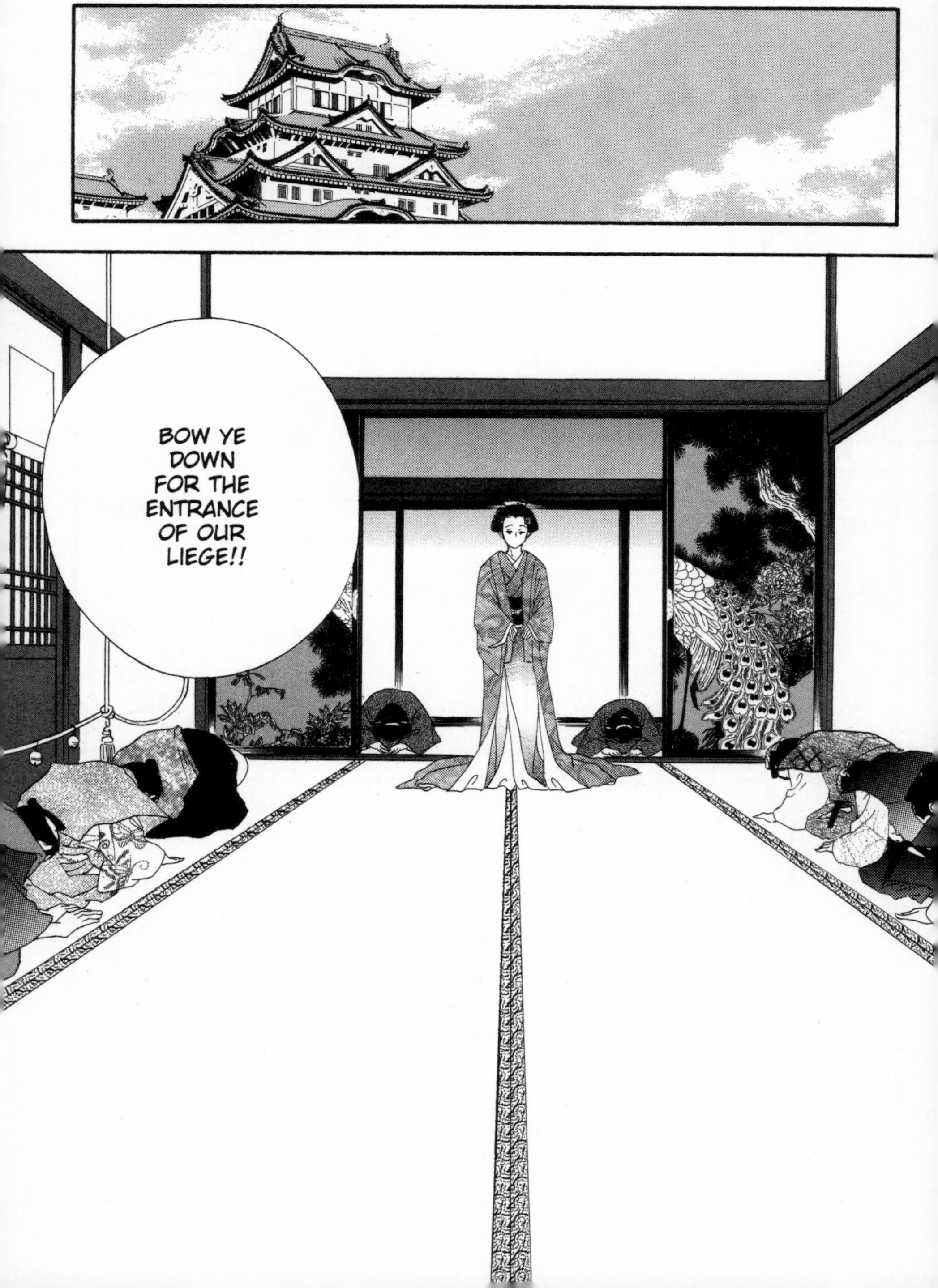
BOW YE DOWN FOR THE ENTRANCE OF OUR LIEGE!!

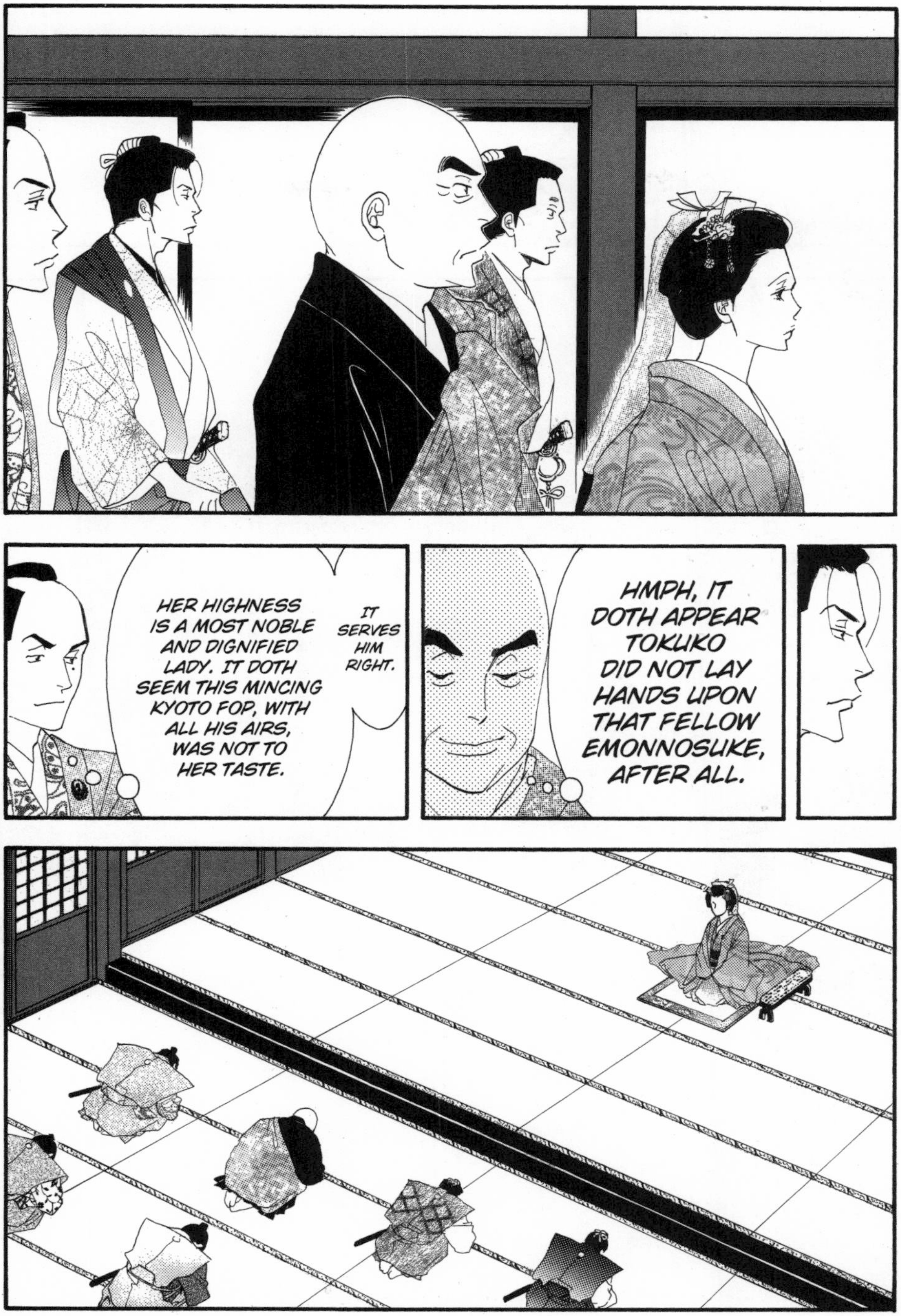
HMPH, IT DOTH APPEAR TOKUKO DID NOT LAY HANDS UPON THAT FELLOW EMONNOSUKE, AFTER ALL.
IT SERVES HIM RIGHT.
HER HIGHNESS IS A MOST NOBLE AND DIGNIFIED LADY. IT DOTH SEEM THIS MINCING KYOTO FOP, WITH ALL HIS AIRS, WAS NOT TO HER TASTE.

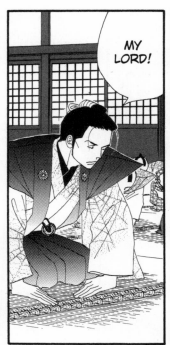

MY LORD!

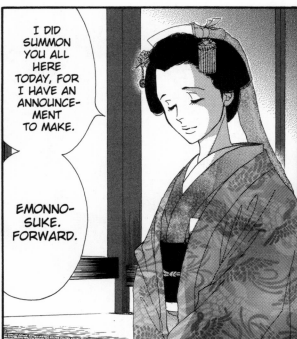

I DID SUMMON YOU ALL HERE TODAY, FOR I HAVE AN ANNOUNCEMENT TO MAKE.

EMONNO-SUKE. FORWARD.

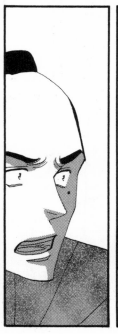

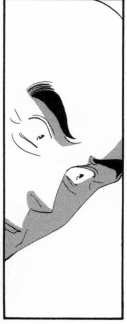

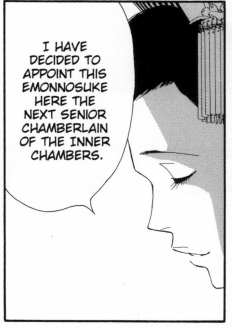

I HAVE DECIDED TO APPOINT THIS EMONNOSUKE HERE THE NEXT SENIOR CHAMBERLAIN OF THE INNER CHAMBERS.

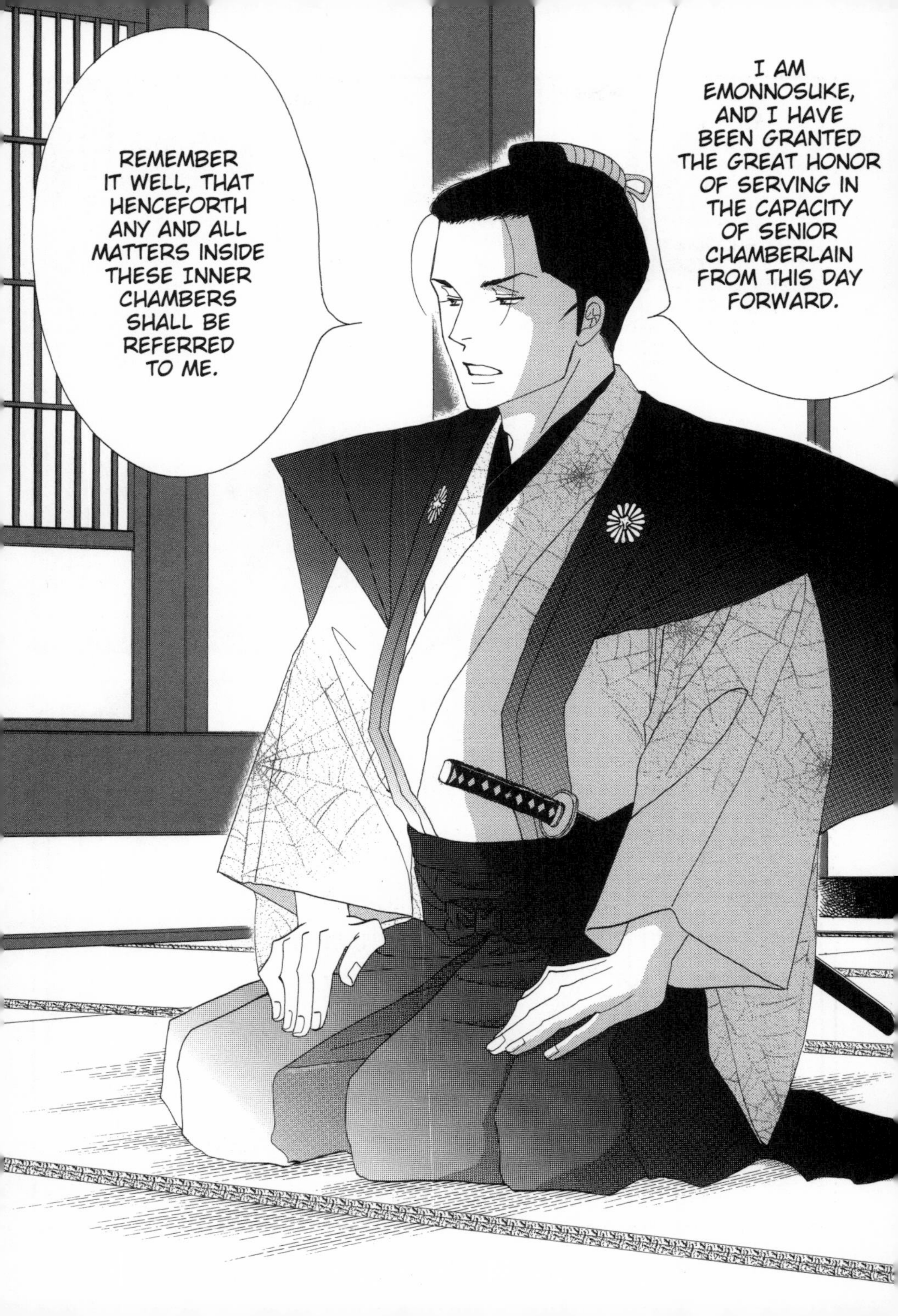
I AM EMONNOSUKE, AND I HAVE BEEN GRANTED THE GREAT HONOR OF SERVING IN THE CAPACITY OF SENIOR CHAMBERLAIN FROM THIS DAY FORWARD.
REMEMBER IT WELL, THAT HENCEFORTH ANY AND ALL MATTERS INSIDE THESE INNER CHAMBERS SHALL BE REFERRED TO ME.

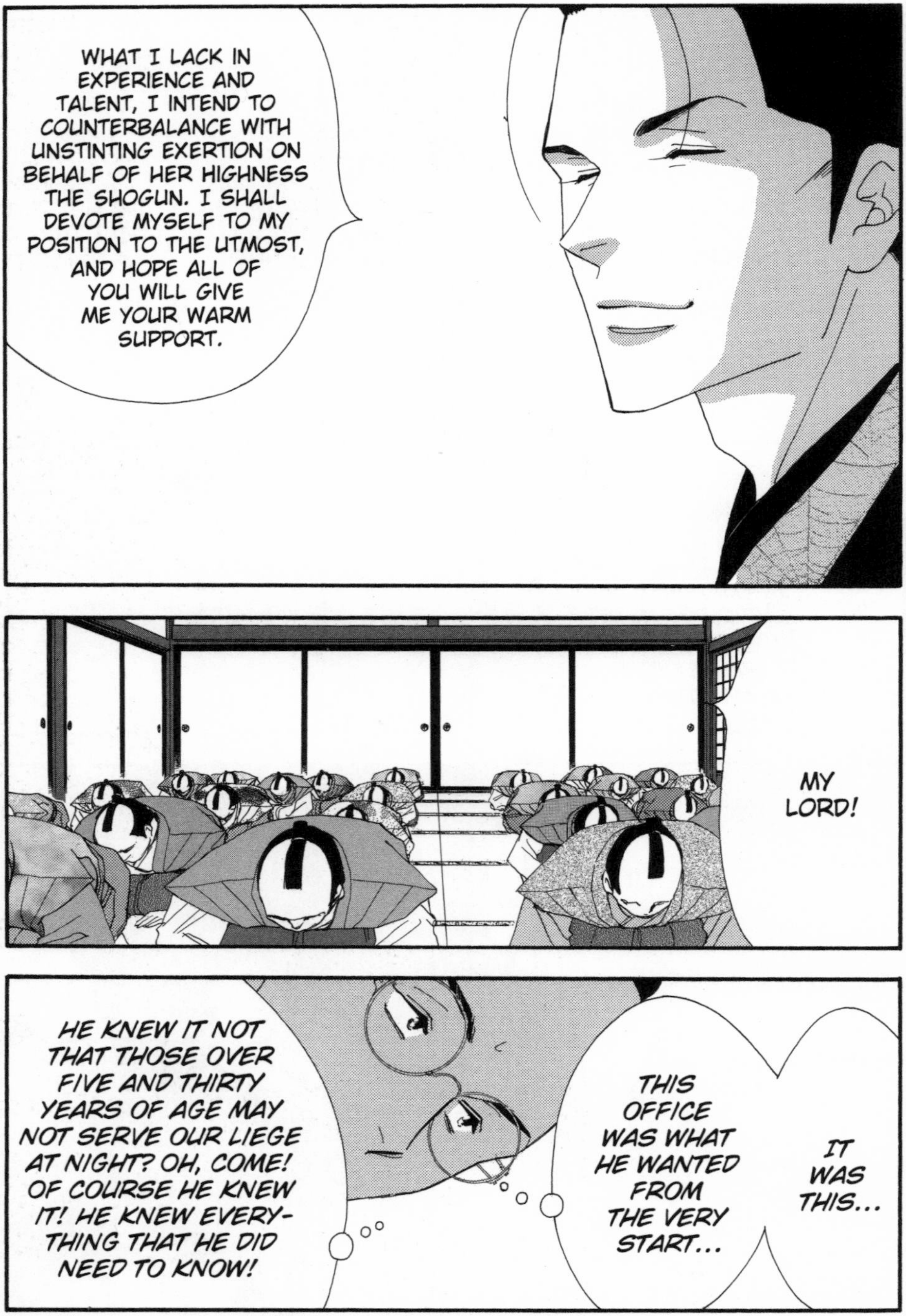
WHAT I LACK IN EXPERIENCE AND TALENT, I INTEND TO COUNTERBALANCE WITH UNSTINTING EXERTION ON BEHALF OF HER HIGHNESS THE SHOGUN. I SHALL DEVOTE MYSELF TO MY POSITION TO THE UTMOST, AND HOPE ALL OF YOU WILL GIVE ME YOUR WARM SUPPORT.
MY LORD!
IT WAS THIS...
THIS OFFICE WAS WHAT HE WANTED FROM THE VERY START...
HE KNEW IT NOT THAT THOSE OVER FIVE AND THIRTY YEARS OF AGE MAY NOT SERVE OUR LIEGE AT NIGHT? OH, COME! OF COURSE HE KNEW IT! HE KNEW EVERY-THING THAT HE DID NEED TO KNOW!

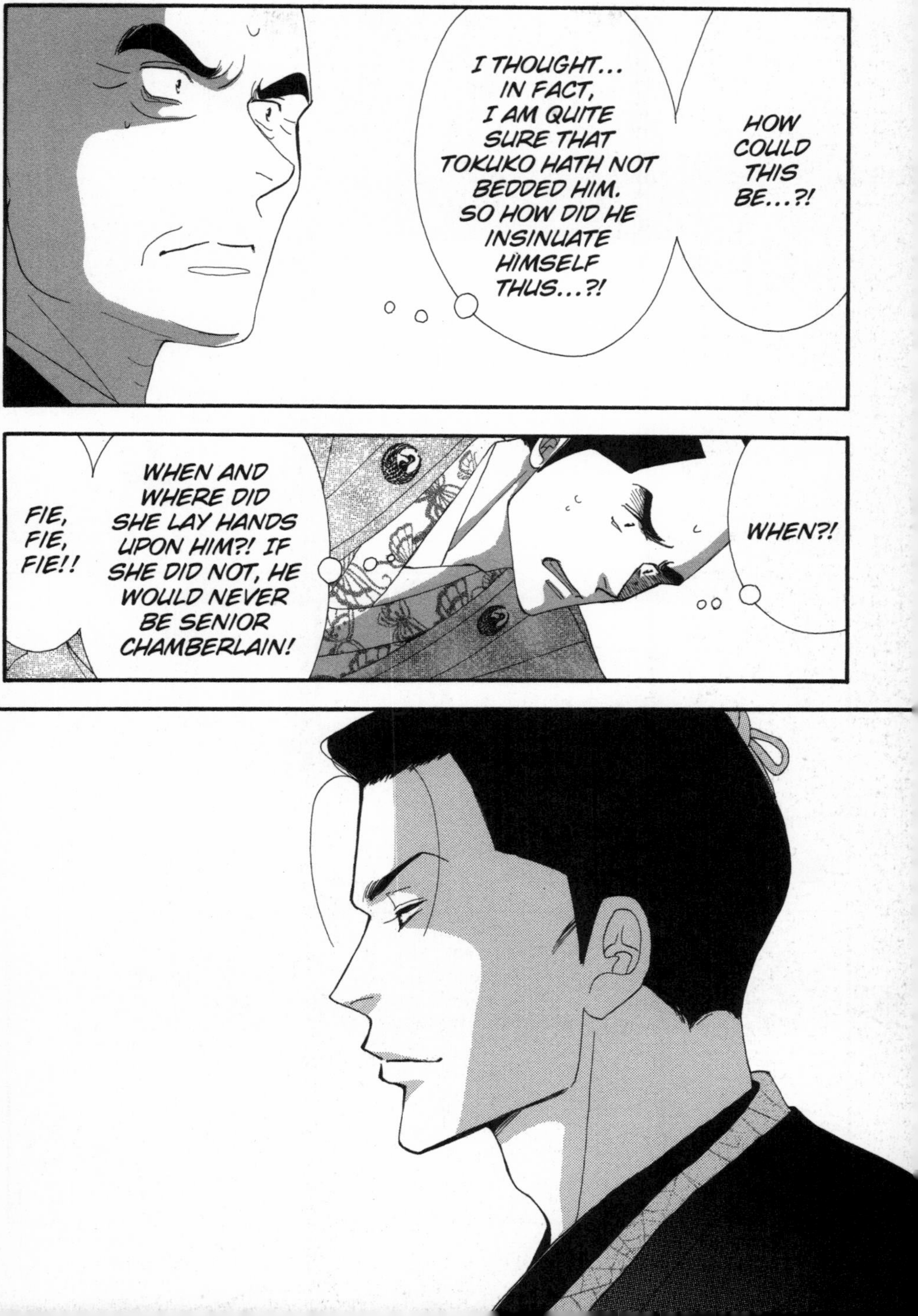
HOW COULD THIS BE...?!
I THOUGHT... IN FACT, I AM QUITE SURE THAT TOKUKO HATH NOT BEDDED HIM. SO HOW DID HE INSINUATE HIMSELF THUS...?!
WHEN?!
WHEN AND WHERE DID SHE LAY HANDS UPON HIM?! IF SHE DID NOT, HE WOULD NEVER BE SENIOR CHAMBERLAIN!
FIE, FIE, FIE!!

In this way, Emonnosuke obtained the post of Senior Chamberlain of the Inner Chambers, which had stood vacant for decades since the retirement of Sir Arikoto.

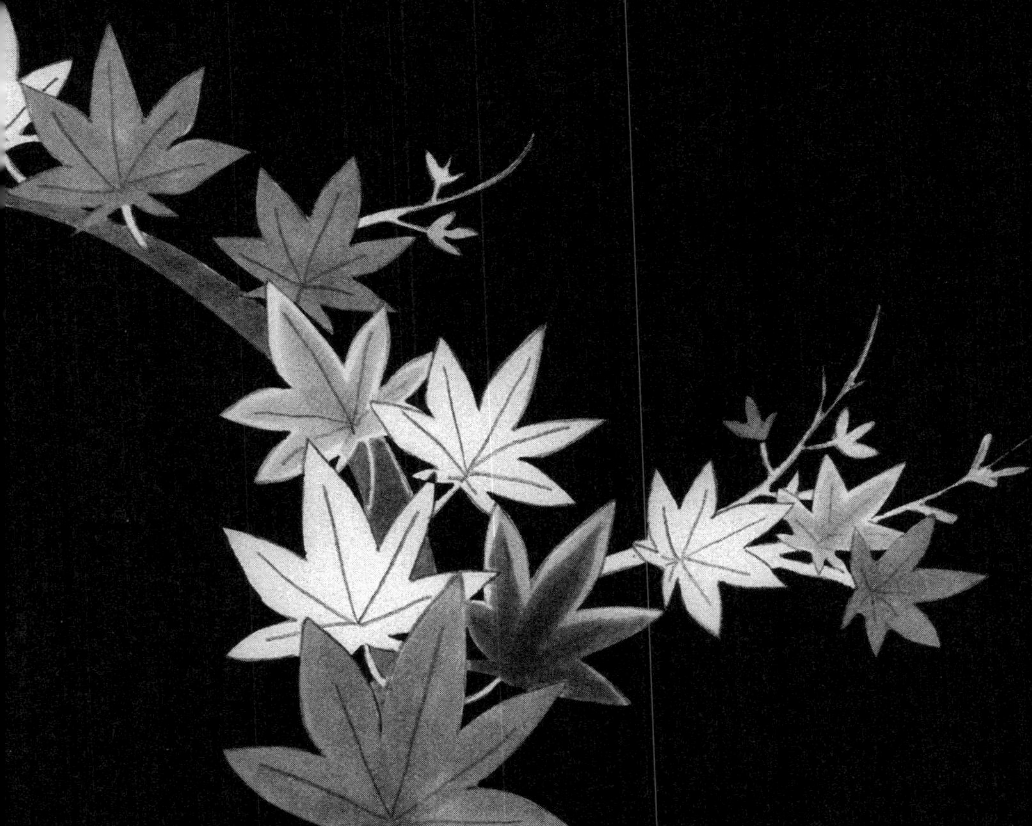

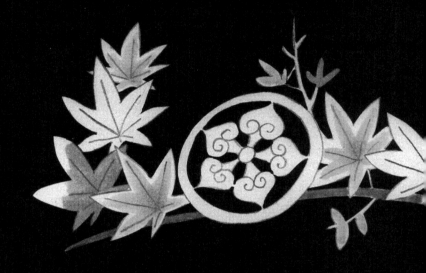

Ōoku

⚛ THE INNER CHAMBERS

Ōoku: The Inner Chambers

VOLUME 4 · END NOTES

by Akemi Wegmüller

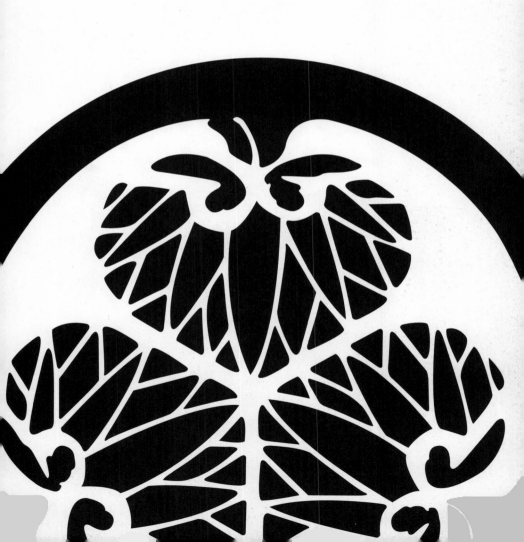

Page 36, panel 1 · OFFICIAL TOKUGAWA HISTORY
An official history of the Tokugawa family giving a daily record of events. The Japanese title is *Tokugawa Jikki*, which literally means "The True Tokugawa Record."

Page 37, panel 7 · FOLLOWED OUR LORD TO THE GRAVE
Junshi was a practice where close vassals followed their master into death either through suicide or forced suicide. The historical Hotta did indeed commit suicide after the death of Iemitsu, with whom he was known to have had a homosexual relationship.

Page 44, panel 4 · SUGOROKU
A Japanese board game.

Page 47, panel 5 · NIGHT-CRAWLING
Yobai literally means "night crawling," and was a practice wherein men snuck into the homes of women they fancied to spend the night with them before marriage.

Page 63, panel 1 · KOISHIKAWA
Located in the Bunkyo area of Tokyo.

Page 67, panel 3 · SUNPU
The present-day city of Shizuoka. Its castle is closely associated with Tokugawa Ieyasu.

Page 68, panel 1 · KUNŌZAN
The Kunōzan Tosho-gu Shrine, near Shizuoka City, is where the historical Tokugawa Ieyasu was first buried.

Page 75, panel 2 · DENGAKU YAKI
Skewered tofu, *konnyaku* (a gelatinous substance made from the konnyaku plant), fish, eggplant, daikon radish, or other ingredients that have been covered in sweet miso paste and grilled.

Page 80, panel 4 · TORA-NO-MON
Literally the "Tiger Gate." At the time this manga takes place it was an actual gate at the south end of Edo Castle. The gate was removed in the late 19th century, and today Toranomon is just a place name.

Page 81, panel 3 · O-BON
The Japanese celebration to honor the dead. It is celebrated in the summer, although the exact day differs by region.

Page 84, panel 4 · AND THEN...
The biwa player is narrating from *The Tale of the Heike,* which is an ancient Japanese text that relates the fall of the powerful Taira family in the 12th century.

Page 94, panel 2 · KAMISHIMO
Formal attire. It literally means "upper and lower" and is an ensemble that goes over the kimono for formal occasions. The upper section is a sleeveless robe with wide starched shoulders, and the lower section is an undivided hakama.

Page 97, panel 1 · SOON AFTER THE NEW YEAR
At this time Japan still followed the lunar calendar, so the New Year did not fall in January.

Page 98, panel 5 · CENTRAL ENCLOSURE
The Central Enclosure, or *honmaru*, is home to the Outer Chambers, the Shogun's Quarters, and the Inner Chambers.

Page 115 · NARITA-YA, DANJURO
The Kabuki actor here is based on the historic Ichikawa Danjuro I, whose stage nickname (*yago*) was Narita-ya. In Kabuki tradition, the audience calls out the actor's name or yago during favorite scenes.

Page 117, panel 3 · AGE OF THE GODS
The gods the woman refers to are Izanagi and Izanami, the divine couple who according to myth gave birth to Japan.

Page 175, panel 2 · NISHIJIN DISTRICT
Nishijin is synonymous with elaborate brocade.

Page 183, panel 1 · KOKU
One *koku* was equal to about five and a half bushels of rice, and this unit was used both to measure rice itself and to measure agricultural land. Domains were always assessed in terms of koku, i.e. how much rice they yielded.

Page 185, panel 3 · AKŌ INCIDENT
Also known as the Forty-Seven Ronin Incident.

Page 187, panel 1 · THREE RANKS OF VASSALS
The three ranks during the Edo period were *shinpan, fudai,* and *tozama.* Shinpan were dynastic lineages descended from Tokugawa Ieyasu. Fudai were hereditary vassals whose families had sworn allegiance to the Tokugawa before the Battle of Sekigahara in 1600. Tozama swore allegiance later, and their status was more precarious.

Page 187, panel 1 · HATAMOTO
Hatamoto belong to the samurai class and are direct retainers of the shogunate. The term literally means "at the base of the flag," and refers to the position of military commander in charge of defending the army camp and flag.

CREATOR BIOGRAPHY

FUMI YOSHINAGA

Fumi Yoshinaga is a Tokyo-born manga creator who de-
buted in 1994 with *Tsuki to Sandaru* (*The Moon and the
Sandals*). Yoshinaga has won numerous awards, includ-
ing the 2009 Osamu Tezuka Cultural Prize for *Ōoku*,
the 2002 Kodansha Manga Award for her series *Antique
Bakery* and the 2006 Japan Media Arts Festival Excel-
lence Award for *Ōoku*. She was also nominated for the
2008 Eisner Award for Best Writer/Artist.

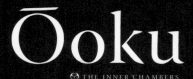

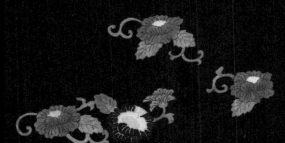

Ooku: The Inner Chambers
Vol. 4

VIZ Signature Edition

Story and Art by Fumi Yoshinaga

Translation & Adaptation/Akemi Wegmüller
Touch-up Art & Lettering/Monlisa De Asis
Design/Frances O. Liddell
Editor/Pancha Diaz

VP, Production/Alvin Lu
VP, Sales & Product Marketing/Gonzalo Ferreyra
VP, Creative/Linda Espinosa
Publisher/Hyoe Narita

Ooku by Fumi Yoshinaga © Fumi Yoshinaga 2008
All rights reserved. First published in Japan in 2008 by
HAKUSENSHA, Inc., Tokyo. English language translation
rights arranged with HAKUSENSHA, Inc., Tokyo.

The stories, characters and incidents mentioned in this
publication are entirely fictional.

No portion of this book may be reproduced or transmitted
in any form or by any means without written permission
from the copyright holders.

Printed in the U.S.A.

Published by VIZ Media, LLC
P.O. Box 77010
San Francisco, CA 94107

10 9 8 7 6 5 4 3 2 1
First printing, August 2010

www.viz.com   www.vizsignature.com

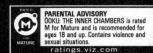

PARENTAL ADVISORY
OOKU: THE INNER CHAMBERS is rated
M for Mature and is recommended for
ages 18 and up. Contains violence and
sexual situations.
ratings.viz.com

RATED
M
FOR
MATURE

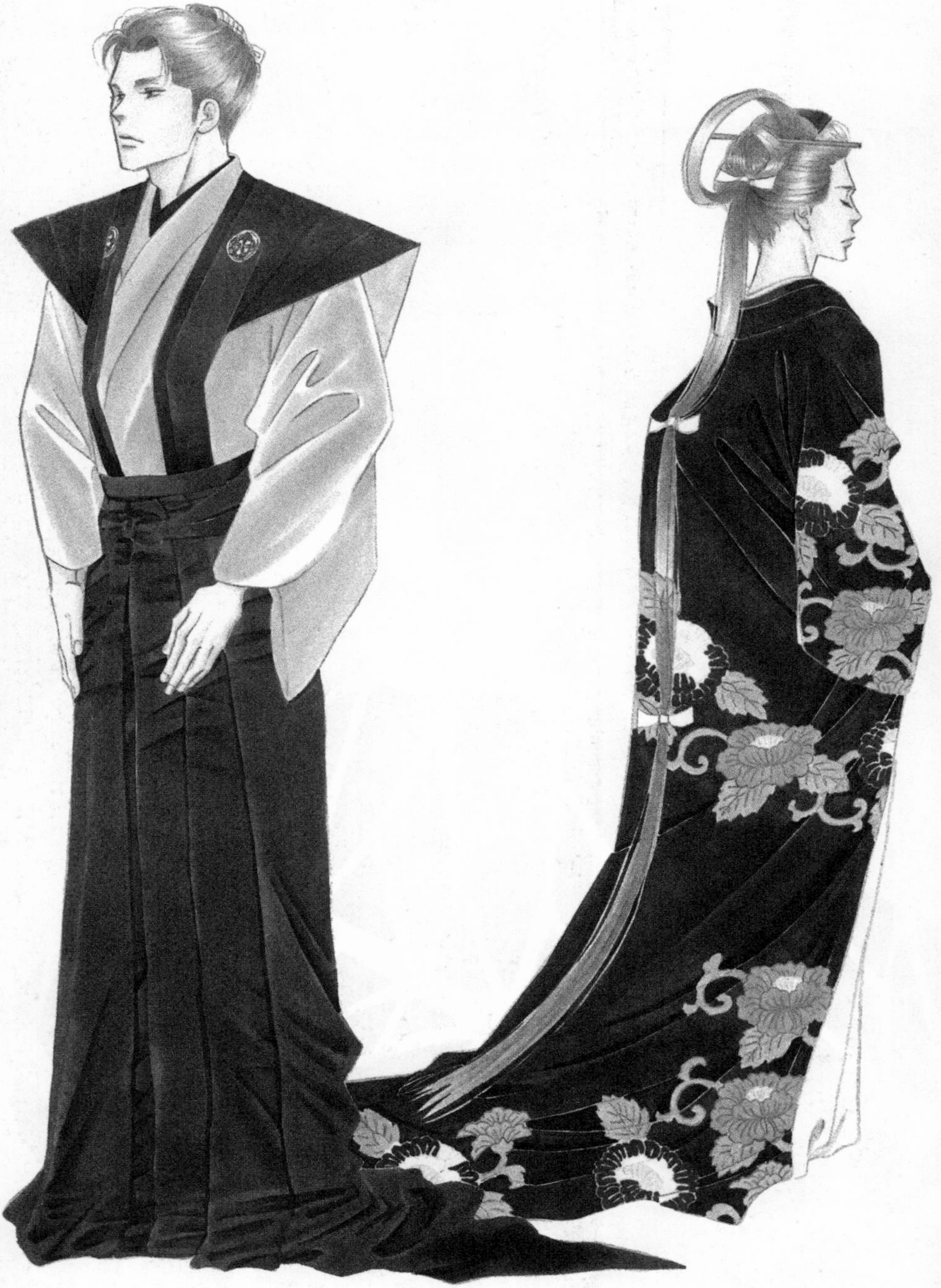

THIS I

Ōoku: The Inne

the original Japa

the orienta

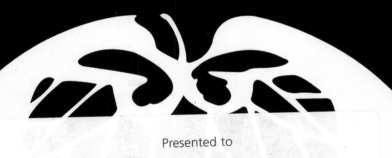